I0754883

SKIDEGATE HOUSE MODELS / Hlg̲aagilda naa gii niijing.a k’ad.dala k̲wan

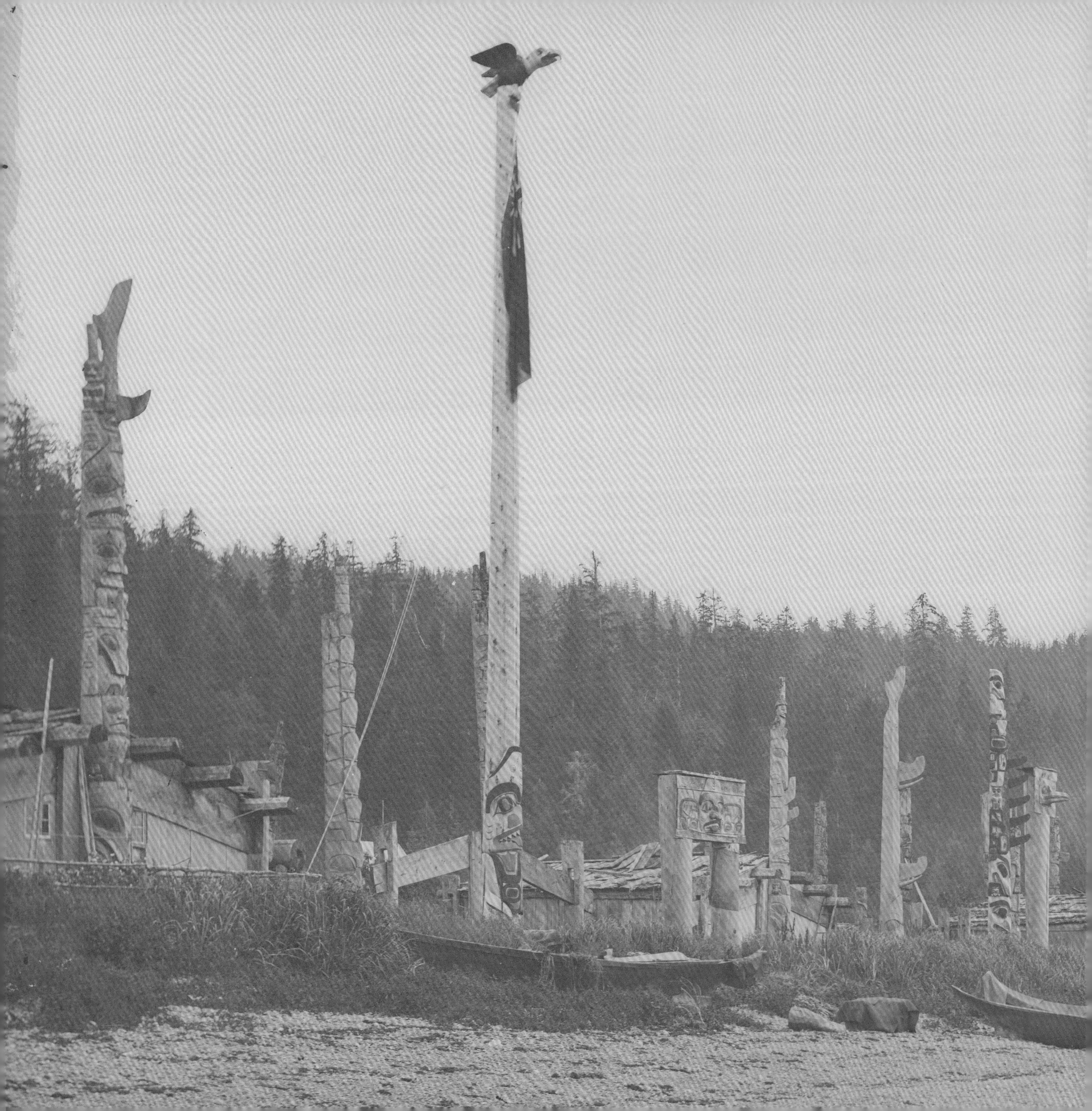

NATIVE ART OF THE PACIFIC NORTHWEST / A Bill Holm Center Series

This series fosters appreciation and understanding of the dynamic cultural and artistic expressions of the Indigenous peoples of the Pacific Northwest.

In the Spirit of the Ancestors: Contemporary Northwest Coast Art at the Burke Museum, edited by Robin K. Wright and Kathryn Bunn-Marcuse

Return to the Land of the Head Hunters: Edward S. Curtis, the Kwakwa̱ka̱'wakw, and the Making of Modern Cinema, edited by Brad Evans and Aaron Glass

Northwest Coast Indian Art: An Analysis of Form, 50th Anniversary Edition, by Bill Holm

Unsettling Native Art Histories on the Northwest Coast, edited by Kathryn Bunn-Marcuse and Aldona Jonaitis

Art of the Northwest Coast, second edition, by Aldona Jonaitis

Painful Beauty: Tlingit Women, Beadwork, and the Art of Resilience, by Megan A. Smetzer

Skidegate House Models: From Haida Gwaii to the Chicago World's Fair and Beyond / HlG̱aagilda naa gii niijing.a k'ad.dala ḵwan: X̱aayda Gwaay.yaay sdaa uu Chicago Tllgaay Ḵ'aaysguux̱an gud ad is, by Robin K. Wright, foreword by Jisgang, Nika Collison

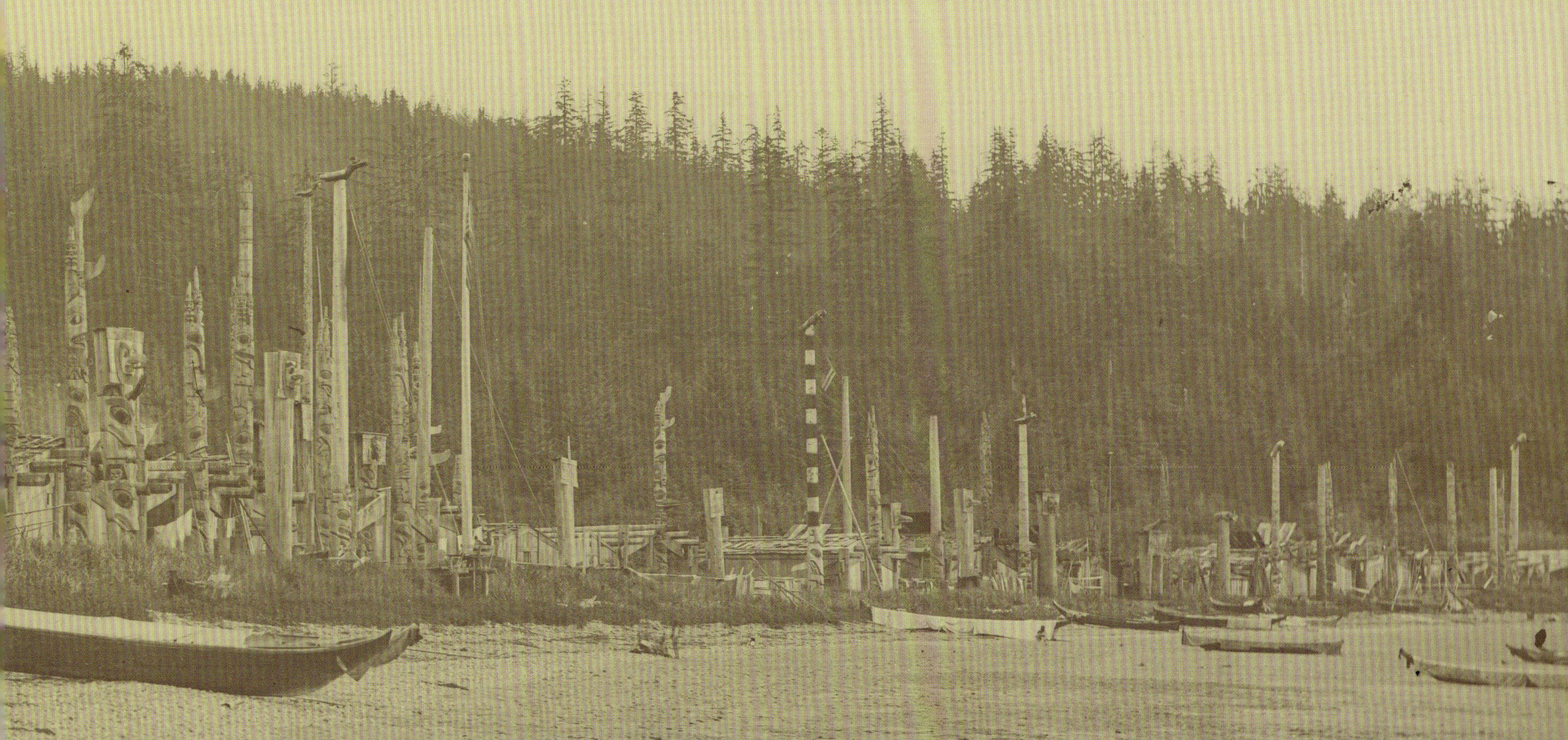

Hlg̱aagilda naa gii niijing.a k'ad.dala ḵwan

SKIDEGATE HOUSE MODELS

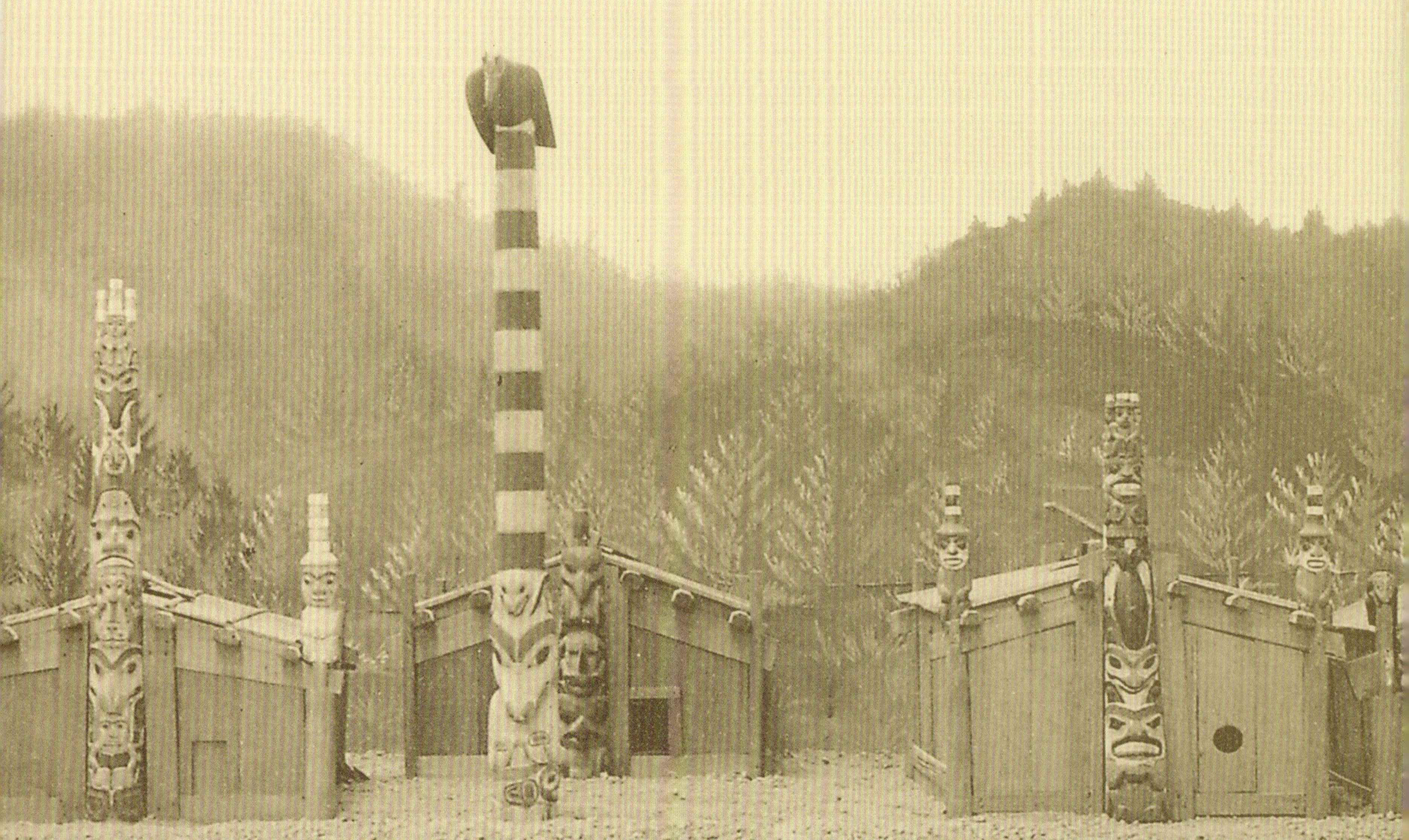

Robin K. Wright / *Foreword by Jisgang, Nika Collison*

FROM HAIDA GWAII TO THE CHICAGO WORLD'S FAIR AND BEYOND

X̱aayda Gwaay.yaay sdaa uu Chicago Tllgaay K̲'aaysguux̱an gud ad is

University of Washington Press / Seattle

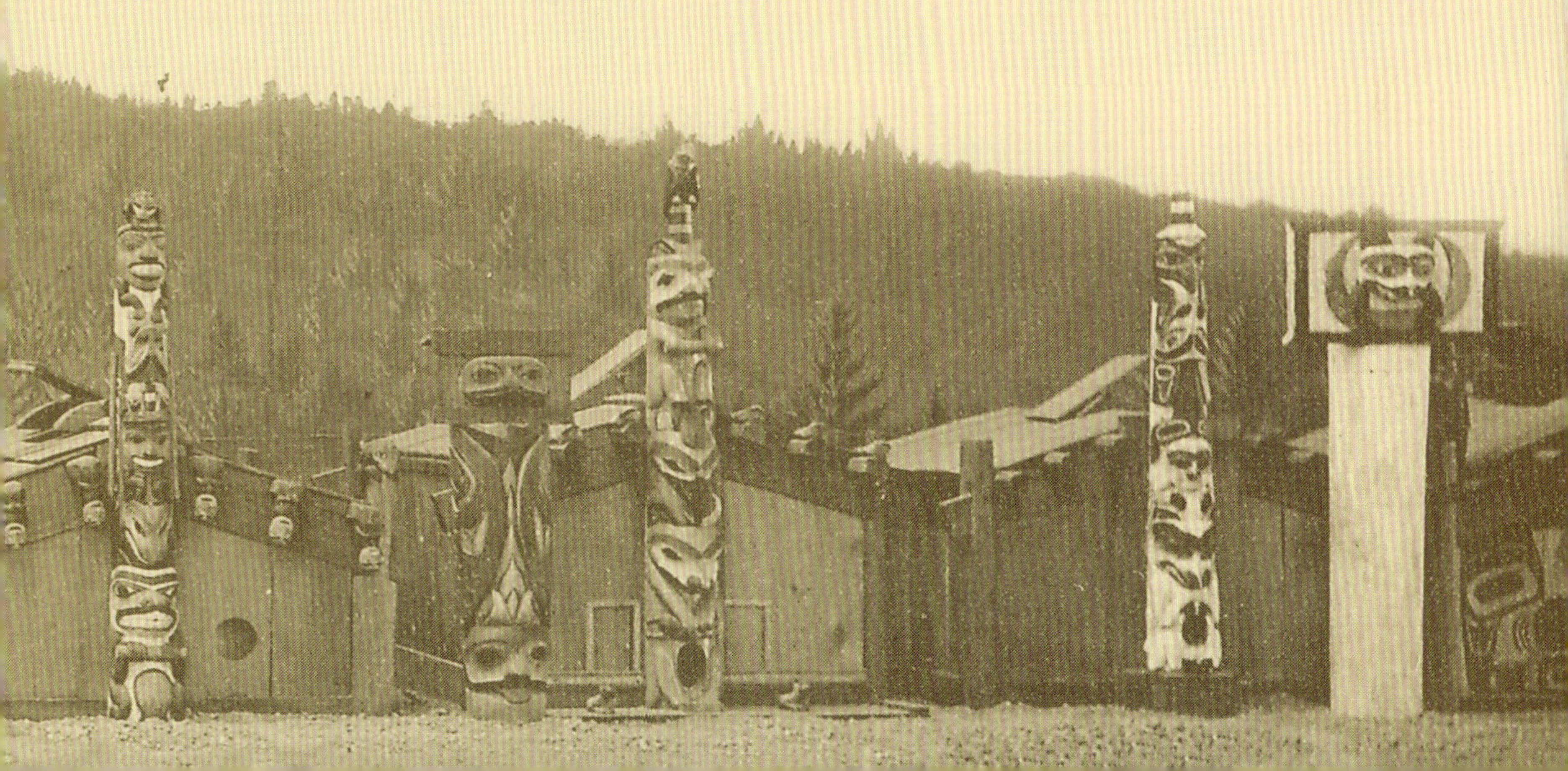

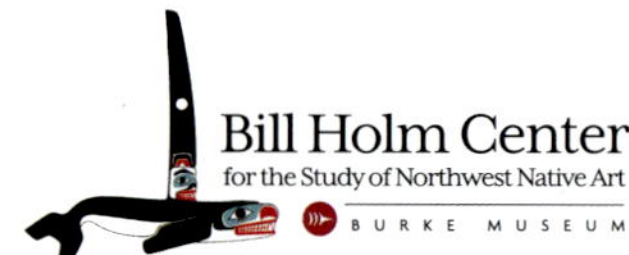

Bill Holm Center for the Study of Northwest Native Art
Burke Museum of Natural History and Culture
www.burkemuseum.org/bhc

A HELEN MARIE RYAN WYMAN BOOK

Helen Marie Ryan Wyman was intelligent, curious, and gregarious; she took great stock in books and reading, and books abounded in her life. The Wyman family is proud to sponsor this book in Native American and Indigenous studies in her name.

Skidegate Houses Models was made possible in part by a grant from the Quest for Truth Foundation.

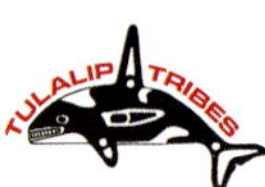

This book was also supported by the Tulalip Tribes Charitable Fund, which provides the opportunity for a sustainable and healthy community for all.

Design by Mindy Basinger Hill
Composed in Minion Pro

27 26 25 24 23 5 4 3 2 1

Printed and bound in China

UNIVERSITY OF WASHINGTON PRESS / uwapress.uw.edu

LIBRARY OF CONGRESS CATALOGING-IN-PUBLICATION DATA

Names: Wright, Robin Kathleen, author. | Collison, Jisgang, Nika, 1971– writer of foreword.

Title: Skidegate house models : from Haida Gwaii to the Chicago World's Fair and beyond = Hlg̱aagilda naa gii niijing.a k'ad.dala ḵwan : X̱aayda Gwaay.yaay sdaa uu Chicago Tllgaay Ḵ'aaysguux̱an gud ad is / Robin K. Wright ; foreword by Jisgang Nika Collison.

Other titles: Hlg̱aagilda naa gii niijing.a k'ad.dala ḵwan | Native art of the Pacific Northwest.

Description: Seattle : University of Washington Press, [2023] | Series: Native art of the Pacific Northwest: a Bill Holm Center series | Includes bibliographical references and index.

Identifiers: LCCN 2022038487 | ISBN 9780295751047 (hardcover) | ISBN 9780295751054 (ebook)

Subjects: LCSH: World's Columbian Exposition (1893 : Chicago, Ill.) | Haida Indians—Dwellings—British Columbia—Haida Gwaii—History—19th century. | Haida wood-carving—British Columbia—Haida Gwaii—History—19th century. | Haida art—British Columbia—Haida Gwaii—History—19th century. | Architectural models—British Columbia—Haida Gwaii—History—19th century.

Classification: LCC E99.H2 W753 2023 | DDC 704.03/9728—dc23/eng/20221014

LC record available at https://lccn.loc.gov/2022038487

♾ This paper meets the requirements of ANSI/NISO Z39.48-1992 (Permanence of Paper).

CONTENTS

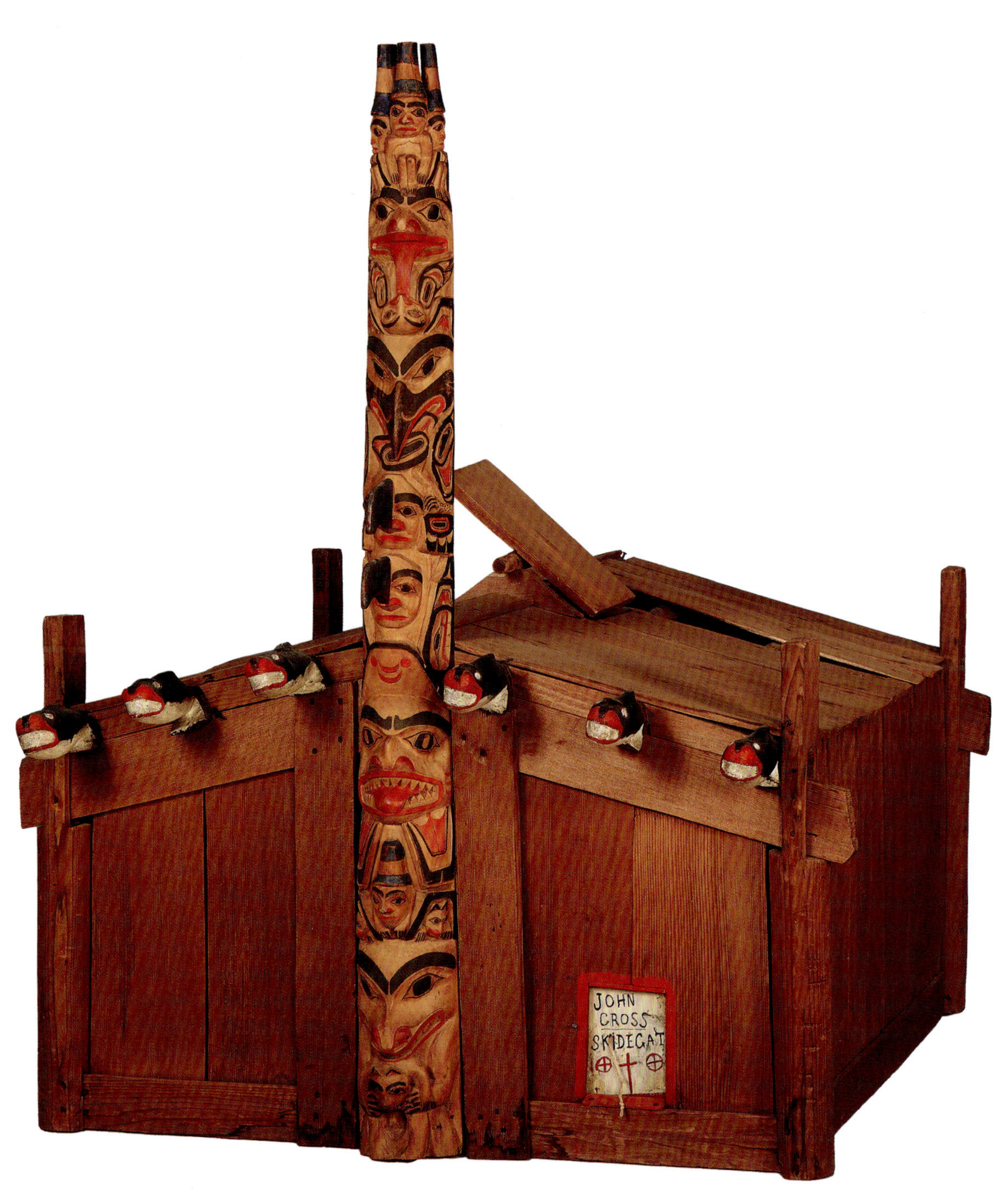
JOHN
CROSS
SKIDEGAT

FOREWORD / *Jisgang, Nika Collison*

My name is Jisgang, I belong to the K̲aay'ahl Laanas clan. Gaahlaay is my chief. My mother is Gid K̲uuyas, my father was Skilay. I grew up in HlG̲aagilda Llnagaay Skidegate Village. I am one of the last generations to receive the smallpox vaccine. I was five or six when I got it. My mom explained the shot would really hurt, and probably scar a lot, showing me hers. She explained why I needed it. That is how I learned my village should have been much bigger than it was.

In 1862 colonizers purposefully introduced smallpox to the Northwest Coast, killing hundreds of thousands of Indigenous people and almost annihilating some Nations, including the Haida.[1] Survivors in northern Haida Gwaii migrated to G̲aw Tlagée Old Massett in order to survive. Chief Skidegate welcomed southern survivors into the village of HlG̲aagilda. Haawa Kilslaay, sah uu dang G̲iida. Before the smallpox epidemic we had successfully kept colonists from our territories. In 1867 the colonial state of Canada was formed, with assigned authority over "Indians and Lands reserved for Indians."[2] In 1876, Canada legislated the Indian Act, which was so effective it informed parts of Apartheid. The year 1876 is also the year missionaries arrived on Haida Gwaii. They shamed and prohibited our ways, often forcing the destruction, sale, or handing-over of our belongings. Desecration of our Ancestors' graves would soon follow "in the name of science." Around 1883, Canada and the Church joined forces to create the horrific Indian Residential School System, which operated for more than one hundred years. In 1884, Canada legislated the Potlatch Ban, which criminalized the legal system of the Northwest Coast from 1885 to 1951. Offenders faced seizure of belongings and up to six months in jail. A final mass exodus of our Ancestors' belongings and funerary remains would follow.

In other words, we were thirty years into the genocide of the Northwest Coast when James Deans traveled to Skidegate to commission a model village for the Chicago World's Fair. Wright notes that when Deans arrived, there were only about eleven poles and three longhouses still standing in Skidegate (families were largely living in colonial-style homes). Fourteen years prior, almost eighty poles of varying purpose stood in Skidegate (see chapter 3 in this book). Deans directed artists to use an early photo of Skidegate to create their replicas. The end result was a massive model village that, while commissioned during times of duress, was built on our peoples' own terms. It was sent to the World's Fair along with a large collection of our peoples' belongings, including a real-life pole, house, and canoe. When the fair ended, the village and greater collection were split up and dispersed willy-nilly around the world, far away from Haida Gwaii.

About 120 years later, Dr. Robin Wright started to piece the village model back together. For more than twenty years she searched the globe tracking down the model houses and poles; scoured archives to sort out the work of early anthropologists, photographers, missionaries, government agents, and museums; and worked with our people to sort these findings out further, along with working on Haida language, genealogies, privileges, and histories. The findings were woven together into this precious book. In piecing back together as much of our model village as she could, Dr. Robin Wright has not only created a fascinating body of critical research, she has assisted our Nation in our greater plight: piecing ourselves back together.

Several years ago, I was listening to a radio program on strategies of war and the annihilation of a people. In addition to destroying lives, destroying heritage was a critical tactic. Shatter identity so that the survivors don't know who they are, where they come from, or their place in the world. I was born in 1971. The population of Skidegate numbered fewer than three hundred people. Growing up, we were called "Indians" and our home, the "Queen Charlotte Islands." I lived with my grandparents behind the only pole left standing in our village.[3] Part of my family lived "off reserve" and part off island, disenfranchised from their community through colonial regimes. Haida was rarely spoken, if at all. The were no masks, dance blankets, songs, or dancing. I didn't have a proper name. Many didn't. It was all silenced—hidden away in minds, archives, museums, and behind closed doors.

That was for the first few years of my life. I also grew up during a time of great cultural and political revitalization. Despite massive population loss and colonial regimes, our Ancestors preserved as much Haida knowledge as possible by employing subversive tactics and by working with anthropologists and other foreigners to record our knowledge. We started coming back out through the art, through the poles. I was seven when I witnessed the first pole to be raised in Skidegate Village in almost one hundred years, the Skidegate Dogfish Pole. Carved by my chinaay grandfather Iljuwas Bill Reid, the pole was raised in 1978, in front of the first longhouse to be built in Skidegate since the late 1800s, with a great community potlatch.[4] A similar event had happened nine years earlier in the village of Old Massett, when Robert Davidson gifted his community a pole to raise. These events awakened much more than I think either artist anticipated.

My children are Haida, not Indians. They live on an archipelago called Haida Gwaii. The population of Skidegate is nine hundred strong, and more than five thousand as a Nation. My children have proper names, given in potlatch. They have attended many pole raisings in their lifetime, wearing their regalia. They are learning and growing up in the art, the language, the culture, the land and water. They are learning their family ties and their clan and nation histories. They were Haida singing and dancing in the womb.

Today there are sixteen poles of varying purpose standing throughout Skidegate.[5] My clan is readied for a memorial pole-raising in September 2022, and by the end of 2023, four new carved house posts will be standing at Xaaynang.nga Naay, the Skidegate Health Centre. There are nineteen poles in G̱aw Tlagée Old Massett, the most recent being raised in August 2022, marked by a two-day potlatch hosted by Christian and Candace White (Yahgu Jaanas/Laanas clan̲) in Old Massett. And more recently, in October 2022, a memorial pole was raised for Tlajang nang kingaas, Benjamin Ray Davidson.

We might be a far cry from eighty poles standing in Skidegate alone, but we are also a far cry from one pole left standing. Our Ancestors did everything they could to preserve our Haida-ness. Each subsequent generation has been dedicated to the same. For decades we have been piecing ourselves, our clans, and our villages back together the same way Dr. Wright pieced the Skidegate House models back together.

Like Dr. Wright's restoring of our model village, the restoration of our world is not fully complete. Not everyone and everything has been located or gathered. There could even be a correction down the road. But we are still here—we are Haida—and we know our place in this world. My friend's book is an important contribution to this journey. So many years of working with our people to bring critical stories together under one roof. So many names, clans, genealogies, houses, and poles reunited. When I hold this book, I am holding a part of myself, my family, our community, our Nation. When I hold this book, I am holding a part of our past, present, and future, all at the same time.

Haawa to my friend Robin for your respect, passion, and

scholarship. Haawa to Haida Gwaii, our home. Haawa to the Ancestors, without your determination we would not be here as Haida. Haawa to our knowledge holders and scholars who scour their minds and the earth to gather the knowledge our Ancestors preserved. Haawa to the Supernatural, who help guide us in this work.

Notes

1. Not just smallpox but also TB, measles, and other diseases.
2. BC joined in 1871.
3. It was raised ca. 1884 by David Shakespeare for his wife, Jane, of the Saang.ahl Staastas; see chapter 3, Model Pole No. 17, for more on that pole.
4. The Shakespeare and Dogfish poles stood side by side for almost a decade before the Shakespeare Pole fell in 1989. The Dogfish Pole was taken down for conservation in 2014. Both now live in the Haida Gwaii Museum. The Longhouse served as the Skidegate Band Council Headquarters through the mid-1990s. In 1998 it became the Hlg̱aagilda Xaayda Kil Naay Skidegate Haida Language House, home to the Skidegtae Haida Immersion Program (SHIP).
5. Haida Heritage Centre-6, Cheexial-1, Lydia Williams-1, Gah Yah-1, Skidegate-1, Sk'aadGa Naay-1, Niis Wes-1, Cumshewa-1, WiiGanad-1, Unity-1, Gidansda-1.

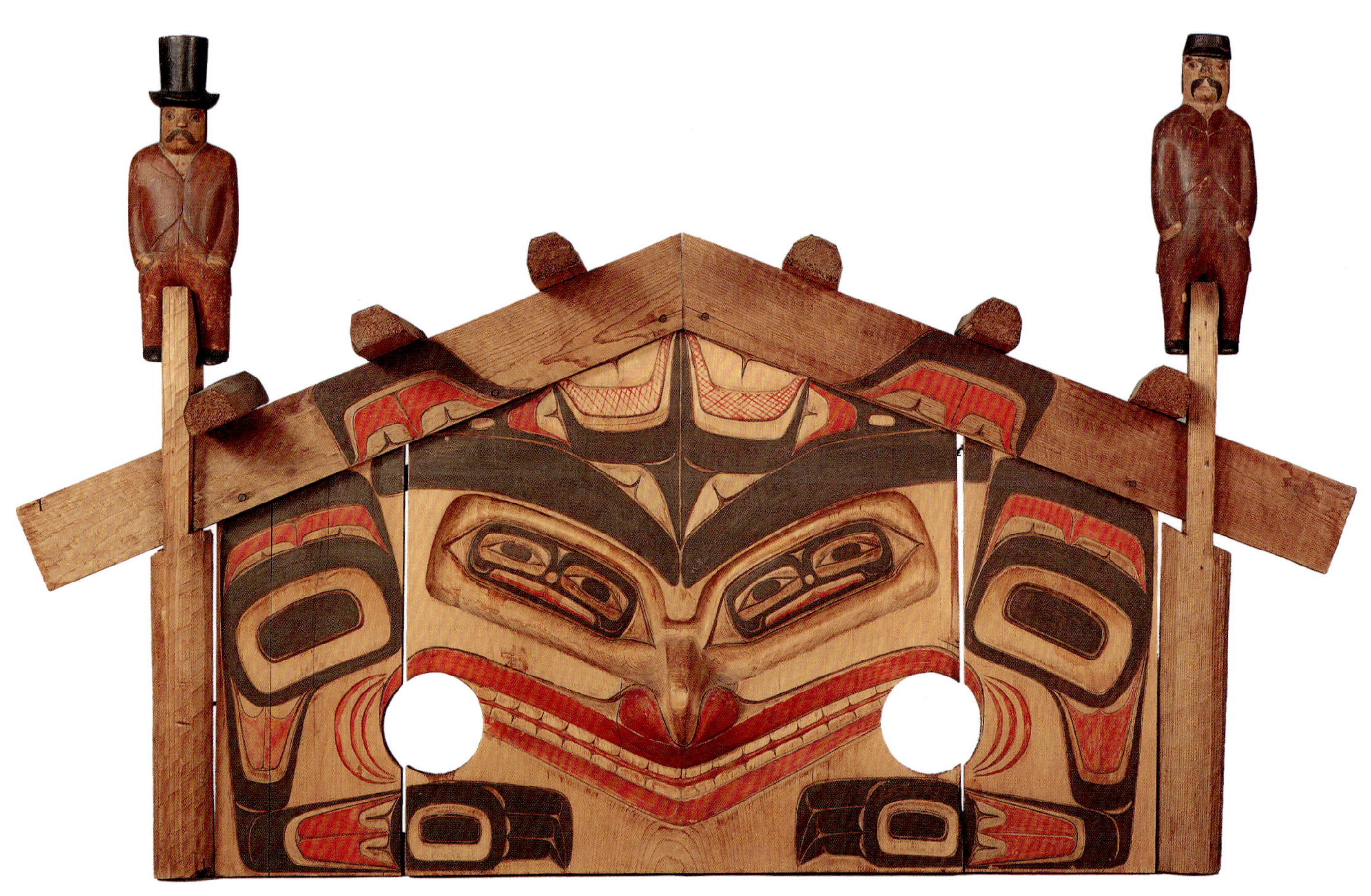

ACKNOWLEDGMENTS

Research for this book began in 2001 and grew out of the previous ten years' research that resulted in the book *Northern Haida Master Carvers* (Wright 2001b). It was through researching that book, which was focused in large part on the extended Edenshaw family and their nineteenth-century contemporaries, that I discovered what a rich historical resource existed in the model houses made for the World's Columbian Exposition, and in James Deans's notes that accompanied them. I promised myself that when I finished that book, I would return to the Field Museum of Natural History in Chicago and work on the full story of the model village.

Thank-yous for this book are first due to many Haida scholars and culture-bearers who have shared their oral history and cultural knowledge with me over the past forty-four years: Haawa, Haawa, Haawa! Thinking back to my first trip to Haida Gwaii in 1979, as a very naïve graduate student working on my master's thesis on argillite pipes, I bravely knocked on the door of Chief Skidegate, Dempsey Collinson. He generously welcomed me into his home with no introduction and showed me his argillite collection. As a 'Waasdan jiina (white woman/non-Haida person), I have tried to correct many of the historical errors that have been published in the scholarly works of my academic predecessors. I could not have done this work without the help of the Haida people who have patiently corrected my errors and generously entrusted their intellectual property with me. I apologize to them for any of my errors, or those of others, that have gone uncorrected here.

I met Richard Wilson at Sg̱ang Gwaay Llnagaay in 1986. He has shared his knowledge of Haida genealogy and history with me for more than thirty-six years. His work with the Haida Gwaii Museum and with the many Haida elders who have shared their clan histories for the Clans of Skidegate document housed there has been invaluable. The Haida Gwaii Museum, under the directorship of Nathalie Macfarlane, facilitated my initial research, and together with Jisgang, Nika Collison, Ḵaay'ahl Laanas, current executive director and curator of the Haida Gwaii Museum, and Jaad ga x̱il ta, Irene Mills, Naa 'Yuuwans X̱aaydaG̱aay, we were successful in receiving a National Endowment for the Humanities Exhibition Planning Grant in 2006. This allowed us to travel to the Field Museum in Chicago with Burke Museum exhibit designer Andrew Whiteman, who also visited Skidegate with me in 2006. We worked together with this team to develop plans for an exhibition (as yet unrealized) that could bring together all the existing Haida house models for a traveling exhibit that could open at that Haida Gwaii Museum at Ḵay Llnagaay. Andrew accompanied us to Haida Gwaii and filmed interviews with Ḵii'iljuus, Barbara Wilson; Richard Wilson; Chief Git'Ḵun, John Williams; Chief Gidansda, Percy Williams; Chief Gidansda, Niis Wes, Ernie Wilson; and Nang King.aay'uwans, James Young. Excerpts from some of these interviews appear in this book. I have not given up hope that an exhibit may, someday, reunite the models and bring them back to Skidegate.

Haawa, Haawa, Haawa to the Skidegate Haida Immersion

Program (SHIP) elders who have worked with me over the years to correct and update Haida spellings and decipher James Deans's misspellings: Gwaaga̱nad, Diane Brown; Nang King.aay'uwans, James Young; Sg̱aana Jaads K'yaga X̱iigangs, Iitl Gaa Tsida T'ahl G̱aguulas, Kathleen (Golie) Hans; Jiixa, 'Lala T'agwa, Gladys Vandal; Jaad Aahl Sing.G̱ang.nga, Kaaniihl, Pearle Pearson; Gaayinguuhlas, Roy Jones Sr.; Yang K̲'aalaas, Grace Wilson Jones; Chief Git'K̲un, John Williams; Chief Gidansda, Percy Williams; and Chief Gidansda, Niis Wes, Skil Kil Xiids, Ernie Wilson. Also, a special thanks to SHIP facilitators Luu G̱aahlandaay, Kevin Borserio; and Denver Cross. Haawa to the many Haida historians who read various versions of the manuscript as it developed and made useful corrections and suggestions. Special thanks to Aay Aay Gidins, research and repatriation coordinator at the Haida Gwaii Museum, whose careful reading of the manuscript caught many typos, spelling errors, and language corrections. Thanks as well to contributing oral historians Chief Gidansda, Guujaaw, Niisdaka.na, Jags Brown and Chief Nang Jingwas, Russ Jones. A special Haawa to Jisgang, Nika Collison, who carefully read multiple drafts, made many insightful editorial suggestions along the way, and contributed the wonderful foreword.

I must also thank Randy Burke and Bluewater Adventures and their crews for taking me so often to Gwaii Haanas National Park Reserve and allowing me to bring a Haida guest with me most years. Since 1993, I have been privileged to be a resource person on the Bluewater Adventures sailboats (the *Island Roamer*, *Island Odyssey*, and *Island Solitude*), visiting Gwaii Haanas on trips partnered with the Bill Holm Center at the Burke Museum. I have witnessed the creation and growth of the park and sat with and learned from many Haida Watchmen who protect the ancient village sites there. These trips began and ended in Skidegate, and I was able to go early and stay on to visit with many Haida people there. These trips enabled my conversations with knowledgeable Haida elders and have been a highlight of my life.

Thanks to my academic and institutional colleagues who have generously shared their research, their collections, and their archives with me. The primary institution that has welcomed my research has been the Field Museum of Natural History in Chicago that houses the majority of the still surviving Skidegate house models. I have worked with the following people over the years: Jonathan Haas, curator of North American Anthropology; Armand Esai, library archives manager and museum archivist; Gordon Ambrosino, collection manager; Jamie Kelley, head of collections; Nina Cumings, photo archivist; David Foster, Temporary Exhibits Department; Angela Steinmetz, registrar; Alan Francisco, registrar; and Ruth Norton, chief conservator. Twenty-seven other museums and archives have also been crucial to this research (see the list following these acknowledgments).

The late Ira Jacknis, research anthropologist at the Phoebe Hearst Museum of Anthropology, University of California, Berkeley, generously shared his research on Franz Boas and the anthropology of world's fairs. He also introduced me to other scholars, including Paige Raibmon, professor of history at the University of British Columbia, who helped me to track down obscure references during the final phases of research. Mary Malloy, research associate at the Peabody Museum of Archaeology and Ethnology, Harvard University, helped to rule out the existence of a whaling captain named Jefferson. My former student Cynthia McGowan, now assistant collections manager at the British Museum, shared her notes on the Newcombe collection of totem poles that clarified a portion of my own garbled record on Newcombe's notes. Emily Moore shared her research on the stolen Tongass pole that came to Seattle, and her book helped locate an image of the engraving of the Wallace pole at the Centennial Exposition.

I could not have accomplished this lengthy project without financial support from a variety of sources, including the University of Washington Royalty Research Fund, a Canadian Embassy Senior Fellowship, Del Lewis and the Quest for Truth Foundation, the National Endowment for the Humanities, and the Bill Holm Center Endowed Professorship and the Bill Holm Center at the Burke Museum.

Thank you also to the Milliman Endowment that funded the beautiful photographs taken by Gail Specht at the Field Museum in 2016, and to Gail Specht, whose sensitive photography has enhanced the visual impact of the Field Museum's house models and poles.

Many thanks to my colleagues who read the manuscript and offered very useful critiques. Of course, I owe a huge debt of gratitude to my mentor and colleague for fifty years, Bill Holm, who set me upon this research path and guided me every step of the way. In particular, I am grateful for his groundbreaking work that identified the styles and bodies of work of several Haida artists, including the "Master of the Chicago Settee." At the time Holm did this research, he did not have access to James Deans's notes that recorded the name Zacherias for the maker of the model of Captain Gold's house. However, he used the model of Chief Skidegate's mortuary pole from the WCE model village as a key piece (see figure 3.21), along with the Chicago Settee (see figure 3.24), in describing the style of the "Chicago Settee Guy."

When I shared the Zacherias name with Holm, we looked closely at the model of Captain Gold's house, and he pointed out subtle elements of style in the painting on the house front that led us to conclude that the model fit with the other pieces he had attributed to the Chicago Settee maker. It was a moment that I will always remember, discovering the real name of the "Chicago Settee Guy." Deans had recorded only the single name Zacherias, and I owe a huge debt of gratitude as well to the Haida contributors: Chief Gidansda, Percy Williams; Nang King.aay'uwans, James Young; SG̱aana Jaads K'yaga X̱iigangs, Iitl Gaa Tsida T'ahl G̱aguulas, Kathleen (Golie) Hans; Jiixa, 'Lala T'agwa, Gladys Vandal; Jaad ga x̱il ta, Irene Mills; and Captain Gold, Richard Wilson, who shared their family genealogies with me and confirmed that there was only one Zacherias in Skidegate, and his full name was Zacherias Nicholas.

Thanks to the staff of the Burke Museum Heritage Department, who care for the Northwest Coast Arts and Cultures Collections. Collections manager Rebecca Andrews and volunteer photographer Doug McTavish were very quick to arrange for a last-minute photograph, and Ashley Verplank McClelland, rights and reproductions manager, helped with the tedious work getting photo permissions and locating elusive publishable photographs.

I owe a special thanks to the Bill Holm Center and the Bill Holm Center Professorship Endowment for funding my research and the publication of this book. Thank you to Kathryn Bunn-Marcuse, and to her associate, Bridget Johnson, for their hard work and support. Katie, as assistant director of the Bill Holm Center for the five years preceding my retirement as director in 2015, freed me from administrative and grant-writing duties that allowed me to find some time for research, and now as director of the Bill Holm Center she is carrying on the work in an inspired way.

Editor in chief Larin McLaughlin, editorial assistant Caroline Hall, senior project editor Joeth Zucco, copyeditor Amy Smith Bell, and art director Mindy Hill at the University of Washington Press and proofreader Judy Loeven and indexer Scott Smiley were wonderful to work with in the final stages of editing and designing the book.

I must also thank my mother, Lorraine Wright, who diligently created a typescript of Deans's notes before the technology existed to do this by scanning. Though we haven't used these in the book, her hard work was appreciated, and I only wish she could have lived long enough to see the book published.

Special thanks to my spouse and life partner, Dr. Carol S. Ivory, who has given me needed emotional support and encouragement since 1984, especially during the past five years of difficult cancer treatments and recovery. I could not have finished this book without her steadfast love and support.

HAIDA ORAL HISTORIANS

The Haida oral history keepers below, listed alphabetically by English name, generously shared their knowledge during the preparation of this book with the author.

Kaalga Jaad, Erin Brillon, Laana Tsaadas
GwaaG̱anad, Diane Brown, Ḵaay'ahl Laanas
Niisdaka.na, Jags Brown, Juus xaade
Giida Ku Juus, Walker Brown, Ḵaay'ahl Laanas
Chief Skidegate, Clarence (Dempsey) Collinson (d. 2008), Naa S'aagaas X̱aaydaG̱aay
Jisgang, Nika Collison, Ḵaay'ahl Laanas

Chief Wiiganad, Sidney Crosby, Naa 'Yuuwans Skidegate Gidins
Aay Aay Gidins, Naa 'Yuuwans Skidegate Gidins
Jaad Aahl Sing.g̱ang.nga, Gladys Gladstone, K̲aay'ahl Laanas
Chief Gidansda, Guujaaw, G̱aag'yals K̲iiG̱awaay
SG̱aana Jaads K'yaga X̱iigangs, Iitl Gaa Tsida T'ahl G̱aguulas, Kathleen (Golie) Hans (1933–2023), matriarch of the Naa 'Yuuwans Skidegate Gidins
Yang K̲'aalaas, Grace Wilson Jones, K'aadaas Gaah K̲'iiG̱awaay
Kwiiahwah Jones, Naa S'aagaas and Ganada clan, Nisga'a
Gaayinguuhlas, Roy Jones Sr. (d. 2020), G̱aag'yals K̲iiG̱awaay
Chief Nang Jingwas, Russ Jones, Naa S'aagaas X̱aaydaG̱aay
Skil Gaahlandaay, Mike McGuire, Staastas
Jaad ga x̱il ta, Irene Mills, Naa 'Yuuwans Skidegate Gidins
Jaad Aahl Sing. G̱ang.nga, Kaaniihl, Pearle Pearson (d. 2018), matriarch of the Naa S'aagaas X̱aaydaG̱aay
Iljuuwaas, Billy Stevens (d. 2007), K'aadaas Gaah K̲'iiG̱awaay
Jiixa, 'Lala T'agwa, Gladys Vandal, Naa 'Yuuwans Skidegate Gidins
Chief Git'K̲un, John Williams (1921–2008), K̲'una K̲iiG̱awaay
Chief Gidansda, Percy Williams (1930–2015), G̱aag'yals KiiG̱awaay
Lalaxaaygans, Terri-Lynn Williams-Davidson, G̱aag'yals K̲iiG̱awaay
K̲ii'iljuus, Barbara Wilson, matriarch of the St'awaas K̲iiG̱awaay
Chief Gidansda, Niis Wes, Skil Kil Xiids, Ernie Wilson (1913–2009), G̱aag'yals KiiG̱awaay
Captain Gold, Richard Wilson, Naayii Kun K̲iiG̱awaay
Nang King.aay'uwans, James Young (1923–2008), Naa 'Yuuwans Skidegate Gidins
Chief Gaahlaay Lonnie Young, K̲aay'ahl Laanas
Gid yahk'ii, Sean Paul Young, G̱aa'yals K̲iiG̱awaay

FUNDERS

The following generously funded the research and publication of this book.

2001 Royalty Research Fund, University of Washington. For research on Skidegate Haida House Models commissioned by James Deans
2006–8 NEH Exhibit Planning Grant, "Skidegate Haida House and Pole Models for the World's Columbian Exposition"
2006–15 Bill Holm Center Endowed Professorship, Burke Museum, funds for research and travel
2003 Canadian Embassy Senior Fellowship to research and prepare a manuscript on Skidegate Haida House Models made for the World's Columbian Exposition in Chicago in 1893
2015 Milliman Endowment Faculty Excellence Award, UW School of Art, Art History, and Design, for Gail Specht photography of Field Museum model poles and houses
2016–22 Bill Holm Center, Burke Museum, funds for illustration publication fees
2021 Quest for Truth Foundation through the Bill Holm Center, Burke Museum, publication funds

MUSEUMS AND ARCHIVES

The following curators and collection managers generously welcomed me into their collections.

American Museum of Natural History: Peter Whiteley, curator; Annibal Rodriguez and Laila Williamson, collections managers; Kathryn Sabella, Repatriation and North American Ethnology, Division of Anthropology; Barry Landua, systems manager and manager of digital imaging, Division of Anthropology; and Gregory Raml, special collections reference librarian
The Art Institute of Chicago: JT de la Torre, archives assistant, Research Center
Beinecke Rare Book & Manuscript Library, Yale University: Moira Fitzgerald, head, Access Services
Bill Holm Center, Burke Museum: Kathryn Bunn-Marcuse, director; Bridget Johnson, associate director
Brooklyn Museum: Susan Zeller, curator; Deirdre E. Lawrence, archivist; Nancy Rosoff, Andrew W. Mellon Senior Curator, Arts of the Americas; Monica Park, rights and reproductions manager
Burke Museum of Natural History and Culture, Arts and Culture Department: Rebecca Andrews, collection manager; Ashley Verplank McClelland, curatorial assistant and rights and reproductions manager; Doug McTavish, photographer
Canadian Museum of History: Andrea Laforet, director, Ethnology and Cultural Studies; Mélissa Duncan, collections information specialist, photo archives; Anneh Fletcher, collections information specialist, library; Jacqueline Vincent, The Brechin Group, Inc.
Library and Archives of Canada

Chicago History Museum Research Center: Ellen Keith, Sarah Yarrito, and Angela Hoover, rights and reproduction

Chicago Public Library: Teresa Yoder, Riva Pollard, and Morag Walsh, archival specialists, Special Collections and Preservation Division

Denver Art Museum: John Lukavic, Andrew W. Mellon Curator of Native Arts; Nancy Blomberg, chief curator and Andrew W. Mellon Curator of Native Arts

Fairbanks Museum and Planetarium, St. Johnsbury, Vermont; Steve Amos, curator

Field Museum of Natural History: Jonathan Haas, curator of North American Anthropology; Armand Esai, archivist; Gordon Ambrosino, collection manager; Jamie Kelley, collection manager; Nina Cumings, photo archivist; David Foster, temporary exhibits; Angela Steinmetz, registrar; Alan Francisco, registrar; Ruth Norton, chief conservator; and Lauren Hancock, anthropology registrar

Florida Museum of Natural History, Gainesville: Elise V. LeCompte, registrar and coordinator of museum health and safety; and Jeffrey Gage, photographer

Haida Gwaii Museum: Nathalie Macfarlane, director; Nika Collison, director and curator; Kwiiahwah Jones, curator; and Aay Aay Gidins, research and repatriation coordinator

Jefferson County Historical Society, Port Townsend, Washington: Ann Welsh, vice president of the Board of Trustees; and Reed Barry, research center assistant

Milwaukee Public Museum: Alex Barker, curator

Museum of Vancouver: Wendy Nichols, curator of collections; Jillian Povarchook, acting curator; and Sharon Fortney, curator of Indigenous collections and engagement

Oakland Museum of California: Carey Caldwell, curator

Peabody Museum of Archaeology and Ethnology, Harvard University: Susan Haskell, curatorial associate for special projects; and Cynthia Mackey, Office of Rights and Reproductions

Philadelphia Museum of Art: Susan Anderson, archivist

Portland Art Museum: Anne Crouchley, associate registrar; and Deana Dartt, curator

Musée du Quai Branly—Jacques Chirac, Paris: Paz Núñez-Regueiro, Conservatrice en chef du patrimione responsable de l'Unité patrimoniale des Amériques

Museum für Völkerkunde, now KHM-Museumsverband, Weltmuseum, Vienna, Austria: Christian Feest and Gerard van Bussel

National Archives, Washington, DC

Royal British Columbia Museum and BC Archives: Martha Black, curator; Dan Savard, collection manager; and Kelly-Ann Turkington, permissions/licensing office

Royal Ontario Museum: Arni Brownstone, assistant curator, Indigenous Americas; and Nicola Woods, rights and reproductions coordinator

Smithsonian Institution: Felicia Pickering, collection manager

Übersee-Museum, Bremen, Germany: Stephanie Walda-Mandel, head of subject area Oceania and America

University of Pennsylvania Museum of Archaeology and Anthropology: William Wierzbowski, assistant keeper; and Alex Pezzati, archivist

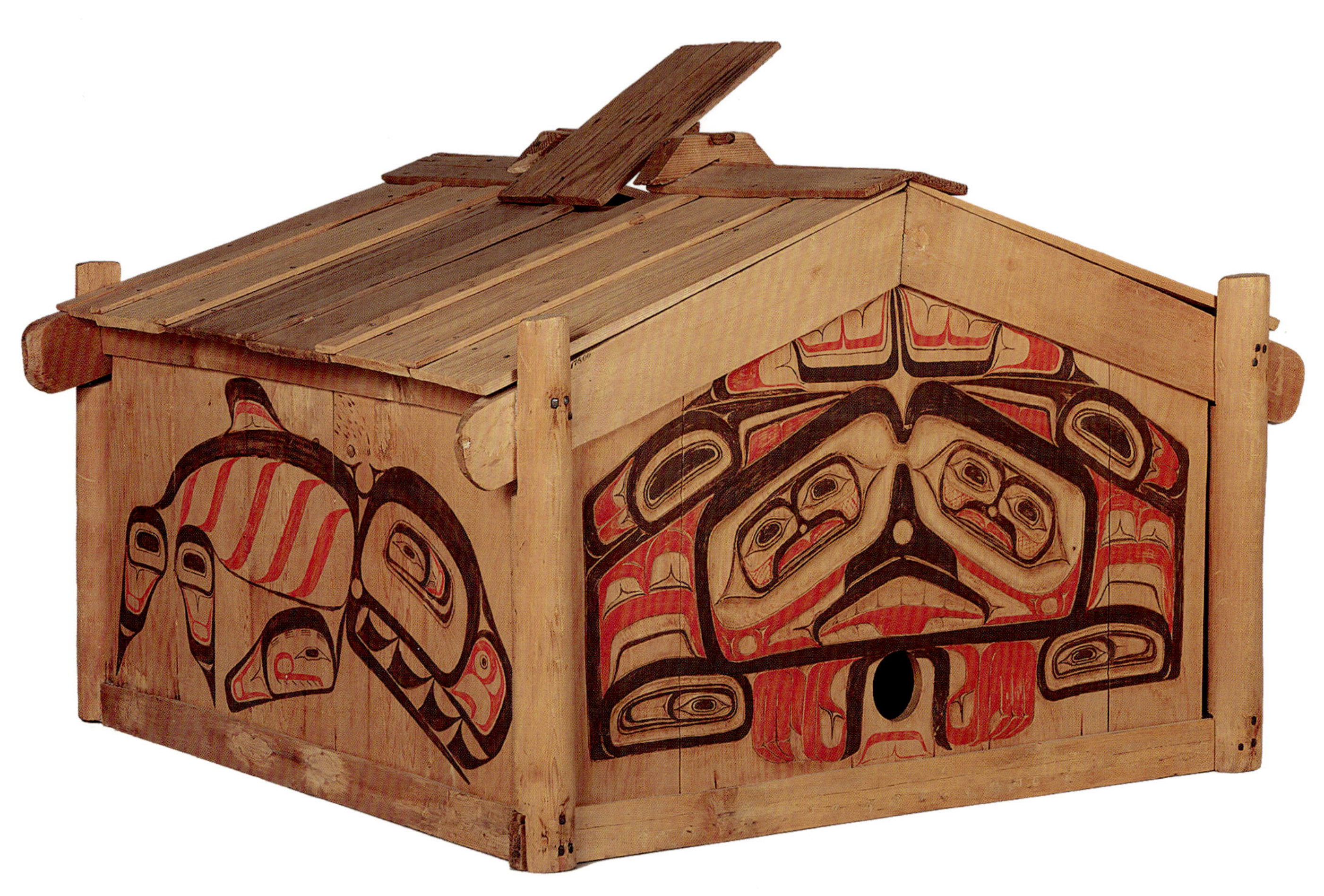

SKIDEGATE HOUSE MODELS / Hlg̱aagilda naa gii niijing.a k'ad.dala ḵwan

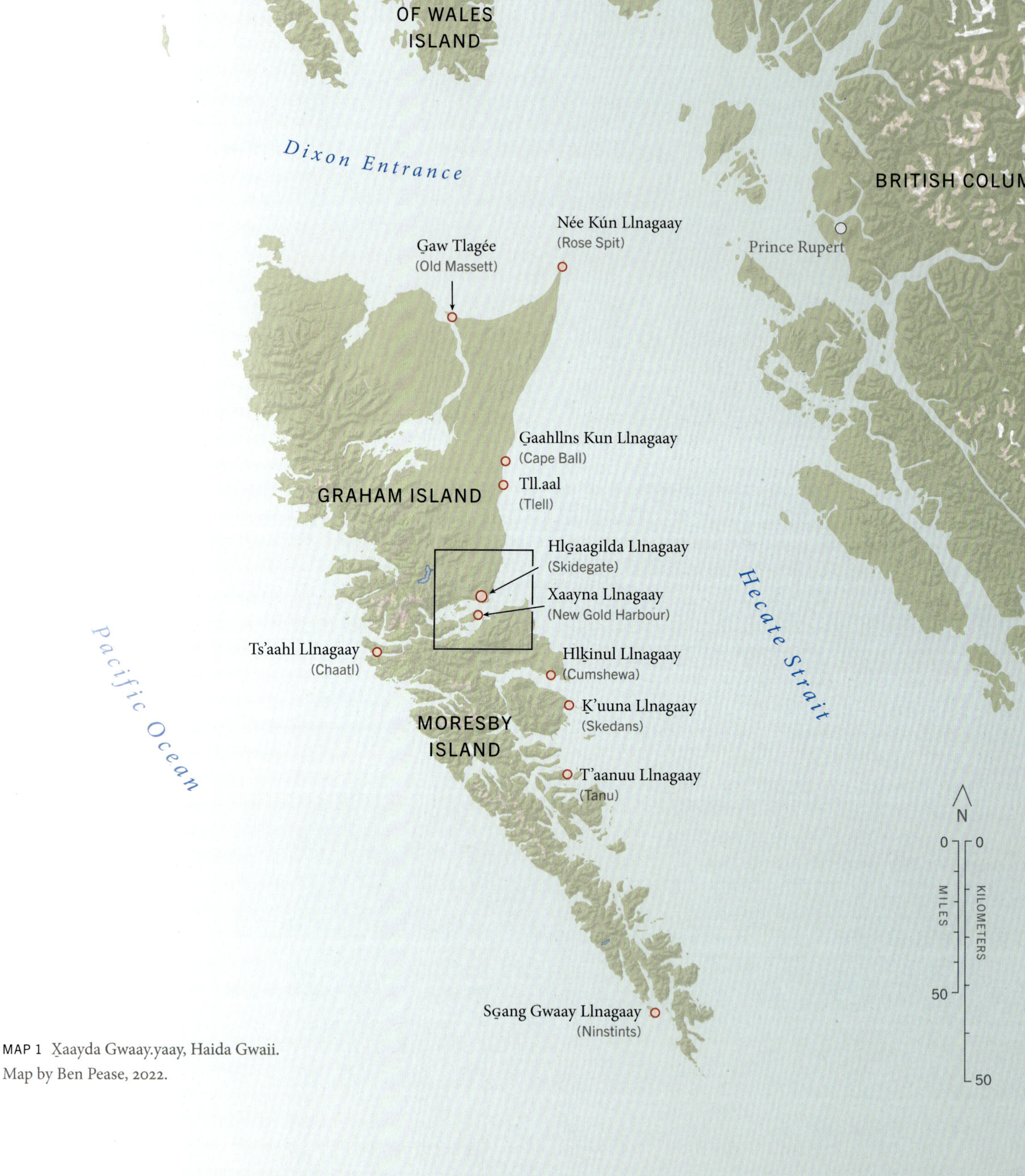

MAP 1 X̲aayda Gwaay.yaay, Haida Gwaii.
Map by Ben Pease, 2022.

INTRODUCTION

My dad was brought up to be a historian, and you had to have somebody to carry on the stories. . . . My dad's name is Gid glaay.yas [Henry Young, d. 1969].[1] Gid means "baby." Glaay.yas means "calm."[2] They wanted his life to be calm. Throughout his life. That's what the name means. . . . He was raised by the bonfire. What do I mean by "the bonfire." The bonfire goes twenty-four hours a day. And it takes the smartest man out of the clan to tell them the story. And the next night, its only gray-haired people can sit at this fire. The next night. He's asked to tell the story. The same story back to these gray-haired people. He misses this one word, just one word, that story's over. The next night they tell them that story again. And the next night it's his turn again. When he gets this one story perfect, word for word, then they will tell him another story. This is how my dad was raised, to carry the history.

—Nang king.aay 'uwans, James Young Interview, Skidegate, August 22, 2006

The X̱aayda had methods for maintaining accuracy from generation to generation. The methods utilized for transmitting the stories were stringent. The teachers/elders would consider all the children of the clan; out of those numbers, one, or possibly two, were selected to be taught all the oral histories of the clan. Only the very brightest children were selected to receive all the information, and those children would be regularly in the company of elders. The elders would tell the oral history and then the child would repeat it word for word. . . . The X̱aayda protect the integrity of the oral histories by allowing only those who are properly trained and have the right to tell their clan stories to do so. The tllsda X̱aayda ḵ'aaygan.ŋga [long, long ago ancient stories] are the intellectual property of the clans.

—Kii'iljuus, Barbara Wilson, matriarch of the St'awaas Ḵiiḡawaay, in "Tllsda Xaaydas K'aaygang.nga: Long, Long Ago Haida Ancient Stories"

The X̱aayda (Haida) are the Indigenous people of Haida Gwaii (map 1).[3] They have long been known for their spectacular totem poles and cedar plank architecture as well as the two-dimensional design system that is recognized as one of the world's most sophisticated art forms. By the last decade of the nineteenth century, the devastating impact of population loss through diseases such as smallpox, along with Christian missionizing and Canadian government policies that made the potlatch illegal in Haida Gwaii, had all put a severe strain on the strict cultural practices that were nevertheless carried on by knowledgeable Haida elders in hidden ways.[4] These Haida culture-bearers also began to work with some outsiders who systematically recorded in written form the oral histories of the Haida clan members who chose to share with them. Some outside collectors purchased the material culture that illus-

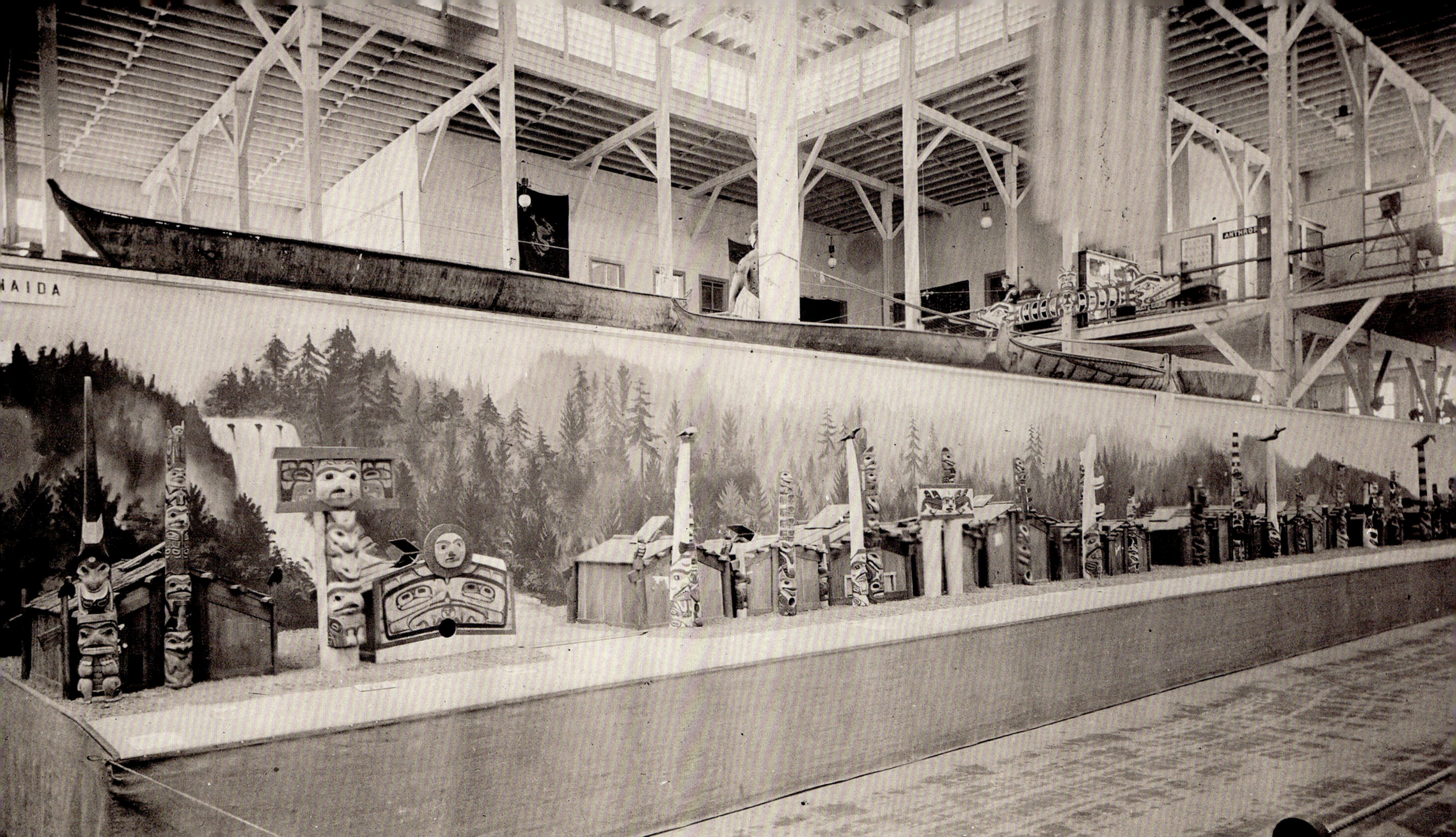

I.1 Model of Hlg̱aagilda Llnagaay, Skidegate village, installed in the Anthropology Building at the World's Columbian Exposition, 1893. Courtesy of the Peabody Museum of Archaeology and Ethnology, Harvard University, 93-1-10/100266.1.39.

trated these histories. It is unfortunate that Haida material culture was often acquired by outsiders with no documentation, sold under duress, stolen from graves, or in other ways separated from the knowledge that should have stayed with it.

Fortunately, in rare cases, objects were commissioned and documented in collaboration with the makers. Part of this preservation of cultural history took the form of a large model village commissioned for the 1893 World's Columbian Exposition in Chicago from at least seventeen Haida artists who were living in Skidegate in 1892 (figure I.1). This set of model houses and totem poles is a unique resource, and this book—a collaborative effort with the Haida people of Skidegate—is intended to document it further. To better understand the place these house models hold in the history of Northwest Coast art and culture, it is useful look at some of the world and local influences that had occurred in the decades immediately before 1892 that impacted their creation.

WORLD'S FAIRS AND EXPOSITIONS

During the late nineteenth and early twentieth centuries a series of international expositions were held in various cities around the world, all celebrating the industrial, technological, and cultural progress of the powerful colonial countries that hosted and participated in them. Beginning with the 1851 Crystal Palace Exhibition in London, these fairs became competitive endeavors, each striving to surpass the previous ones in grandeur. Growing out of the Industrial Revolution, they featured the technological accomplishments of the competing nations as well as lavish displays of cultural diversity. At these expositions the cultures of nonindustrial nations were displayed as a way of dramatizing the "progress of civilization," reinforcing the concept of cultural evolutionism that was prevalent in that era. A significant body of literature has arisen analyzing issues of colonialism and the representation of race at these fairs (see, for instance, Beck 2019; Benedict 1983; Fogelson 1991; Hinsley and Wilcox 2016; Jacknis 1991, 2016; and Rydell 1978, 1980, 1984, 1989).

The Indigenous cultures of the Pacific Northwest Coast were first represented in such a setting at the 1876 Centennial Celebration in Philadelphia, which was the first American international fair. The Smithsonian Institution was responsible for preparing an exhibit intended to document the history and present conditions of the American Indian. A significant collection of Pacific Northwest Coast material culture was assembled for this exhibition by the Washington Territory pioneer and collector James G. Swan. After the fair these objects became part of the Smithsonian Institution's collections (Cole 1985, 19–33).

A Paris Exposition was held two years later, in 1878, and the Trocadero Museum in Paris dates its founding collections to this event. Subsequently, the Smithsonian exchanged a number of objects with the Trocadero Museum, including some Haida objects collected by Swan for the Philadelphia Exposition (Walsh 2002). A decade later, the Paris World's Fair of 1889 set the standard for the planners of the Chicago Fair to supersede. In this Paris fair, villages from various French colonies were constructed and inhabited with Indigenous peoples who were brought to Paris to become a living part of the display (Fogelson 1991, 74). The display of Indigenous peoples in Europe has a long history going back to the late eighteenth and early nineteenth centuries, when traveling shows of Indigenous peoples from North and South America, organized by people such as Samuel Hadlock (1824) and George Catlin (1850s), performed to entertain European royalty and for amusement at local community fairs (Feest 1987; Wright 1987).

In 1891 planning began for the World's Columbian Exposition (WCE) to be held in Chicago in the summer of 1893. With the goal of promoting Chicago as a center of industrial and cultural achievement, the WCE would celebrate the four-hundredth anniversary of Christopher Columbus's first voyage (figure 1.2). Frederic Ward Putnam was hired as the chief of

1.2 World's Columbian Exposition, the Basin and the Court of Honor with Agriculture, Machinery, Administration, Electricity, and Manufactures Buildings seen from behind the Statue of the Republic, Chicago, 1893 (Arnold and Higinbotham 1893).

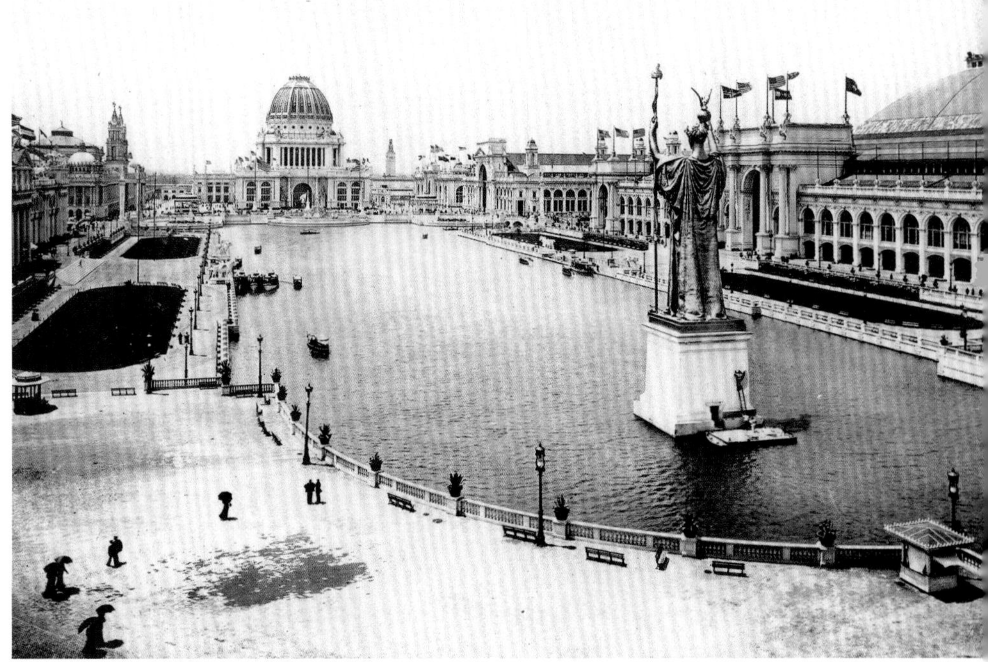

the fair's Department of Ethnology and Archaeology, and he in turn hired Franz Boas as his chief assistant. Putnam was professor of anthropology at Harvard University and director of the Peabody Museum of American Archaeology and Ethnology. His goal for the exhibits at the WCE was to:

> secure and place in the Exposition a perfect ethnographical exhibition of the past and present peoples of America and thus make an important contribution to science, which at the same time will be appropriate, as it will be the first bringing together on a grand scale representatives of the peoples who were living on the continent when it was discovered by Columbus. (Jacknis 1991, 92, cited in Dexter 1966, 316)

Many Native North Americans did attend the fair, not only to be put on display, but as workers and interested visitors. There were such attractions as Buffalo Bill's Wild West Show, a very popular independent enterprise located outside the fairgrounds, and the Midway Plaisance, the amusement park of the fair. Initially intended to serve as a bazaar and center of popular entertainment with displays that would have some redeeming educational, cultural, or historical content, it was placed under the oversight of Putnam's "Department M, Ethnology, Archaeology, Progress of Labor and Invention, and Collective Exhibits" (Fogelson 1991, 75). Their lofty educational goals were rapidly overwhelmed by entertainment and entrepreneurial forces. Found in the Midway were such attractions as the first Ferris wheel, Sitting Bull's daily war dances performed by a variety of Indian troupes, a Bedouin encampment, the "Street of Cairo" with the "danse du ventre," belly dancing, a Chinese theater, a German beer hall, a Javanese village with puppet plays, an exhibition of South Sea Islanders, and a variety of other money-making sideshows. It was after visiting the Midway Plaisance that Potawatomi leader, activist, and writer Simon Pokagon, wrote *The Red Man's Rebuke*, later retitled *The Red Man's Greeting*. In it he stated:

> In behalf of my people, the American Indians, I hereby declare to you the pale-faced race that has usurped our lands and homes, that we have no spirit to celebrate with you the great Columbian Fair now being held in this Chicago city, the wonder of the world. No; sooner would we hold high joy-day over the graves of our departed fathers, than to celebrate our own funeral, the discovery of America. (Pokagon 1893, 1)

After the publication of this "greeting," which Pokagon had printed on white birchbark to honor the tree and strengthen his political statement, he met with fair organizers and urged that they counter the stereotypical views of Native Americans that were put forward in the Midway displays. Pokagon became friends with the mayor of Chicago, Carter Harrison Sr., who was so impressed with Pokagon that he invited him to speak in front of thousands of people who attended the Chicago Day celebration at the fair on October 9. Pokagon intended his speech not only to rebuke the fair organizers and attendees but also to urge payment for Potawatomi lands, including the very land on which the fair was built, that had been negotiated by his father, Leopold Pokagon, in the 1833 Treaty of Chicago but never fully paid. Pokagon's goal was never achieved, however; Mayor Harrison was assassinated on October 28, two days before the end of the fair (Beck 2019, 5–7).

In addition to the exhibits on the Midway Plaisance, within the so-called White City (WCE) fairgrounds proper, there were a number of model villages that featured Indigenous cultures occupied by living people on display, including an Eskimo village from southern Labrador, a Penobscot village with three birchbark tepees, an Iroquois settlement sponsored by the state of Illinois with four traditional dwellings and a longhouse occupied by twelve Tuscaroras and Senecas, as well as the Kwakwa̱ka̱'wakw group discussed below.

The Smithsonian Institution's exhibits were housed in the Government Building and did not include living people, featuring instead the various culture areas with life-size mannequins wearing traditional clothing and surrounded by artifacts. Also in the Government Building was an Alaska exhibit sponsored by the Bureau of the Interior featuring one of George Emmons's Tlingit collections that later went to the American Museum of Natural History. Many of the state buildings also included exhibits of Indigenous artifacts to represent their histories, notably Washington State's display of artifacts collected by James G. Swan and Myron Eells that later became part of the Washington State Museum (now the Burke Museum of Natural History and Culture). Interestingly, the Michigan Building displayed Pokagon's poem "Red Man's Rebuke" just as it was printed on white birchbark (Fogelson 1991, 78–84).

Unfortunately, displays representing the indigenous North American peoples at the fair did not educate fairgoers about such contemporary issues as Native sovereignty, as Simon Pokagon would have wished. Instead they were guided by the colonial attitudes that promoted the exploitation of Indigenous peoples and their lands. To illustrate the benefits of "civilization," a model Bureau of Indian Affairs (BIA) school building was constructed on the fairgrounds north of Putnam's outdoor villages. It contained workshops, classrooms, sitting rooms, a dining room, kitchen, dormitories, and apartments for employees. BIA commissioner T. J. Morgan brought delegations of Indian students from government and religious schools to occupy the model school and be put on display to showcase "Indian progress" to the tourists attending the fair. Richard Henry Pratt, the founder of the Carlisle Indian School, was very critical of Putnam's exhibits, which he felt put too much emphasis on traditional Indian cultures at the expense of showing Indian "progress." Pratt brought more than five hundred Carlisle students to Chicago to troop in military fashion under the banner "Into Civilization and Citizenship" (Fogelson 1991, 86).

The discipline of anthropology was in its infancy at this time. Frederic Putnam was instrumental in founding the anthropology departments in Cambridge, Chicago, and San Francisco museums. One of his goals was to establish a great museum in Chicago after the fair, which he felt would grow in importance as the American tribes were absorbed into the dominant colonial cultures (Jacknis 1991, 92). As with his contemporaries, Putnam's belief in "vanishing cultures" was coupled with an evolutionist approach to anthropology. According to Harlan Smith, one of Putnam's assistants: "From the first to the last the exhibits of this department will be arranged and grouped to teach a lesson; to show the advancement or evolution of man" (Smith 1893, 117, quoted in Jacknis 1991, 92). Toward this end, Putnam hired nearly one hundred paid and volunteer assistants to assemble a massive collection of artifacts for the Anthropology Building exhibits. One of these was Franz Boas, hired as Putnam's chief assistant.

According to Ira Jacknis, the World's Columbian Exposition had a profound effect on the subsequent development of Northwest Coast anthropology: "This single event was so influential that almost all subsequent work was related to it in some way" (Jacknis 1991, 91). Boas was teaching at Clark University until June 1892, when he left this position to work full-time on the WCE. Boas was put in charge of the Northwest Coast and physical anthropology exhibits. He hired James Deans, a Victoria, BC, resident, to commission a set of model houses from the residents of the Haida village of Hlg̱aagilda Llnagaay (Skidegate) and assemble a collection of other Haida objects.

THE EARLIER MODEL HOUSES AND POLES ON THE NORTHWEST COAST

The Haida house models made for the World's Columbian Exposition are some of the earliest known on the Northwest Coast and are the only set that attempted to represent an entire village.[5] However, Haida carvers had been making objects for sale to Europeans for more than one hundred years by this time and were the first on the Northwest Coast to create an art form specifically for the trade with explorers and entrepreneurs who arrived on fur trading ships in the late eighteenth and early nineteenth centuries. For this trade they used a soft black argillaceous stone found in a quarry near Skidegate to carve tobacco pipes that displayed traditional Haida figures as well as portraits of the foreign seamen and their ships (Wright 1977, 1979, 1980, 1982, 1985, 1986, 2001a). After the devastation wrought by the last of several smallpox epidemics in 1862, the form of these carvings evolved from tobacco pipes made as souvenirs to models of totem poles, houses, and figural groups depicting Haida stories, carved both in wood and argillite. This shift happened at a time during the combined effects of the many lives lost to disease, changing economies, missionary activities, and the colonial government that made it illegal to potlatch the raising of new houses and totem poles that displayed hereditary crests. The carving of models of these poles and houses became a way for the Haida to preserve their traditions and stories during these repressive times.

Tlingit, Tsimshian, Nuxalk, and Kwakwa̱ka̱'wakw artists also carved model poles and houses, but the Haida models made in the late nineteenth century far outnumber them. Model houses often include attached frontal poles, but many more freestanding model poles than model houses were made during this time and later, primarily for sale to visiting tourists. Thousands of model poles exist (I know of no one who has attempted to count them).[6] However, model houses from all tribal regions of the Northwest Coast number fewer than a hundred examples known to me at this time. Models of houses and poles sold to outsiders can only be documented dating back to the early 1870s. The very earliest collection of a model pole is one accessioned into the Smithsonian Institution in 1870 (figure 1.3). It was collected by Lieutenant Franklin M. Ring, who was serving with the US Army when the forts at Wrangell and Tongass were established in 1868. He served at Fort Tongass between November 7, 1869, and March 5, 1870. The model pole Ring collected is based on the Tongass pole that had recently been raised in honor of "Chief-of-All-Women," Aanséet, Taant'a ḵwáan G̱anaax̱.ádi. She was Chief Ebbets's wife and Mary Ebbets Hunt's mother. This pole became famous when it was stolen by a group of Seattle businessmen in 1899 and erected in Seattle's Pioneer Square (figure 1.4). It was copied many more times in the form of model poles made as tourist souvenirs after its arrival in Seattle, largely due to its becoming a symbol of Seattle through the promotion of Joseph E. Standley and his Ye Olde Curiosity Shoppe during the Alaska Yukon Pacific Exposition in 1909 (see Moore 2018, 110; Garfield 1980; Duncan 2000, 162–66).

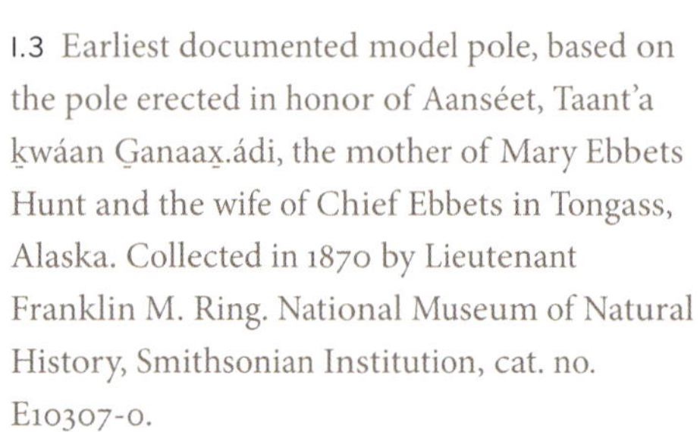

1.3 Earliest documented model pole, based on the pole erected in honor of Aanséet, Taant'a ḵwáan G̱anaax̱.ádi, the mother of Mary Ebbets Hunt and the wife of Chief Ebbets in Tongass, Alaska. Collected in 1870 by Lieutenant Franklin M. Ring. National Museum of Natural History, Smithsonian Institution, cat. no. E10307-0.

There is one case in which models of house posts were made in the late eighteenth century for use within a Tlingit community by the Tlingit artist Ḵadjisdu.ax̱ch', who is said to have carved

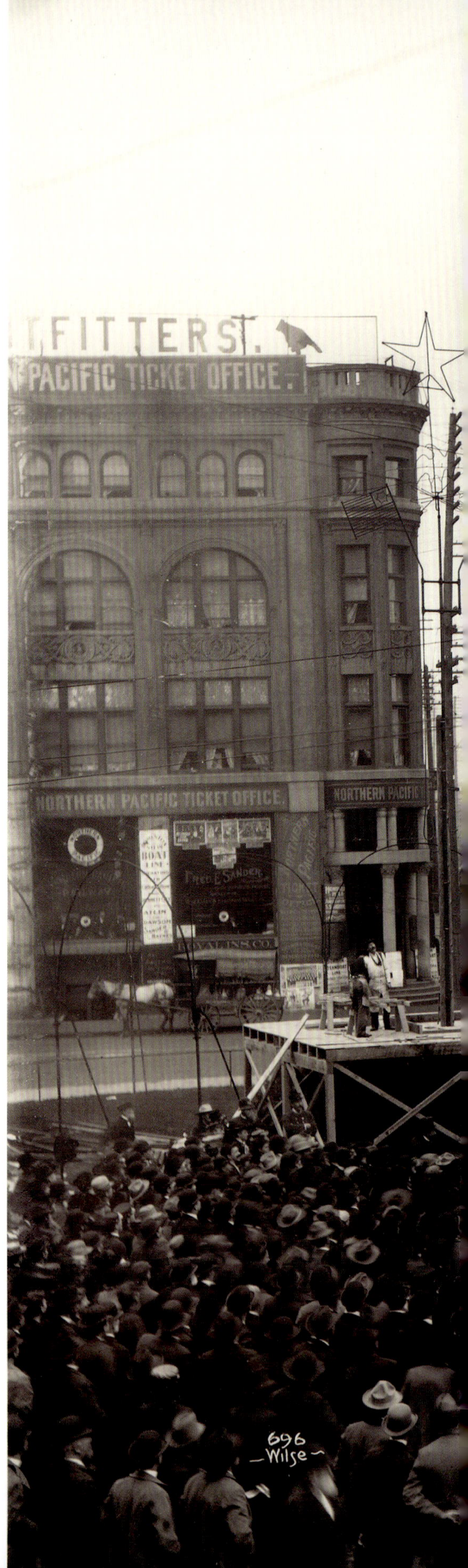

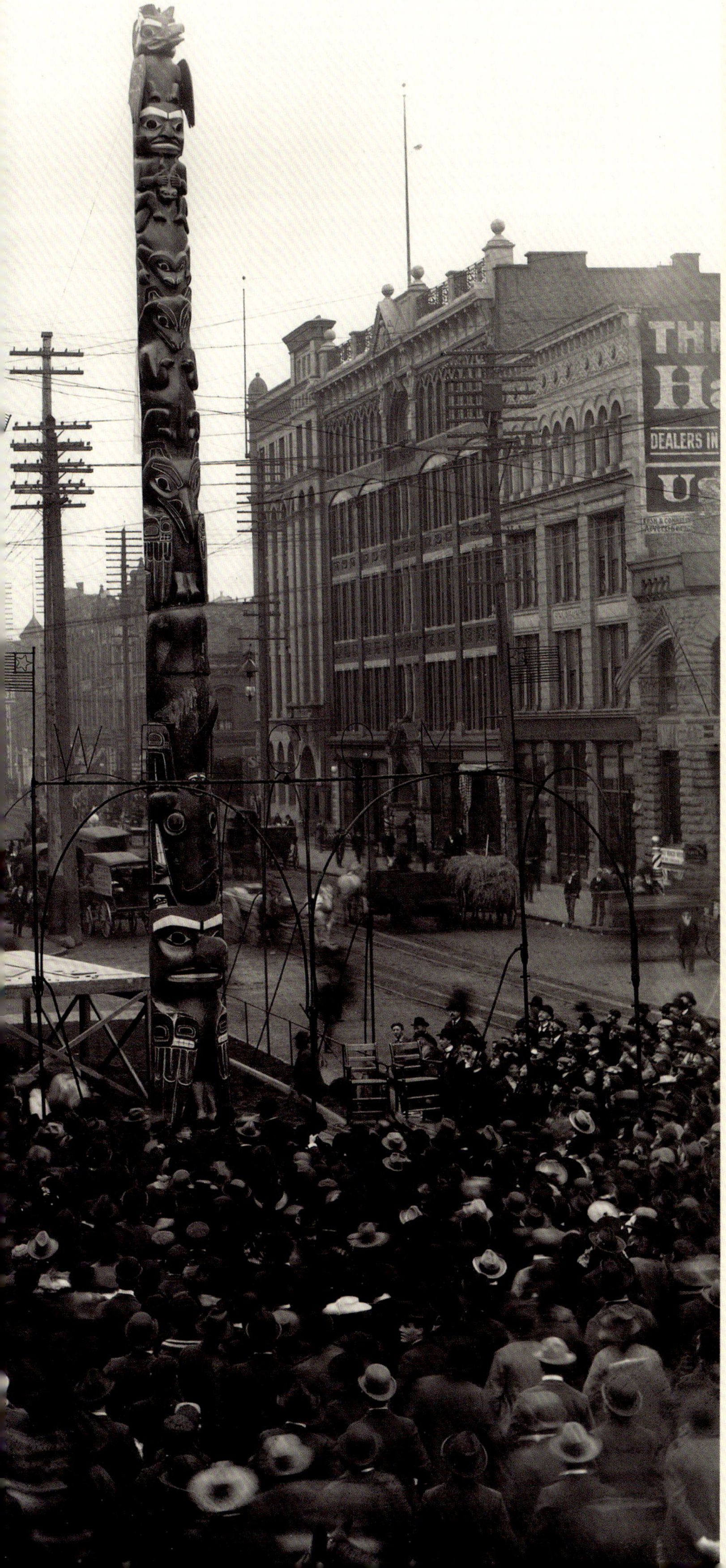

I.4 "Unveiling the Seattle Totem," at the raising ceremony in Seattle's Pioneer Square, October 18, 1899. The so-called Seattle Pole is known as the "Chief-of-All-Women Pole" honoring Aanséet, Taant'a ḵwáan G̱anaax̱.ádi, Tlingit from Tongass, Alaska. It was stolen by a group of Seattle businessmen and taken to Seattle. Museum of History and Industry neg. no. 88.33.146.

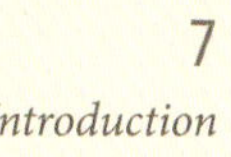

maquettes of the Klukwan Whale House interior posts during his canoe trip north from his home in Old Wrangell, as the house owners were describing what they wanted on their house posts (Enge 1993).[7]

Speaker's staffs, also known as "talking sticks" on the Northwest Coast, are like miniature poles that display the crests of the owner and are held by the speaker on ceremonial occasions. These chief's staffs date back well before the appearance of model totem poles. Sometime in the 1850s or earlier, a chief's staff was gifted from the 7IDANsuu family on Haida Gwaii to the Kadashan family in Wrangell during a marriage ceremony. This staff became a family crest and was subsequently reproduced as a full-size totem pole raised in front of John Kadashan's house in Wrangell (see Wright 1992).[8]

Several early model poles were collected for the Smithsonian Institution by Washington Territory pioneer James G. Swan. In 1873 he sent a model Haida pole to Spencer Baird at the Smithsonian (figure I.5). This pole has a beaver at the base and an eagle at the top and may have been based on one of the Skidegate or Skedans poles of this type (see figures 3.117, 3.121, 3.123, 3.124, 3.125; MacDonald 1983, 83). Swan would have purchased this model pole either in Victoria or from the visiting Haida who were camping and trading on the beach at Port Townsend in 1873, with whom Swan became friendly. At this time Swan had not yet visited the Haida in their home islands. He had begun collecting ethnological objects in Washington Territory during his time in Port Townsend in the 1860s, sending plant and animal specimens to Spencer Baird, assistant secretary at the Smithsonian, initially at his own expense (McDonald 1972, 150–51).

In 1866, Swan inherited some funds and invested in trade goods that he had sent to Sitka, Alaska, for the purchase of furs

1.5 *right* Model pole collected by James G. Swan, 1873. National Museum of Natural History, Smithsonian Institution, cat. no. E13096-0.

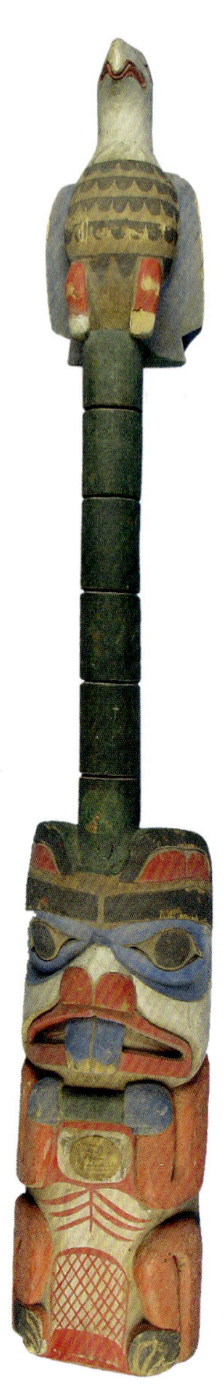

and "curiosities" (boxes, baskets, robes, a bracelet, and a cane). He picked these up on his first trip north in 1869 from Captain A. J. Whitfords (or A. T. Whitford, according to Cole 1985, 23), a trader in Sitka. No model poles or houses were included among the objects he acquired in 1869, according to his diary (Swan 1869). Swan was hired in 1875 by Baird to collect Northwest Coast objects for the Centennial Exposition held in Philadelphia in 1876. This allowed Swan to make another trip north to Alaska, where he acquired about five hundred objects that were exhibited in Philadelphia and later became part of the Smithsonian's earliest Northwest Coast collections (Cole 1985, 28). Two of these were Tlingit house models acquired upon his return to Sitka in 1875 (figure 1.6). It is possible that he had ordered these during his visit in 1869 and picked them up on his return trip six years later. We know that one year after Swan's initial visit to Sitka, when Sophia Cracroft visited Sitka in 1870, she observed in the quarters of a military officer "a curious model of the front of an Indian house, extremely well done & painted. Major Bell will endeavour to get us another, equally well done" (Wyatt 1984, 48; DeArmond 1981, 20).

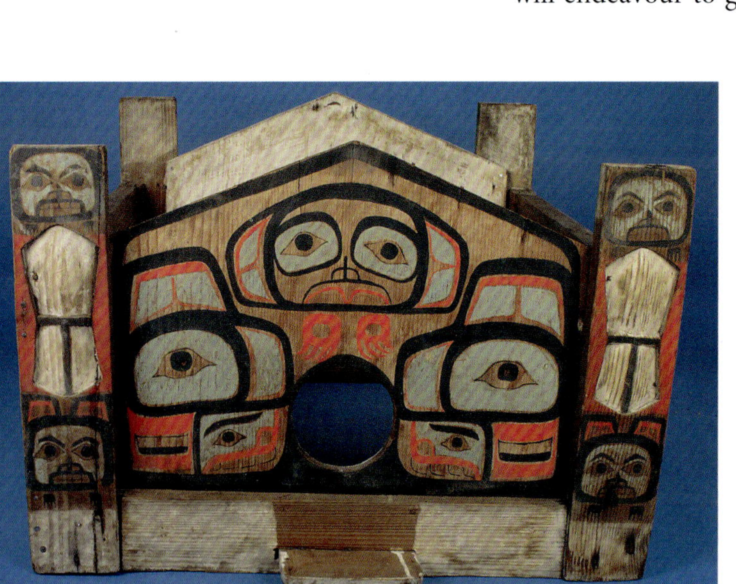

1.6 One of two Tlingit house models collected by James G. Swan, 1875, in Sitka, Alaska. National Museum of Natural History, Smithsonian Institution, cat. no. E18905-0. Swan also collected five small figures (cat. no. E18907) carved of wood with leather robes that were part of this house.

Swan was keen to collect full-size totem poles on his 1875 trip and was able to acquire six, all of which were exhibited in 1876 in Philadelphia and became part of the Smithsonian's collections.[9] The Haida whom Swan visited in Howkan and Klinkwan refused to sell him any of their full-size poles on this trip, but Swan did succeed in commissioning a new one to be carved specifically for the exhibition through the trader Alexander Baronovich at Karta Bay (figure 1.7) (see Wright 2001b, 206–9). This pole is shown in an engraving of the Centennial displays in the US Government Building exhibition hall, and showing faintly in the background to the left of this pole is a model house with corner posts and a tall frontal pole (figure 1.8). It may be that this model is one that has lost its original number at the Smithsonian but does have "Q. Charlotte Is. Swan" written on one of the boards (figure 1.9a). It has two human watchmen figures wearing hats on the corner posts of the painted house front. This model combines features of two Skidegate houses—one with a fully painted house front, and one with human figures on the corner posts

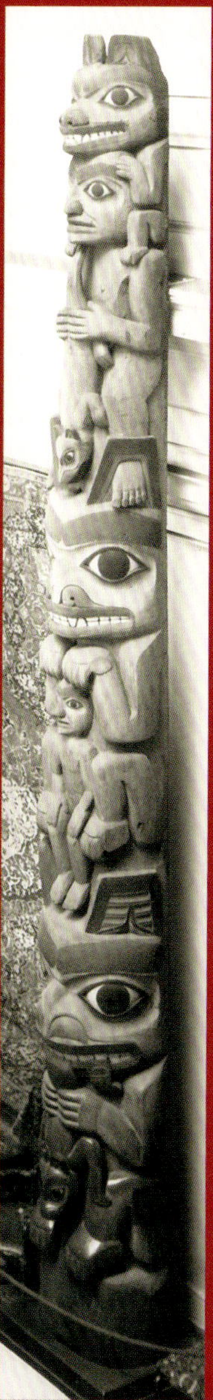

1.7 Kaigani Haida pole commissioned by James G. Swan, 1875, for the Centennial Exposition in Philadelphia, 1876, 9 m h. Likely carved by gid k'w. ajuss, Dwight Wallace, perhaps with his son, John Wallace. It is similar to an older Sukkwan pole, now in the Denver Art Museum (cat. no. 1946.251) that was carved by Dwight Wallace and brought by John Wallace to the Golden Gate International Exposition in San Francisco in 1939 (see Wright 2001b, 199–203, figure 4.27; Moore 2018, 88–89, figures 4.5 and 4.6). National Museum of Natural History, Smithsonian Institution, cat. no. 54298, neg. no. 38-109A.

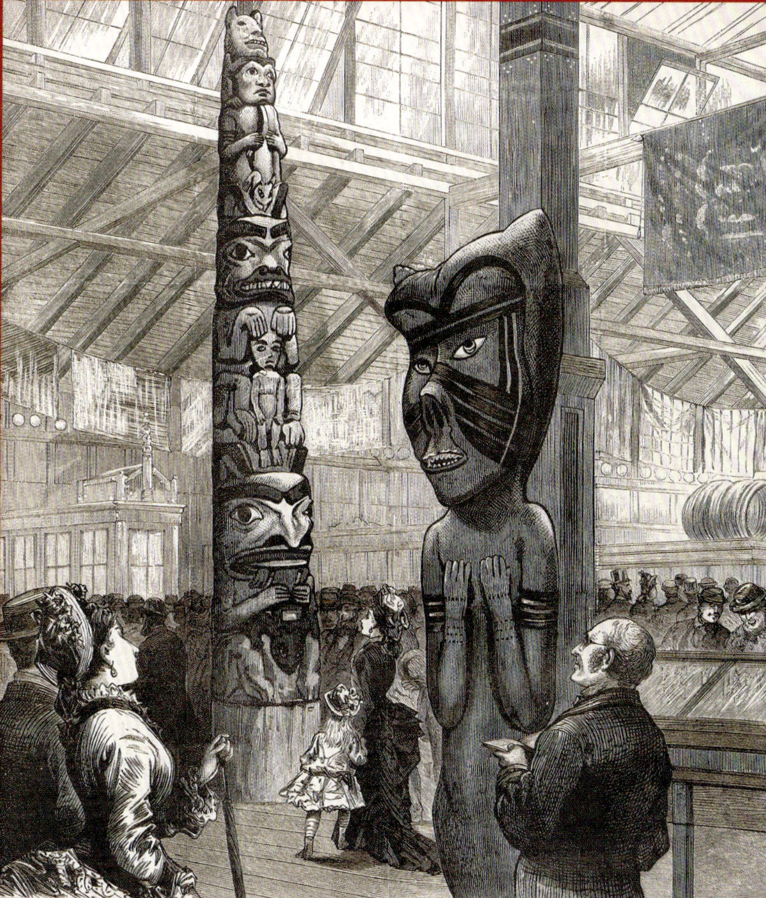

1.8 Engraving from Frank Leslie's Historical Register of the United States Centennial Exposition, showing the interior of the US Government Building's exhibit hall at the Centennial Exposition in Philadelphia, 1876. Note the model house displayed on top of an exhibit case to the left of the large Haida pole. Courtesy of the University of Illinois Rare Book and Manuscript Library, Q051 FRA (see Wright 2001b, 206–9, figure 4.33).

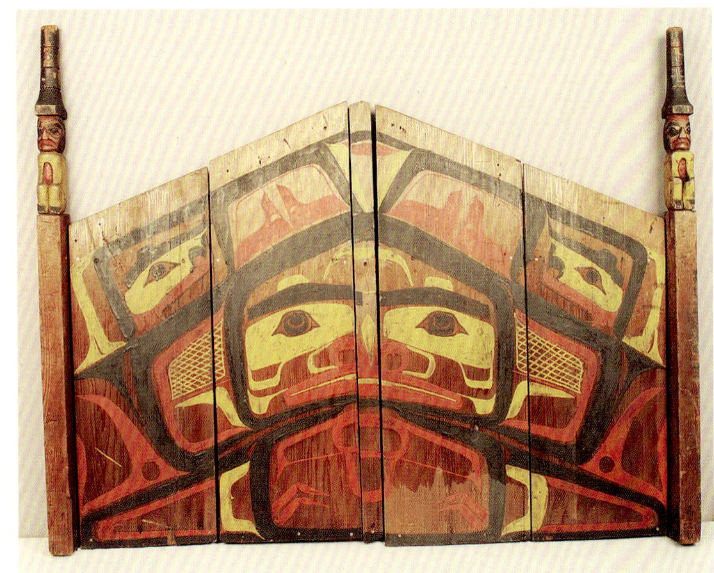

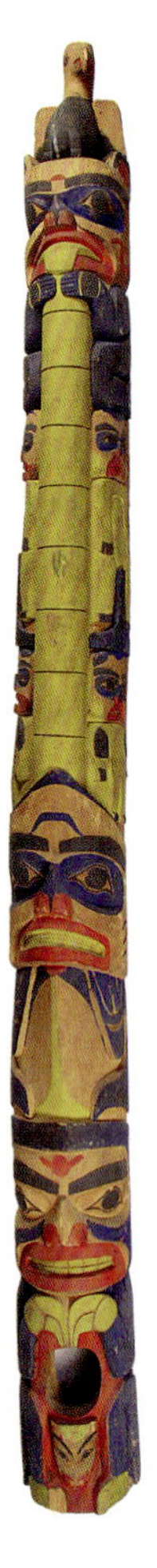

I.9 A & B Model house and frontal pole exhibited together at the Centennial Exposition in Philadelphia, likely collected by James G. Swan before 1876. National Museum of Natural History, Smithsonian Institution, cat. nos. ET14554-0 and ET24468 (pole, 88 cm h × 15 cm w). These were given "T" or temporary catalog numbers when they were found in the collection with no numbers. The house was stored as four separate walls. The three unpainted walls were formerly T14557, but the number was changed to T14554 when it was determined they are a set of four walls. Two loose boards are with the house front, and one of them has writing in pencil: "Q. Charlotte Is. Swan." See model house and pole to the far right in figure I.10.

(a rare thing on Haida houses, known only from the village of Skidegate—see figures 3.85, 3.97). The tall frontal pole shown in the engraving in front of this model house may be another Smithsonian pole with a temporary number (figure 1.9b) that depicts a Haida flood story.[10] Swan had tried desperately but unsuccessfully to get Baird to fund a trip for him to help install his collection at the Philadelphia Exposition. This may explain why the model houses were exhibited with frontal poles that were not originally associated with them, both in Philadelphia and subsequently, which has continued to confuse the Smithsonian records.

This same model house together with the pole also show at the back to the far right in a photograph that was taken a few years after the Philadelphia Exposition, when the objects had been moved to the Smithsonian Building in Washington, DC, most likely around 1884 (figure 1.10).[11] Cropped from a much larger photo, this detail shows them on top of an exhibit case to the right side of the full-size Tsimshian painted house front that was collected by Swan with the help of Rev. Crosby in Fort Simpson in 1875.[12] Though difficult to make out, there are six more house models visible in this photograph. A careful examination of the enlarged detail shows, working from left

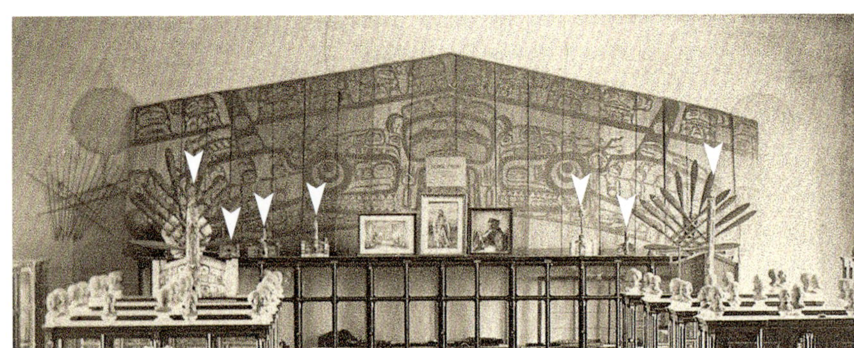

I.10 Photograph of Fort Simpson painted house front and seven model houses displayed in the Prehistoric Archaeology exhibit in the Smithsonian Building, Washington, DC, sometime after the Centennial Exposition objects were sent there after the fair (perhaps 1884). National Museum of Natural History, Smithsonian Institution, neg. no. MNH-2962. Note that this image is cropped from a much larger photograph.

to right, in front left is a large Tsimshian model house (figure I.11a) with a Haida model pole (figure I.11b) positioned as its frontal pole. This Haida pole also depicts the flood story, and most likely was collected separately from the model house, though they were exhibited together and have retained the same catalog number.

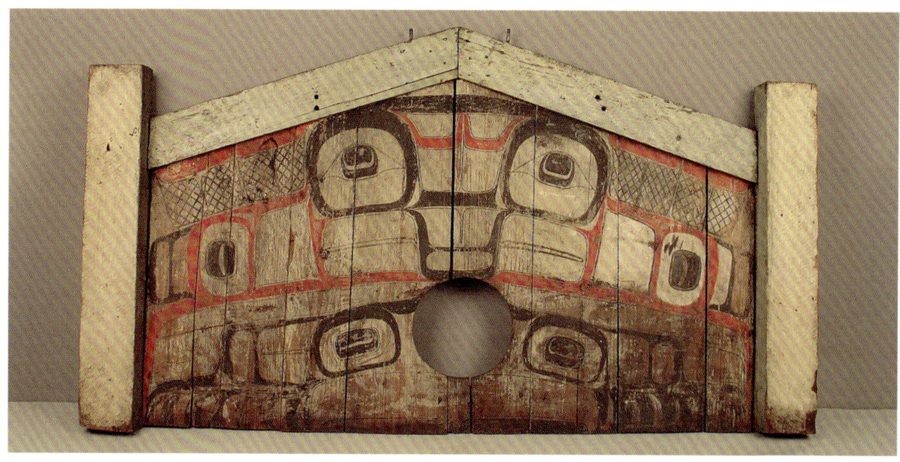

In the back row to the left of the framed pictures are likely the two Tlingit houses Swan collected in Sitka, the plain one to the left, and between them, second from the left in the back row, appears to be a model house that has a salmon-boy frontal pole (figure I.12).[13] Its original catalog number couldn't be found, so it was given a temporary number, and its collection history is undocumented. If this is the model, it was most likely collected by Swan in Skidegate on his 1883 trip to Haida Gwaii. This house model has an unusual frontal pole in the form of a salmon transforming into a human figure. Whales are painted on the sides and front of the house, and four whales extend out on the beam ends. No houses in Skidegate match this configuration, but there was a freestanding memorial pole in the form of a transforming salmon that stood at the northern end of the village (see figure 3.139, the WCE model of this pole).

I.11 A & B Tsimshian model house and Haida frontal pole (displaying the flood story figures) that share the same catalog number and were displayed together at the Smithsonian (see figure I.10). National Museum of Natural History, Smithsonian Institution, cat. no. E23547. See model house and pole to the far left in figure I.10.

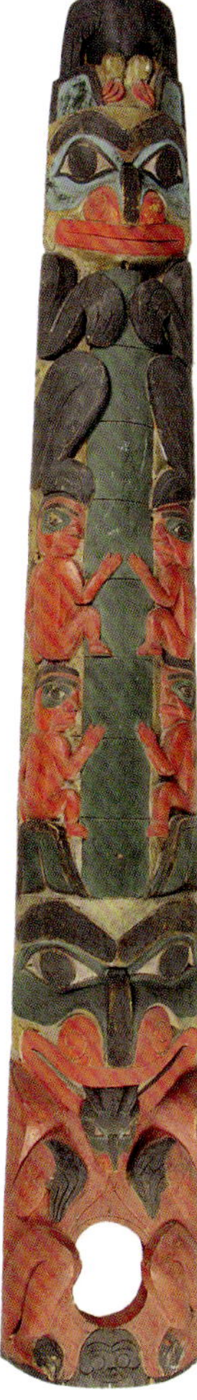

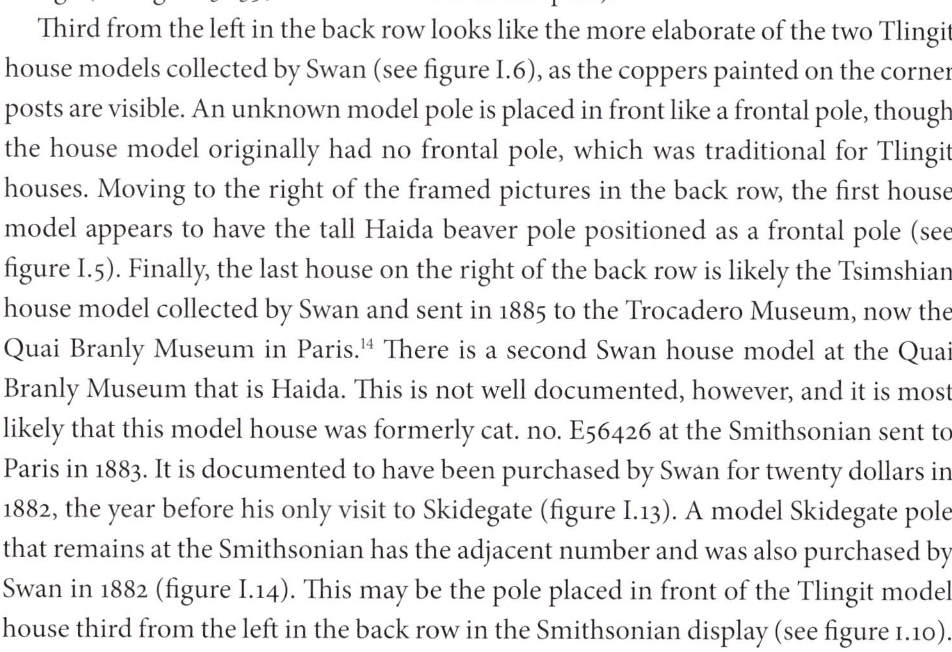

Third from the left in the back row looks like the more elaborate of the two Tlingit house models collected by Swan (see figure I.6), as the coppers painted on the corner posts are visible. An unknown model pole is placed in front like a frontal pole, though the house model originally had no frontal pole, which was traditional for Tlingit houses. Moving to the right of the framed pictures in the back row, the first house model appears to have the tall Haida beaver pole positioned as a frontal pole (see figure I.5). Finally, the last house on the right of the back row is likely the Tsimshian house model collected by Swan and sent in 1885 to the Trocadero Museum, now the Quai Branly Museum in Paris.[14] There is a second Swan house model at the Quai Branly Museum that is Haida. This is not well documented, however, and it is most likely that this model house was formerly cat. no. E56426 at the Smithsonian sent to Paris in 1883. It is documented to have been purchased by Swan for twenty dollars in 1882, the year before his only visit to Skidegate (figure I.13). A model Skidegate pole that remains at the Smithsonian has the adjacent number and was also purchased by Swan in 1882 (figure I.14). This may be the pole placed in front of the Tlingit model house third from the left in the back row in the Smithsonian display (see figure I.10).

Spencer Baird hired Swan again in 1883, this time in the capacity of assistant to the Fish Commissioner, to visit Haida Gwaii and collect natural history specimens as well

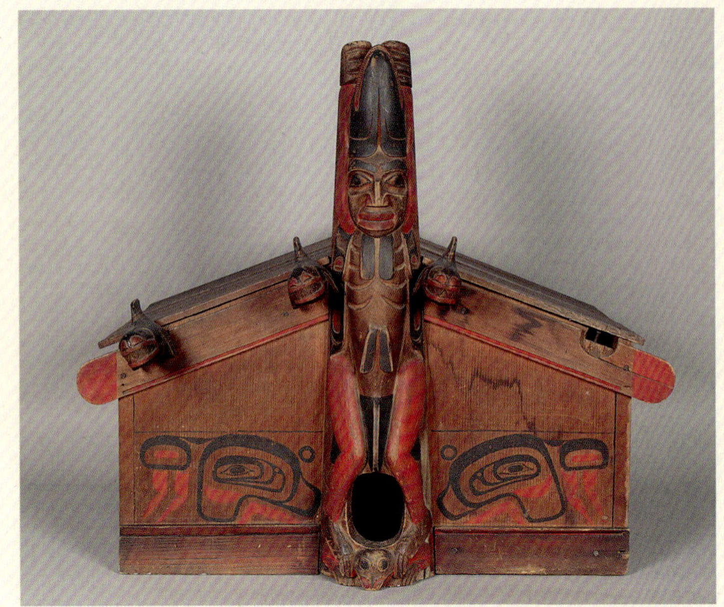

I.12 Model Haida house with whales on the roof beams and painted on the sides of the house, likely 1883. The frontal pole has a salmon transforming into a human figure. Frontal pole: 54 cm h. National Museum of Natural History, Smithsonian Institution, cat. no. ET24565-0.

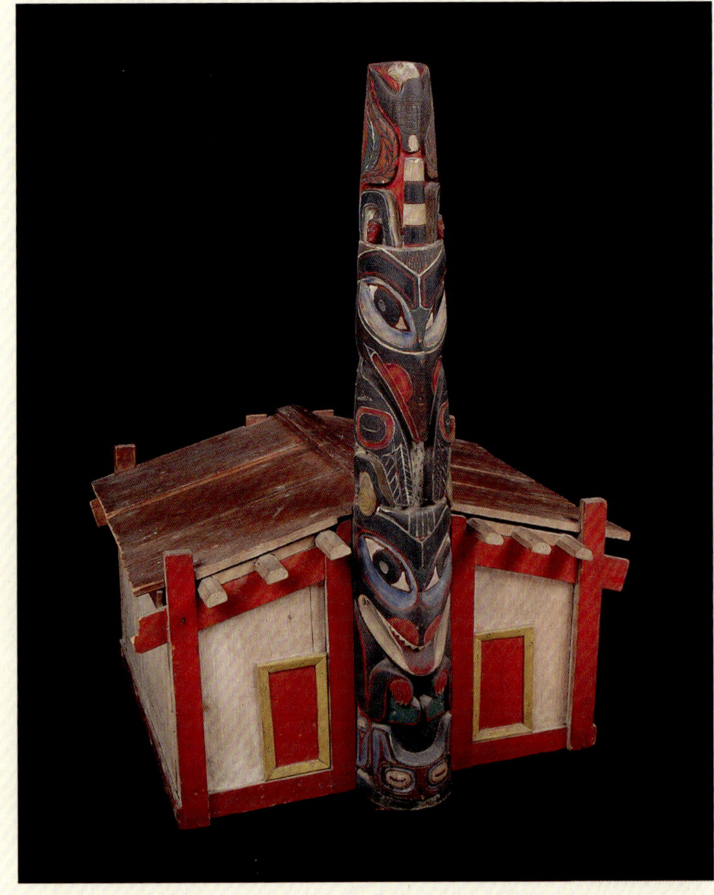

I.13 Skidegate Haida house model purchased by James G. Swan for twenty dollars and sent to the Smithsonian in 1882, 100 h cm × 69 w cm × 61 d cm, now at the Musée du Quai Branly—Jacques Chirac, Paris, cat. no. 71.1885.78.11 (formerly Musée de l'Homme and National Museum of Natural History, Smithsonian Institution, cat. no. E56426?).

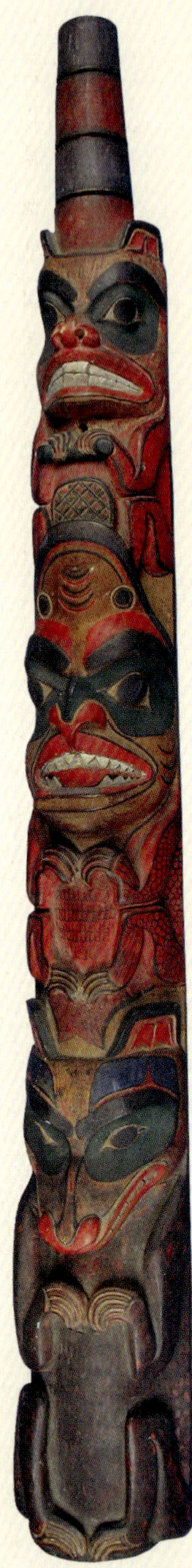

I.14 Haida model pole model purchased by James G. Swan in Skidegate, 1882, National Museum of Natural History, Smithsonian Institution, cat. no. E56427-0.

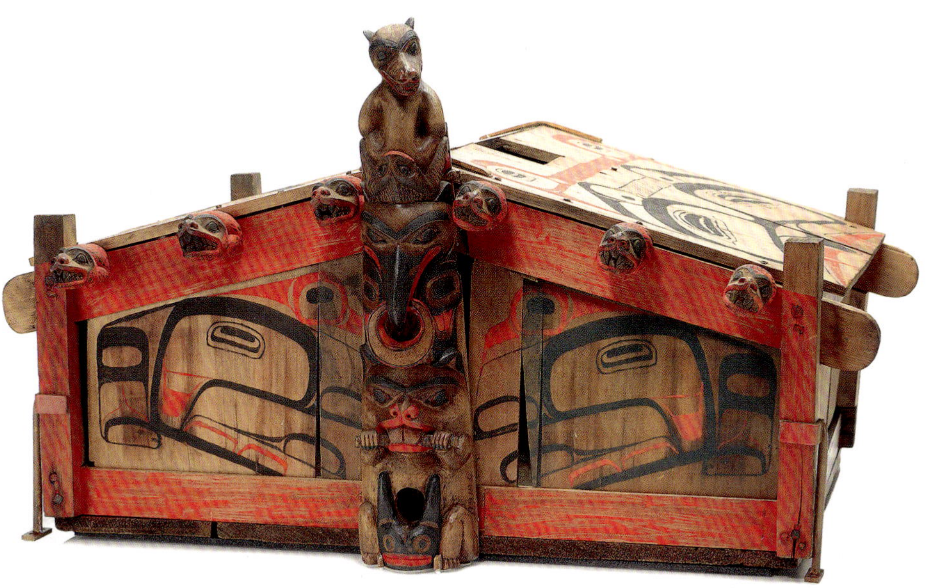

I.15 Model Haida house collected by Swan in 1883, attributed to John Robson, 59.8 cm h. National Museum of Natural History, Smithsonian Institution, cat. no. E89184–0.

as Haida artifacts for the Smithsonian's growing collections. This was Swan's only trip to Haida Gwaii, during which he was accompanied by a Haida interpreter, Johnny Kit Elswa, and James Deans (who later returned to Skidegate to commission the model houses for the Chicago World's Columbian Exposition). During this trip Swan collected hundreds of objects, including several (at least twenty-five) argillite model poles, three wooden model poles, and one house model. The model house from Skidegate (figure 1.15) may be based on Xuuajii Naas (Grizzly Bear House) in Skidegate that had bears on the roof beams (see figure 3.128); however, the frontal poles are different, having only a beaver in common. The frontal pole on this model has a beaver at the bottom, a raven with the crescent moon in his beak above, and frog facing up below a wolf with its back forward, twisting its head around front, with its long tail turned up on its back that shows at the top front. It can be attributed to John Robson's hand, based on its style.[15]

Also on Swan's 1883 trip he hired Johnny Kit Elswa to carve several models, one in argillite, based on Albert Edward Edenshaw's house frontal pole in K'yuusda (see Wright 2001b: 146–48), and one said to be a model of a T'aanuu pole (figure 1.16).

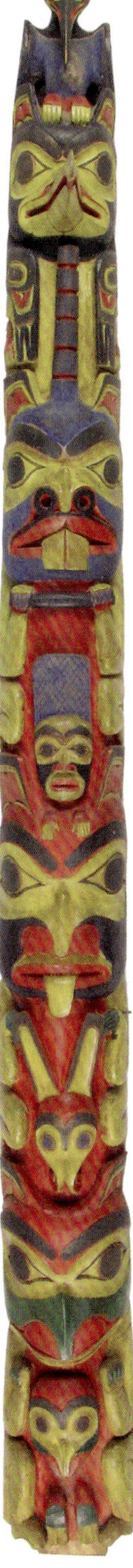

I.16 *right* Model pole collected by James G. Swan, 1883, made by Johnny Kit Elswa, said to represent a chief's house frontal pole from T'aanuu, but the figures more closely resemble a pole from K'yuusda, also copied by Kit Elswa in argillite and sketched by James G. Swan (see Wright 2001b, 147–49, figures 3.32, 3.33, and 3.34). National Museum of Natural History, Smithsonian Institution, cat. no. E74748–0.

This pole was said by Swan to have been made by Johnny Kit Elswa: "model of totemic column in front of chief's house Laskeek [T'aanuu], Queen Charlotte Id., B.C." This pole has a raven at the top, a beaver in the middle, a butterfly and a bear at the bottom. Although there were three poles at the north end of T'aanuu that did have beavers, none is exactly like this model. It appears, in fact, that this pole by Kit Elswa is another version of the K'yuusda pole he carved in argillite with the butterfly at the bottom. This model is very similar in style and color to the flood pole discussed earlier (see figure I.9b). This is likely based on GitK̲un's frontal pole and may have been carved by Kit Elswa as well, though it has lost its original documentation.

By the time James Deans returned to Skidegate in 1892 to commission the set of model houses and poles for the World's Columbian Exposition, only eleven house models of any tribal style are known to have been collected earlier on the Northwest Coast. All but one of these had been acquired by James G. Swan.[16] Of the ninety-nine known house models (of any date or any tribal style), sixty are Haida, and more than half (thirty-two) of these were commissioned by Deans in 1892.[17] Seen in this context, the set of Skidegate house models holds a unique place in the history of Northwest Coast art. No other Indigenous village in North America was so systematically documented in this way by its own residents, and for these reasons it deserves further study.

ONE / Haida House Models in the White City

The organizers of the anthropology exhibits in Chicago would have been well aware of the displays of Northwest Coast material that had been shown in Philadelphia, which had been criticized for their general disorganization and lack of educational interpretation (Cole 1985, 27; Jacknis 2016, 265). To assure that the Chicago exhibit would be superior in every way, it was determined to make much more systematic collections. James Deans's assignment was to commission a model of the village of Skidegate as it appeared nearly thirty years earlier, in 1864, fourteen years before the first photographs of the village were taken by George Dawson (Cole 1985, 123; Jacknis 1991, 95). It is unclear why this specific date was chosen, although this would have been immediately after the devastation of the 1862 smallpox epidemic, a turning point in Haida history. The organizers of the fair wanted to represent Native cultures in their "pristine" condition, before the impact of Europeans, as a way to highlight the differences between the Euro-Americans' forward-looking "civilization" and what they perceived to be "primitive" cultures, and thus contrast and highlight the successes of the American industrial age. This ignored the fact that the Spaniard Juan Perez made contact with the Haida in 1774, more than one hundred years before the World's Columbian Exposition (WCE).

Upon his arrival in HlG̱aagilda Llnagaay (Skidegate village) in 1892, Deans reported that only three old-style cedar plank houses were still standing (Deans 1899b, 17). He purchased one of these for the Chicago fair, leaving two. Most people were living in colonial-style milled lumber houses, and only a few poles remained standing in the village. The re-creation of their now missing poles in model form must have appealed to the Haida carvers who sought to preserve their traditions and stories. The Haida were looking back to their ancestral histories while the fair organizers were looking toward the future of the American colonial "civilization." Thus the Haida and the fair organizers had diametrically opposed agendas when the model village was made.

In less than a year this model village was carved and shipped to Victoria aboard the steamer *Danube*, and then on to Chicago by boat and train, arriving there in the fall of 1892. There it was assembled in the Anthropology Building, which opened late, several months after the official opening of the fair. In addition to the model village, Deans collected three boxcar-loads of Haida material, including a full-size house and frontal pole and a forty-two-foot Haida canoe. The house and two more full-size Haida poles (loaned by E. E. Ayer) were erected on the bank of South Pond next to the Tlatslasikwala (Nuwitti) house collected by George Hunt, and the Haida canoe was pulled up on the beach there (figure 1.1). Also at the South Pond there were a Nuxalk memorial bear figure and house frontal pole (seen to the right), a Tsimshian pole (seen to the far left), Salish house posts, and two Tlingit poles loaned by E. E. Ayer (out of the photo to the left) (Cole 1985, 123–27; Jacknis 1991, 98).

A group of Kwakwa̱ka̱'wakw people led by George Hunt were brought from Alert Bay by Franz Boas to demonstrate

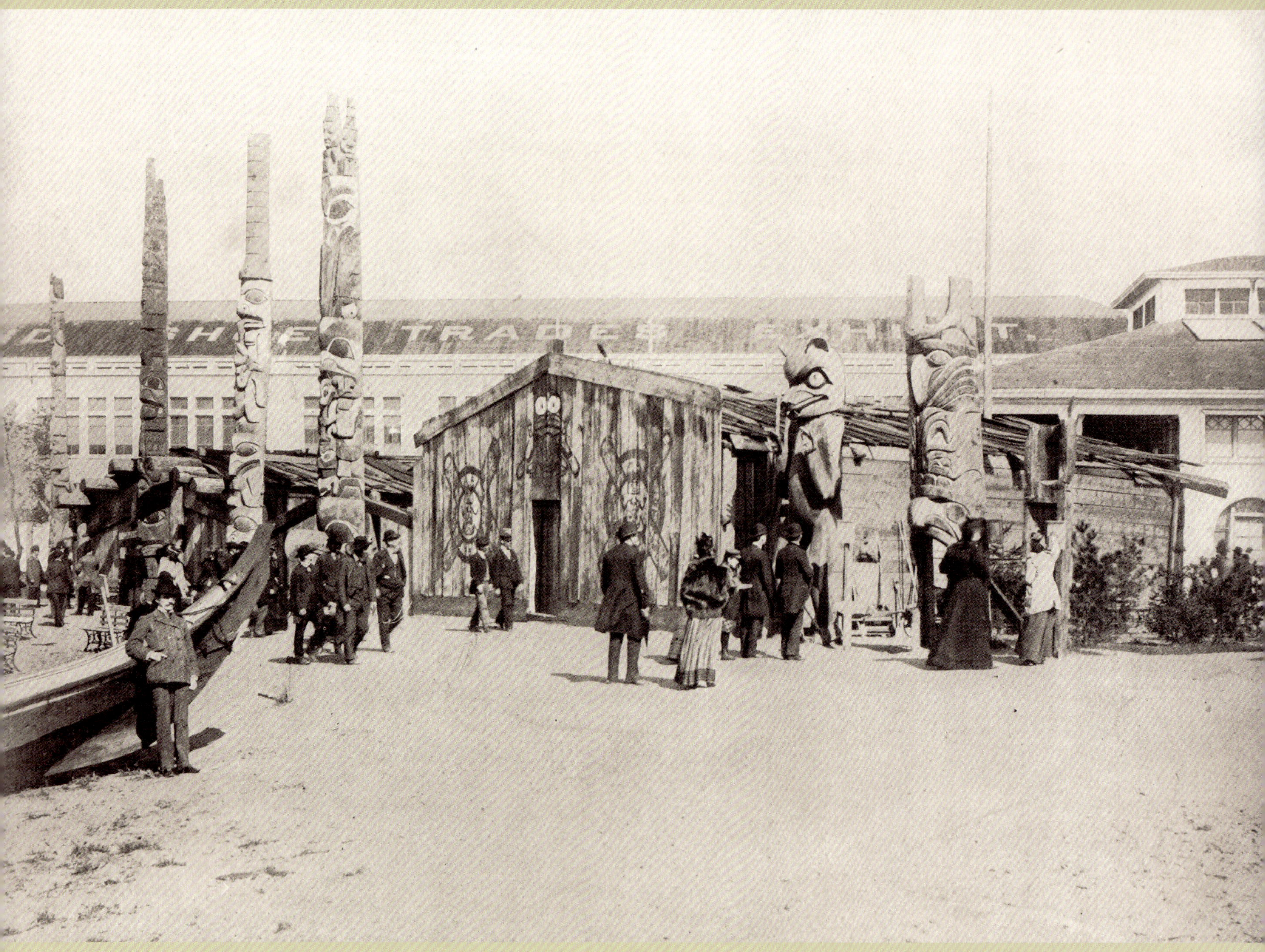

1.1 Tl'aajaang quuna's house and frontal pole (pole at far left, house with six extended beams) at the World's Columbian Exposition in 1893, from *The Glories of the World's Fair, Chicago: The Fair*, 1894. Courtesy of the Chicago History Museum, cat. no. ICHi-68016.

their songs and dances. They lived in the big houses on the fairgrounds, but no Haida people were invited to participate, and the only public interpretation of their model village was conducted by James Deans. Deans's interpretation of the model village at the fair was based on his own written record of the stories he had acquired from the Skidegate carvers telling the history of each house and model pole. He recorded the names of seventeen of the Haida artists whom he commissioned. Their names are: Adam Brown [Cowgill], Peter Brown, John Cross [Niislant], George Dickson [Dixon], William Dickson [Dixon], Daniel Ellguwuus [Iljuuwaas], Phillip Jackson, Joshua Kinna-jesser [Tait], Moses McKay [Lansing], Phillip Pearson, John Robson [Gyaawhllns], Amos Russ [Gidansd], David Shakespeare [Skilduunaas], Peter Smith, Tom Stevens [Tl'aajaang quuna], George L. Young, and Zacherias [Nicholas].

We are indebted to James Deans for recording these names and associating them with the house models they made. Five of these artists—John Cross, William Dixon, Moses "Makay," John "Robison" (Robson), and George Young—had been discussed by Marius Barbeau in his 1950s books on argillite carvers (Barbeau 1957, 1958). The carving styles of John Cross, John Robson, and a then unnamed artist dubbed the "Master of the Chicago Settee" had been analyzed by Bill Holm (Holm 1981). Leslie Drew and Douglas Wilson list John Cross, George and William Dixon, Moses McKay, John Robson, David Shakespeare, and George Young in their book on argillite (Drew and Wilson 1980), but by the time the research for this book was done, nothing had been published about the other nine carvers' work (Adam and Peter Brown, Daniel Iljuuwaas, Phillip Jackson, Joshua Tait, Phillip Pearson, Amos Russ, Peter Smith, and Tom Stevens). Unfortunately, Deans didn't put names with the freestanding model poles in the set, with the exception of one by Tom Stevens. His efforts were primarily focused on recording the stories associated with the poles, but his goal in recording these stories was to prepare an exhibition, and later a publication that would appeal to the non-Haida public (Deans 1899b).

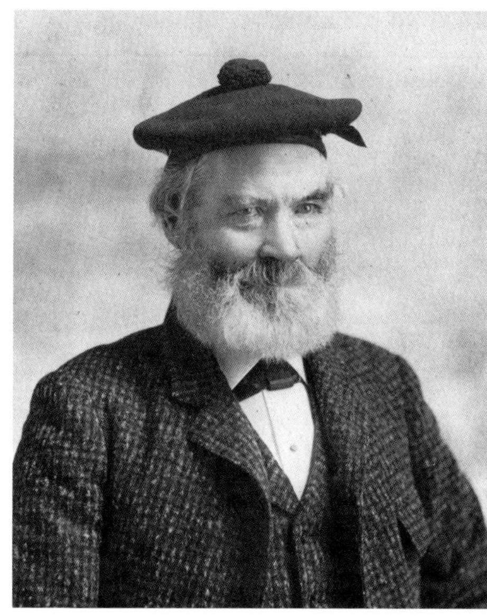

1.2 James Deans. Image F7472. Courtesy of the Royal BC Museum and Archives.

To better understand how James Deans arrived at his position of recorder/collector, some biographical information is presented here. He was born in Aimisfield, Haddingtonshire, Scotland, on June 17, 1827 (figures 1.2, 1.3). He left London on August 17, 1852, on the Hudson's Bay Company's barque *Norman Morrison*, and arrived in Victoria, BC, on January 16, 1853. With him were about two hundred settlers, including Deans's brother George and George's wife, Annie, all brought by the Puget Sound Agricultural Company, a branch of the Hudson's Bay Company, to settle Vancouver Island. The Hudson's Bay Company post had been established in Victoria in 1849. Deans worked for five years at seventeen pounds per year and board, after which time he received a grant of land of twenty-five acres. Deans was employed for the first few weeks at the company's store and was later sent to work on the HBC farm at Craigflower near Victoria. He spent two-and-a-half years there and was then sent to Lake Hill Sheep Station, where there were seventeen hundred sheep, to work the rest of his term (Bunyan 1982).

Deans was skilled at languages and quickly learned the Chinook Jargon trade language that allowed him to converse with the local Indigenous population. His linguistic abilities allowed him to serve as interpreter not only with the First Nations people but with the occasional Russian visitor. He also became known as a botanist, geologist, fisheries expert, ethnologist, and anthropologist—all self-taught skills (Bunyan 1982). In 1857, Deans left the HBC and became a farmer with his brother George on their property, which was named Oak Vale Farm, near Mount Tolmie and Victoria. In 1864 he married Catherine Bullion, from Edinburgh, Scotland. They had no children. Shortly after his marriage, Deans reported on his placer-mining at the Bullion Claim on the Leech River. His mining activities were continued in Haida Gwaii, during 1869, 1870, and 1872, working for the Queen Charlotte Coal Company in Skidegate Inlet (Cole 2003). Deans returned there again in 1882 for more coal exploration.

Deans also worked during this time for the Indian Commissioner in BC, Israel W. Powell, which led to his accompanying James G. Swan on his circumnavigation of Graham Island, Haida Gwaii, in 1883, as discussed in the introduction. Swan was collecting for the Smithsonian Institution, and Powell introduced him to Deans, suggesting that someone from the British Columbia Indian Service should join Swan on the trip. However, when Powell did not come up with the funds to pay for Deans's trip, Deans took it upon himself to travel there on his own funds, joining Swan several weeks later in Massett. From there they circumnavigated Graham Island in a canoe with Albert Edward Edenshaw as their guide. Swan and Deans did not get along well on this trip, leading Swan to comment in a letter: "the most *cultus*, useless incubus I ever was cursed with" (McDonald 1972, 184–93).[1] Albert Edward Edenshaw would likely have agreed with Swan's opinion, given that Deans later led the Field Museum collector and infamous grave robber George Dorsey back to graves shown to them by Edenshaw, from which Edenshaw had expressly forbidden them to remove anything (see discussion below).

Deans returned again to Haida Gwaii in 1884, where he surveyed a company's coal claim. While there he became acquainted with an American man named Benjamin Gibbs and nine others who had been taken as slaves by the Haida for about a year (Deans 1878). He was also an amateur archaeologist and excavated several burial mounds near Victoria. Though he had little schooling, Deans was a prolific writer and poet who wrote as many as sixty letters to the editor and articles for *The Colonist*, the Victoria newspaper. He published twenty-five articles on the Haida, Northwest Coast myths, and archaeology in the *American Antiquarian* between 1886 and 1895 (Deans 1884?, 1888?, 1890, 1892). Several of these articles were republished in two

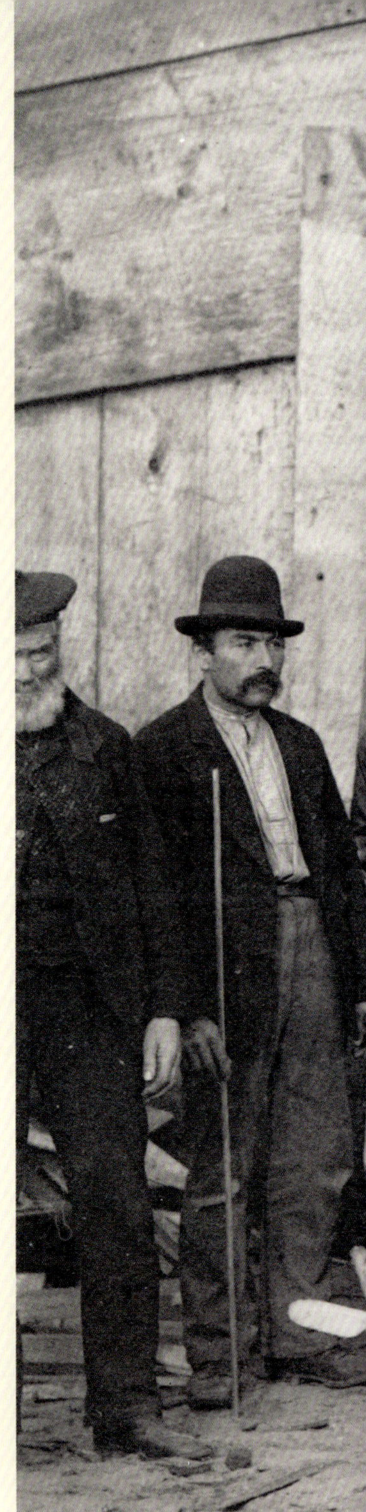

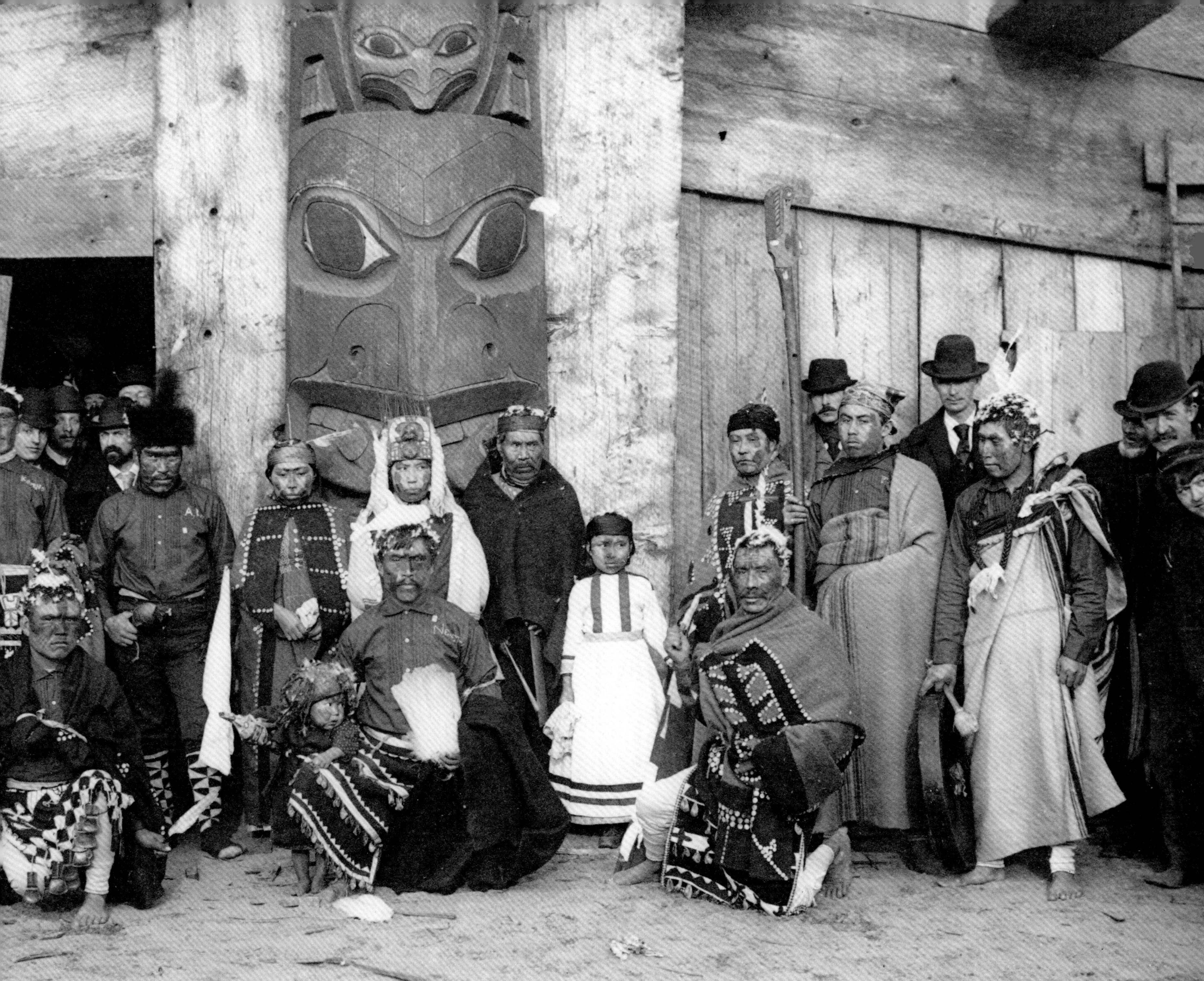

1.3 James Deans (far left edge of photo) and George Hunt (next to Deans) with a Kwakwaka̱'wakw group in front of Tl'aajaang quuna's Haida House at the World's Columbian Exposition, 1893. "Quackuhl Model Village, World's Columbian Exposition, Chicago, Illinois." Photograph by Charles Dudley Arnold, 1893. World's Columbian Exposition Photographs by C. D. Arnold, Ryenon and Burnham Art and Architecture Archives, Art Institute of Chicago, Digital File # 198902_140619-E20989.

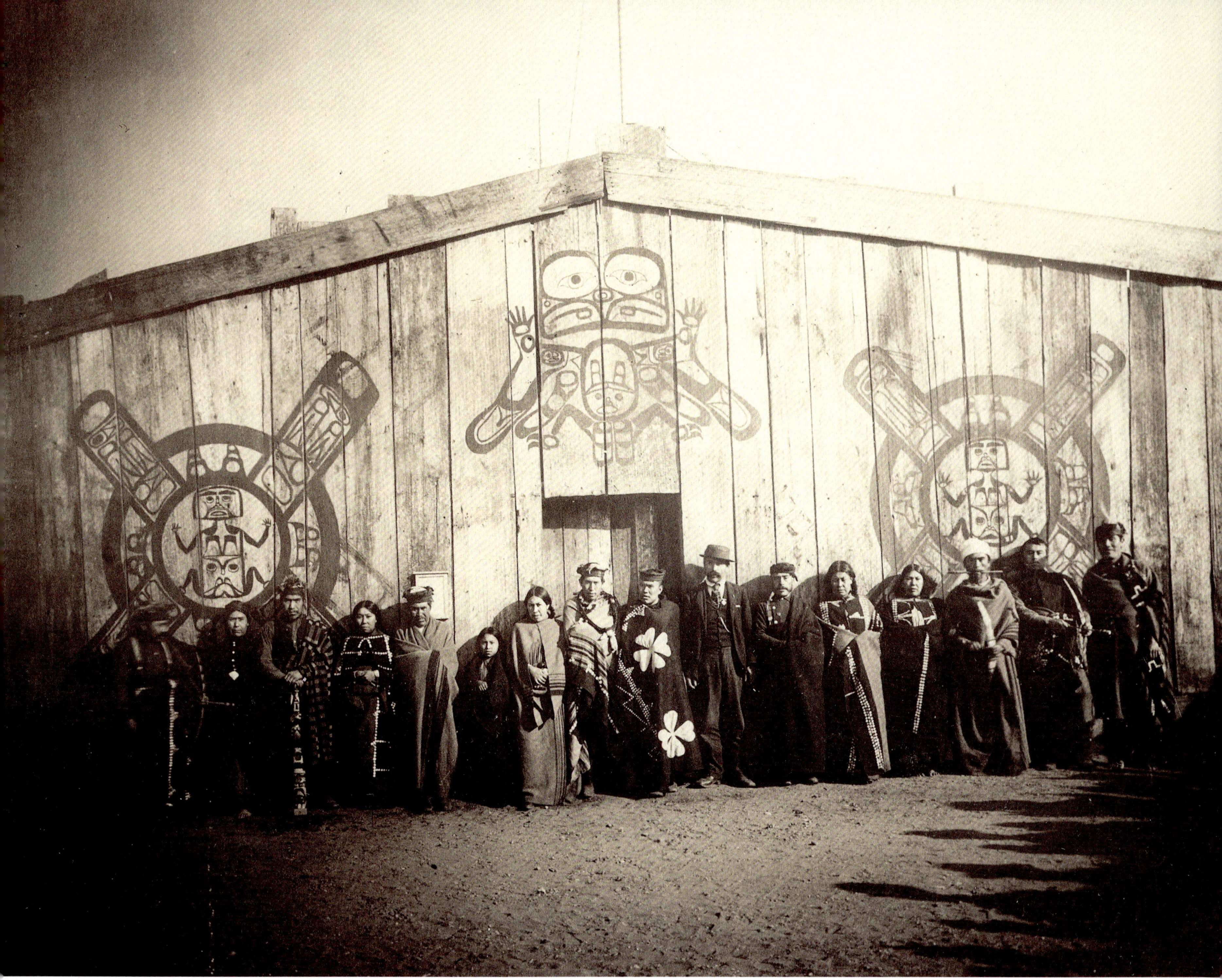

1.4 Kwakwa̱ka̱'wakw group posing in front of Nakumgilisala's house, brought from Tlatslasikwala (formerly known as Nuwitti) to the World's Columbian Exposition, Chicago, 1893. Courtesy of the Peabody Museum of Archaeology and Ethnology, Harvard University, 9-1-10/100266.1.30.

limited-edition volumes in 1899 by the International Folk-Lore Association (Deans 1899a, 1899b).

When James Deans was hired by Franz Boas to collect Haida material for the Chicago fair, he arranged to go to Haida Gwaii again. He spent over two months there in early 1892, returning to Victoria on the steamer *Danube* on May 27, as reported in the *Victoria Daily Colonist*. He brought with him the complete 28- × 29-foot Haida house and 40-foot frontal pole belonging to Tom Stevens (Tl'aajaang quuna) (see figure 1.1 left and figure 3.105 left). According to the newspaper account:

> Mr. Deans has obtained a collection before which the most critical connoisseur of fine arts must stand in mute amazement. . . . As all the models were not finished, they were not brought down. It is Mr. Deans intention to return with the steamer next trip and after all is finished, he will return to Victoria at the first opportunity, bringing the remainder of the collection with him. Such a collection as has been made will doubtless take the lovers of fine arts by surprise. (*Victoria Daily Colonist* 1892a)

The house and frontal pole were sent to Chicago immediately. It wasn't until September 9, 1892, that Deans was able to return to Victoria with the complete collection of model houses. In addition, he had the forty-two-foot canoe and an ermine skin headdress (*Victoria Daily Colonist* 1892b). Mary Watson Tulip told Marius Barbeau: "My father [Amos Watson] carved for the Chicago Fair, and he sold his big canoe there to Chicago fair" (Barbeau 1916–1954, BF 256.17).

Boas had arranged for George Hunt, Boas's collector/collaborator from Fort Rupert, to bring a group of fifteen adults and two children, all Kwakwa̱ka̱'wakw people, to the fair to be the living components of his anthropology exhibit.[2] They included George Hunt's oldest son, David, and also George Hunt's brother William Hunt, William's wife, and his father-in-law (Jacknis 2002, 85).[3]

In April 1893 they set out for Chicago, escorted by James Deans, who stayed the entire length of the fair with them in Chicago until it closed in October. It is said that Deans gave daily "readings" of the totem poles at the fair (Twigg 2005). The group was housed temporarily in three small rooms in the stock pavilion, until they could move into the two traditional cedar plank houses (Tl'aajaang quuna's Skidegate house, and a Tlatslasikwala (formerly Nuwitti) house belonging to Nakumgilisala) that were erected on the fairgrounds (figures 1.3 and 1.4). At the end of the fair the Kwakwa̱ka̱'wakw group, including Deans, returned to the Northwest by Canadian Pacific rail. Putnam's attitude toward these people is revealed in his correspondence with the railway company, arguing that they should "be free like other exhibits, as they were exhibits in every sense of the term" (Cole 1985, 133, 335n52). At one point Deans was left behind at a dinner stop and wired ahead that the Indians be put off at the next stop to wait for him. George Hunt reported that after that Deans "acted Bad to us. I did not like his way at all." The Kwakwa̱ka̱'wakw were paid $20 per month for 7.5 months, for a total of $150 each, plus expenses from Alert Bay. Hunt was paid $90 per month for eight months plus expenses. It is unclear how much Deans was paid for his time (Cole 1985, 335n52).

Deans did profit from his collecting on Haida Gwaii. It is unclear what Boas's budget was for this collection. A. W. Vowell (1892), Indian Superintendent for British Columbia, claims to have been "credibly informed that about $4,000 has been appropriated for the purchase of articles" from BC by unnamed agents collecting for the World's Fair. By May 1892, James Deans had received $750 for the WCE collecting, but this apparently did not include the cost of the model village (Beck 2019, 71). I have found only a partial document that is an invoice of specimens sent by Deans for the WCE collection, just one page of what was apparently a longer document that totals $177.[4]

Before Deans left for the fair, he sold several items that he had acquired while collecting for Boas to the new British Columbia Provincial Museum. The *British Colonist* reported in April 1893 that Deans was paid $298.65 for this Haida Collection (Cole 1985, 348n27). This included two full-size interior house posts from Skidegate (RBCM 1, 2), a model of Daniel Iljuuwaas's house, which duplicates one sent to the WCE (RBCM 232), a model grave house, also a duplicate of one set to Chicago (RBCM 224), and several model poles, three of which are duplicates of poles sent to Chicago (RBCM 227, 228, 230, 231, 237). We know that two of these house models, collected with the WCE material, were sold to the Provincial Museum in Victoria for $25 and $29 each (this according to the Royal British Columbia Museum, James Deans's September 1892 invoice for the Skidegate collection). At this rate the full WCE model village may have been purchased by Boas from Deans for around $1000. Certainly Deans would have paid the artists considerably less than this amount, keeping a portion for his time and efforts.

After the fair Deans continued to profit beyond the Boas WCE commission and Provincial Museum purchases. The frontal pole from one other model house collected by Deans at this time, now attributed to John Robson, is at the Fairbanks Museum and Planetarium in Saint Johnsbury, Vermont. It was acquired in 1894 in Victoria from Deans.[5] During the following years, Deans was temporarily hired by the BC Provincial Museum to arrange the Indian materials in its collection (Cole 1985, 226). He continued to publish articles on Haida stories through the 1890s and continued to benefit from his experience with the Haida people and the World's Columbian Exposition throughout his life. Most infamously, in 1897, Deans accompanied George Dorsey from the Field Museum and the photographer Edward P. Allen on their collecting trip to Haida Gwaii (Cole 1985, 170–75). Twenty-two cases of objects were subsequently shipped to the Field Museum (Bunyan 1982). During this trip several graves in Haida Gwaii that Deans had seen in 1883 while there with Swan and Albert E. Edenshaw were looted. Edenshaw had specifically forbidden their collecting in these sites in 1883. When Deans led Dorsey there in 1897, the graves were stripped of their valuable contents, and unwanted items were strewn carelessly around. This trip has become infamous, due to the number of graves that were looted, and has gone down in history as one of the most egregious examples of looting on the Northwest Coast. Thanks to the efforts of the Haida people, in October 2003 the ancestors that were taken from these graves by Deans and Dorsey were returned and have now been reburied (Krmpotich and Peers 2013; Ross 2003).

James Deans passed away on July 17, 1905, at age seventy-eight, at Oak Vale Farm on Richmond Avenue, Victoria, BC. According to his obituary, Deans's only living relatives were his brother, George, and George's children (Bunyan 1982), but we know Deans had other siblings in England, who emigrated to Australia.[6]

PUBLIC RESPONSE TO THE HAIDA HOUSES AT THE WORLD'S COLUMBIAN EXPOSITION

The full-size houses and poles installed outside the Anthropology Building and the Kwakwa̱ka̱'wakw families who lived in them during the fair received far more attention in the Chicago press than the displays inside the Anthropology Building. This press coverage was largely very racist and sensationalized the appearance of the poles, the people, and the dance performances put on by the Kwakwa̱ka̱'wakw, reflecting the attitudes of the late nineteenth-century fairgoers (Jacknis 1991, 101–6; Jacknis 2002, 83–89). Boas intentionally featured the Kwakwa̱ka̱'wakw at the fair because he felt: "they have exerted an influence over all the tribes on the north pacific coast. It is my belief that the peculiar culture of the whole region has had its origin among the tribes of Fort Rupert, the Kwakiutl" (Johnson 1898, 344, cited in Jacknis 1991, 93; Rydell 1978). Because the people in residence in the Northwest Coast houses (including the Haida one) were all Kwakwa̱ka̱'wakw, the public incorrectly assumed that the houses and poles were also all Kwakwa̱ka̱'wakw. They were aided in this misunderstanding by newspaper accounts and the guides at the fair.

An account of the house opening ceremonies held on May 6, 1893, in the *Chicago Sunday Post*, illustrated the Haida house and frontal pole with the caption: "The Quacquhl Home and Home Gods." In another article in the *Sunday Inter Ocean* an illustration of the poles and houses on the south pond is titled "Totem Poles in Qhag Gulth Village." The houses are described as being "built of drift wood, ship timbers, the wreckage of unfortunate vessels." Of course, this misrepresents the highly developed woodworking skills of Northwest Coast carvers who felled, carved, and split their own cedar trees and crafted elegant canoes by steaming and spreading using sophisticated techniques. The article goes on to describe the poles in a way that insults both Northwest Coast and Chinese artists:

> rudely carved posts on which monsters of the deep, beasts of the forests and field and birds of the air have been caricatured in more horrid and hideous shapes than ever beset the opium-enlivened brain of a Chinese artist. . . . In front of each door and about them are heraldic posts, some thirty feet high, and totem poles fifty feet in height, on all of which are carved rude figures, hideous in outline, gigantic in size, and great glaring eyes, ferocious paws, and huge bodies of bears and frogs and men are made luridly hideous with paint, daubed and streaked to intensify the ugliness of the carving. (*Sunday Inter Ocean* 1893)

An article in the *Chicago Sunday Tribune* includes portraits sketched of "Hamaseloq, Claclasequala" and "Qhany, Koskimo" members of the Kwakwa̱ka̱'wakw group, and gives a brief review of the Skidegate house models in the Anthropology Building:

> Over in the building devoted to anthropology there are representations of almost every type of natives of the American continent, but many of them are representations only, and the folks who go there to study man and his works find it pretty abstruso. However, Prof. Putnam has given them some chance of seeing the living types. Many of the visitors spend an hour before the reproduction of the village of Skidegate, in British Columbia, which the canny Scot, James Deans, has arranged. After they have studied the queer looking huts with their heraldic columns, topped off almost invariably by the raven, they go away wondering where the "heathen" of the Northwest coast learned so much about wood carving. It is a pleasing surprise when they cross over to the South Pond and find some of those huts no longer in miniature, but big enough to contain a score or more of savages, with the big heraldic columns stuck right up in front. There are half a dozen tribes represented, but the visitors simply are told that these are the Quackuhls, the Indians of the Northwest coast who spread along the coast from Southern Alaska to Central Vancouver. (*Chicago Sunday Tribune* 1893)

Finding most of the Anthropology Building exhibits to be "abstruso," this reviewer goes on to give quite a backhanded compliment to the carving skills of the Haida, while expanding the territories of the "Quackuhls" all the way to Alaska.

In Jewell Halligan's *Illustrated World's Fair*, James Deans is credited with actually making the model village of Skidegate, not just commissioning it:

> REMARKABLE TOTEM POLES: In the north end of the Anthropological building may be found a model of the village of Skidgate [*sic*] Queen Charlotte Islands, British Columbia, in 1864. The model was made by James Deans, who was present with the exhibit to explain the methods of the historian in detailing by rude and conventional carvings the lineage of the house owner. The tribe, phratry, and gens are shown, and color plays an important part. The man with the highest pole became a prominent citizen, for the carver charged dearly for his labors. It is to be understood that the tribal array here shown was made in three villages, and in actual life did not present the poles so nearly together. (Halligan 1894, 700)

In this same photo book, Tl'aanjaang quuna's Haida house and frontal pole on South Pond is shown with the caption "The Quackuhl Totem Pole" (Halligan 1894, 564). In fact, the only Kwakwa̱ka̱'wakw house at the fair had no frontal pole and had only painted designs on the front (see figure 1.4).

It is unfortunate that none of the artists who made the Skidegate model village were invited to attend the fair, and that James Deans was the only person there who interpreted it to the public. In fact, there is evidence that some of the Haida had asked to be allowed to go to Chicago but were denied by Arthur Vowell, superintendent of Indian Affairs in British Columbia, who was acting as their guardian under the Indian Act, when Putnam declined to pay the wages and expenses for them, as he had promised to do for the Kwakwa̱ka̱'wakw (Raibmon 2000). Certainly, if any Haidas had been present, one would expect that at least Tl'aanjaang quuna's Haida house would have been identified as such, and the Haida artists rather than Deans would have gotten credit for their creations.

Putnam had not planned for the WCE exhibits to be racist.

Rather, he intended "the presentation of native life [to] be in every way satisfactory and creditable to the native peoples, and no exhibition of a degrading or derogatory character will be permitted" (Rydell 1978, 266). But one of Putnam's own staff members was actually fired for objecting to the treatment of Native peoples at the fair in her letter to the *New York Times*, charging that the Indian exhibits were meant to mislead the American people: "It has been used to work up sentiment against the Indian by showing that he is either savage or can be educated only by Government agencies. . . . Every means was used to keep the self-civilized Indians out of the Fair" (Rydell 1978, 266).

Judging from the newspaper accounts of the Kwakwa̱ka̱'wakw's dance demonstrations, the fair-going public was appalled at what they perceived to be "barbaric" displays of "primitive" culture that they witnessed: "Wildly gesticulating, dancing along the road, wearing feathers, shaking stones inside a rudely carved rattle-box, they sung and marched along. Interpreter Hunt led the way. It was a most barbaric-looking spectacle, these savages, with faces smeared with black, red, and yellow colors till they looked like devils, yelling, dancing, throwing themselves about to the weird music of the tom-tom and their song" (*Daily Inter Ocean* 1893). The totem poles were described as "rude, horrid and hideous" in comparison with the pseudo neoclassical structures that housed the majority of the exhibits at the fair. Most of these grand fair buildings were meant to be temporary and were constructed of chicken wire and plaster with a coating of white paint, thus the Chicago fairgrounds came to be known as the "White City."[7]

The model of Hlg̱aagilda Llnagaay was used by the WCE anthropologists to promote their own "scientific" agenda, the founding of an important museum collection, and the comparative analysis of Indigenous cultures. The WCE fair promoters used the model of Hlg̱aagilda Llnagaay for their own civic and colonial agenda, to glorify the industrial achievements of Chicago in comparison with what they perceived to be the less "advanced" nations and cultures of the world. Nowhere at the WCE were the voices of the Haida heard, except as they were imbedded in the carvings themselves. This book explores the model of Hlg̱aagilda Llnagaay that was made as an act of empowerment by the carvers for the Haida people at a moment in time at the end of the nineteenth century, when the Haida were faced with many outside factors that sought to disempower them.

TWO / Hlg̱aagilda Llnagaay / *Early Descriptions and Views*

The oral histories kept by the Haida go back to a time even before the Haida, to the travels of Nang Kilslas (the supernatural being, Raven, "the one whose voice is obeyed") and other supernatural beings who brought Haida Gwaii into existence. The most comprehensive written record of these oral histories, to date, was recorded by the linguist John Swanton, one of Franz Boas's students, and a member of the Jessup North Pacific Expedition, sent by Franz Boas to Haida Gwaii for ten months in 1900 and 1901. Swanton spent most of his time in Skidegate working with Walter McGregor of the Sealion Town People, K̲aay'ahl Laanas (E9), and Abraham from T'aanuu Llnagaay of those born at K'aadasg̱uu creek, K'aadaas Gaa K̲'iig̱awaay (R3), with the services of Henry Moody, G̱aag'yals K̲iig̱awaay (R4), as interpreter (Swanton 1905a, 9).[1] Edward of the Daayuu'ahl 'Laanas (R8) provided the list of Skidegate houses to Swanton (Swanton 1905a, 286–87). Mrs. James Watson, Xaagyah Laanas (R1), provided the house names for Sg̱ang Gwaay (Swanton 1905a, 282–83), and Walter, K̲aay'ahl Laanas (E9), Lucy, Skoa'laadas (R10), and Richard, Yaku Gitanee (E8b) provided the house names for Ts'aahl Llnagaay and Xaayna Llnagaay (Swanton 1905a, 288–89).[2] Today, Haida historians are using Swanton's records of their oral history, correcting and adding to them.[3]

As explained to Swanton by his Haida consultants, the Haida divide themselves into two matrilineal moieties, Eagle and Raven, and each of these is divided into named lineages that refer to places of origin or to special properties of the clan. Each lineage controlled property such as the right to fish or gather in certain places as well as the right to display certain crests on poles and tattoos or on regalia such as headdresses, hats, and robes. Lineage property also includes names (both personal and house names), songs, and dances. A chief at the head of each lineage inherits his place from his uncle, his mother's brother. If no matrilineal nephew exists, the chief's sister's daughter could take his place and hold the position in trust for her own son. Lineages could be divided into subgroups, each with a chief of these divisions, and the owner of each large cedar plank house was a house chief who had authority over the members of the household that could include their noble family members as well as associated commoners and slaves who lived in the house. Traditionally each Haida winter village was the home of only one lineage with its in-marrying spouses and their children. Over time with the amalgamation of several lineages in a village, the position of "town chief" evolved. The town chief would be the highest-ranking, wealthiest house chief of the lineage that owned the town site (Blackman 1981, 16–17).

By 1878 in Hlg̱aagilda there were ten Eagle houses grouped toward the middle, and Raven houses at both the south and north ends of the village. This included seven older Raven houses (R5, R6) to the south end. Many of these were occupied by Raven men married to the high-ranking Naa 'Yuuwans X̱aaydaG̱aay or Naa S'aagaas X̱aaydaG̱aay women (E6a or E6b). At the north end of the village were at least nine more recent Raven houses belonging to families that had emigrated from the north, Naikun and Cape Ball (R13). Families from western villages had also moved in to HlG̱aax̱id Llnagaay (First Beach) and Xaayna Llnagaay (New Gold Harbour). In the Haida matrilineal social system, people were expected to marry outside of their moiety.[4] Each household would include both an Eagle (husband or wife) and their spouse of the opposite Raven side (or moiety). The children of the house have the same clan as their mother, and the nephew of the husband (his sister's son who had their same clan) would live with his uncle when he came of age and would be expected to take the uncle's place when he died. The house frontal poles would typically include the crests of both the husband's and the wife's clans, signaling who lived inside. Wives' crests were often at the bottom of the frontal pole. The freestanding memorial poles, however, generally had only the crests of the deceased persons who were memorialized by the poles, although in some cases secondary figures representing the spouse's crests were included.

Swanton recorded a story about the history of the village of Skidegate when its old name was HlG̱aay.yuu, going back to when it was a Raven village. At this time the most important families in Skidegate Inlet were Ravens, the Seaward Sḵaahladas (R5) (Jiaaxwii SḵaahladasG̱aay), who occupied the village of Xaayna Llnagaay on Maude Island, and the HlG̱aay.yuu Laanas, Skidegate Town People (R6). This story says that in very old times there was a town on the southeast side of Maude Island named Xō'tao lnagā'-i (X̱uutuu Llnagaay). The daughter of the town chief here committed some grave offense and was abandoned by her people. She wandered away to a place that had a rocky shore, where she met "two good fellows" and married one of them. These were Cormorants, and they settled the village of Łgai-u' (Old HlG̱aay.yuu). Their children were the HlG̱aay.yuu Laanas, Skidegate Town People (R6). They came to settle at another village and took the name HlG̱aay.yuu with them to the village that later had the name of Skidegate, HlG̱aagilda Llnagaay. Part of them later came to be called HlG̱aagilda ḴiiG̱awaay, Those Born at Skidegate (R6a) (Swanton 1905a, 80–81). At a later time, HlG̱aagilda Llnagaay became an Eagle village and came to be known by an Eagle chief's name SG̱iidagiids (map 2).

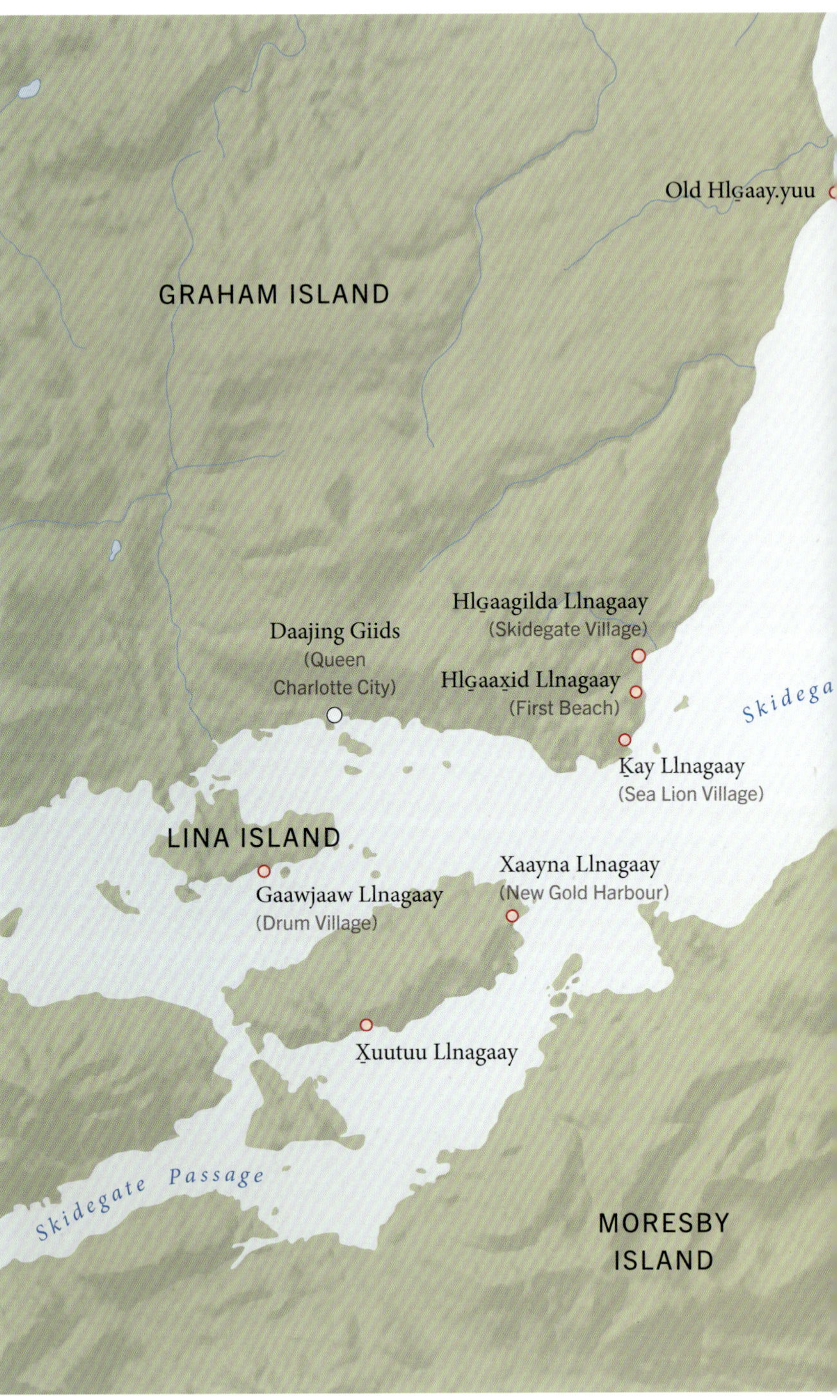

MAP 2 HlG̱aagilda Llnagaay and nearby villages. Map by Ben Pease, 2022.

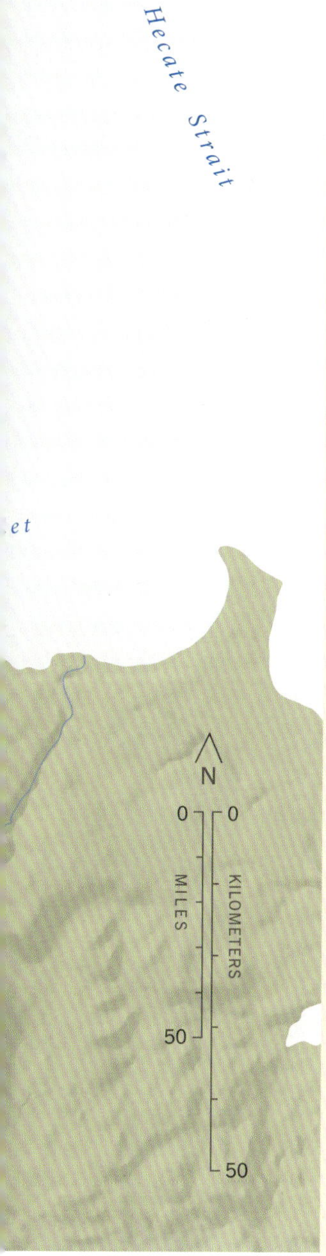

Hecate Strait

et

N
0 0
MILES KILOMETERS
50
50

How HlG̱aagilda Changed from a Raven to an Eagle Village

The ancient name of Skidegate is HlG̱aagilda. It was a Raven village. My ancestors lived in the big village of Naay Kun. There was a dispute over a blue hawk. So it started a big argument and it escalated into a village war. That's how the big village at Naay Kun split up, and half of the people moved along the north shore and eventually ended up in Massett, and my ancestors moved down the east coast of Haida Gwaii and stopped in Cape Ball and Tllall.

When they were living in Tllall, one of the young Eagle ladies married one of the Raven men from HlG̱aagilda. She went to live in HlG̱aagilda with him. They had a daughter. In the old days our ancestors used to go up into the forest and build fires under the big spruce trees, and they'd have kelp stuck into the bark, and the heat of the fire would start heating up the pitch and it would start dripping down into containers. It was one of the major medicines of our ancestors. And so one day they were doing that, and the Raven dad and the Eagle mom with a little Eagle girl were up in the forest there. And the little girl was looking up at what they were doing. She got too close and a big gob of hot pitch fell and landed right in her eye and blinded her. And so, the Eagle mother come down to Skidegate with the chiefs, you know, the Naay Kun chiefs. And they met with the Raven chief of HlG̱aagilda and they demanded payment for the injury to their Eagle girl. And so the Raven chief offered them so much, and they refused and he offered them more, but they refused. And so I guess he made the last offer and they refused, so the Raven chief nodded at his nephew. The chief's nephew, he was next in line to be the chief of the Ravens of HlG̱aagilda. So he grabbed the chief's talking stick and he went to the front of the longhouse, the doorway, and he threw the stick out of the longhouse and that's representing they gave up the village. So then all the Ravens packed up all their stuff and loaded their canoes and they paddled up the inlet to Lina Island and they built their new village there called Gaawjaaw Llnagaay drum village.

And then, so all our ancestors from Tllall and Cape Ball moved down into HlG̱aagilda, and they took over the village and it become an Eagle village. And then in the old days, even nowadays, people, Haidas, get nicknames over things that happen, you know. The chief of the Eagle village, his two nephews used to come and visit him, and out of respect it's customary to bring a gift for your auntie, and these two nephews never ever brought his wife a gift. And when they left she was all upset. And she told her husband, the chief, she said your nephews come to visit and they never give me a gift, not even a sG̱iida. And a sG̱iida is a giant red chiton and we eat it, we get it off the rocks at low tide and we cook it up and eat it. And so later on, he is walking through the village and he met up with some of the guys and he stopped and he was telling them about how upset his wife was over his nephews never bringing her a gift. And he told them what she said, not even a sG̱iida. And so they were chuckling away and they started calling him son-of-a chiton. And in Haida, how you say that is sG̱iidagiids, that's son-of-a chiton. So then that name stuck to him. They started calling him SG̱iidagiids and then it become his chief's name and it become a real powerful name, a hereditary name that's been passed down, so Chief SG̱iidagiids. And so when the first sailing ships reached outside of Skidegate, out past the bar, and the Haidas paddled out there to meet them to trade and that, the white explorers usually named the village after the chief from the village. They wrote it as "Skidegate."

—Niisdaka.na, Jags Brown, Juus xaade, March 7, 2022

EARLIEST EUROPEAN DESCRIPTIONS OF SKIDEGATE

In the late eighteenth- and early nineteenth-century journals of explorers and fur traders, written descriptions of the village of HlG̱aagilda Llnagaay and the people who lived there appear less frequently than several of the other Haida villages. HlG̱aagilda Llnagaay was not approached by the first Europeans to arrive at Haida Gwaii in 1774. At that time the Haida and Juan Perez on the Spanish ship *Santiago* made first contact at sea off the northwest corner of Haida Gwaii near the villages of K'yuusda (Kiusta), Daadans (Dadens), and Yaak'u (Yaku) (Wright 2001b, 16–31). It was not until thirteen years later, in 1787, that George Dixon on the *Queen Charlotte* sailed from K'yuusda south along the west coast, around Cape Saint James and up the east coast of Haida Gwaii near HlG̱aagilda Llnagaay. Dixon's journal, published in 1789, described the great success he had in trading with the Haida for sea otter pelts, which sparked a fur trading rush to the spot he named Cloak Bay, at the west side of K̲'iis Gwaay (North or Langara Island). Subsequent trade was centered both there and at the southern tip of the islands, off SG̱ang Gwaay, and farther south at Nootka Sound on Vancouver Island, these places being easiest to reach from the open sea.

In the early explorers' journals, as explained above, HlG̱aagilda Llnagaay (Skidegate village) was called by the name of a town chief instead of the Haida name for the village, as was the case with many Haida villages ("Ninstints," "Cumshewa," "Skedans," etc.). There was a chief SG̱iidagiids in this village at the time of first contact in the late eighteenth century, and so it came to be known by the fur traders by that chief's name.[5] Many other chiefs SG̱iidagiids succeeded him throughout the next two centuries (see Appendix I). The Haida name for the village, HlG̱aagilda, refers to a place of stone or a rock at the base of a waterfall that the current makes spin (Elders of HlG̱aagilda X̱aayda Kil Naay 2016, 758).

The earliest explorers' and fur traders' journals contain very few descriptions of the village of Skidegate or its residents, but there are a few accounts of their trading interactions. George Dixon's journal from July 1787 describes two encounters with an old man who may have been one of the old chiefs of Skidegate described as an old, tall, thin man with wrinkles and hollow cheeks, who had a "natural ferocity of temper," though his name was not recorded. He was met first on the west coast near the entrance to Skidegate channel and then again on the east side. Dixon gave him a light horseman's cap on the first encounter and acquired a labret from an old woman who may have been this man's wife:

> In one of the canoes was an old man, who appeared to have some authority over the rest, though he had nothing to dispose of: he gave us to understand, that in another part of these islands (pointing Eastward) he could procure plenty of furs for us, on which Captain Dixon gave him a light horseman's cap: this present added greatly to his consequence, and procured him the envy of his companions in the other canoes, who beheld the cap with a longing eye, and seemed to wish it in their possession.
>
> There were likewise a few women amongst them, who all seemed pretty well advanced in years; their under lips were distorted in the same manner as those of the women at Port Mulgrave, and Norfolk Sound, and the pieces of wood were particularly large. One of these lip-pieces appearing to be peculiarly ornamented, Captain Dixon wished to purchase it, and offered the old woman to whom it belonged a hatchet; but this she refused with contempt; toes, basons, and several other articles were afterwards shewn to her, and as constantly rejected. Our Captain began now to despair of making his wished-for purchase, and had nearly given it up, when one of our people happening to shew the old lady a few buttons, which looked remarkably bright, she eagerly embraced the offer, and was now altogether as ready to part with her wooden ornament, as before she was desirous of keeping it. This curious lip-piece measured three and seven-eighth inches long, and two and five-eighth inches in the widest part: it was inlaid with a small pearly shell, round which was a rim of copper.[6] (Beresford 1789, 198–209)

After rounding Cape Saint James and turning north, Captain Dixon realized that Haida Gwaii was a group of islands. He encountered the same chief:

> Amongst these traders was the old Chief, whom we had seen on the other side these islands, and who now appearing to be a person of the first consequence, Captain Dixon permitted him to come on board. The moment he got on the quarter deck he began to tell a long story, the purport of which was, that he had lost in battle the cap which we had given him; and to convince us how true this story was, he shewed us several wounds he had received in defending his property; notwithstanding this, he begged for another cap, intimating at the same time, that he would never lose it but with his life. Our Captain, willing to gratify his ambition, made him a present of another cap, and we presently found it was not bestowed in vain, for he became extremely useful to us in our traffic; whenever any dispute or mistake arose in the unavoidable hurry occasioned by so great a number of traders, they always referred the matter to him, and were constantly satisfied with his determination. W.B. [William Beresford]
>
> —Off Queen Charlotte's Islands, July 30 (Beresford 1789, 216–19)

In 1791, Captain Gray on the *Columbia* sailed around Haida Gwaii. An account of this voyage was recorded by John Hoskins. This includes a description of heraldic poles in front of the houses but does not indicate specific village names.[7] Hoskins does give us the first clear documentation of the Skidegate chief's name, Skediates, included with his list of chiefs (Howay 1990, 236):

> list of words and the names of the Chiefs of the various tribes which inhabits the Islands that I have yet seen or heard of:
>
> Cunniah [Gaanyaa]
> Needen [Niidan]
> Cuddah [K'udee]
> Skediates [Sg̱iidagiids]
> Comsuah [Kunx̱alas]
> Caswhat [Kaxius? from K̲'uuna Llnagaay]
> Ugah [? from Skincuttle Inlet (Sk̲'in K̲aahlii)]
> Coyah [X̱uuya]

Captain Joseph Ingraham's 1791 journal describes chief "Skutkiss" (Skidegate?) while visiting Cumshewa, a village to the south of Skidegate, as "a chief of the first consequence among these people, as at every place we visited they spoke of him as a man of great power and of whom they were afraid. He is a man of low stature and seemingly a feeble constitution, his countenance mild and agreeable" (Kaplanoff 1971, 129). This description differs considerably from Dixon's, so perhaps they were not dealing with the same chief. Ingraham made the remarkable trade with this man of a Hawaiian feathered cap and two feathered cloaks (gifts acquired in the Sandwich Islands), in exchange for five skins. The chief decided he wanted to return the feathered items, but Ingraham refused, valuing the Haida's sea otter furs more highly than royal Hawaiian regalia.

> I showed everything which I thought would induce them to trade, among which were some feathered caps and cloaks I had received as presents at the Sandwich Islands. With these they seemed vastly enamored. I sold a cap and two cloaks for five excellent skins. Skatzi praised them highly, which induced Skutkiss to buy them, but after possessing them a little while he repented his bargain and asked for his skins again. But as sea otter skins were to me much better curiosities than caps and cloaks, I chose to adhere to the bargain. Although I always gave these people the fairest chance in trade, yet to return skins after once bought would be to commence a custom tending to lose time and which could have no end. Seeing I was determined not to return the skins, the old chief threw those he had on board into the canoe and followed himself, where he sat for a while looking sullen. However, a small present reconciled us again. (Kaplanoff 1971, 131)

Several years later in November 1809, a Skidegate chief known as "Estakunah" (Niisdaka.na) came on board the *Otter* and tried to quarrel with the captain, according to the *Otter* journals kept by Robert Kemp and Samuel Furgerson. Later in 1811 this "Estakunah" is described as the head chief (Malloy 1998, 199). James Deans's notes about the World's Columbian Exposition model village say that "Nastacanna" was a name used by the Skidegate chiefs before they became chief (Deans 1893c, 35). The first known specific mention of totem poles in the village of Skidegate was that of the first Christian missionary to visit this place, Reverend Jonathan S. Green, on the fur trading bark *Volunteer* (under Captain Charles Taylor) in 1829:

> June 24—Today we ran round "Point Rose," the northeastern part of Queen Charlotte's Island, and sailed down the eastern side of the island to Skidegas. The day was pleasant, and the prospect, for this part of the coast, delightful. Just before we cast anchor, we passed the village of Skidegas. To me the prospect was most enchanting, and, more than any thing I had seen, reminded me of a civilized country. The houses, of which there are thirty or forty, appeared tolerably good, and before the door of many of them stood a large mast carved in the form of the human countenance, of the dog, wolf, etc., neatly painted. The land about the village appeared to be in a good state of cultivation. The indians did not raise much, excepting potatoes, as they have not a variety of seeds; yet, from the appearance of the land, I presume they may greatly vary their vegetable productions. Several of the tribe met us before we cast anchor, and remained till evening. To these I soon made known my object. They appeared pleased, and most earnestly solicited me to go on shore. They offered four or five of their principal men as hostages, and they repeatedly assured me that all would be well. Though I am anxious to see the country, and visit this village, yet I am not quite clear that I ought to go. I could not effect much by a single visit, and there are too many chiefs here, to ensure safety from the fact of having on board a hostage. (Green 1915, 84–86)

Whether it was one or more Skidegate chiefs who were described by late eighteenth-century explorers, by the end of the nineteenth century one of them was dubbed "Skidegate the Great" by James Deans:

> It was he whose name the first white visitors about [before] the beginning of the present century gave the name Skidegat's Town to this village. These white visitors named him Jaques. He was named The Great because he was large in body and wealth, if not in good deeds. The following description of him and his connections I had from old people who knew him well. He was a man about six feet in height had a very small head on an exceedingly large body, so large that a belt he wore round his waist could go around three ordinary sized men. His wealth. He was the richest chief of this day. It is said he had thirty slaves, male and female. (Deans 1893b, 77)

PROSPECTORS AND SMALLPOX

By 1835 the sea otter population had been decimated by the fur trade and smallpox had already struck the Haida. The maritime fur trade was replaced by land-based fur-trading posts run by the Hudson's Bay Company (Fort Simpson on the Nass River, established in 1831; Fort Stikine at Wrangell, leased from the Russians in 1839; and Fort Victoria, established in 1843). Visitors to Haida Gwaii came on steamboats delivering goods and people up and down the coast. Fur traders were replaced by prospectors and entrepreneurs as the gold rush was sparked in British Columbia in the mid-nineteenth century. The first report of gold on Haida Gwaii came in 1850 from the family of Nang kilslas "The one whose voice is obeyed," who became known as "Captain Gold," chief of the Pebble Town People (R9), while they were living in K̲aysuun Llnagaay on the west coast of Moresby Island (see Wright 2001b, 159–60).[8] This set off a flurry of gold mining efforts that all ended in failure for the gold miners by 1853 (Dalzell 1968, 59–62).

In subsequent years, mining efforts in Haida Gwaii turned to copper and coal, which resulted in tragedy for the Haida. Francis Poole, a civil and mining engineer, kept a diary of his time in Haida Gwaii that was published in 1872. Most of his time there was spent in the southern part of the islands near Skincuttle Inlet (Sk̲'in K̲aahlii) prospecting for copper, but he had occasion to interact with the Chief Skidegate of that time, who spent the winter camped near Poole's copper mining operation, apparently to keep an eye on his operations and assure his status among the southern chiefs.

Smallpox broke out among the Haida who were with Poole on Sk̲'in G̲aadll (Skincuttle Island) in the summer of 1862, which forced him to burn all of Sk̲'in G̲aadll and move across to SG̲way Kun Gway.yaay (Burnaby Island) (Poole 1872, 134, 158–59, 221). Smallpox spread from here and from other sources coming through and from Victoria, resulting in a tragic loss of Haida lives. There were several smallpox epidemics on the Northwest Coast starting in the late eighteenth century. It is estimated that an 1836 epidemic killed one-third of the population on the northern Northwest Coast. The Haida population plummeted from an estimate of about ten thousand, some say as high as thirty thousand in the early nineteenth century to less than a thousand by the turn of the twentieth century (Steedman and Collison 2011, 18). In the 1830s Skidegate was estimated to have had a population of 738, and by 1880–83 only 100 people. At this time, some of the surviving southern Haida were still living in their villages and had not yet moved into Skidegate. By the end of the nineteenth century, most were forced to move north to maintain their survival. By 1915–20 the population of the village was 238 (Boyd 1999, 208, 217, 219).

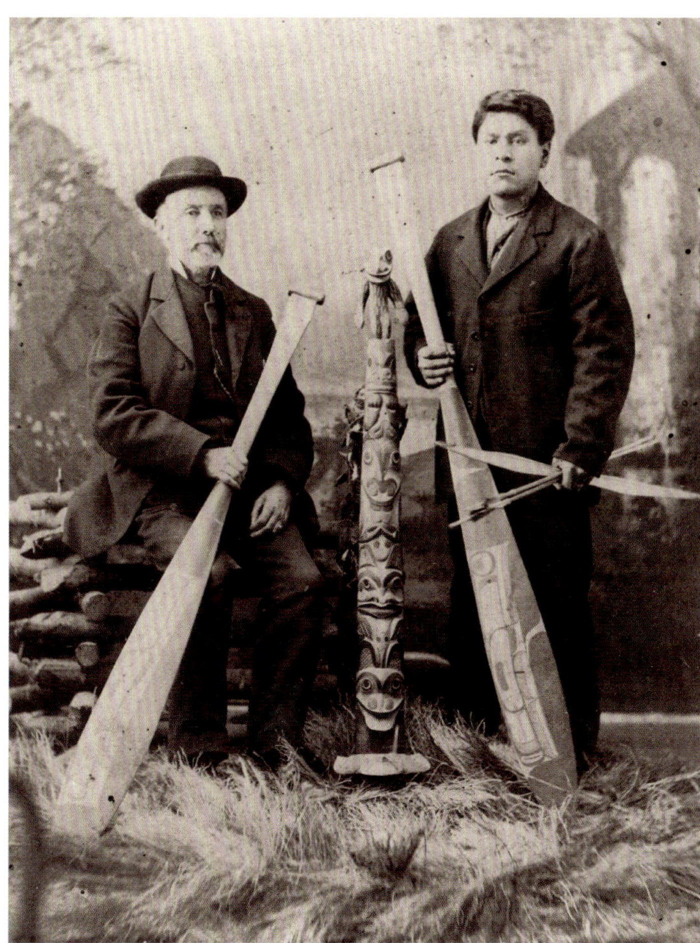

2.1 James G. Swan and Johnny Kit Elswa posing with Heiltsuk model pole and paddles, October 1883. Spencer & Hastings Studio, Victoria, BC. University of Washington Libraries Special Collections, NA 1412.

EARLY WATERCOLORS

James G. Swan, who worked variously as a school superintendent, judge, lawyer, and customs agent in Port Townsend, first visited Haida Gwaii in 1883 with his Haida interpreter, Johnny Kit Elswa, whom Swan had hired in Victoria (figure 2.1), although he had been collecting Haida objects for ten years before this (see the introduction). Swan's official position in 1883 was assistant and collector for the Fish Commission, but he was charged with collecting all he could acquire that illustrated the ethnology and archaeology of the Northwest (Cole 1985, 39). As mentioned above, James Deans took it upon himself to join Swan in Massett on July 21, 1883. Swan hired Albert Edward Edenshaw to be their guide for the first part of the trip. They set out on Monday August 6, 1883, to circumnavigate Graham Island in Edenshaw's canoe, accompanied by Edenshaw's wife, Amy, their son Henry and two of Edenshaw's nephews (Swan 1883a). After a twenty-day paddle they arrived in Skidegate, and the Edenshaw family and James Deans departed. Swan was very happy to be without them. In a September 3 letter from Skidegate to Alexander McKenzie, the HBC factor in Massett, Swan reported of Deans:

> He has been an encumbrance to me ever since he joined me at Massett. He has not been of the slightest assistance to me and I made up my mind on my arrival here

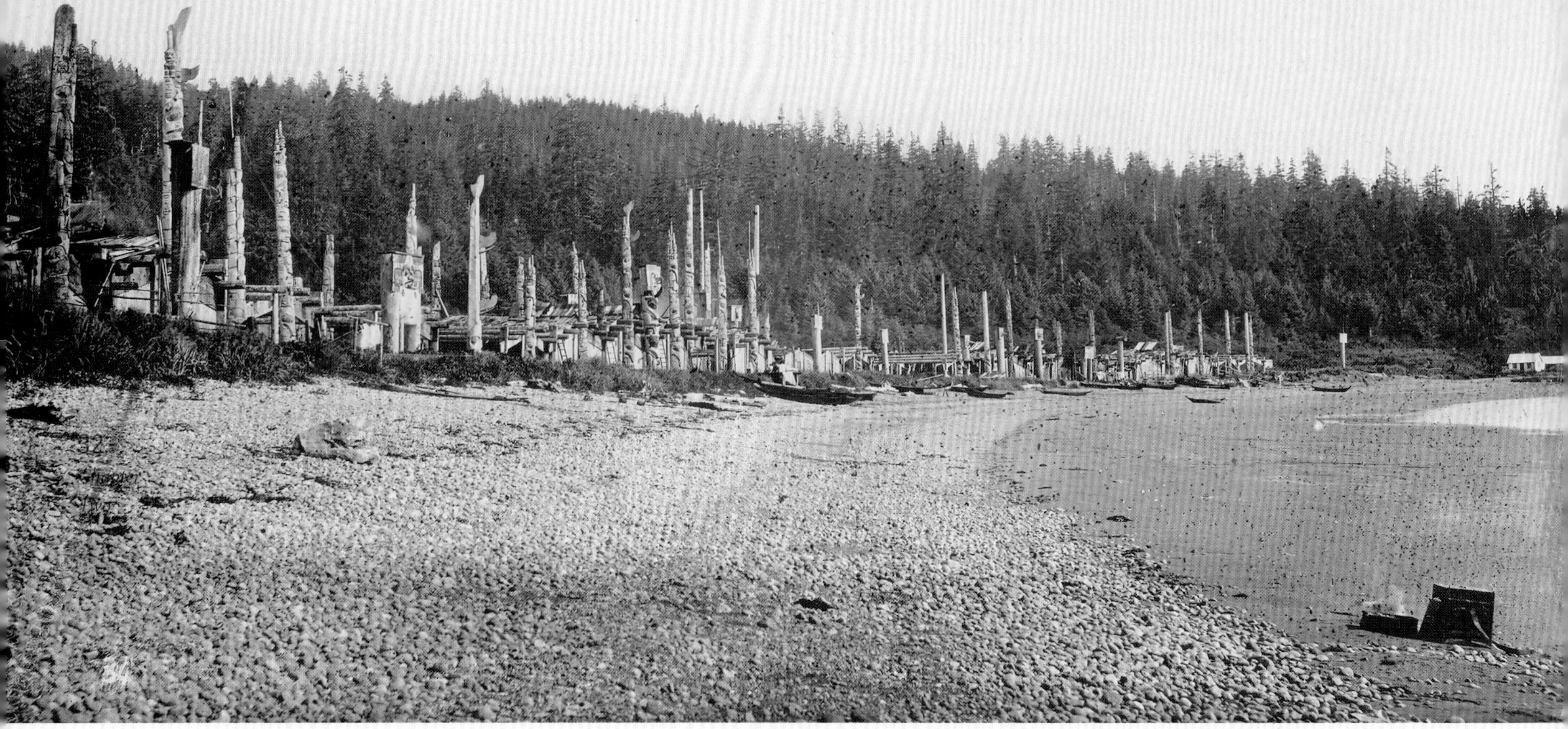

2.2 *above* Hlg̱aagilda Llnagaay from the south end, 1878. Photograph by George M. Dawson. Courtesy of the Canadian Museum of History, neg. no. 253.

2.3 *right* Hlg̱aagilda Llnagaay, 1878. Photograph by George M. Dawson. Courtesy of the Canadian Museum of History, neg. no. PA-37756.

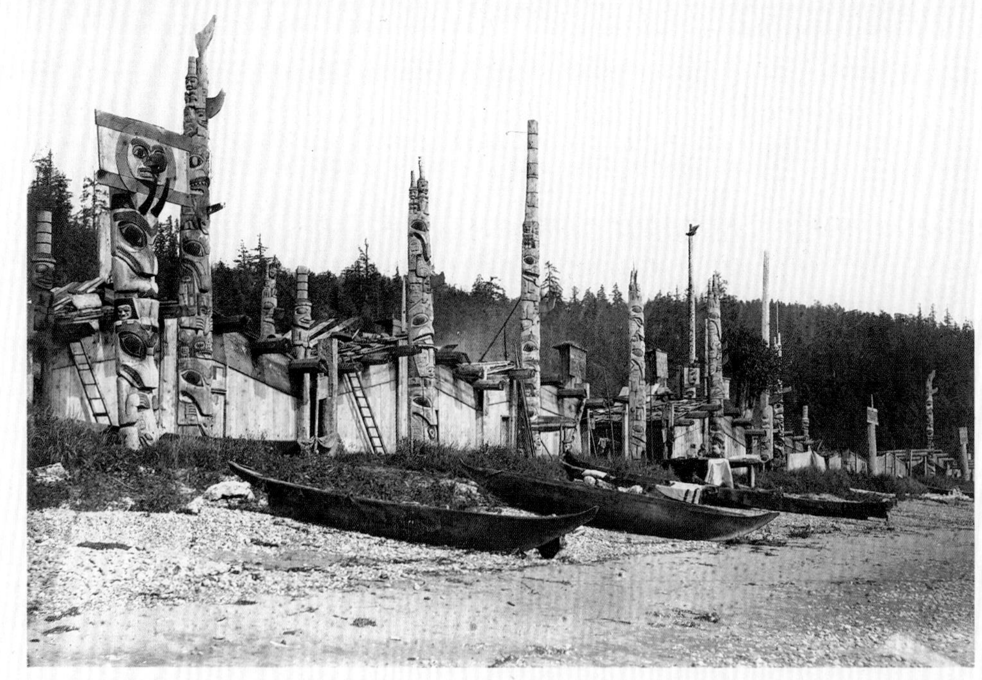

> to do the rest of my work alone. I think if he had not been with me I would have had less trouble with Edinsu who was disposed from the time I started to consider Mr. Deans as the man to be consulted and myself as a sort of [super?ary]. Certain facts came to my attention after my arrival here which have forced me to conclude that he had better not be with me on my future business with Indians. (Swan 1883b)

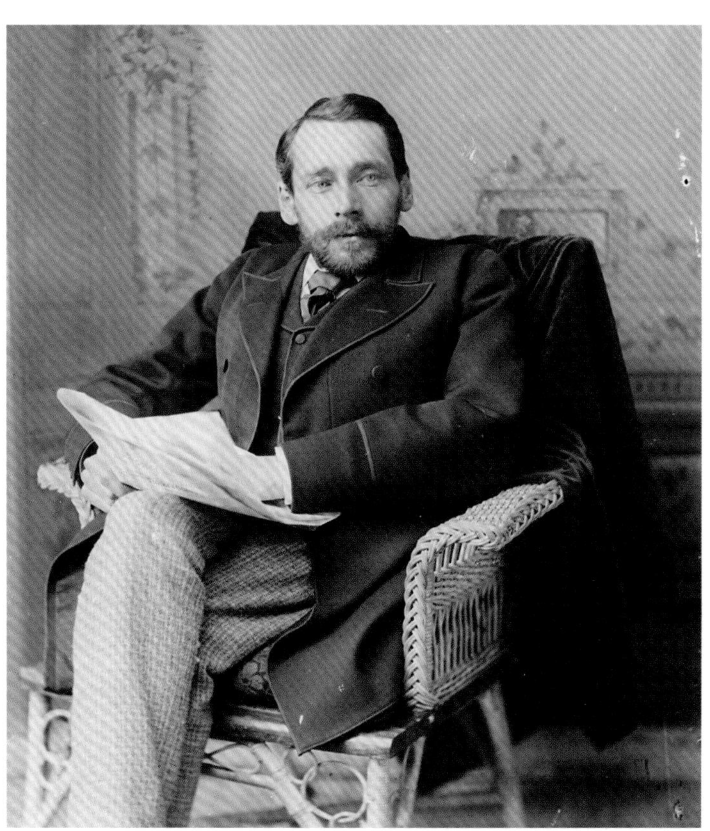

2.4 George Mercer Dawson, ca. 1885. Photograph courtesy of the Library and Archives of Canada, neg. no. PA-25521.

During Swan's visit in Skidegate he stayed with William Sterling, the superintendent of the Skidegate Oil Works (dogfish oil) and his partner, Alexander McGregor, two miles south of the village. Swan spent several days there and described his visits with a Haida man whose name he spelled "Ellswarsh" (Iljuuwaas) and his wife and children (Soo-datl [Suudaahl], Sam, and Ellen). This family had visited him two years earlier at Swan's home in Port Townsend, where Iljuuwaas worked making silver bracelets and other jewelry. Swan reported that in 1883 Iljuuwaas's older daughter, "Soo-datl," was married to "Kit-ha-gunda" (William), who was an argillite carver, and Swan purchased several pieces from him. Swan also bought a rattle and two silver bracelets from Iljuuwaas (see figure 3.99). In September, Swan contracted with Iljuuwaas to take him in his canoe on a collecting trip to K̲'uuna Llnagaay (Skedans), Hlk̲inul Llnagaay (Cumshewa), and T'aanuu Llnagaay (Tanu). On their return to Skidegate late on the evening of September 10, Swan was invited to spend the night in the home of Iljuuwaas. While in Skidegate earlier in August, Swan had the occasion to draw two of the houses there, including Grizzly Bear's Mouth House (see figure 3.118) and Box House (see figure 3.111). These drawings are very useful, even though by this time photography had arrived in Haida Gwaii. We do have photographs of these two houses, but not all of the details of Box House visible in Swan's drawing are visible in the photographs. Other drawings by Swan, done in K'yuusda (Kiusta) and Yaak'u Llnagaay (Yaku), are extremely valuable, as they record two houses that were never photographed (see Miles 2003, 121–24).

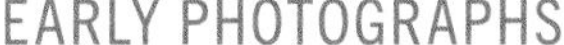

EARLY PHOTOGRAPHS

The first photographs of Skidegate had been taken five years earlier on July 26, 1878, by George Mercer Dawson (1849–1901) (figures 2.2, 2.3, 2.4; see figure 3.44). Dawson worked as a geologist with the Geological Survey of Canada, responsible for surveying British Columbia. He suffered from Pott's disease as a boy, a tuberculosis of the spine, which permanently deformed his upper spine and stunted his growth (Cole and Lockner 1989, 3–4). Despite his disability, Dawson excelled in his career. Beyond geology, he had a keen interest in natural history and ethnology. He was present in T'aanuu (Laskeek) when GitK̲un raised the last totem pole to go up in that village, which Dawson photographed (MacDonald 1983, 90–91, plate 114). Dawson collected many objects now housed at the McGill University Museum and described ceremonial activities that he witnessed during his voyage up the east coast of Haida Gwaii (Cole and Lockner 1989; Cole and Lockner 1993; Dawson 1880). His work in British Columbia brought him the reputation as "one of Canada's foremost contributors to ethnology" and as a "father of Canadian anthropology" (Zeller and Avrith-Wakeam 2003).

Oregon Columbus Hastings was an amateur astronomer and photographer. In 1879 he was the official photographer on an inspection trip to several reserves in BC on the HMS *Rocket*, hired by Dr. Israel Wood Powell, the superintendent for Indian Affairs in British Columbia. Hastings had photography studios both on Fort Street in Victoria, BC (partners with Stephen Allen Spencer) and in Port Townsend, Washington (his father Loren Hastings was one of the founders of that city), specializing primarily in portraiture (see figures 2.1, 3.36, 3.87, 3.102). In 1894 he was hired by Franz Boas to take photographs in Fort Rupert and again in 1898 for the Jessup North Pacific Expedition.[9]

Edward Dossetter was a British professional photographer who lived in Victoria, BC, from 1881 to 1885. Born in England, where he photographed the entire Bayeux Tapestry for the South Kensington Museum (now the Victoria and Albert Mu-

2.5 Hlg̱aagilda Llnagaay, 1881. Photograph by Edward Dossetter. American Museum of Natural History Library, Image #42268.

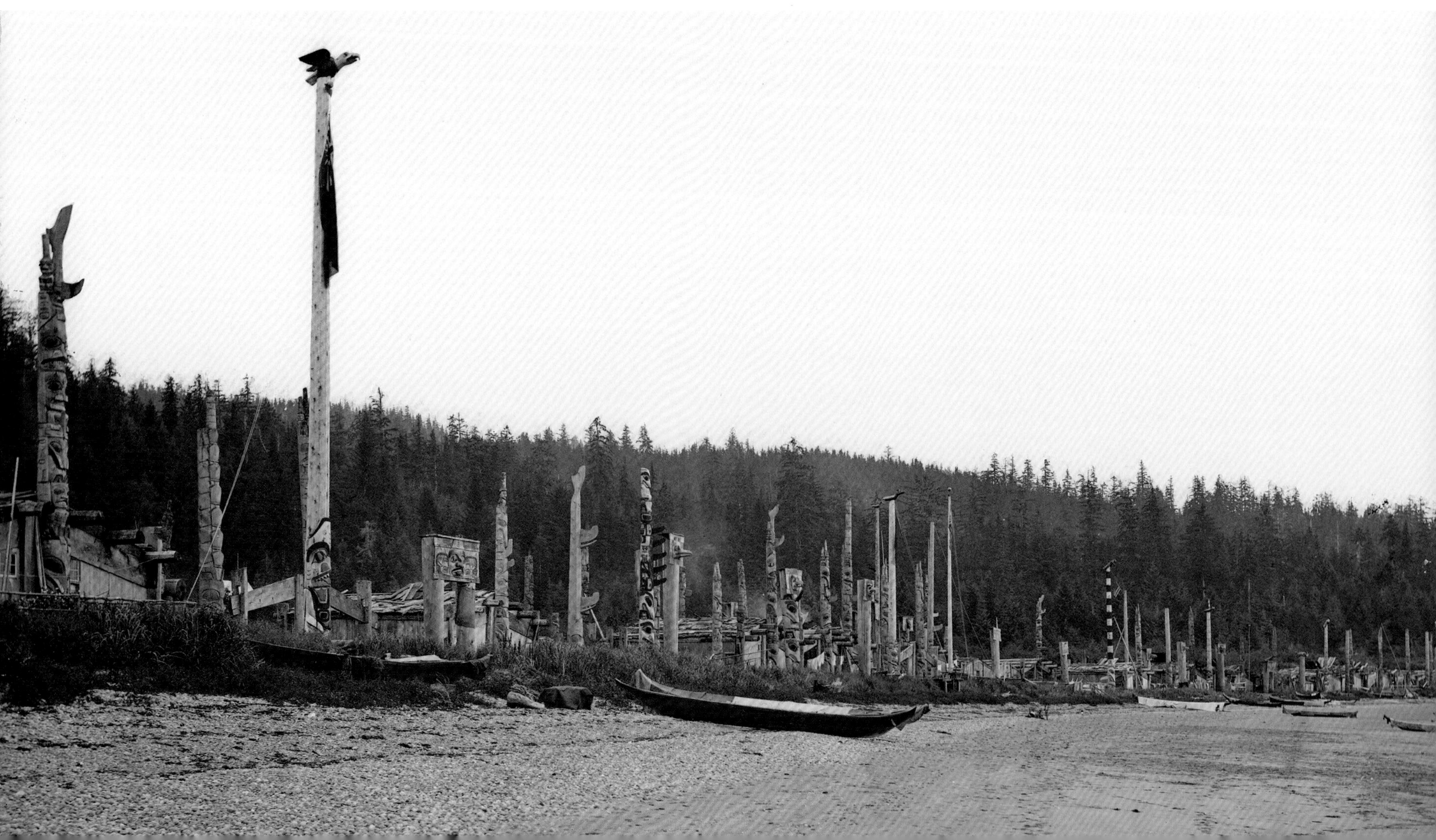

seum), Dossetter moved to New Zealand in 1876 and then to Victoria, BC, in 1880–81. In 1881 he accompanied Dr. Israel W. Powell, on another inspection trip to villages up the BC coast aboard the HMS *Rocket*. He produced sixty-four glass plate negatives from that trip that he gave to Powell, who then sent them to the American Museum of Natural History.[10] These include some of the most stunning photographs of the village of Skidegate. These photographs and their details have been very helpful in comparing the old houses with the models (figures 2.5, 2.6; see figures 3.68, 3.70, 3.72).

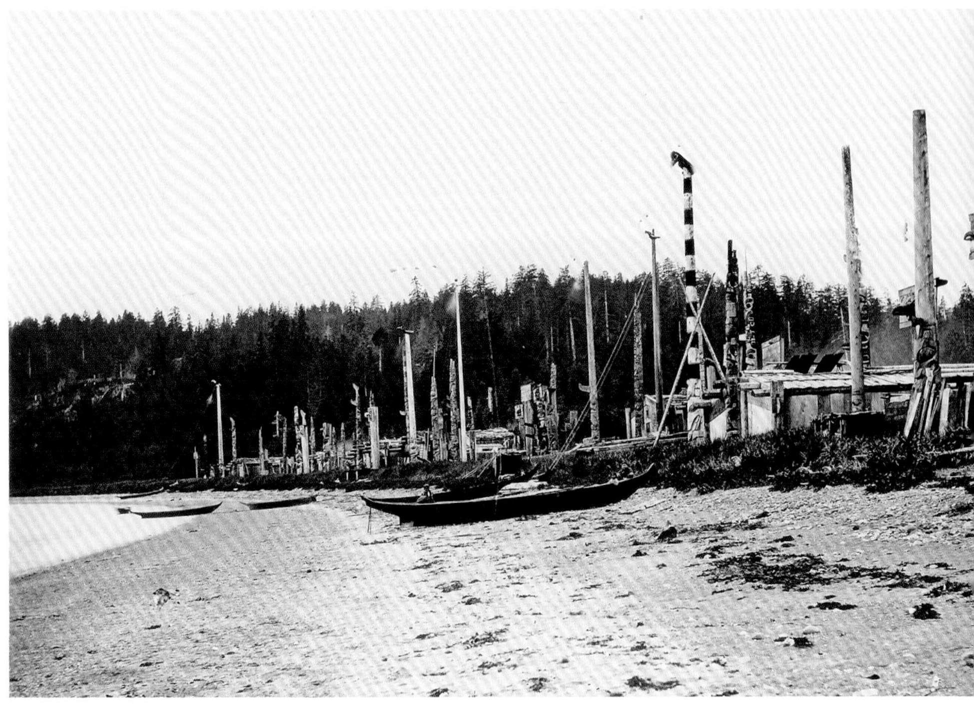

2.6 Hlg̱aagilda Llnagaay, 1881. Photograph by Edward Dossetter. American Museum of Natural History Library, Image #42264.

Hannah Hatherley Maynard (1834–1918) and Richard Maynard (1832–1907) visited Haida Gwaii in 1884 and 1888. They had been married in Bude, Cornwall, England, in 1852 and moved to Bowmanville, Ontario, Canada, where they had four children. Richard opened a shoemaking business in Bowmanville but in 1859 was lured to the gold fields on the Fraser River in British Columbia. He returned to Bowmanville to close his business and moved his family to Victoria, BC, in 1862. While Richard had been prospecting out west, Hannah learned the trade of photography. After their move Richard pursued placer mining in the Caribou and Stikine country, and Hannah opened the city's first portrait studio in Victoria. Their fifth child was born in Victoria. After giving up on prospecting after a year, Richard opened a shoemaking and boot business next door and also learned photography from Hannah (figure 2.7) (Watson 1996).

According the May 17, 1918, issue of the *Colonist*, "Everyone was astonished. And like many women who start anything new she was for a long time boycotted by the public . . . until Victoria got used to a woman photographer, Mr. Maynard frequently pretended that he had taken pictures, whereas in actual fact it was his wife who had done the job." Richard is generally credited with taking the outdoor landscape photographs, and Hannah with the portraits, but Hannah frequently accompanied him on his trips, and it is likely that Hannah participated in the outdoor photography as well, although they are mostly credited as "R Maynard Photography." Richard was commissioned to take photographs in 1873 and 1874 along the west coast of the BC mainland on the HMS *Boxer* with superintendent of Indian Affairs, I. W. Powell. Richard traveled for the first time to Haida Gwaii in April and May 1884 with the American explorer Captain Newton H. Chittenden (figure 2.8). Hannah did not accompany him on these trips, but shortly after his return from Haida Gwaii, she made a solo trip to Haida Gwaii on the *Princess Louise* in August 1884 (Wilks 1980, 7).

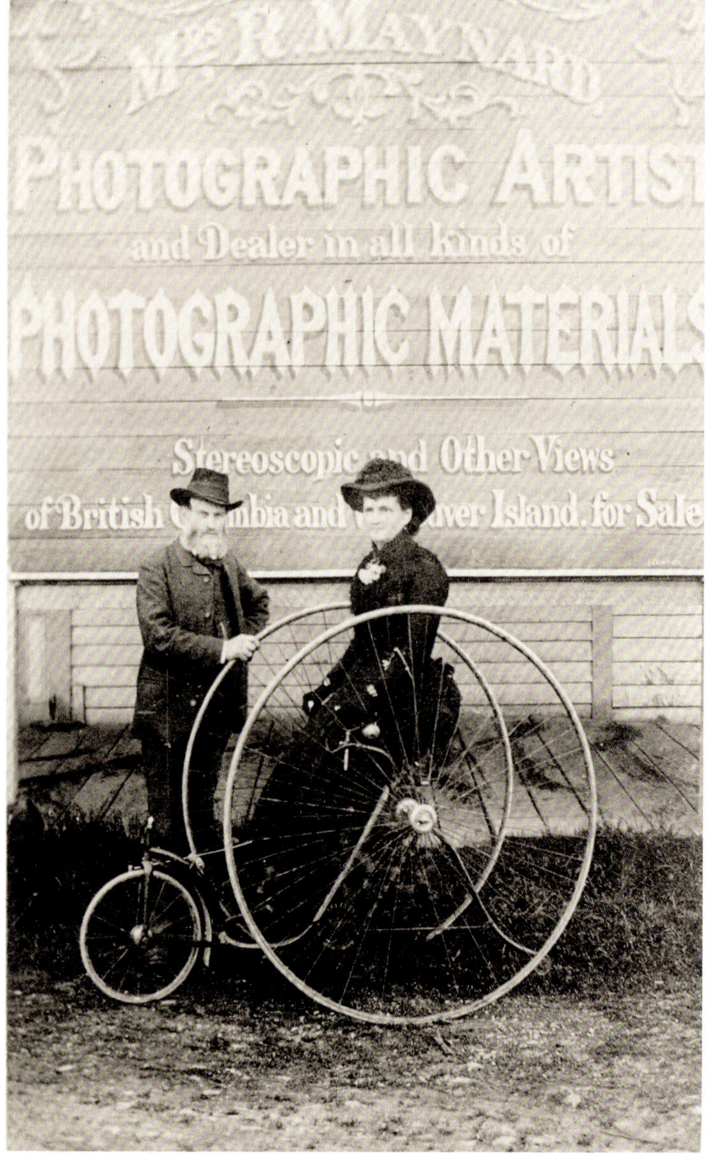

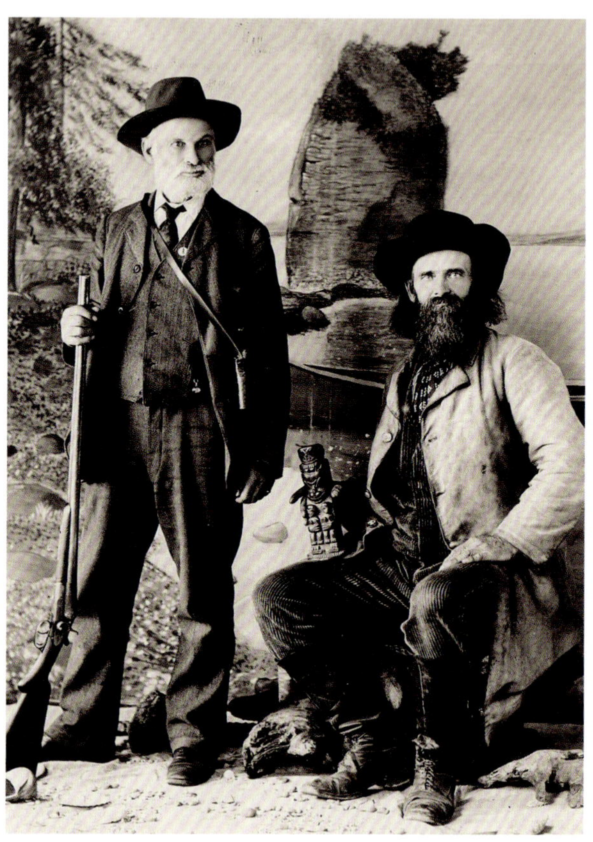

2.7 *left* Hannah and Richard Maynard outside of Mrs. Maynard's studio, 1880s. Image #C-08673. Courtesy of the Royal BC Museum and Archives.

2.8 *below* Richard Maynard and Captain Newton H. Chittenden, 1884. Image #A-01505. Courtesy of the Royal BC Museum and Archives.

In August 1888, Richard and Hannah went back to Haida Gwaii, their second visits, but together for the first time (Mattison 1985, 121). It is unclear which of them took the famous photograph of Captain Gold's house, Skidegate the Great's mortuary pole, and Grizzly Bear's Mouth House, among many others (figures 2.9, 2.10; see figures 3.20, 3.22, 3.33). According to Dan Savard, who managed the Anthropology Audio Visual collection at the Royal British Columbia Museum for over twenty years, "it is impossible to determine who created every Maynard photograph" (Savard 2010, 170).

Captain Newton H. Chittenden (1840–1925) had served in the Union army during the Civil War and later earned a law degree. In 1884 he offered his services to the British Columbia government to explore Haida Gwaii. Unfortunately, most of his writings, including the only copy of his autobiography, were destroyed during the San Francisco earthquake and fire.

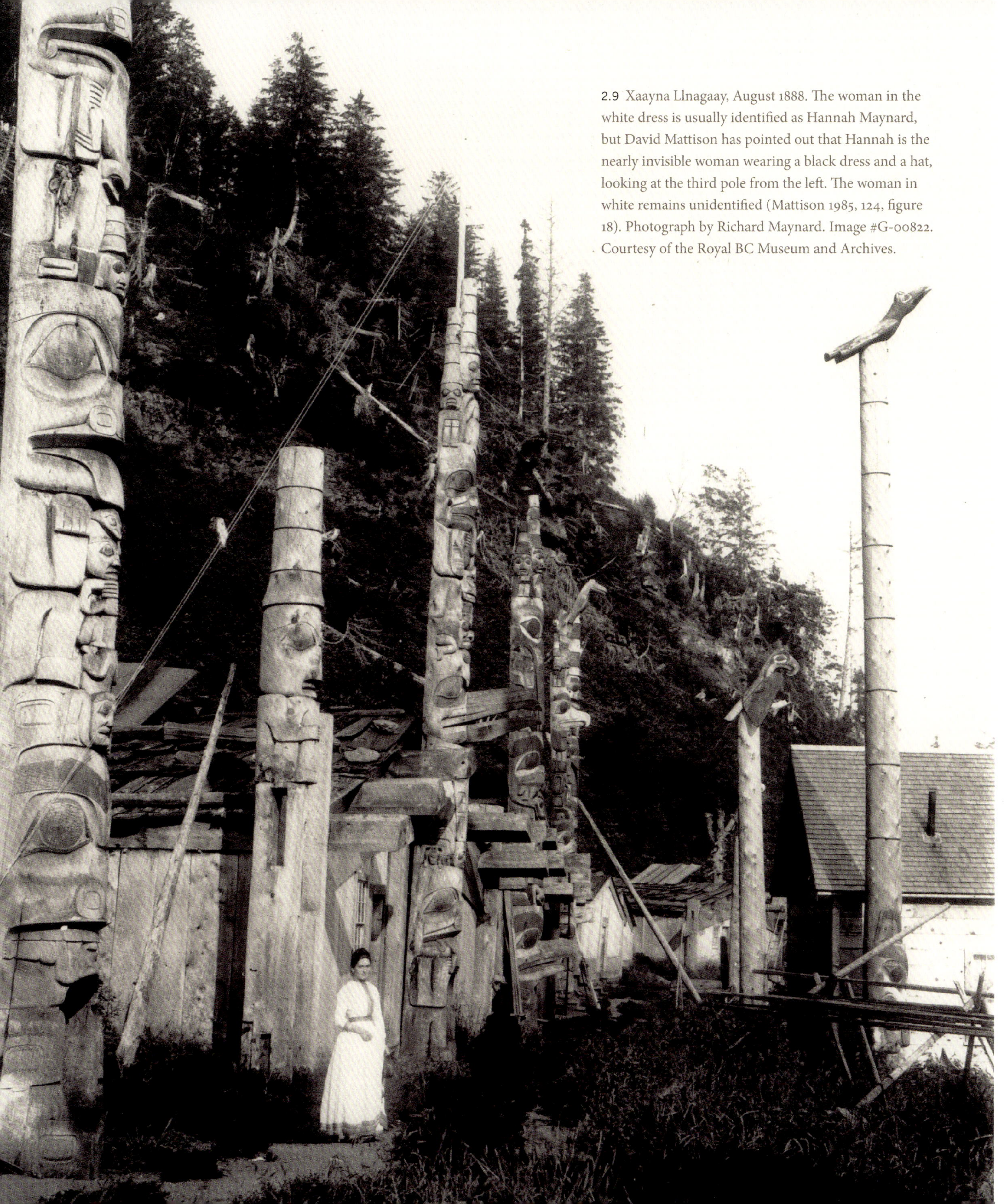

2.9 Xaayna Llnagaay, August 1888. The woman in the white dress is usually identified as Hannah Maynard, but David Mattison has pointed out that Hannah is the nearly invisible woman wearing a black dress and a hat, looking at the third pole from the left. The woman in white remains unidentified (Mattison 1985, 124, figure 18). Photograph by Richard Maynard. Image #G-00822. Courtesy of the Royal BC Museum and Archives.

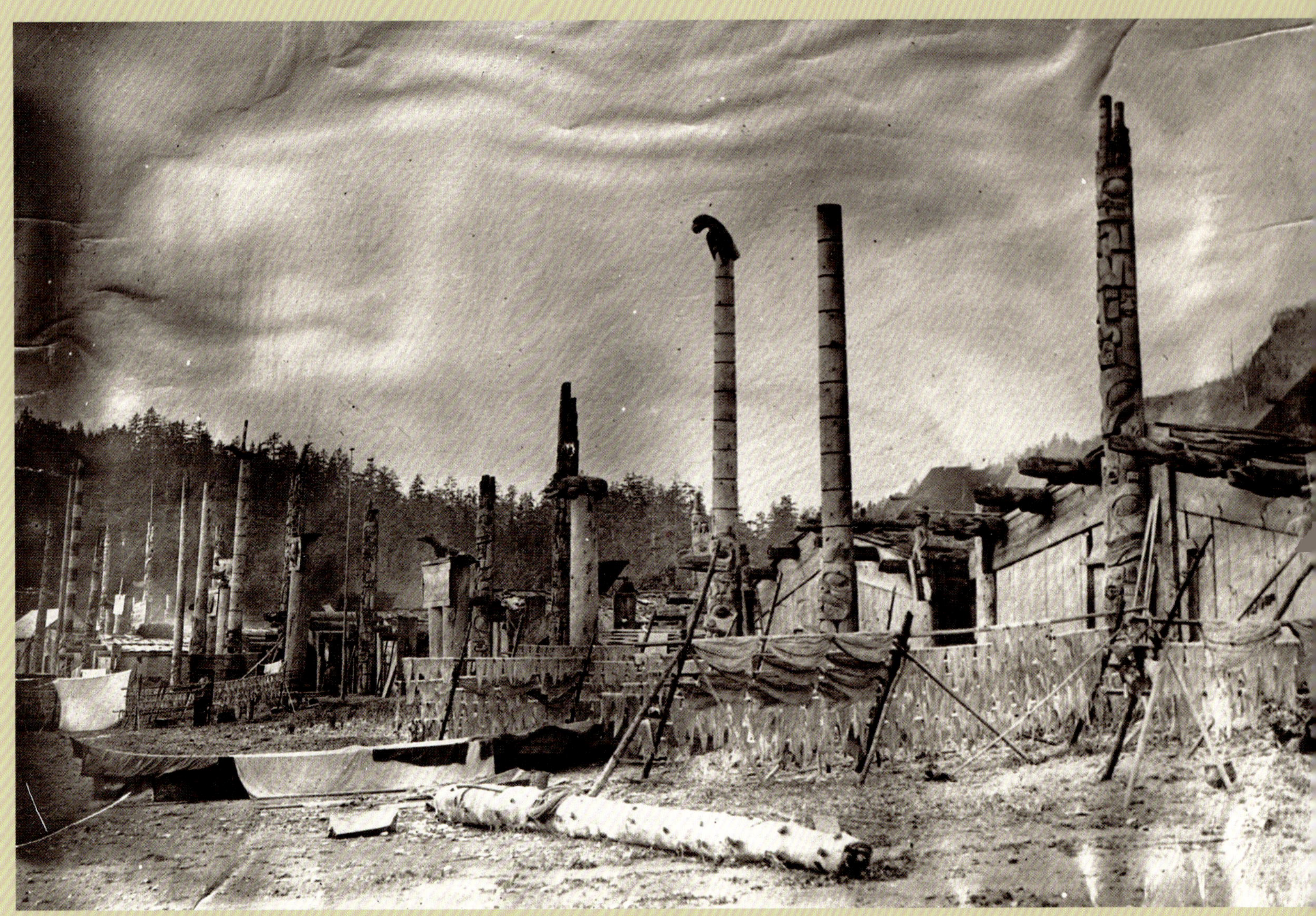

2.10 Grizzly Bear's Mouth House and Grizzly Bear House (right). Photograph by the Maynards, 1884. Canadian Museum of History, neg. no. 71-3087.

Fortunately, the *Official Report of the Exploration of the Queen Charlotte Islands for the Government of British Columbia* (1884) has been reprinted as *Exploration of the Queen Charlotte Islands* (Chittenden 1984 [1884], 11). Chittenden held an official appointment at the WCE as British Columbia's special commissioner to the exhibition, and he exhibited his large collection near the Skidegate village display (Cole 1985, 131). After the fair he toured this collection to the California Mid-Winter Exposition before depositing it at the Provincial Museum in Victoria in 1884 (Cole 1985, 133).

Charles F. Newcombe (1852–1924) was a physician, botanist, and ethnographer. He took many photographs in his travels but is best known for the Northwest Coast collections he acquired for several museums. Working closely with community members, Newcombe purchased at least sixty-seven totem poles on the Northwest Coast between 1897 and 1924, more than any other collector (figure 2.11). Thirty-one of these poles (or parts of poles) are Haida. Of the Haida poles he collected, only two are from the village of Skidegate (McGowan 2003, 23), an inside house post collected in 1897 and sent to the Übersee Museum in Bremen, Germany (see figure 3.92), and the frontal pole of the house on the extreme north end of Skidegate that had the name Naa G̱a Gayhlas, "House to which the tide comes" according to Newcombe. It was sent to the Field Museum in Chicago and then to Melbourne, Australia, in 1911 (see figures 3.134, 3.135). Also, the mortuary panel from Captain Gold's house near Skidegate was purchased by Newcombe for the Field Museum in 1905. Twenty-seven other poles collected by Newcombe from other Haida villages were sent to many museums around the world: the Royal British Columbia Museum in Victoria, BC, the Pitt Rivers Museum at Oxford, the British Museum, the Royal Botanic Gardens at Kew, Cambridge, and Liverpool Museums in England.

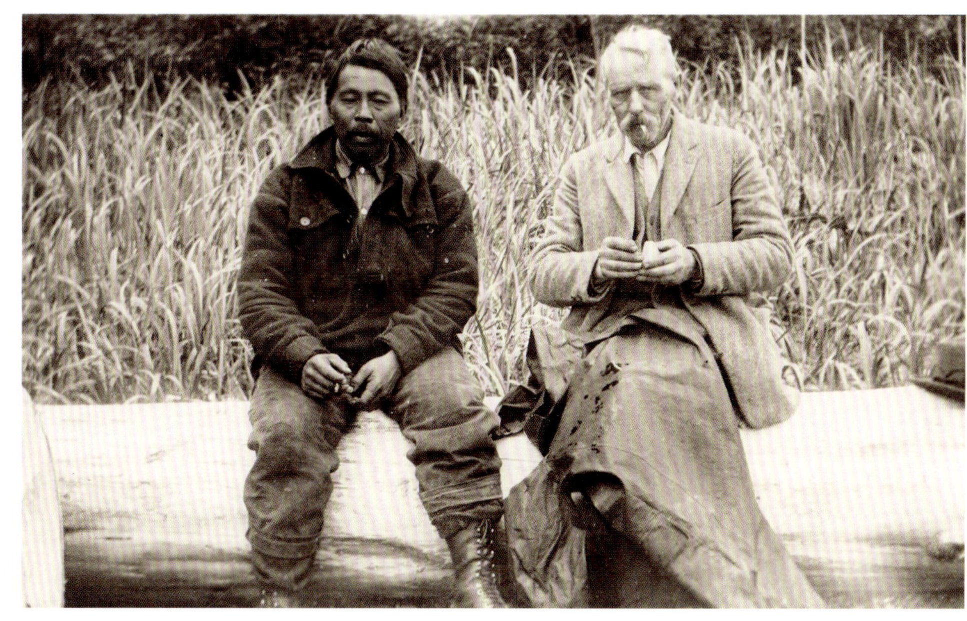

2.11 Chief Gidansda Henry Moody and Dr. Charles F. Newcombe, 1923. Photographer unknown. Image #F-05403. Courtesy of the Royal BC Museum and Archives.

Newcombe moved with his wife and children to Victoria, BC, in 1885. After the death of his wife in childbirth in 1891, he took the oldest of his six children back to England to school, where he also studied geology and natural history at the British Museum and the University of London before returning to British Columbia. His first trip to Haida Gwaii was in 1895 with Francis Kermode of the Provincial Museum. Newcombe was asked by George Dorsey to collect for the Field Museum in Chicago, and in 1897 he returned again to Haida Gwaii on his own boat, the *Pel-*

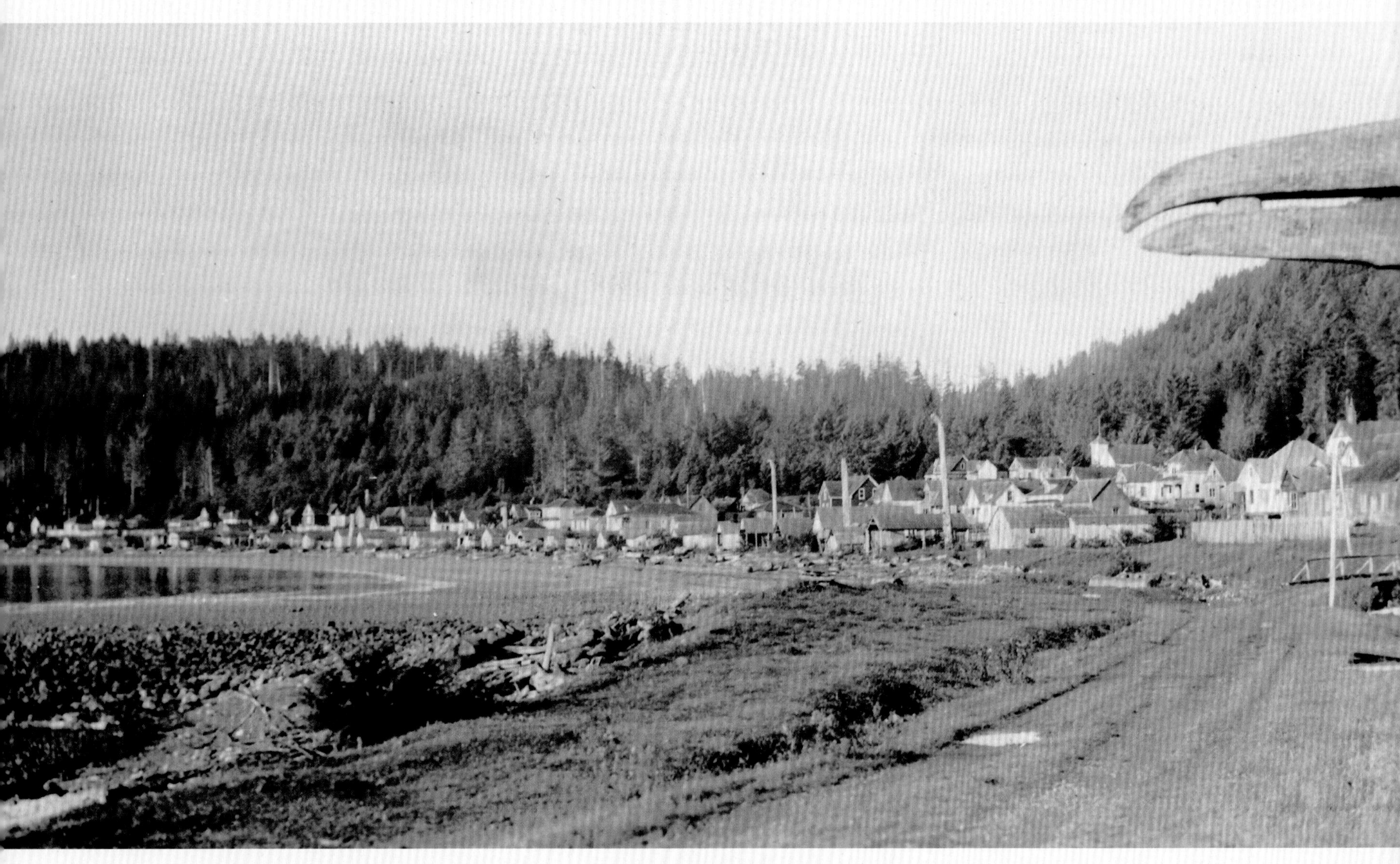

2.12 Hlg̱aagilda Llnagaay looking south from the Millas pole (beak in foreground). Collection of Mrs. Doreen Jones. Photograph by Catherine Tranter, 1920–30. Image PN17312. Courtesy of the Royal BC Museum and Archives.

ican, which he used for many trips into the 1920s. From 1901 to 1905, Newcombe worked full-time for the Field Museum in Chicago, collecting and documenting their collections (Neary 2003). During this time he worked with James Deans's notes, making margin notes on the typescript, and linking Deans's notes to the Field Museum's catalog numbers. It is Newcombe's lists of poles and their owners, correlating to the photographs of Dawson, Dossetter, and the Maynards, that were most useful in confirming the identities of the model poles collected by Deans. In 1904, Newcombe was commissioned to assemble ethnological exhibits at the Louisiana Purchase Exposition in Saint Louis. In 1911 he became an agent for the Provincial Museum in Victoria, BC, and published a guide to the Anthropological Collection in the Provincial Museum (Newcombe 1909).

By 1892, when the model houses were commissioned, only about eleven poles still stood in Skidegate, and James Deans acquired two inside house posts and an entire house with its frontal pole at that time (see figures 3.68, 3.77, 3.104). Later, Newcombe acquired two poles in Skidegate in 1897 and 1911. By the 1920s the village had only a few old poles still standing (figure 2.12). The frontal pole of Fort House stood until the 1940s (MacDonald 1983, 44). Skiu'lun awG̱a X̱aad (see figure 3.82) stood across the road from Billy and Clara Russ's house until it was taken down due to safety concerns in 1958 (Russ Jones and Betty Richardson, personal communication, August 16, 2020).[11]

Forty-eight poles are visible in Dawson's 1878 photograph of HlG̱aagilda (see figure 2.2). This includes partial views of the six poles in the old row of houses behind the south end of the village. MacDonald's mapping survey of the village between 1966 and 1970 documents seventy-eight poles, including the six corner posts, three interior house posts, and six frontal poles on the eight unnumbered houses in a row behind the southern end of the village. Little is known of these eight older houses, and no models are known to have been made of these. Only one old pole remained standing in the village by 1990, and it is now housed at the Haida Gwaii Museum at K̲ay Llnagaay (see figure 3.125). Of the more than seventy-eight poles known to have been raised in Skidegate during the nineteenth century, only six are known to be preserved in museum collections. The others have survived only in the photographic record, and in 1892 only a handful of photographs existed that documented the HlG̱aagilda poles between the first photos in 1878 and 1892. This makes the work of these nineteenth-century photographers and the work of the Haida carvers who made the World's Columbian Exposition models especially valuable. Of the models that were carved for the WCE in 1892, at least six represent gyaaG̱ang (totem poles) that were erected after 1878. The photographs of HlG̱aagilda Llnagaay were used by the carvers who made the model houses and poles in most cases after the original poles were missing from the village.

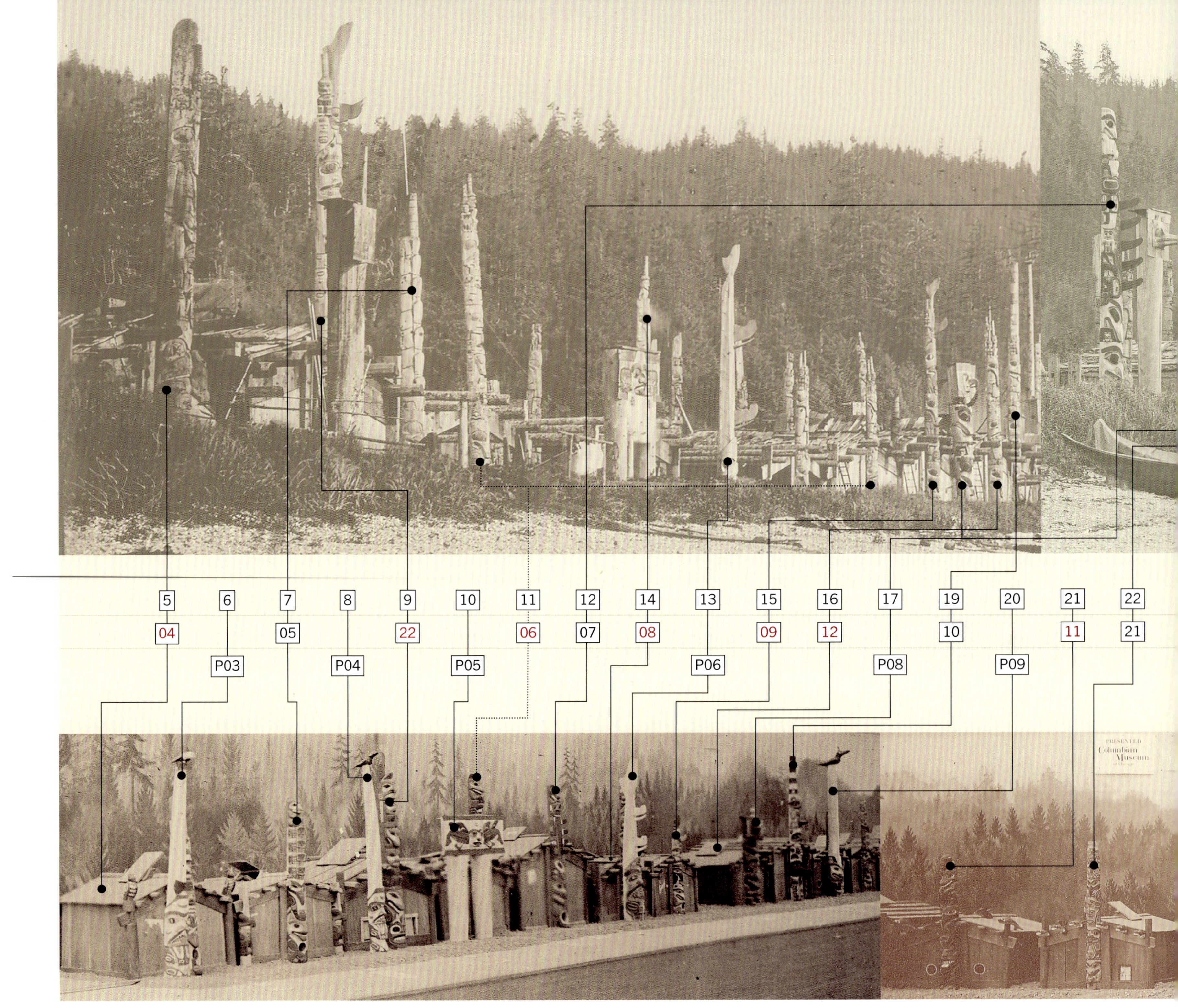

COMPARISON BETWEEN THE OLD VILLAGE AND THE MODEL VILLAGE

This panorama illustrates the correlations between the old village Hlg̱aagilda Llnagaay, as shown in two historical photographs and the model village as it was installed at the World's Columbian Exposition. Solid lines connect the models with the related old houses, dotted lines

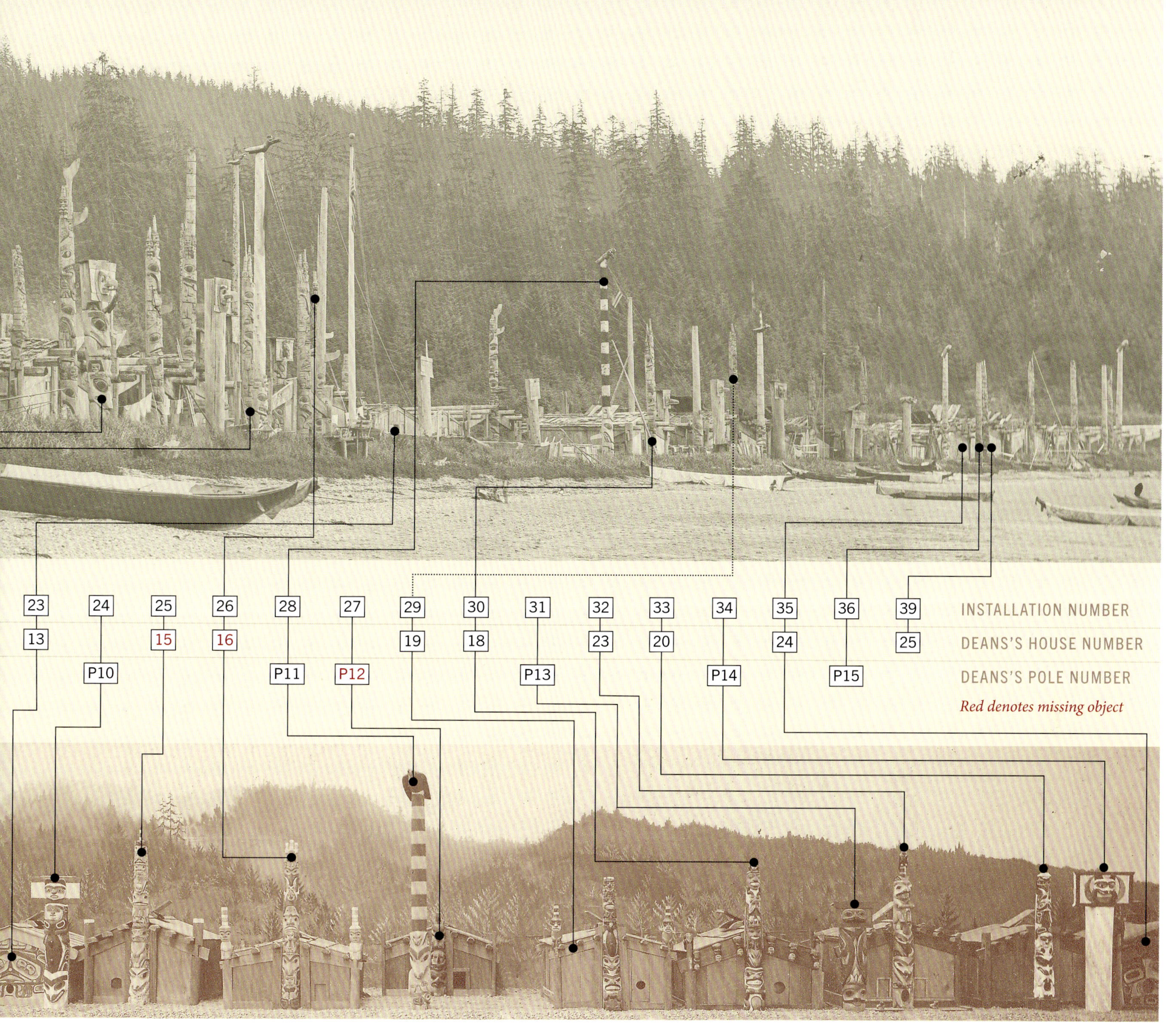

indicate uncertainty. Top (left to right): Hlg̱aagilda Llnagaay Dawson 1878 (detail of figure 2.2); Dossetter 1881 (detail of figure 2.5). Bottom (left to right): Model of Hlg̱aagilda Llnagaay at the World's Columbian Exposition (detail of figure I.1); C. D. Arnold 1893 (detail of figure 3.2).

COMPARISON OF NUMBERING SYSTEMS

This table compares several of the numbering systems used for the World's Columbian Exposition (WCE) model houses and poles with the numbering systems used for the old houses.

DEANS'S NUMBER	INSTALLATION NUMBER	FIELD MUSEUM CATALOG NUMBER	SWANTON'S NUMBER	NEWCOMBE'S NUMBER	MACDONALD'S NUMBER	WHERE NOW
01	1	17823	6 Xaayna		6 Xaayna	FM
02	46	nn 17801?	15? Sg̱ang Gwaay		13 Sg̱ang Gwaay	Welt
03	4	17819			31 Hlg̱aax̱id	FM
04	5	17818 to BKLN	17/19?	1	30	BKLN owl only/missing house
05	7	17816		4	28	FM
06	11	17812 to UPenn		5	27? or 24?	missing
07	12	17811 to UPenn	8?	12a	25M	PAM pole only, missing house
08	14	17809 to UPenn	17/19?	9	24	missing
09	15	17808 to BKLN	21	16	23	missing
10	19	17805 to BKLN		18	21	missing
11	21	17803 to UPenn	20	19	20	missing
12	17	17806 to UPenn	21	17	22	missing
13	23	17800	16	nn?	18	FM
14	37	17828 to BKLN	9	?	1B?	missing
15	25	17827 to UPenn	13? or 15	23	17	missing
16	26	17833 to MF	8	21	16	missing
17	45	17825 to UPenn	7		6	missing
18	30	17834	9		12	FM
19	29	17832		nn	10	BKLN
20	33	17837 to BKLN			8	BKLN house only, missing pole
21	22	17802	14	20	19	FM
22	9	17814 to UPenn	18	3	29	missing
23	32	17822			7	FM
24	35	17990	5		5	FM
25	39	17836	6		4	FM
26	41	17829 to UPenn				missing
27	43	17835 to UPenn				PC
P01	3	17820			31X	FM
P02	2	17821			12M Ts'aahl	FM
P03	6	17817			29M2	FM
P04	8	17815			29M1	FM
P05	10	17813		8	27X	FM
P06	13	17810			26M	FM
P07 g.h.	?	17824				FM
P08	16	17807			23X	FM
P09	20	17804			21M	FM
P10	24	nn			18X2	Welt
P11	28	17842			12M2	FM
P12 g.h.	27	17991 to BKLN				missing
P13	31	17839			11X or 12 X	FM
P14	34	17841			9X	FM
P15	36	17840			5M2	FM
P16	38	17830		20a	18M1	FM
P17	40	17838			5M1	FM
P18	42	17831				FM
P19	44	17843				FM
nn	46.5	17801 figures that go with Sg̱ang Gwaay house				FM

Note: Model pole numbers are listed after model house #27 indicated by "P" to distinguish from the sequence of model houses. Included with the model pole numbers are two model grave houses indicated "g.h." following the number to distinguish from the poles. The Field Museum number column indicates if there was an exchange with another museum. The Where Now column indicates current location or missing status.

"Installation no." indicates the order that the houses and poles were installed at the WCE; "Swanton #" are from John Swanton's *Contributions to the Ethnology of the Haida* (Swanton 1905a, 286); "Newcombe #" are from C. F. Newcombe notes, BC Archives (Newcombe 1900–1911); "MacDonald #" indicates the number used in George MacDonald's *Haida Monumental Art* (1983, 38–57).

Abbreviations: BKLN = Brooklyn Museum of Art; FM = Field Museum, Chicago; MF = Marshall Field Department Store; nn = no catalog number; PAM = Portland Art Museum, Oregon; PC = Private Collection; UPenn = University of Pennsylvania Museum; Welt = Weltmuseum, Vienna, Austria.

CHAPTER 3 / Model Houses, Poles, and Their Makers

This chapter presents each of the twenty-nine house models, the seventeen freestanding model poles, and the artists who were commissioned by James Deans for the World's Columbian Exposition (WCE) in Chicago, 1893. Deans sketched a map of twenty-seven house models (including the three not from Skidegate) to represent the 1864 village as he thought the house models should be installed at the WCE (figure 3.1a,b).[1] This sketch does not include the two grave houses.

The WCE model village had fewer houses and poles than the historical village of Hlg̱aagilda Llnagaay. John Work, the Hudson's Bay Company's chief factor (chief trader) at Fort Simpson, reported forty-eight houses in Skidegate in 1835 (Cole and Lockner 1993, 158). The wife of Chief Skidegate told Swanton in 1901 that Dawson's number of houses (forty) was likely correct (Swanton 1905b, 286fn1). The government census report for 1881 recorded only fifteen occupied Skidegate houses, but Edward of the Daayuu'ahl Laanas (R8) gave Swanton the names of twenty-two Skidegate houses in 1901 (see Appendix II, Swanton's Skidegate House List). MacDonald described thirty houses in 1966–80, but his map indicates thirty-eight houses, eight of which are unnumbered (MacDonald 1983, 38). The wife of Chief Skidegate told Swanton: "Before the last row of houses was built, the houses stood farther back, and were more numerous" (Swanton 1905b, 286fn1).

There have been no fewer than five different numbering systems for the model houses: Deans's original list, the order of installation (documented in the photos and written on the back of the models), Boas's lists from two of his manuscripts, the Field Museum's accession list, and the Field Museum's catalog numbers written on the models. There have also been three different numbering systems for the original full-size Skidegate houses: John Swanton's 1901 list, Charles F. Newcombe's lists, and George MacDonald's 1983 list. For a comparison of some of these numbers and a panorama comparing the placement of the old full-size houses with the installation of the models at the WCE, see the panorama between chapters 2 and 3 and "Comparison of Numbering Systems."

After comparing his list of Skidegate houses to the sequence of the WCE house models listed by Deans a decade earlier, Swanton lamented that "there seems to be considerable confusion about the order in which these should stand. In only a few cases do the names agree with those which I obtained myself, but both may nevertheless be right, for houses might bear two or more names. There are four more houses in Skidegate proper than I learned of, but I am not satisfied that all of these were contemporaneous" (Swanton 1905a, 286). Neither Deans's list nor the installation order of the house models accurately reflects the actual order of houses as they stood in the village. Some houses and poles had no models made for the WCE, but other models of them do exist (see figure 3.124).

James Deans's sketch (see figure 3.1a, b) shows certain geographic features around Skidegate such as salmonberry bushes and the gardens behind the houses with each of the model houses and their numbers indicated below. This includes three

3.1 A & B James Deans's sketch, 1893, with the numbered model houses drawn in the order that he intended them to be installed at the World's Columbian Exposition. Courtesy of the Field Museum, Anthropology Archives Acc. File 21, drawn by James Deans.

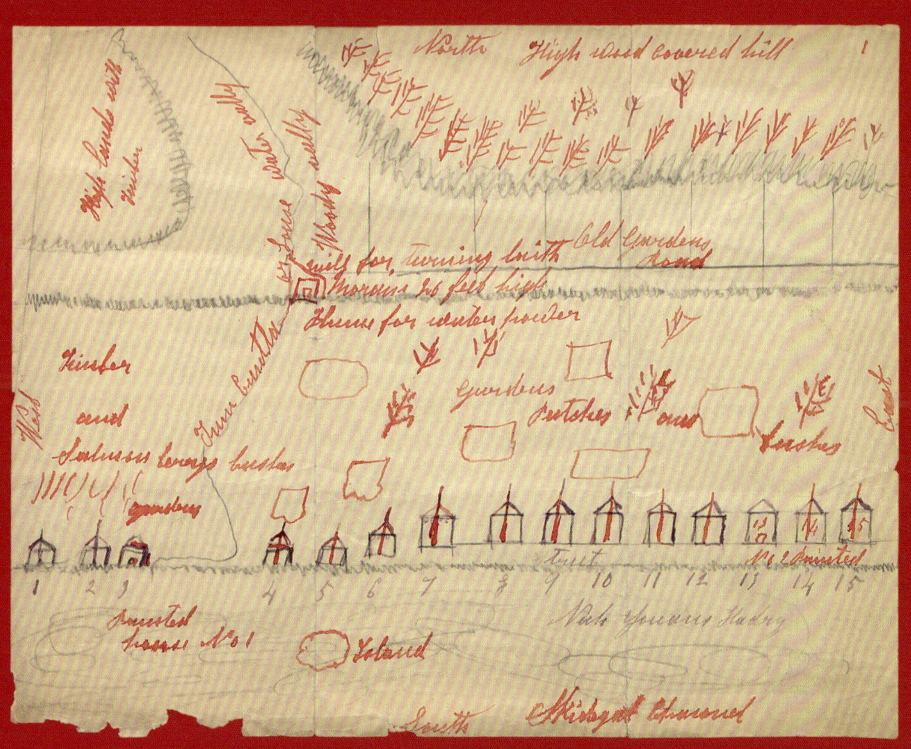

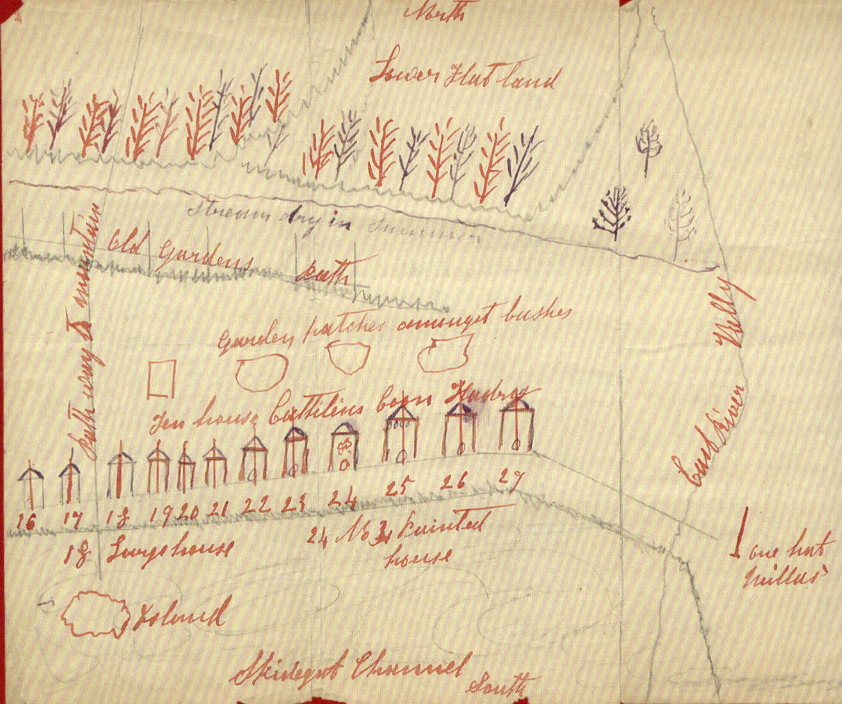

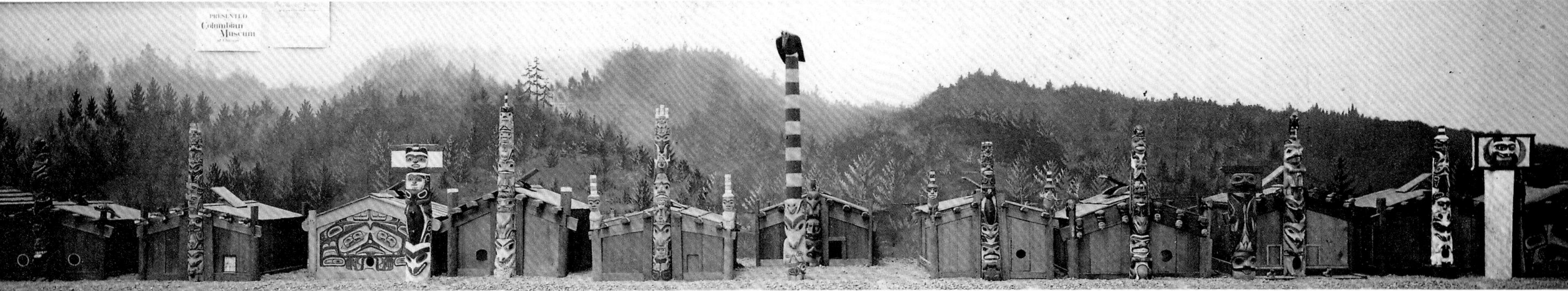

houses separated to the left that are from different villages, Xaayna Llnagaay, Sg̱ang Gwaay Llnagaay, and Hlg̱aax̱id Llnagaay. Deans wanted the WCE installation of the houses to follow this order, but when the models were installed, Boas deviated from Deans's sketch by leaving out the Sg̱ang Gwaay Llnagaay house model and repositioning "High Crest House" (Deans's No. 22).[2] Deans's written lists include twenty-seven model houses and two grave houses, but apparently there was no room for three of these on the platform, and it is believed that they were exhibited elsewhere in the building since they do have installation numbers painted on the back. Based on the installation numbers and the existing photographs, only twenty-five of the model houses and only one of the two model grave houses were installed with the model village.

3.2 Hlg̱aagilda Llnagaay, Skidegate, Model Village installed in the Anthropology Building, World's Columbian Exposition, 1893. Note that the original label for this photograph says: "Anthropology and Ethnology Building, Alaskan Village in miniature, 1893," despite the fact that Skidegate is in Canada, not Alaska. Photograph by Charles Dudley Arnold. Chicago Public Library, accession #WCE/CDA, Vol. VII, C. D. Arnold album, plate 108.

The most published photo of the Skidegate house model exhibit shows the left (south) end of the village at a raking angle, as they were installed inside the Anthropology Building on a fifty-foot-long bench with a painted backdrop meant to represent the Skidegate landscape (see figure I.1). A photo of the WCE model house installation that had not been published before 2009 was discovered at the Chicago Public Library (figure 3.2) (Wright 2009). This photo confirms that one of the model grave houses was exhibited in the middle of the village (Model Grave House No. 12), and that the model mortuary pole now in Vienna, Austria, was exhibited at the WCE (Model Pole No. 10). Another photo of the extreme right end of the model village shows the last two house models and model pole that appear in the exhibit (figure 3.3, far left). There may be an additional photo showing the houses at the extreme right end of the village, though none has yet been found, and it may be that none was taken of this section. There is a dip in the tree line of the forest backdrop just as the exhibit extends under the ceiling of the upper level. This section to the right of the Chicago Public Library photo should contain at least two additional houses before the two that show at the end in figure 3.3, based on the installation numbers.

An exhibit guide shows a map of the Anthropology displays (figure 3.4), which indicates that the Skidegate model village was located near the south entrance to

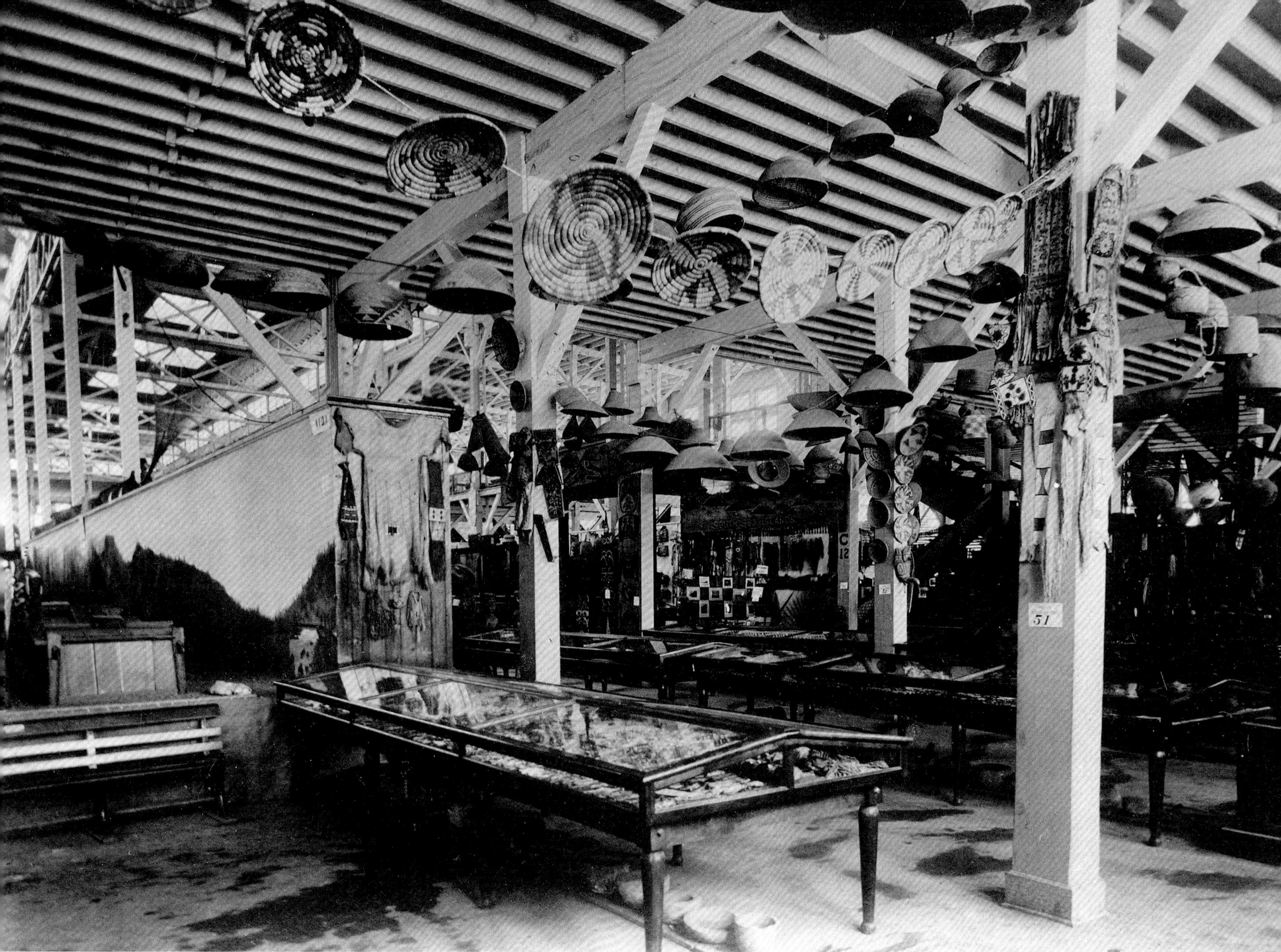

3.3 World's Columbian Exposition, 1893. Anthropology Building exhibits showing the Edward E. Ayer's collection to the right (baskets hanging from the ceiling and behind) and the right end view of the Hlg̱aagilda model village (to the far left, see figure 3.137). Courtesy of the Peabody Museum of Archaeology and Ethnology, Harvard University, 93-1-10/100266.1.33.

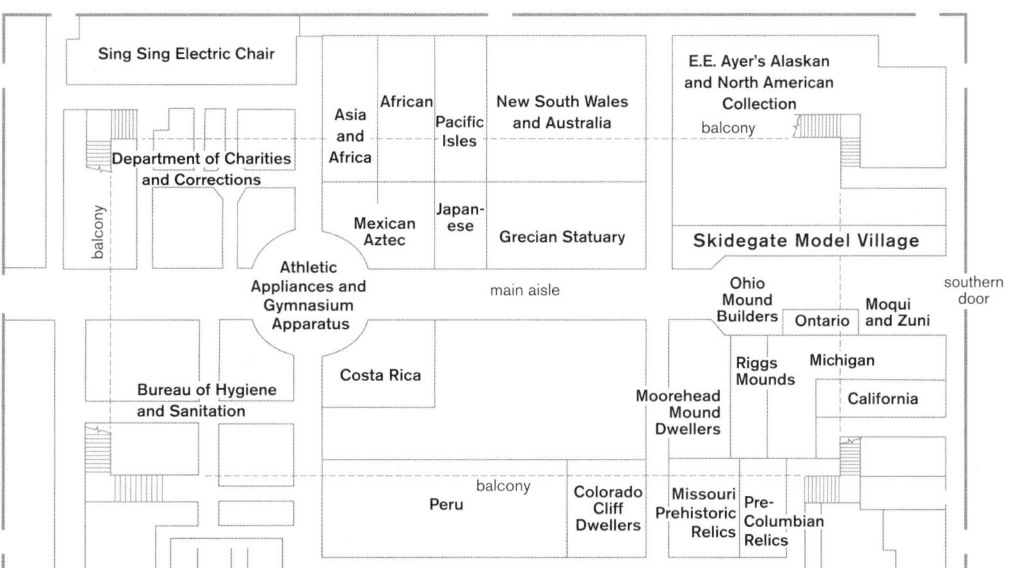

3.4 Floor plan of displays inside the Anthropology Building at the Worlds' Columbian Exposition, 1893. Redrawn by Ben Pease based on the Ground Plan in Wade and Wrenn, 1893, 37. Courtesy of Chicago History Museum, cat. no. F38MZ1893.A2W.

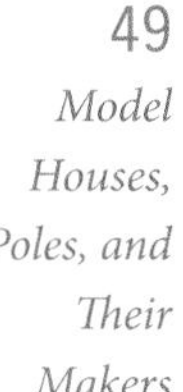

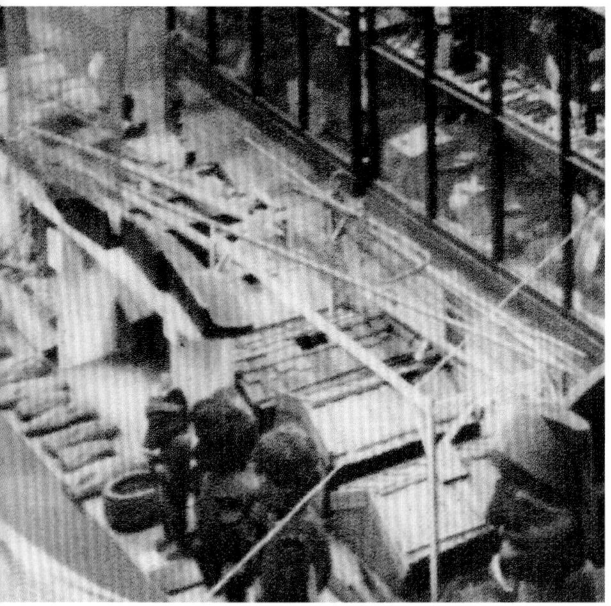

3.5 View of Edward E. Ayer's displays located behind the installation of the Skidegate model village. This detail from the extreme lower left of the full photo shows a row of eleven model houses from their back side, including the Tsimshian, Nuxalk, and extra Haida houses facing right. American Museum of Natural History Library, Image #337268s.

the building with its painted backdrop screening the Edward E. Ayer collections of Alaskan and Native American objects that were displayed behind it near the stairs to the balcony exhibits. Facing the house models were displays of Pueblo, Ontario, Michigan, and "Mound Builder" Mississippian exhibits. At least two if not all three Haida houses that did not fit—the SG̱ang Gwaay house now in Vienna (House Model No. 2), Earthquake House (House Model No. 17), and the shed roof grave house (Model Grave House No. 7)—were likely installed in the area that included Ayer's collection of Alaskan and North American material, behind the painted mural. A close-up detail of the lower left-hand corner of a photograph of that area (figure 3.5) shows a row of eleven model houses, three of which have a visible frontal pole. Two of these may be either Earthquake House or the SG̱ang Gwaay house. However, the SG̱ang Gwaay house has three watchmen at the top and doesn't resemble the visible poles. The tallest of these has an eagle-like bird as the top figure, so this is probably not Earthquake House either (see No. 17 below).[3]

They were joined there by four Tsimshian house models collected by Odille Quintal Morison in Fort Simpson and five Nuxalk house models collected by Fillip Jacobsen for Boas (figure 3.6) (see Atkinson 2011, 153–55; Beck 2019, 61–62; Cole 1985, 123–24).[4] Four of the Nuxalk models had short frontal poles, and at least two of the Nisgaa houses also had short frontal poles. Based on their prominent gable panels, the Nuxalk house models appear to be placed at the right end of this display (as seen from the back).

After the close of the fair in the fall of 1893, all of these models became part of the collections of the newly established Field Museum of Natural History in Chicago. Between 1900 and 1907 the Field Museum deaccessioned two of the Tsimshian models,

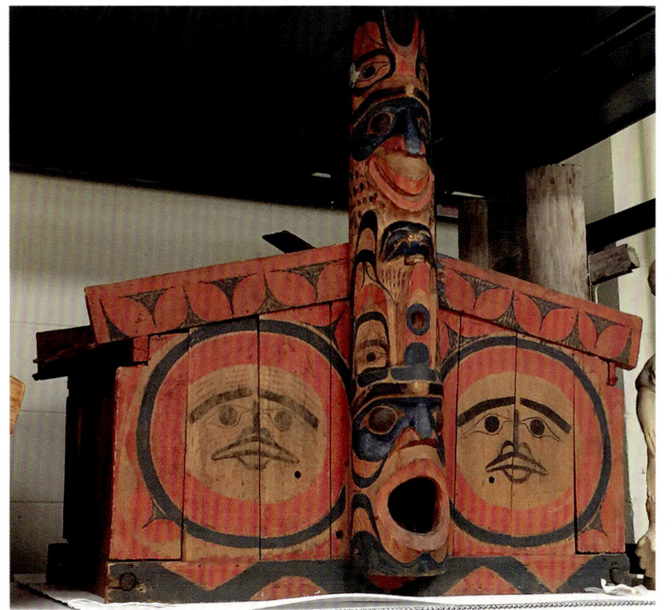

3.6 Nuxalk house model collected by Phillip Jacobson for the World's Columbian Exposition, 1893. Courtesy of the Field Museum, cat. no. 18645. Photograph by the author.

nineteen of the Haida model houses, and one model mortuary pole, which were exchanged, sold, and gifted to the Brooklyn Museum (nine model houses—two of them Tsimshian), the Free Museum of Science in Philadelphia (later the University of Pennsylvania Museum of Archaeology and Anthropology, ten house models), the Museum für Völkerkunde in Vienna, Austria (one house model and one model mortuary pole), and the Marshall Field Company in Chicago (one house model). The Field Museum may have deaccessioned these models thinking they were repetitious and used them as a means of acquiring objects that were not represented in their collection. Of the Haida houses, only two complete houses and parts of six others remain in these other museums, and fourteen remain missing in 2023.

It is likely that these model houses were not seen by the museums as works of art or valuable historical documents but instead as "museum dioramas" of the type being made by museum exhibit designers and were considered to be temporary and expendable.[5] They were large and difficult to store, and often only the pole was retained and the house itself destroyed. They were also seen as educational tools suitable for children's museums. The University of Pennsylvania Museum loaned two of the house models to the Boy Scouts in 1919, and eight were loaned to Memorial Hall in Fairmount Park that same year. At Memorial Hall the eight houses became part of a Children's Museum. No records were found of the return of these loans.[6] The location of eight of the ten house models sent to Philadelphia remains unknown, but parts of two of them got out onto the market. One house frontal pole is now at the Portland Art Museum, acquired by the dealer Julius Carlebach (see figure 3.51). Another frontal pole was auctioned by Sotheby's in Paris in 2009 and is now in a private collection in Vancouver, BC (see figure 3.138).

The model that represents a house from the village of SG̱ang Gwaay Llnagaay (Ninstints) and a model mortuary pole from the Skidegate set were sent from the Field Museum to the Ethnographic Museum in Vienna (now the KHM-Museumsverband, Weltmuseum), where they remain today (see figures 3.13, 3.83). Several other model Skidegate houses were commissioned by Deans, but never made it to Chicago, including one now in the Fairbanks Museum and Planetarium in Saint Johnsbury, Vermont, and two in the Royal British Columbia Museum in Victoria, BC. Nine Haida house models and one model grave house remain at the Field Museum, along with sixteen of the original freestanding model Haida poles and the five Nuxalk and two of the four Tsimshian house models.

A few of the models remaining at the Field Museum have been exhibited over the years. The southern half of the model village, fourteen of the model houses, and eight model poles were displayed at the Jackson Park Museum, as recorded in three photographs sometime before the museum was moved in 1921 (figures 3.45, 3.55, 3.64).[7] The original painted backdrop was displayed, and exhibit cases with artifacts were placed in front of the platform. Another partial display took place in 1971, long after the nineteen Haida model houses had been exchanged with other museums. By then the painted backdrop had been replaced by faux evergreens.[8] Only seven houses and the shed roof grave house were included along with four Nuxalk models placed at the right end. Most of the models that remain at the Field Museum are in storage today, with the exception of Skidegate the Great's mortuary pole (Model Pole No. 1) and the two dogfish memorials (Model Pole Nos. 3 and 4).

Though some of the stories Deans collected have been published (Deans 1899b), his complete collection notes have never been systematically analyzed until now and have remained unpublished in the archives of the Field Museum of Natural History in Chicago (Deans 1893a; Deans 1893b). Questions still remain as to the exact identity of some of the original houses on which the model houses were based. These include Mountain House (House Model No. 8), Earthquake House (House Model No. 17), Copper House (House Model No. 26), and Cah Guintt (House Model No. 27).

In the remainder of this chapter, each house discussion will combine the primary documentation from several sources: James Deans's original notes (Deans 1893b; Deans 1893c), John R. Swanton's list of Skidegate houses (Swanton 1905a), Charles F. Newcombe's notes on Skidegate houses (Newcombe 1900–1911), George MacDonald's compilation of those sources (MacDonald 1983), and my own comments on the discrepancies in these records. Both Deans and Boas had hoped to represent the historical village as it stood, but neither Deans's numbering system nor Boas's installation actually accomplished this. The models are therefore presented here in the order that they should have been displayed, if they had been arranged as closely as possible according to the houses in the village. Explanations are given where this was not possible. Since some of the houses have not been associated with any full-size house, these are presented near the end.

The discussion of each model will include Deans's creative names and spellings of the names in quotation marks, and, if possible, the current spelling in X̱aayda kil and the English translation of that name. Where known, the artists are discussed near the models that they made with their genealogy charts following. In many cases the artists are closely related and so have been included together on one genealogy chart. Where possible, photographs that compare the original Skidegate houses and poles with the models, photos of the model village installation at the WCE, and photos of the house models as they appear today are included. Figure captions include the original Field Museum catalog number, and if transferred, the other museums' catalog numbers, and status (if missing).

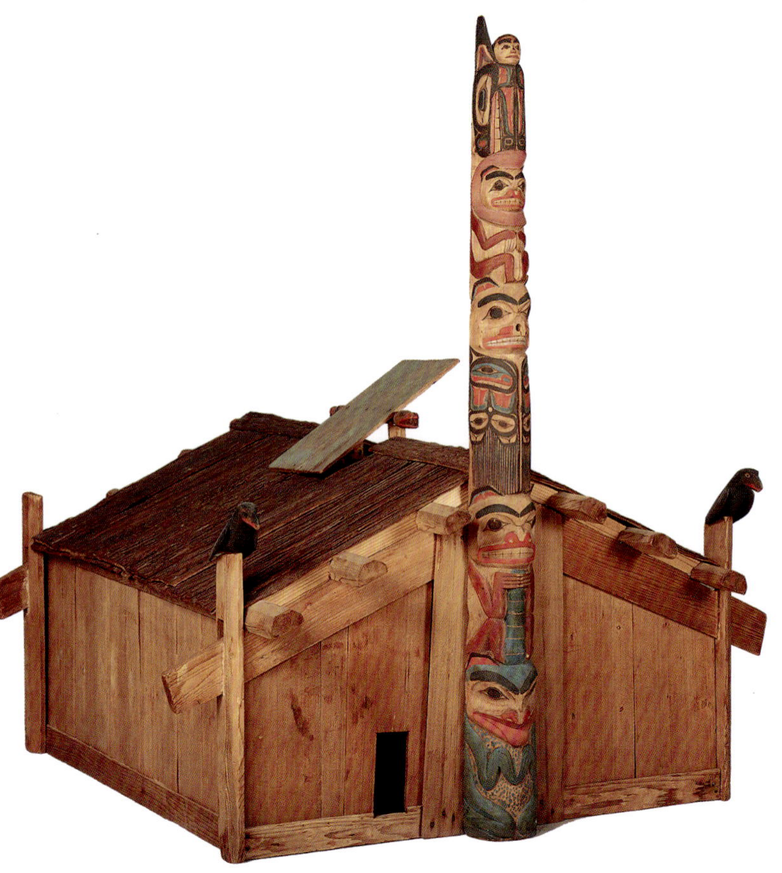

3.7 *above* House Model No. 1, X̱uuya Naas, from Xaayna Llnagaay (New Gold Harbour), 1892, made by Peter Smith, 48.5 in. × 4.75 in. × 3.5 in. (pole). Courtesy of the Field Museum, cat. no. 17823, photograph by Gail Specht.

3.8 *right* House No. 1 and Model Pole No. 2 installed at the extreme left end of the model village at the World's Columbian Exposition, 1893. Field Museum, cat. nos. 17823 and 17821. Detail of figure 1.1. Courtesy of the Peabody Museum of Archaeology and Ethnology, Harvard University, 93-1-10/100266.1.39.

HOUSE MODEL NO. 1 / *Made by Peter Smith*

Deans described this model as "Chooah Nass, from the village of Heenii," the current spellings being X̱uuya Naas, "Raven House" from Xaayna Llnagaay (figures 3.7, 3.8). It was made by Peter Smith, who used to live in the original house (Deans 1893b; Deans 1893c). Xaayna Llnagaay is located on Maude Island, near Skidegate (see Map 1 and Map 2). The original house in Xaayna Llnagaay is described by MacDonald as House No. 6, "House Waiting for Property" (MacDonald 1983, 65) (figure 3.9). His information was drawn from Newcombe and Swanton, though Newcombe recorded different information from his two sources, William Woods and Moses McKay.[9] The old pole is now on display in the Grand Hall at the Canadian History Museum in Hull, Quebec, in front of a reconstructed house (figure 3.10). This original pole has an oval door opening through the belly of the bottom figure. The model of this pole does not, but instead has a rectangular door to the left of the frontal pole. The old house also had rectangular doors to either side of the pole, as can be seen in the photograph (see figure 3.9), so the model was accurate in this way. There are many other differences between the model and the original pole, as there are with most of the models. On the model, ravens are placed on the outside corner posts, but there were none on the original house. This would have given rise to Deans's name, "House of Ravens." There are varying descriptions of the figures on the poles. W. Woods identified the figures on the original old pole as the Ts'aamus on the bottom and thunderbird at the top.[10] The Ts'aamus is a supernatural snag (a log that lies just below the surface and is a danger to seafarers) and can be represented in many different forms. It is depicted here as a bear-like figure with a stack of sgil (spruce root basketry hat rings, signs of status) above the head. Moses McKay agreed that the bird at the top is a thunderbird but identified the bottom figure as a killer [whale].[11] The arms and legs on the lower figure suggest that Woods's Ts'aamus identification is likely correct, rather than a killer whale.

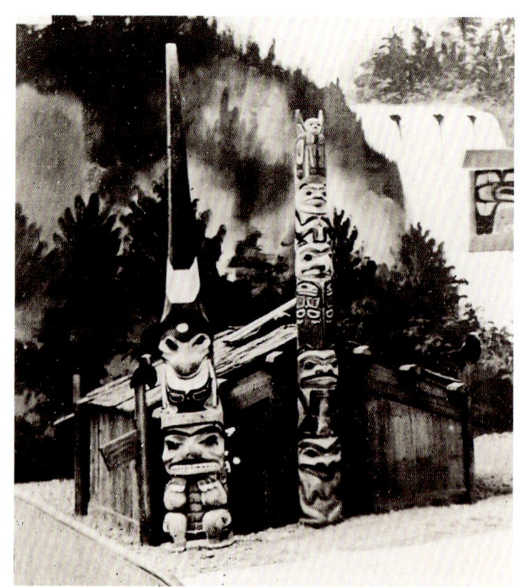

Neither Woods nor McKay identified the figures in the middle of the pole, but Deans provides a lengthy description of the figures on the model of this house, which are somewhat different than those described for the original pole. He calls the figure on the bottom a brown bear and the figure above as a beaver, referring to the sgil it is holding as "6 or 9 degrees of tuden skeel." He describes the figure above as a mountain thundershower in the form of a thunderbird with the rain shower and rainbow indicated by the wings and extended lines representing rain seen on the model. The model is missing the beak of the thunderbird (Deans 1893c). He describes the figure above the bird as the sun that comes out after the thunderstorm. Above the sun is a woman from the Tsimshian story of Nanasimget (spelled by Deans "Nach noo Simgate"), whose wife is taken away by a killer whale and later rescued by him. Deans recounts this story in great detail (Deans 1893c, 16–19).[12] On the model she is shown as a human face above a killer whale. Deans's story ends with an account of the two sea lion heads carved on the pivot ends of the smoke hole cover, which he says were put there for decoration only (see figure 3.7) (Deans 1893b). In fact, the sea

3.9 *below left* Xaayna Llnagaay (New Gold Harbour) showing in the center "House Waiting for Property." Photograph by Brooks, ca. 1890. Image G-02447. Courtesy of the Royal BC Museum and Archives.

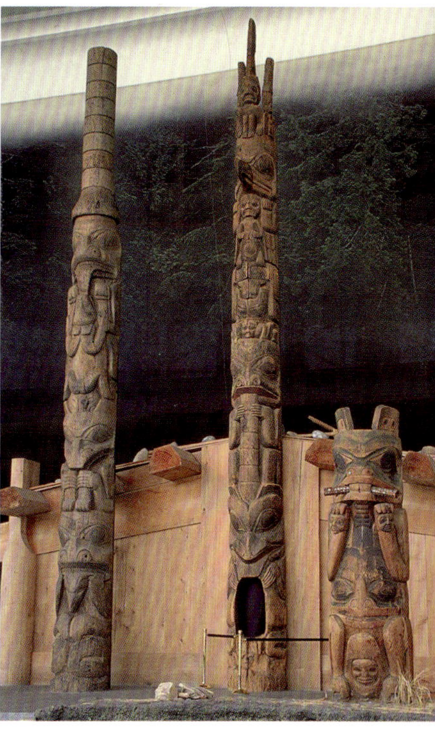

3.10 *below right* Frontal pole (center) from "House Waiting for Property," Xaayna Llnagaay, now installed at the Canadian Museum of History. Courtesy of the Canadian Museum of History, neg. no. S92-4409.

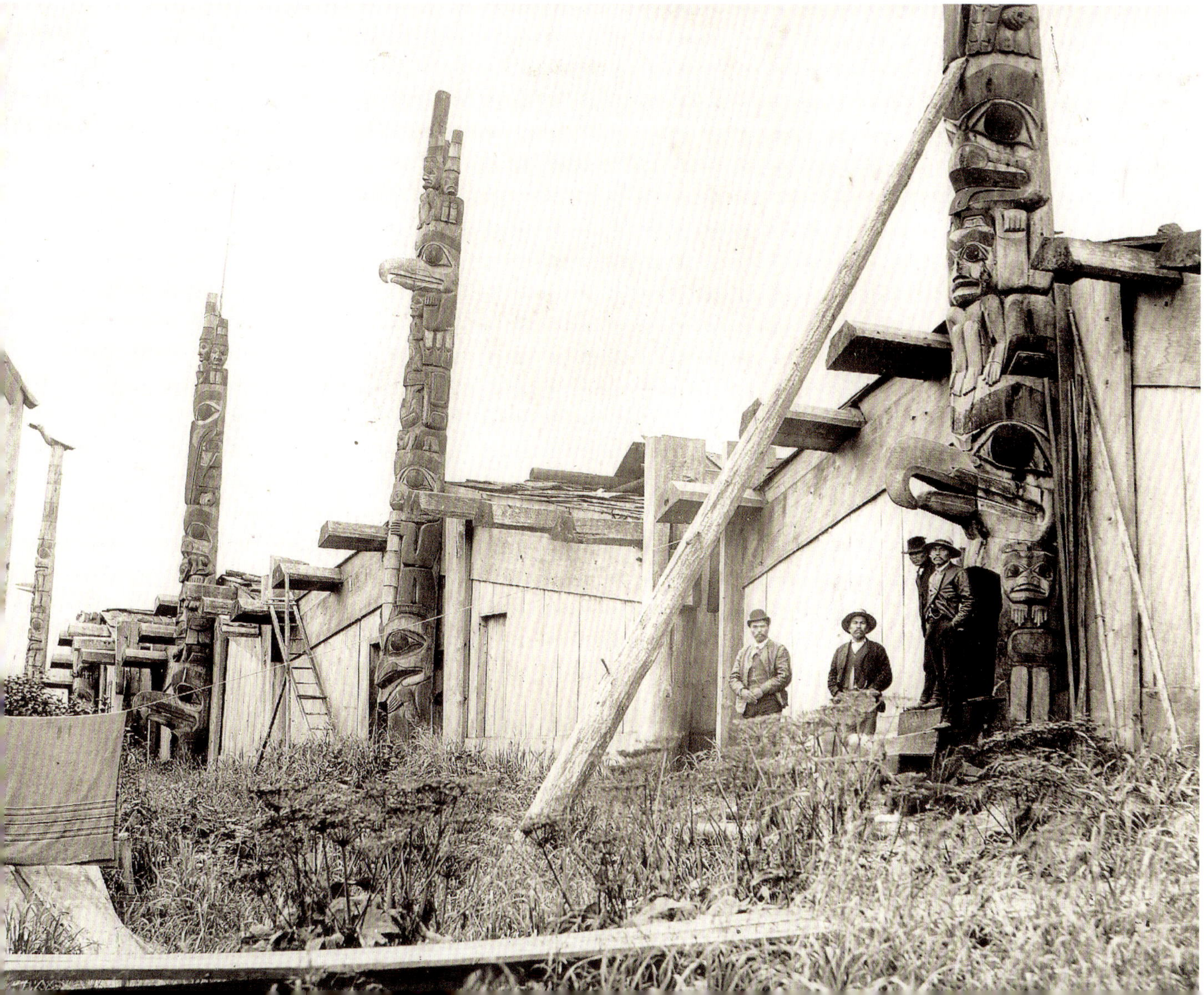

lion is one of the crests of both the Hlg̱axiidgu Laanas (R9) and Naasduu K̲iig̱awaay (R10a) clans, one of which owned the original house, so their use here was meaningful.

I believe that Deans's brown bear and beaver identifications for the two figures at the bottom are not correct. As with many of Deans's explanations, his understanding of the clan system and their crests is confused in many cases. If we are to believe either of Newcombe's advisers, Woods and McKay, the house either belonged to the Pebble Town Ravens (R9) or Those Born at Hippa Island (R10a). According to Swanton (1905a, 270), the R9 crests are moon, thunderbird, rainbow, killer whale, sea lion, and the R10a crests are killer whale, thunderbird, sea lion, rainbow, Ts'aamus, dogfish, and the tree to commemorate Xā'gi. Neither brown bear nor beaver are listed as crests of either of these clans, though Deans incorrectly says that the bear is a crest of the owner of the house. Deans also stated that Raven was the crest of both the owner of the house and his wife. Here again, Deans is probably incorrect, since given Haida marriage customs, the Raven owner would likely have been married to a woman from an Eagle clan.[13]

The full-size pole has a figure with a tall dorsal fin placed between the two watchmen figures at the top. The thunderbird has human arms with long wing-feathers extending down, and a whale facing backward with two profile heads at each side with their snout pointing downward is curled beneath the thunderbird. Between the whale heads is a shared tail with flukes pointing upward toward two angular pectoral fins that meet below a shared single short dorsal fin. The fin is grasped by a human figure on the chest of the thunderbird. The original old pole lacks the sun figure entirely but includes a small figure crouched between the ears below the whale. The model pole shows the whale only at the top. This whale also has two heads shown in profile at the sides, an unusual feature, and places a human head with the single dorsal fin at the top, representing, according to Deans, the wife of Nanasimget.

Peter Smith / *See Genealogy Chart 1*

Peter Smith, Naasduu K̲iig̱awaay (R10a), was born ca. 1856 and died May 5, 1906 (May 6?) (Skidegate gravestone). He is listed (age thirty) in the 1891 census for Skidegate (Family #386), living with his wife, Loisa (age twenty-one), and their daughter Minnie (age five), a nephew, Mr. Jackson (age twenty-five), a brother George Smith (age twenty-three), and John Michael (age twenty-two). Peter Smith was baptized in 1890 (age thirty-

GENEALOGY CHART 1.
The family of Peter Smith, Naasduu K̲iig̱awaay (R10a)

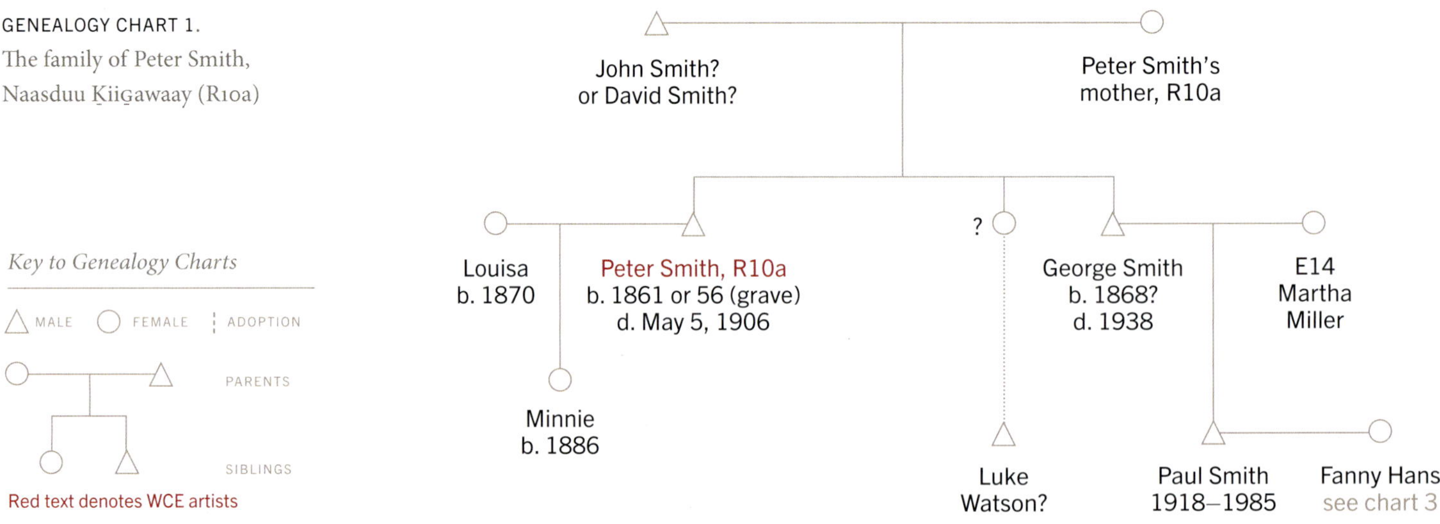

one) at Gold Harbour, and after his baptism was a local preacher of the Epworth League, an association of the United Methodist Church at Skidegate.

Peter Smith was said by Deans to have lived in the original Xaayna house that he copied but had moved to Skidegate by 1891. As mentioned earlier, there is some confusion over who owned this house (see note 9), but the pole from the original house was purchased by Newcombe from George Smith, Peter's brother. Peter and George Smith were both Naasduu K̲iiG̲awaay, Those Born at Hippa Island. No one is known to have survived from these two clans today (Haida Gwaii Museum, Clans of Skidegate), although both brothers had at least one child (Minnie and Paul Smith).

Peter's brother, George Smith (b. 1868?, d. 1938), was known as an argillite carver and was discussed by both Marius Barbeau (1957, 95–101) and Leslie Drew and Douglas Wilson (Drew and Wilson 1980, 250).[14] Barbeau confirms their clan as the "Children of Neesto," Those born at Hippa Island (R10a). Luke Watson told Barbeau that George Smith was his uncle and that George Smith's family migrated to Ts'aahl Llnagaay (Chaatl) and then Xaayna Llnagaay (New Gold Harbour) during the nineteenth century, and then to Skidegate when he was about twelve years old (Barbeau 1916–1954, B. F. 314, file 1). Their father was identified as John Smith by Erna Gunther (Gunther 1966, 174) and possibly as David Smith by Amos Watson (Barbeau 1916–1954, B. F. 257.1).

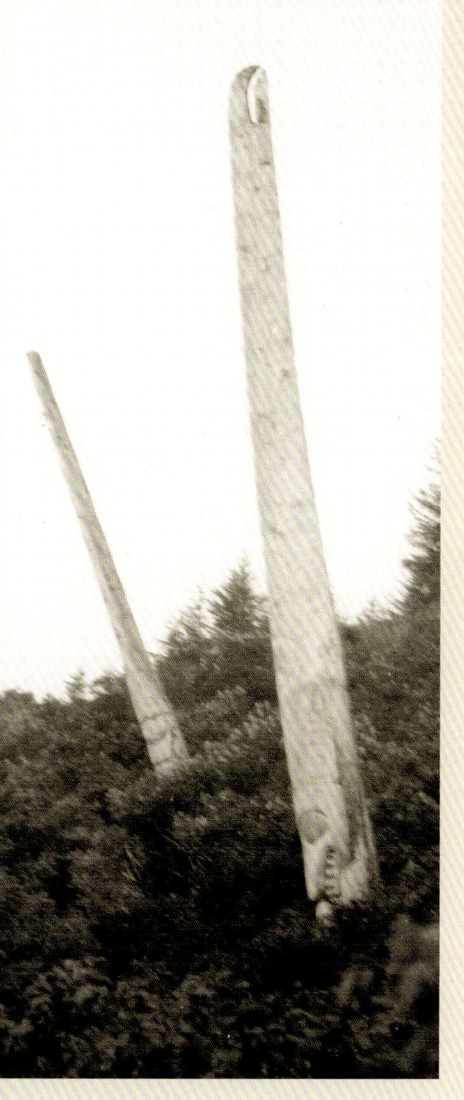

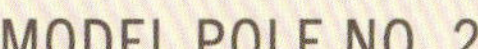

MODEL POLE NO. 2

A freestanding memorial pole model was placed just to the left of the Xaayna house model at the WCE (figure 3.11; see figure 3.8, left). Deans identified this pole as a memorial belonging to the west coast tribes representing the "Cheel Yeelas." He says: "In form it represents the beak of a bird, whence its name. This bird frequents the west coast of those islands, its name is Kiswit" (Deans 1893b). In Newcombe's copy of Deans's account, he has written "?!" in the margin next to this explanation, strongly suggesting that he didn't believe this. In fact, the Tsil X̲iilas is a supernatural killer whale with a raven-beaked dorsal fin. The original for this memorial is probably one of the two poles representing

3.11 *above* Model Pole No. 2 representing SG̲aana Tsil X̲iilas pole from Ts'aahl Llnagaay (Chaatl Village), 1892, 55 in. h × 8.5 in. w × 8.5 in. d. Courtesy of the Field Museum, cat. no. 17821, photograph by Gail Specht.

3.12 *left* Ts'aahl Llnagaay (Chaatl Village), two memorial poles representing SG̲aana Tsil X̲iilas, photograph by C. F. Newcombe, 1901. Image PN63. Courtesy of the Royal BC Museum and Archives.

Tsil X̱iilas that once stood at Ts'aahl Llnagaay at the western end of Skidegate Inlet. According to MacDonald, one "was for the cousin of 'Great supernatural power,' the chief of those Born on the Stasaos Coast," Sdasaaws K̲iiG̱awaay (R11) and the other was erected to the memory of "Great supernatural power" (MacDonald 1983, 125, 12M, 13M) (figure 3.12). The photo of these two memorial poles does not show the bases, but the model pole has a whale with its tail curled up below its raven-beaked dorsal fin and a human figure at the base. Deans identifies the original owner as a Raven man named Abraham (Deans 1893b). There was an Abraham Green (age seventy-seven) living in New Gold Harbour, listed in the 1891 census (Family #336). This was likely the Abraham who owned this pole.

3.13 House Model No. 2, SG̱aana Naas made by Joshua Kinna-jesser, SG̱ang Gwaay Llnagaay (Ninstints Village), 1892. Courtesy of the KHM-Museumsverband, Weltmuseum (formerly the Museum für Völkerkunde), Vienna, Austria, cat. no. MVK VO 51775.

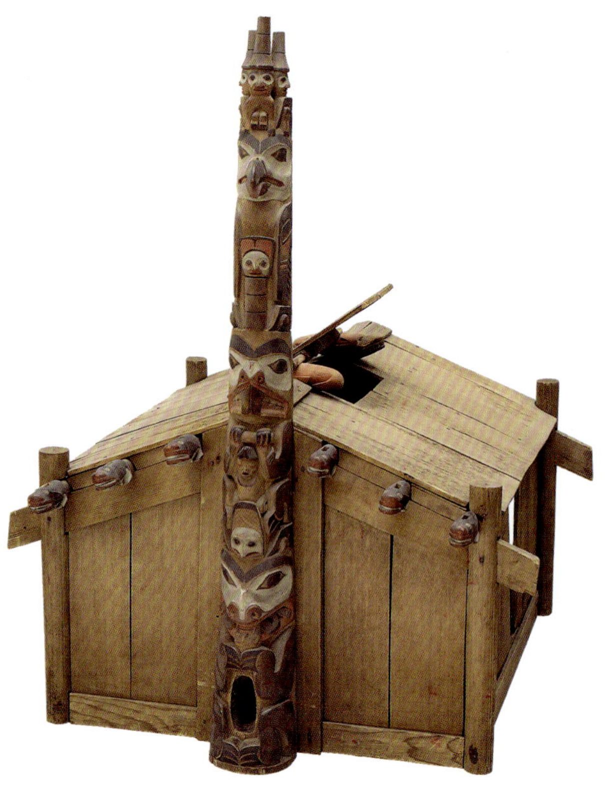

HOUSE MODEL NO. 2 / *Made by Joshua, Kinna-jesser [Tait]*

According to Deans, this is a model of SG̱aana Naas, a SG̱ang Gwaay Llnagaay house that he called "Scannah Nah or House of the Scannahs fin-backed whale crest," that was made by Joshua or Kinna-jesser, owner of the house and resident of Skidegate for many years (figure 3.13).[15] Newcombe identified the owner of this house (the tallest pole pictured in the center of his photograph, figure 3.15) as Joshua Tait. The notes associated with this photograph in the BC Archives identify the owner of the mortuary pole (#1) in the photo to the left of this house as James Watson's wife. The house frontal pole (#2) owner is identified as Giaf (?) Joshua Tait, and the owner of #3 as Giaf (?) T. Tait. It is unknown what the "Giaf" may mean. In Newcombe's 1901 diary, he lists the same information, referring to a photo of Ninstints, omitting the word "Giaf" but listing the figures on Joshua Tait's pole as eagle, cormorant, beaver, and bear, and noting that Joshua Tait was deceased.[16] This confirms the identity of Joshua/Kinna-jesser as Joshua Tait.[17]

MacDonald identifies both the Joshua Tait house and the one next to it, belonging to Timothy Tait, as belonging to Those Born at the Southern Part of the Islands, Gangx̱id K̲iiG̱awaay (E2) (MacDonald 1983, 111), likely basing this clan identification on the information in Swanton's list of houses at SG̱ang Gwaay. The sequence of houses doesn't match Swanton's list of houses, which places another house belonging to the Qayjuu K̲'iiG̱awaay (R2a), Those Born at Songs-of-Victory-Town, between the two Eagle houses (Swanton 1905a, 283, house nos. 15–17).[18]

Deans included this model with his set of models to show the similarity in Haida carving throughout the islands. This house, No. 2 on Deans's list, was not installed at the WCE with the other Skidegate models. Instead, it may have been displayed elsewhere in the Anthropology Building since it does have the installation number "A46" written right on the front gable, the very last one in the installation order (see figure 3.5).

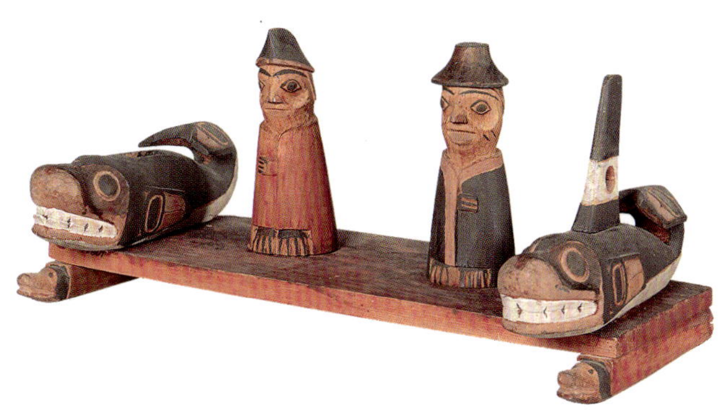

3.14 *left* Two figures representing a man wearing a peaked (shaman's) hat and red robe and a woman with a labret (lip plug), spruce root hat, and black robe (right) placed on a platform flanked by Sg̱aana (killer whales, one missing dorsal fin) meant to have been exhibited together with House Model No. 2, Sg̱aana Naas, likely made by Joshua Kinnajesser [Joshua Tait], 1892, 40 cm × 23 cm × 20 cm. Courtesy of the Field Museum, cat. no. 17801. Photograph by Gail Specht.

3.15 *below* Sg̱ang Gwaay Llnagaay (Ninstints Village), showing the house with the tallest pole in the center belonging to Joshua Tait. Photo by C. F. Newcombe, 1901. Image PN62. Courtesy of the Royal BC Museum and Archives.

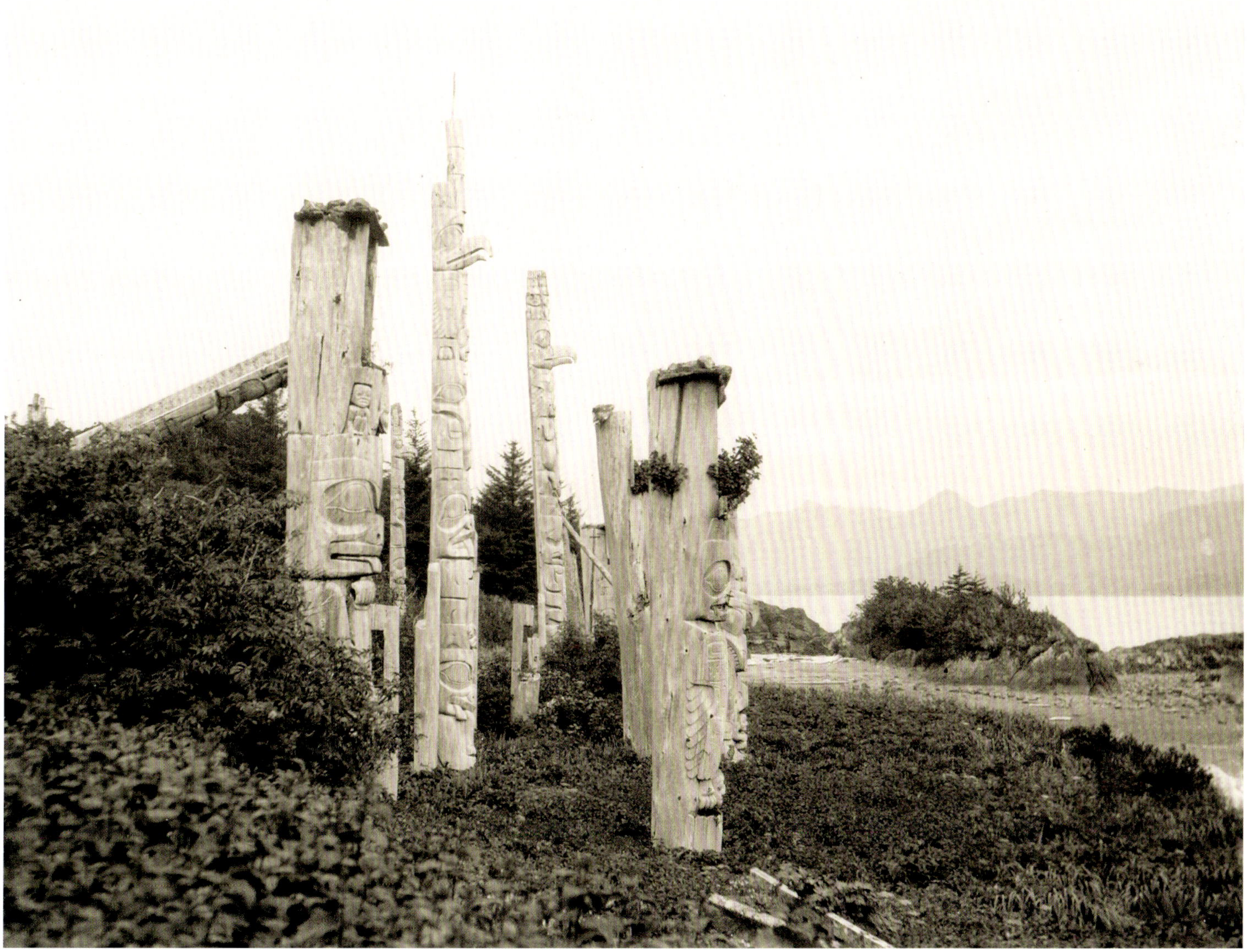

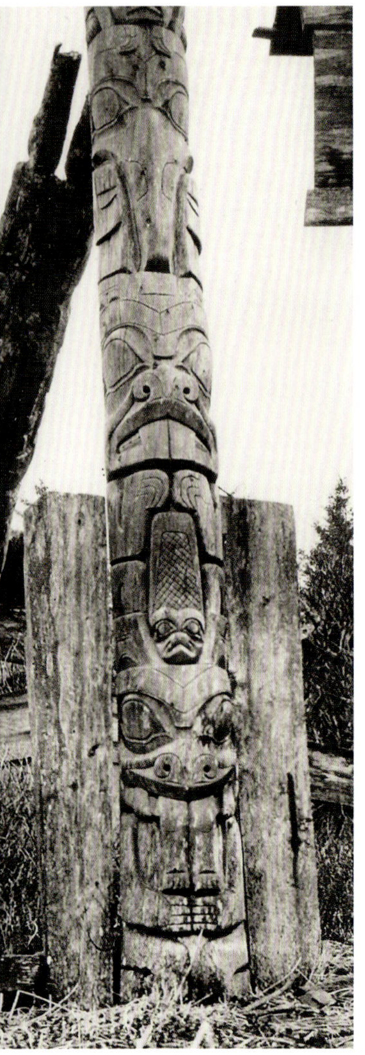

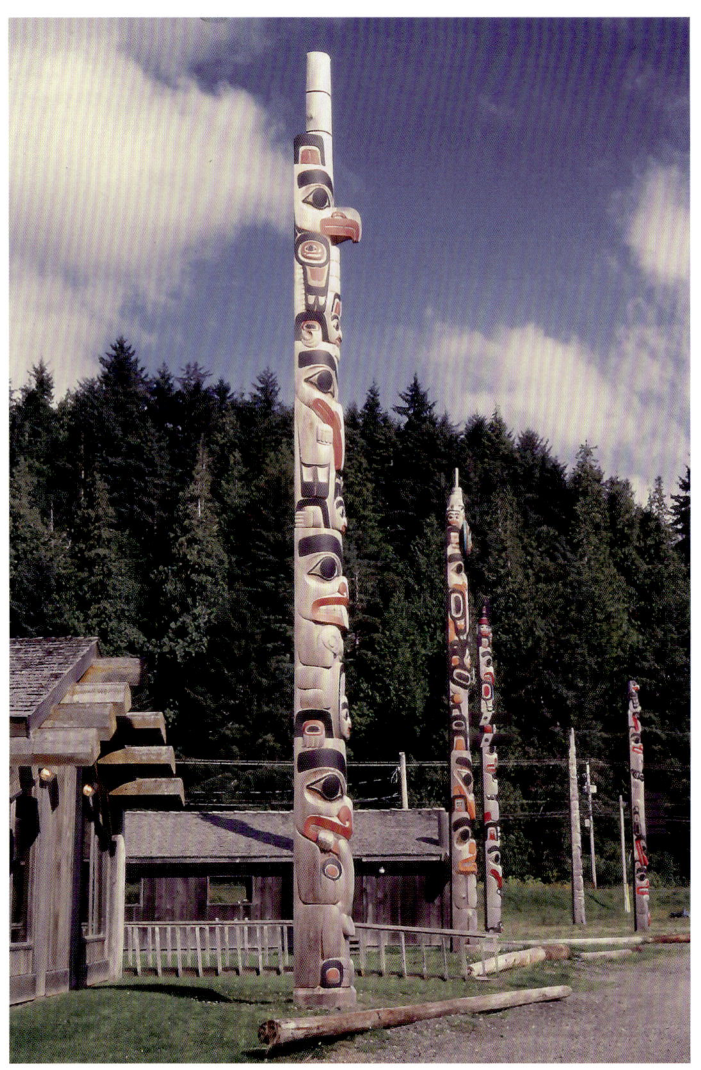

3.16 *above left* S̱gang Gwaay Llnagaay (Ninstints Village) showing the bottom three figures from Joshua Tait's frontal pole. Image PN7781. Courtesy of the Royal BC Museum and Archives.

3.17 *above right* S̱gaang Gwaii pole (left) replica by Tim Boyko, Haida Heritage Centre at Ḵay Llnagaay, raised 2001. Photograph by the author, 2002, courtesy of the Haida Heritage Centre at Ḵay Llnagaay.

According to Deans's description, House No. 2 has a "bear eating a boy at bottom, little face, man, beaver w/stick and 3 sgil above."[19] Deans's description fits the description of the model house that was sent to the Museum für Völkerkunde in Vienna in 1894. It was apparently never given a Field Museum catalog number. The full-size old pole (figures 3.15, 3.16) has an eagle with sgil, a long-beaked bird (cormorant), beaver, and bear eating a human. According to Deans, this bear figure represents "Chuchan Chootsa" [Tciakan Huadji] and tells the story of a boy who wandered into the woods and was eaten by a bear (Deans 1893c).

This old frontal pole was taken to Prince Rupert in the 1920s, then sent to the Royal British Columbia Museum where it remains (cat. no. 1974–18, B). A replica of this pole was carved by Tim Boyko and raised with five other poles in 2001 (figure 3.17). It stands today in front of the Haida Heritage Centre at Ḵay Llnagaay. Freda Diesing also made a replica of this pole in the 1970s that still stands in Prince Rupert (Ramsay 2011, 21). The model of this house differs in having three watchmen figures above the eagle and a doorway carved in the belly of the bear.

Associated with this model house is a figural group with two human figures wearing hats and robes standing on a platform flanked by whales. These figures have been separated from the house for more than a century. They were not sent to Vienna and remain at the Field Museum (see figure 3.14). According to Deans's notes for the S̱gang Gwaay house: "the little figures standing on a piece of board should be placed in front of this house."

Joshua, Kinna-jesser (Tait) / *See Genealogy Chart 2*

As discussed above, the maker of the S̱gang Gwaay house model, Joshua (Kinna-jesser), is probably Joshua Tait, based on the Newcombe identification of the owner of the original house. This man may be the Joshua (age fifty-five, no last name) listed in the 1891 census for Clew (Family #436), with a wife named Maria (age thirty) and a brother-in-law named Moses (age twenty-four).[20] The 1891 census for Clew also lists Peter Tate, age sixty, living with his wife Martha (age fifty-eight) and his brother, Captain Skedans (age fifty-eight) (Family #432). The title "Captain" was often used by town chiefs as a signal of their status. Another brother of Captain Skedans, Jacob (fifty-five), and his wife Jennie (fifty-three), were also living there with two other men named Skye (fifty) and Koonass (eighty). Peter Tate later became "Captain Skedans" before Henry Moody became Chief Skedans (Haida Gwaii Museum, Clans of Skidegate). The town chiefs of K̲'uuna Llnagaay are G̲aag'yals K̲iiG̲awaay (R4) (see Model Pole No. 8). It is unknown if Joshua or Timothy Tait were related to Peter Tate, although their father would have been a Raven.

Timothy Tait was living in Skidegate in 1911 (1911 Skidegate Census), married to Louisa. They had a son named Joshua, born in 1909, perhaps named for the older Joshua Tait who had passed away by 1901. Timothy Tait later married Laura (R13), the mother of Flora Marks (father Fred Marks). Flora married Louie Collinson (E6a). Timothy Tait is likely the T. Tait, listed by Newcombe as the owner of a pole that stood next to Joshua Tait's house. We know that Timothy Tait was Saagi K̲iiG̲awaay, Those born at Sgaagi, Flamingo Inlet (E1), the same clan as the town chief Nang Sdins (Tom Price) (Haida Gwaii Museum, Clans of Skidegate). But Swanton tells us that the owner of the house that the model was based on was G̲angx̲id K̲iiG̲awaay (E2), Those Born at the Southern Part of the Islands, and this man was Joshua Tait, according to Newcombe. It may be that Joshua (E2) and Timothy Tait (E1) were half-brothers with different mothers.

HOUSE MODEL NO. 3 / *Made by Zacherias Nicholas*

Deans called this model house "Kung Nass, Moon House" (now spelled K̲ung Naas) (figures 3.18, 3.19). According to him, "this is the first house in Skidegate on the west side," and belonged to Captain Gold. Captain Gold's house was actually not located in HlG̲aagilda Llnagaay (Skidegate village) proper but was located to the south at HlG̲aax̲id Llnagaay (known as First Beach) (figure 3.20). This house had a fully painted front, one of only three houses on Haida Gwaii to be decorated in that way. Attached to the gable was Captain Gold's mortuary pole panel representing the moon with a hawk face that had been

GENEALOGY CHART 2
The family of Joshua Kinna-jesser (Tait), G̲angx̲id K̲iiG̲awaay (E2)

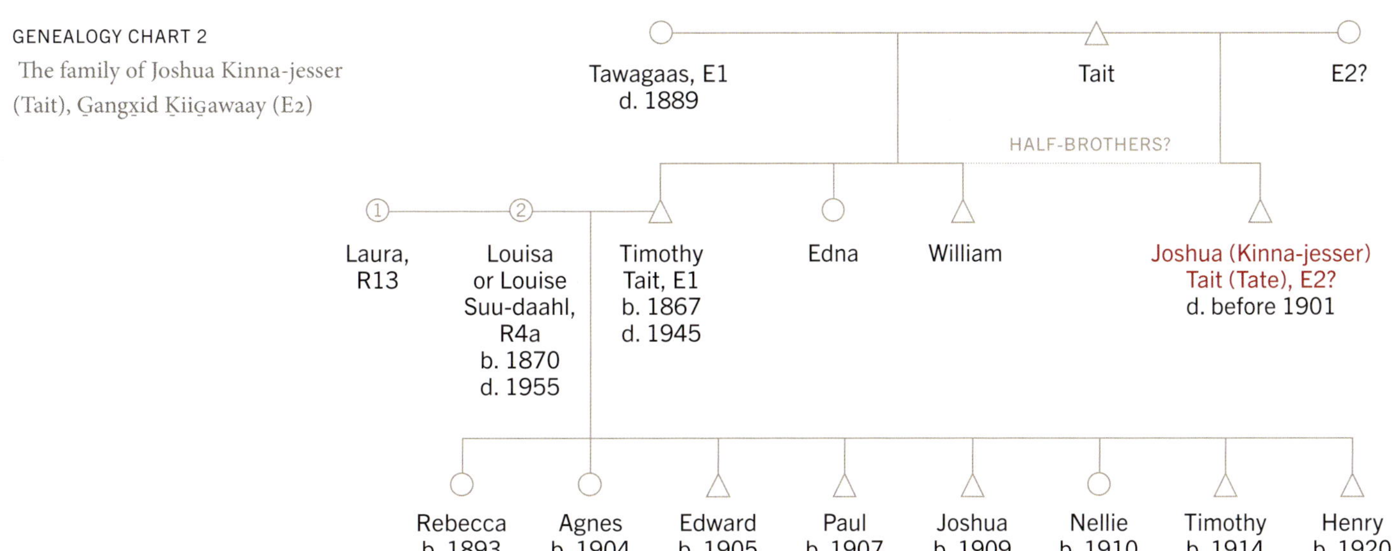

3.18 House Model No. 3, Ḵung Naas from Hlg̱aax̱id Llnagaay (First Beach), made by Zacherias (Nicholas), 1892, 32 in. w × 28 in. h × 8 in. d (façade only). Courtesy of the Field Museum, cat. no. 17819. Photograph by Gail Specht.

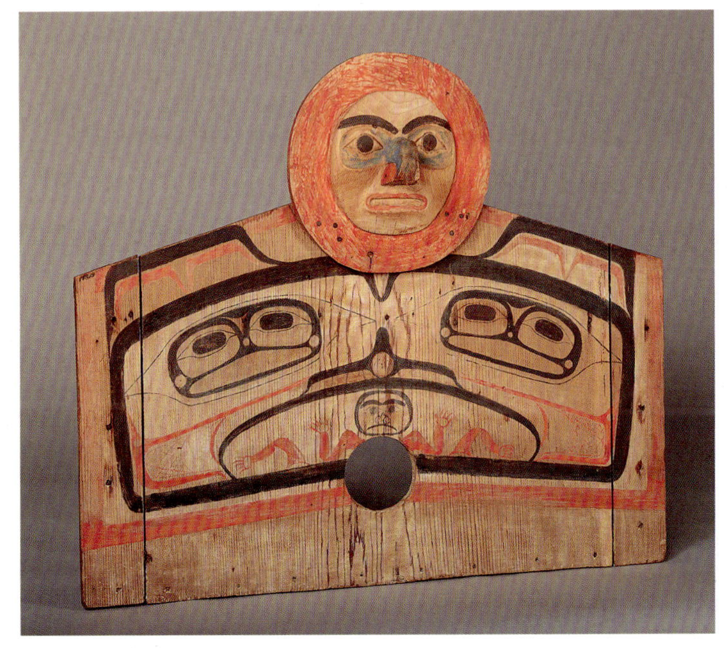

brought from the west coast to this site when the house was built. According to Richard Wilson, the First Beach house was built sometime after 1862 by the second Captain Gold, or "The one whose voice is obeyed" (Nang Kilslas) chief of the Pebble Town People, Hlg̱axiidgu Laanas (R9).[21] The first Captain Gold died ca. 1862, before the move to Xaayna Llnagaay, and his name passed to his young nephew who built this house.

Referring to the model house, Deans says: "This house was made by a Skidegate man named 'Zacherias.' I told him to paint everything belonging to it, so he made a mistake by painting it too true to nature" (Deans 1893b, 22). I'm not sure why Deans felt that Zacharias had made a mistake. We are in fact indebted to Zacharias for painting the model "true to nature" because it has allowed us to understand how Zacharias may in fact have been the artist who painted the full-size house front, an artist who had been known only by the descriptive name, "The Master of the Chicago Settee" (Holm 1981, 197–99). I believe that Zacherias was a man named Zacherias Nicholas, the only Zacherias we have been able to identify in Skidegate (Wright 2009). The close similarity between the painting on the house and the model suggests the same artist painted both, as well as the model of Chief Skidegate's mortuary pole, Sg̱iidagiids X̱aad (Model Pole No. 1), which was placed to the left of Captain Gold's house in the WCE installation (see figure I.1; figure 3.21).

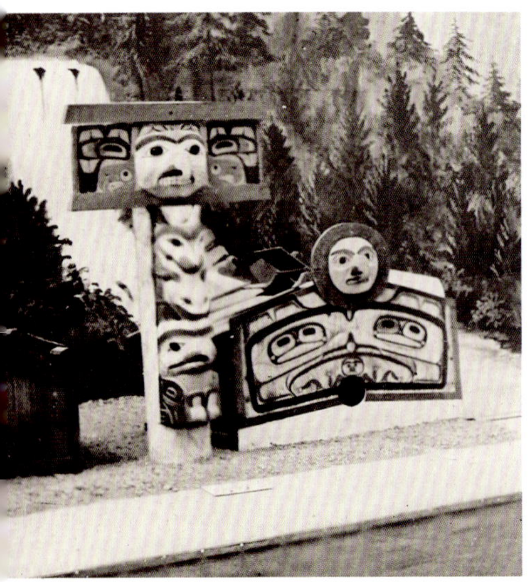

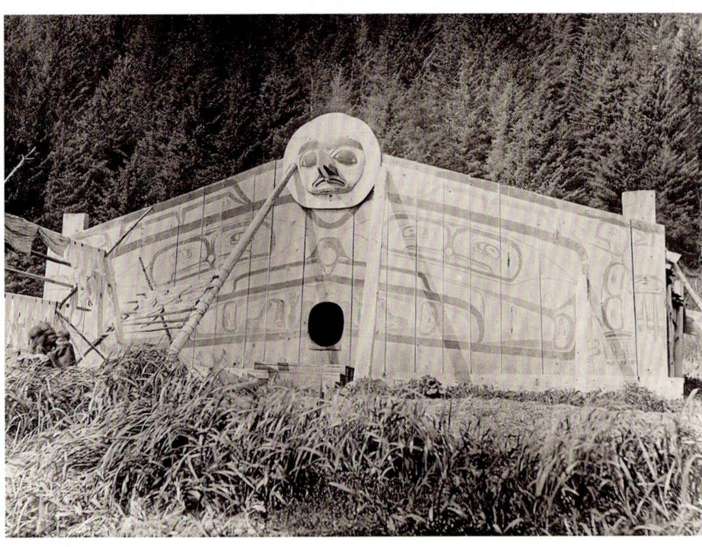

3.19 Detail of figure I.1, Ḵung Naas, "Captain Gold's House" model, 1892, installed at the World's Columbian Exposition in 1893. Photograph by Charles D. Arnold, 1893. Courtesy of the Peabody Museum of Archaeology and Ethnology, Harvard University, 93-1-10/100266.1.39.

3.20 Captain Gold's house at Hlg̱aax̱id Llnagaay, erected after 1862. Photograph by the Maynards, 1884. Image PN9059. Courtesy of the Royal BC Museum and Archives.

3.21 Model Pole No. 1, Sg̱iidagiids X̱aad, "Tomb of Skidegate the Great (Jacques)," attributed to Zacherias Nicholas, 1892. Courtesy of the Field Museum, cat. no. 17820. Photograph by Gail Specht.

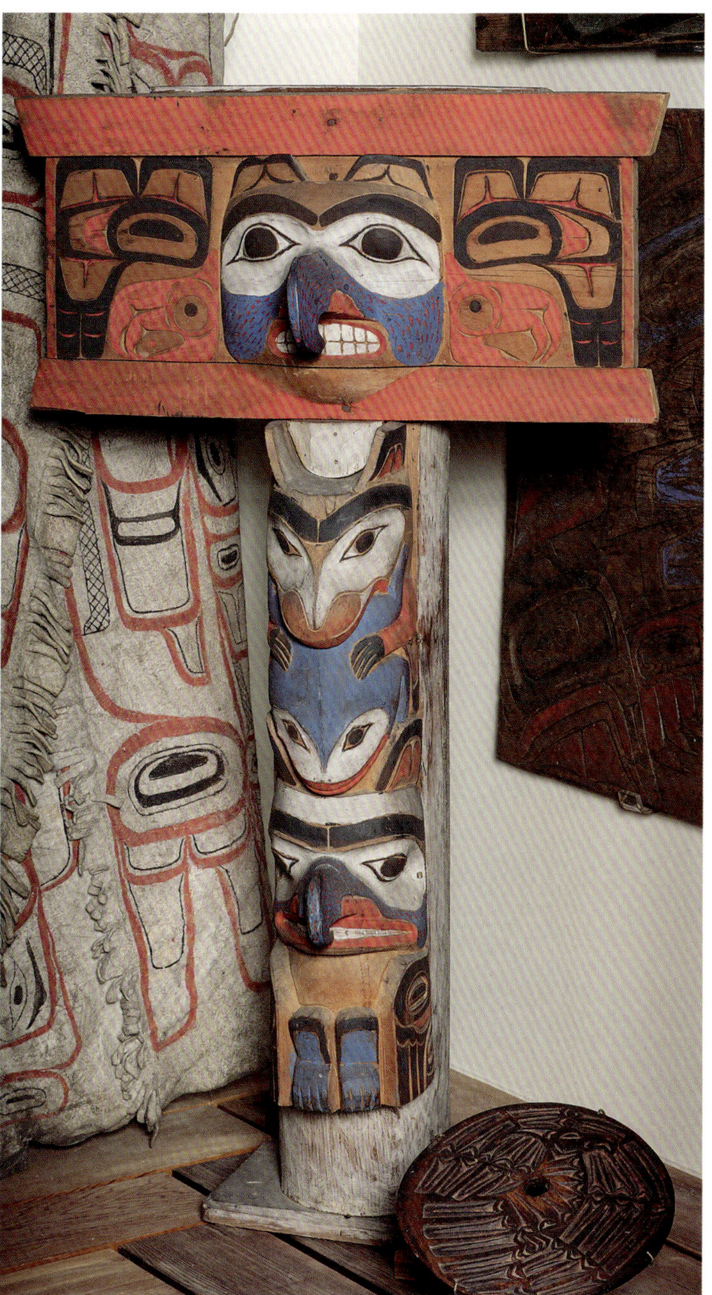

Except for Model Pole No. 11, made by Tom Stevens, Deans did not record the names of the makers of any of the freestanding model poles for the WCE, but the style of the carving on this model mortuary is very clearly that of the artist formerly known as the Master of the Chicago Settee, now Zacherias Nicholas.

MODEL POLE NO. 1 / *Attributed to Zacherias Nicholas*

The mortuary pole of Chief Skidegate "the Great," Sg̱iidagiids X̱aad or Sahlln Gyaag̱ang, stood at Hlg̱aax̱id Llnagaay (known as First Beach), near where Captain Gold's house was located (figures 3.21, 3.22). The 1884 photograph of this pole shows the carved panel that covered the burial cavity fallen to the side, and a naaxiin robe nailed over the mortuary niche at the top.[22] The carved thunderbird panel that would have covered both the naaxiin robe and the niche has fallen away. By the time this photograph was taken, the remains of Chief Skidegate had been buried nearby. This Chief Skidegate is thought to have died sometime in the 1830s. It is unclear whether he is the Chief Skidegate first mentioned in late eighteenth-century explorers' journals (see chapter 2). One of his names was apparently Gunwhat (a note on back of a Maynard photo). Deans explains that he was called "Jacques" by the first white men who met him in the early nineteenth century. Deans gives a long account of the figures carved on his mortuary pole:

Tomb of Skidegat the Great

This is a model of the Suthlingun [saahlln gyaag̱ang] of Skidegat called The Great. He was the founder of the dynasty of that name and the first chief the Illth-Cah-geetla [Hlg̱aagilda] had after their immigration from Chino kundel (Chino Stream) [Chinukundle on navigational charts, Miller Creek, Ts'iinuu G̱andlaay] to where they are now. It was he whose name the first white visitors about [before] the beginning of the present century gave the name Skidegat's Town to this village. These white visitors named him Jaques. He was named The Great because he was large in body and wealth, if not in good deeds. The following description of him and his connections I had from old people who knew him well. He was a man about six feet in height had a very small head on an exceedingly large body, so large that a belt he wore round his waist could go around three ordinary sized men. His wealth. He was the richest chief of this day. It is said he had thirty slaves, male and female. In his day the fleet of whalers from Boston, Mass. and other ports, had their rendezvous in the channel near his house, from which by trade he got lots of money and goods, aided no doubt by his female slaves. He also had all the neighboring tribes under his tribute. In the middle of the Channel (Skidegat) and opposite his house as it stood in those days was a little island. On this island he always had a number of slaves on the watch for any of the West Coast or any other Indians who might make bold enough to pass without his consent or bringing something for him. Often they eluded him by passing under cloud of night. It always pleased him to know they did so, because by their doing so he believed they feared him. He used to have a habit of sleeping by day and running about by night. His totem post in front of his house was covered with carving from bottom to top, and on its top were images of three men as his Tuden Skeel [Daajing sgilgaay].[23] He was the first to adopt the three men tuden skeel. How one of this sort came to be chosen, its origin and signification, is a problem rather difficult of solution, owing to conflicting stories. From observation I find that many of the carvings were a record of the doings of their god Ne-Kilot-lass [Nang Kilslas], known as the raven god. One of these records tells how at one time he Ne-Kilot-lass turned himself into a beautiful woman and while as such three men fell in love with her one by one and married her. I have also been told by one or two parties that this was the origin of the three men on top of the gayring [GyaaG̱ang] or totem post. Having chosen them for his tuden skeel he would allow no one to use any part of it as such, excepting his own family. The remainder of the carvings on his gayrings are the same as are shown on this model of his suthling-un. These carvings are different from all others. How they came to be so the following, well known to the old folks, will show.

When he, Skidegat, considered it time to have a gayring of his own, he sent for the best carver in the village and told him he wanted one made and wished to have a design shown him before it was carved. Fearing to give offense and thereby run a risk of losing his life, he hardly knew what to do, after thinking the matter over he decided to make one following the lines laid down as a rule by the Haida. To his surprise when he took the design home, in order to show it to his employer, he said, that will make a good gayring it shows my crest and my connection very well, but it does not show me nor my principles as chief. Go and make another one which shows me better and when finished bring it here. Glad to get off so easy he went and prepared his design thinking all the while what to put on it, well knowing if he made anything which the old man might consider an insult a slave would be sent to kill him. So with fear and trembling he decide on the following. First, the thunder bird; 2nd, a bat; 3rd, an owl and lastly again the thunder bird. When it was finished and taken home to its owner he looked at it a while then asked for the meaning of the figures, which was given as follows: The upper figure is the Elanga [Hiilang.nga x̱idid] or thunder bird, the Chief's Ton or Crest of the raven Phratry. The 2nd is the Coot-coeg-dochum-thla̱l [bat] [G̱uudagii gamhlG̱ahl], this means that like the bats you sleep by day and when it begins to grow dark you, like the bats, begin to move about looking into everybody's house. 3rd the Frog or Kimquestan [Hlk'yan ḵ'uust'an]. Your neighbors call you a frog, because you claim the water and make them pay tribute. 4th the owl, because like that bird you seem to see best in the dark after blinking and sleeping all day. 5th and lowest. This is again your crest and shows that like the thunder and lightning you are great and terrible. After having this explanation of the carvings he was so well pleased that he paid the carver well and had them engraved on his gayring and on his Suthling-un. I have never seen his gayring, it having fallen before my day. I have often seen his Suthlingun before it was cut down a number of years ago, in order to give his bones a resting place in mother earth. It was not less than 23 feet in height and not less then [*sic*] 3 feet in diameter. Unlike all other Suthlinguns which have a carving on the box and on the post, cut out of solid wood, this one had the carving on the box but instead of the carving on the post being part of it, a large slab containing the carvings had been nailed on the post, as is plainly shown by the model. How the exception came to be made the following will explain: I have already said this Skidegat was a man with a very small head placed on an enormous body. When it was placed in the box after he died the whole strength of the town was unable to place the lot upright. Then a number of the neighbors were invited to help, making a force not less than 500 men strong, then they were unable to pull it on end. Failing to raise it, a receptacle was cut in the post a little above ground, then a slab was cut and carved and made to fit like a door over all. When ready the body was taken out of the box and put away. After this they were able to lift it and put it in the desired position. Then the body was put into the receptacle, the slab firmly nailed on and the body of the great Skidegat left to decay. During the summer of 1889 or 90 a day or two was set apart by the people in the village in order to gather together all the bones of their relatives and have them put in the grave yard. About the same time the descendants of this Skidegat called the villagers together who with pomp and ceremony befiting so great a chief took his bones out of their wooden receptacle, in which they had been so long, and consigned them to mother earth in a garden patch near by. Sic transit gloria Skidegat Magna. (Deans 1893b, 77–80)

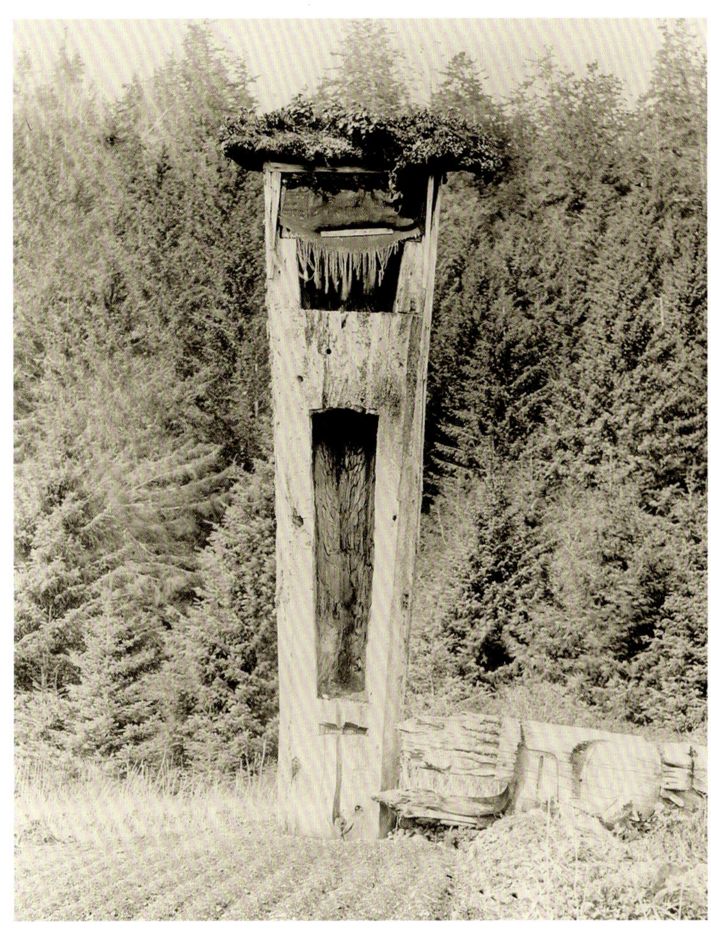

3.22 "Skidegate the Great's" mortuary pole at Hlg̱aax̱id Llnagaay. Photograph by the Maynards, 1884. Image PN5163. Courtesy of the Royal BC Museum and Archives.

This model has been attributed to Zacherias Nicholas (Wright 2009). Two other models of this mortuary pole exist, both collected by James Deans at the same time he commissioned the WCE models, one now in the Royal British Columbia Museum, and one in the Museum of Vancouver (figure 3.23). Though Deans described the figures on the full-size mortuary pole from top to bottom as a thunderbird, bat, frog, owl, and a second thunderbird on the bottom, the models have fewer figures. Both the Royal British Columbia Museum and the Museum of Vancouver models have the bottom thunderbird holding a whale in its talons and a human figure crouching on the head of the bottom thunderbird.[24] The whale is missing on Zacherias's model.[25] It is interesting that the figures on this mortuary pole are not crests of the Eagle clan to which "Skidegate the Great" is assumed to have belonged, since the subsequent Sg̱iidagiids were of that clan.[26] In fact, the thunderbird is a Raven crest (R9 and R10), and Deans's story identifies it as "the Chief's Ton or Crest of the raven Phratry." Deans's story also suggests that the bat and owl figures related specifically to the nocturnal character of "Skidegate the Great." Why the thunderbird (a blue hawk—see note 3.10) appears on

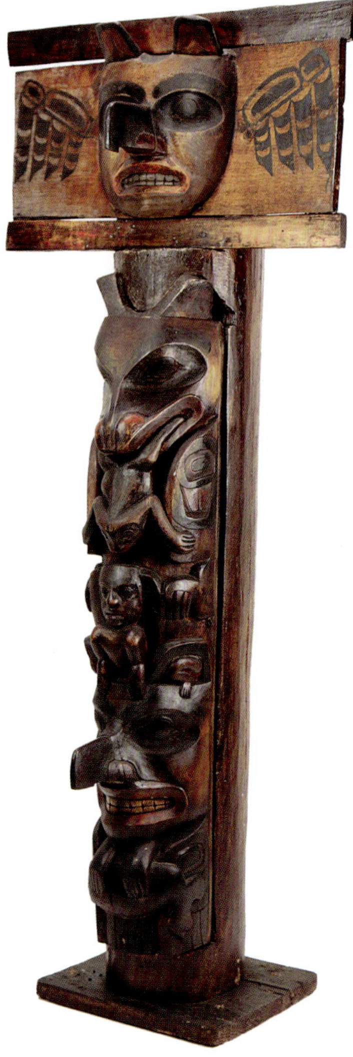

3.23 Model of Skidegate the Great's mortuary pole, attributed to John Robson, 105.4 cm h × 44.5 cm w × 27.9 cm d. Museum of Vancouver collection, AA584.

the pole is less clear. However, these thunderbird and frog figures appear on the grave house poles of subsequent chiefs Sg̱iidagiids (see figures 3.30, 3.31).

Zacherias (Nicholas) / *See Genealogy Chart 4*

Zacherias (Nicholas) is believed to be the artist formerly known as the "Master of the Chicago Settee." Thanks to James Deans, who recorded the name Zacherias as the maker of Ḵung Naas, "Moon House" (House Model No. 3), and members of the Skidegate community who remembered this man, we now know much more about this prolific artist's family. He was baptized on January 8, 1888, in Skidegate (age thirty-one). He was the second husband of Isabella Stevens (Tom Stevens's widow) and married her on February 5, 1906. His occupation was listed as a hunter at that time, and his place of birth Nang Sdins Llnagaay (Ninstints Village). He was also described as a widower in 1906, so had been married previously (BC Archives microfilm #B11387).[27] He died around March 12, 1927 (age eighty), again a widower (BC Archives microfilm #B13361). He had gone hunting and his body was found in a cabin at Slate Chuck (Percy Williams, personal communication, 2006). It is believed that he was from a Raven clan, given his marriage to Isabella Stevens, who was an Eagle, Naa 'Yuuwans Skidegate Gidins (E6a). Her mother, Isabella, was Jiiaxwii Gidin.naay (E11), but was adopted into the Naa 'Yuwans clan.

Zacherias's known carvings include the chief's seat that gave rise to his nickname, the Master of the Chicago Settee (figure 3.24). This chief's seat was purchased for $4.50 by C. F. Newcombe from a chief at the village of Xaayna Llnagaay in the summer of 1901. A second older and larger settee back, also purchased by Newcombe (for $3.00), was said to have belonged to "Scotsgaai." This settee can also be attributed to Zacherias based on style (Field Museum, cat. no. 79597; neg. nos. EC 40 a,b). Scotsgai was the town chief at Ḵaysuun Llnagaay on the west coast of Moresby Island, where he had three houses (MacDonald 1983, 118–20). The older settee back is displayed today in the same case with the newer settee. Also in the same display case is a double-wide coffin chest that can be attributed to Zacherias Nicholas. It displays designs that simulate two chests side by side (figures 3.25a,b).

Zacherias's style of design is characterized by broad angular formlines, very thin negative reliefs, complicated cheek designs, angular and sharply tapering U-forms, and hands that have fingers attached to the concave side of the ovoid. His claws are distinguished by the small circular joint ovoid with two toes and an opposing "thumb" that are curled and tapered with a distinctive "knuckle" at the bend. Also characteristic of his style are U-forms with ovoid reliefs in the ends and salmon trout-head inner ovoids that have the corner of the mouth curving back rather than forward. He made asymmetrical eyelid lines with short points in the front and longer ones on the back. Though simpler than the original large-scale design on the Captain Gold's

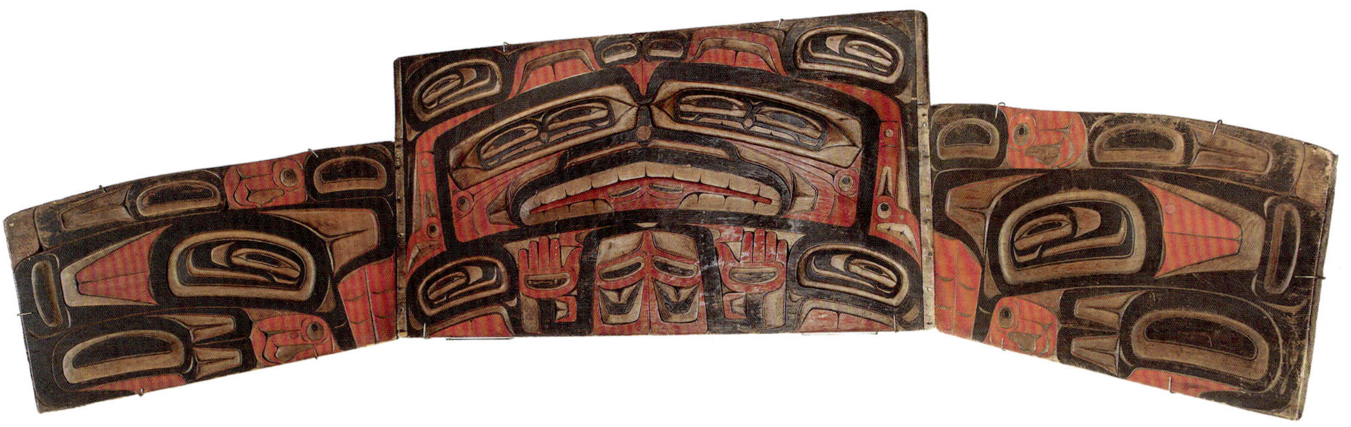

3.24 "The Chicago Settee," collected by C. F. Newcombe from a chief at Xaayna Llnagaay in summer 1901, 121 cm × 66 cm (back); 79 cm × 16 cm (arm). Courtesy of the Field Museum, cat. no. 79595, attributed to "the Master of the Chicago Settee," now known as Zacherias Nicholas (see Wright 2009, 2001b, 74, 342–43n300).

house front, and perhaps more hastily painted, the design on the small model house has some of Zacherias's design elements. The double-Us in the ears are angular and sharply tapered, and the eyelid lines in the inner ovoids are asymmetrical (see Holm 1981; Wright 2009).

Based on the objects that have so far been attributed to him, Zacherias Nicholas worked primarily in wood, ranging in size from monumental in scale such as the painting on Captain Gold's house front (see figure 3.20) and full-size poles such as a house frontal pole from Xaayna (see figure 3.105 right), to smaller-scale objects like chests and rattles (figure 3.26), all likely made for use within the Haida community.[28] Other smaller-scale objects would have been made primarily for sale, such as paddles and model poles.[29] Many argillite objects have been attributed to him, among them a model house (figure 3.27), an argillite chest in the American Museum of Natural History, and an argillite model canoe now in a private collection.[30]

Kathryn Bunn-Marcuse (2007) has linked the floral designs on the lid of the American Museum of Natural History argillite chest attributed to Zacherias to a silver bracelet in the Burke Museum's collection (figures 3.28, 3.29).[31] In addition to the floral designs on the sides, this bracelet has the "American" eagle drawn from the designs on American silver dollars. Floral designs like these, inspired by Euro-American silver, pressed glass, and ship's architecture, were favorites of Haida artists going back to the early nineteenth century (see Bunn-Marcuse 2000, 2007; Wright 1979, 1982). Engraved silver jewelry and argillite carvings with foliate designs were made by a number of Haida artists, including Duncan Ginaawaan, Charles Edenshaw, and John Robson among others.[32]

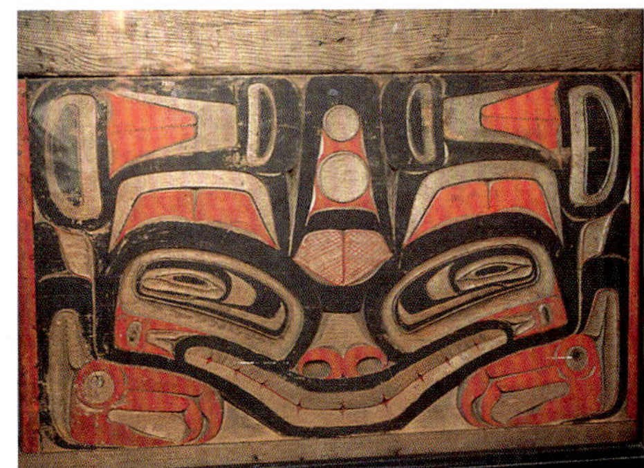

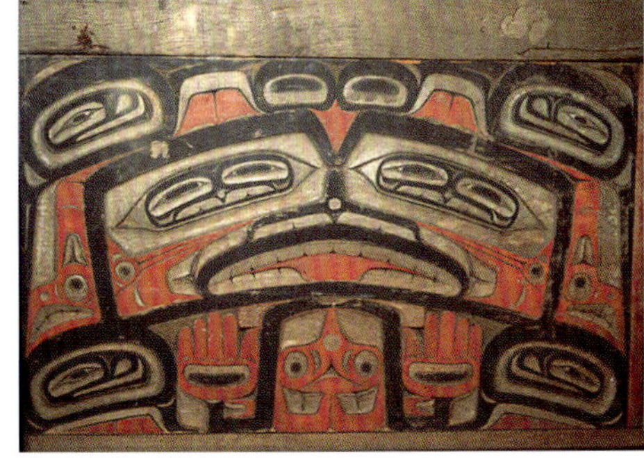

3.25 A & B Double coffin chest, attributed to Zacherias Nicholas, purchased in Skidegate by Charles F. Newcombe for seven dollars, 1901. Courtesy of the Field Museum, cat. no. 79711, two photographs by the author (above is the left side and below is the right side of the double chest).

3.26 Round rattle attributed to Zacherias Nicholas. Collected by James G. Swan, 1883. National Museum of Natural History, Smithsonian Institution, cat. no. 89081. A similar rattle, also attributed to Zacherias Nicholas and collected by James G. Swan, was exchanged by the Smithsonian with the Peabody Museum of Archaeology and Ethnology, Harvard University, cat. no. 88-51-10/50485.

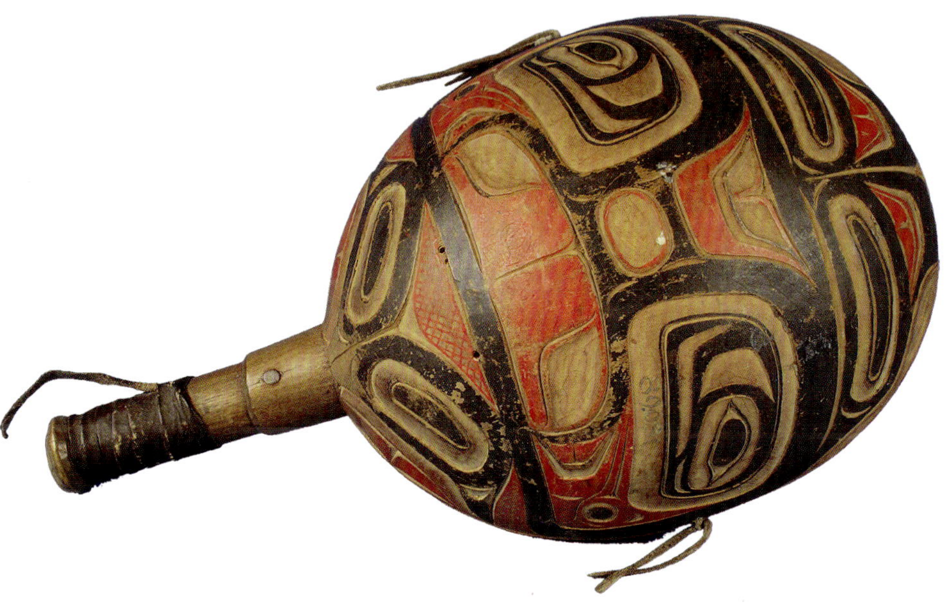

Except for the Ḵung Naas model, documented by Deans to be by Zacherias, all of these objects are attributed to him based solely on style and are the educated guesses of a few interested students of his work. Not all of us agree, and these opinions may be discounted or overturned in future but can serve as a foundation upon which to further study Zacherias's prolific work.

Zacherias Nicholas

Zacherias Nicholas is a name I used to hear all the time. I'm surprised there was nobody named after him. It's a beautiful name. . . . Important name. Even not meeting him or hearing about him, I feel he was a very important man. . . . Zacherias, I like that name. I wonder if that's same fellow that used to like hunting a lot. Is it? They found an old man dead on the beach in Slatechuck one time. He used to be out all the time hunting and fishing. Was it that Zacherias?

Yeah. He used to love hunting and fishing like me. My two speed boats are laying idle out there. But they did it, for years and years.

—Chief Gidansda, Percy Williams, G̱aag'yals Ḵiig̱awaay, August 22, 2006

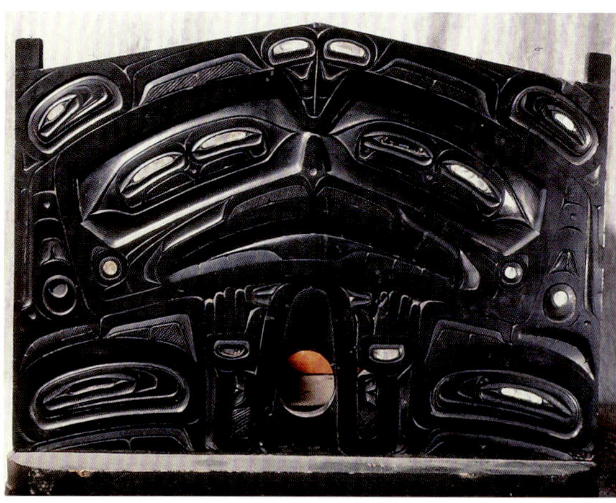

3.27 Model house of argillite with inlaid shell, attributed to Zacherias Nicholas, gift of Heber R. Bishop 1869–1890, frame: 55 cm × 51 cm × 43 cm h. Photograph by Bill Holm. Courtesy of the Division of Anthropology, American Museum of Natural History, cat. no. 16/543.

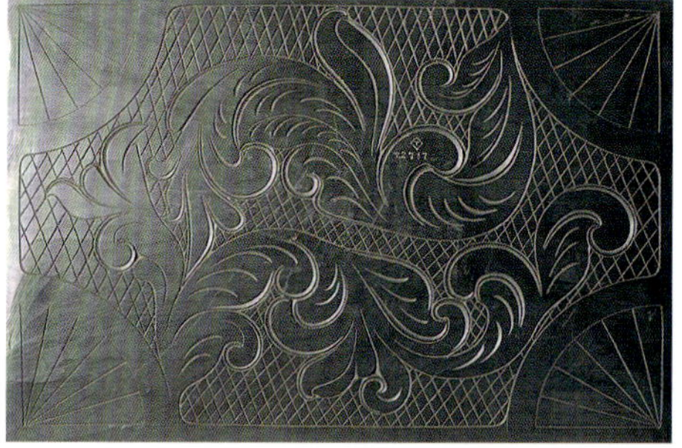

3.28 Argillite chest lid, attributed to Zacherias Nicholas, accession date 1891–1893, 34.5 cm × 19.5 cm. Photograph by Bill Holm. Courtesy of the American Museum of Natural History, cat. no. T/22717.

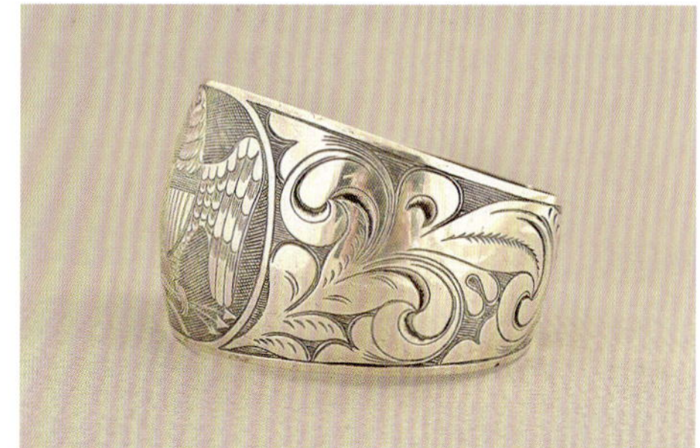

3.29 Silver bracelet, attributed to Zacherias Nicholas, 2.625 in. dia. × 1.625 in. h. Courtesy of the Burke Museum of Natural History and Culture, cat. no. 2005-102/2. Gift in memory of Delbert L. Brink.

GENEALOGY CHART 3

Zacherias (Nicholas), Tl'aajaang quuna (Tom Stevens), Gyaawhllns (John Robson), and Skilduunaas (David Shakespeare)

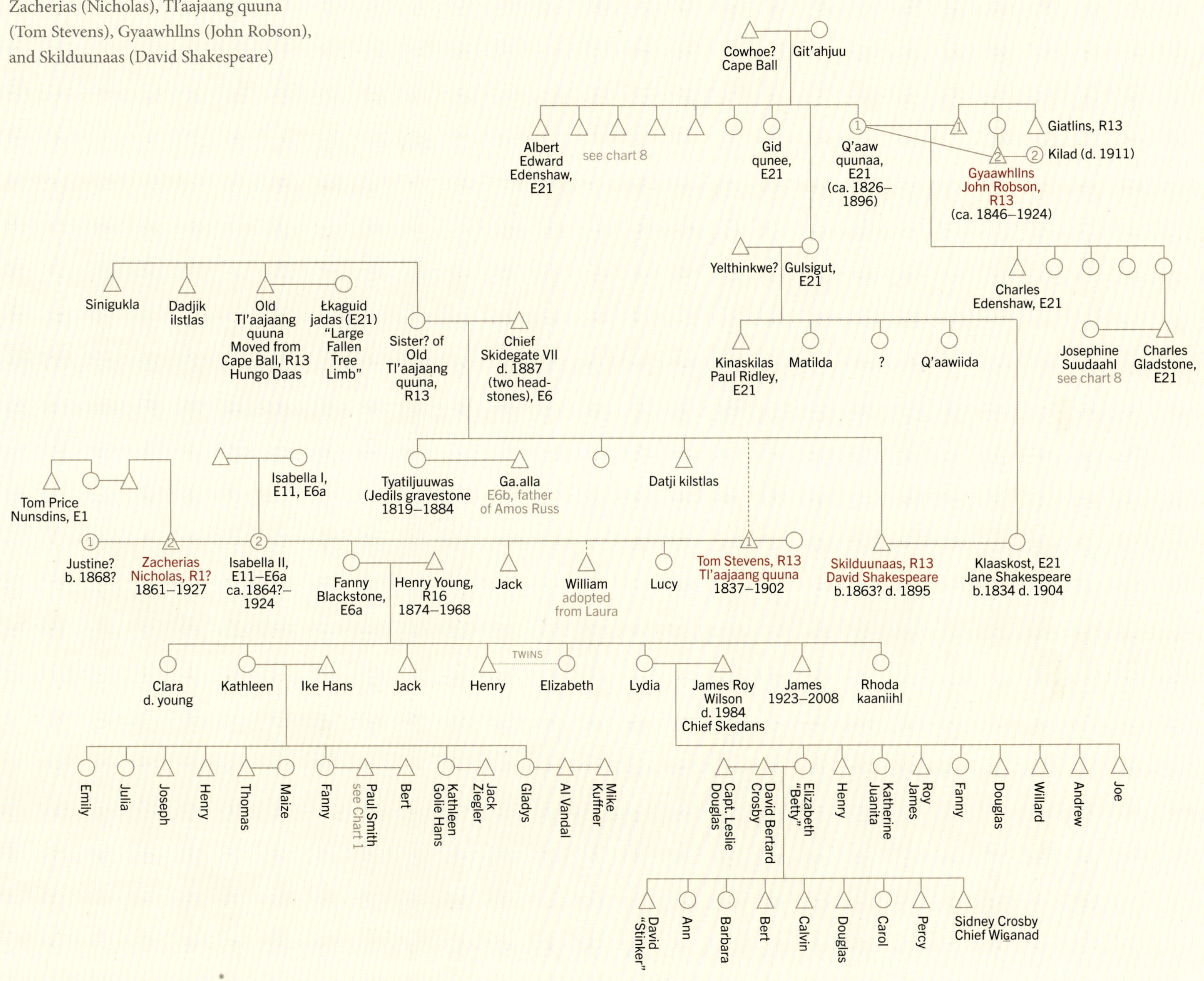

GRAVE HOUSE MODEL NO. 12

Model Grave House No. 12, "Sg̱iidagiids and Niisdaka.na Grave House," was positioned in the center of the Hlg̱aagilda Llnagaay village in the WCE installation, set back from the other house models (figure 3.30; see figure 3.2). Grave houses were normally placed behind the row of inhabited houses. Deans reports this was "Sthlingun Nah Skidegat Youan es Tossen Nastasana, Tombs of The Great Skidegate and his Brother, Nastasana"; however, Deans explains that "this is a model of the tombs of Skidegat the Third and his brother Nastacana, who upon this chief's death became, as far as I understand, Skidegat the Fourth."[33] He describes the house as having two coffins resting on two 'Waasg̱uu (sea wolves). The left coffin was for Sg̱iidagiids, the other his brother's. The short frontal pole had a hawk at the base, a sea frog with a fin on its back, and a raven at the top.

3.30 Detail of figure 3.2, Missing Model Grave House No. 12, Saahlln Naas (Grave House) of Sg̱iidagiids and Niisdaka.na, 1892. Courtesy of the Field Museum, cat. no. 17991, exchanged with the Brooklyn Museum, 1903, new no. 7793.

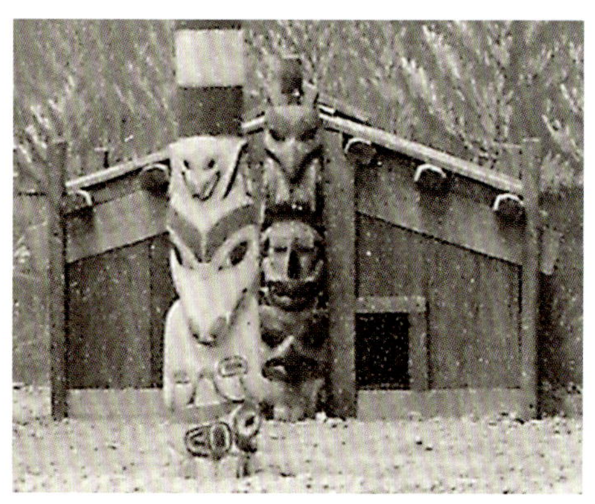

This model grave house is missing from the Brooklyn Museum, where it was sent after the World's Columbian Exposition, but Deans collected another model of this grave house that is very similar (figure 3.31). Though the lower beak and fin on the frog's back are broken off, this model gives us a sense of what the colors on the missing model might have been. Two model mandas and their coffins stayed at the Field Museum (figure 3.32). They were incorrectly associated in the Field Museum records and given the same catalog numbers as Ḵung Naas, Captain Gold's House Model (No. 3). These two model mandas should have been placed inside and numbered with Skidegate's grave house (No. 12) rather than Captain Gold's house model. Mandas are carved crest figures, naturalistic quadrupeds, carved to hold the coffin of a chief on their back. The first known use of this word "mandA" is in Swanton's *Contribution to the Ethnology of the Haida* (1905a, 132) and also in a letter from Newcombe to Swanton

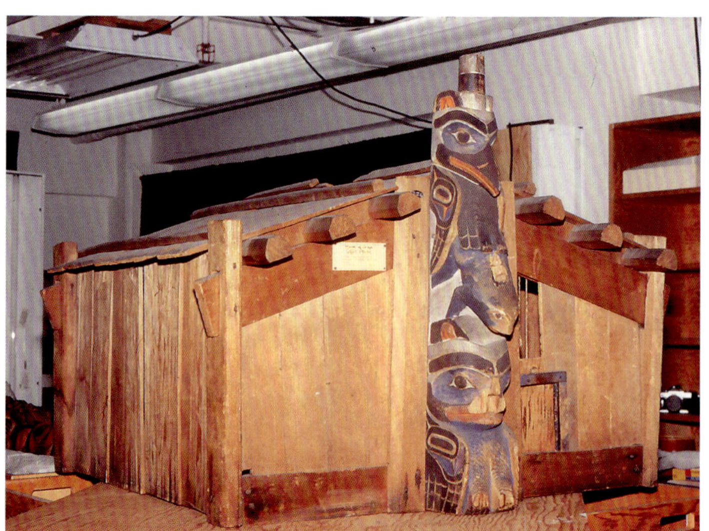

3.31 Model Grave House that was not part of the World's Columbian Exposition exhibit but very similar to the missing Grave House Model No. 12 (see figure 3.30). Collected by James Deans, 1892, at the same time that he collected the WCE models. Cat. no. 224. Courtesy of the Royal BC Museum and Archives. Photograph by the author.

(February 6, 1906) quoting information he received from Moses McKay describing a manda he collected from McKay.[34] The two original mandas, upon which these were based, show just below Nang Jingwas's dogfish memorial pole at the extreme lower left in a Maynard photograph of Skidegate taken in 1884 (figure 3.33). Their position here suggests that the original grave house where the mandas would have been placed with the chiefs' coffins on their backs, might have been nearby.

In referring to the Maynard's photograph of the original mandas, Henry Moody (to Newcombe) identified them as having been moved from a grave house: "one is ga.â la's monument, 'Cry Easy,' the other 'YesdAqana's' (a Tsimshian name) both were of the Eagle clan" [Naa 'Yuuwans X̱aaydaG̱aay (E6a)].[35] The original grave house, then, must have been positioned somewhere to the back of the south end of the village, near these mandas, rather than in the center where the WCE model was placed.

3.32 'Waasg̱uu manda models, 1892. Courtesy of the Field Museum, cat. nos. 17819.1 and 17819.2. Photograph by Gail Specht.

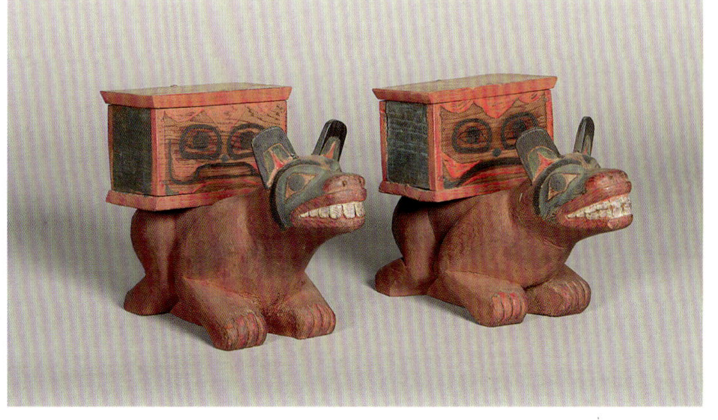

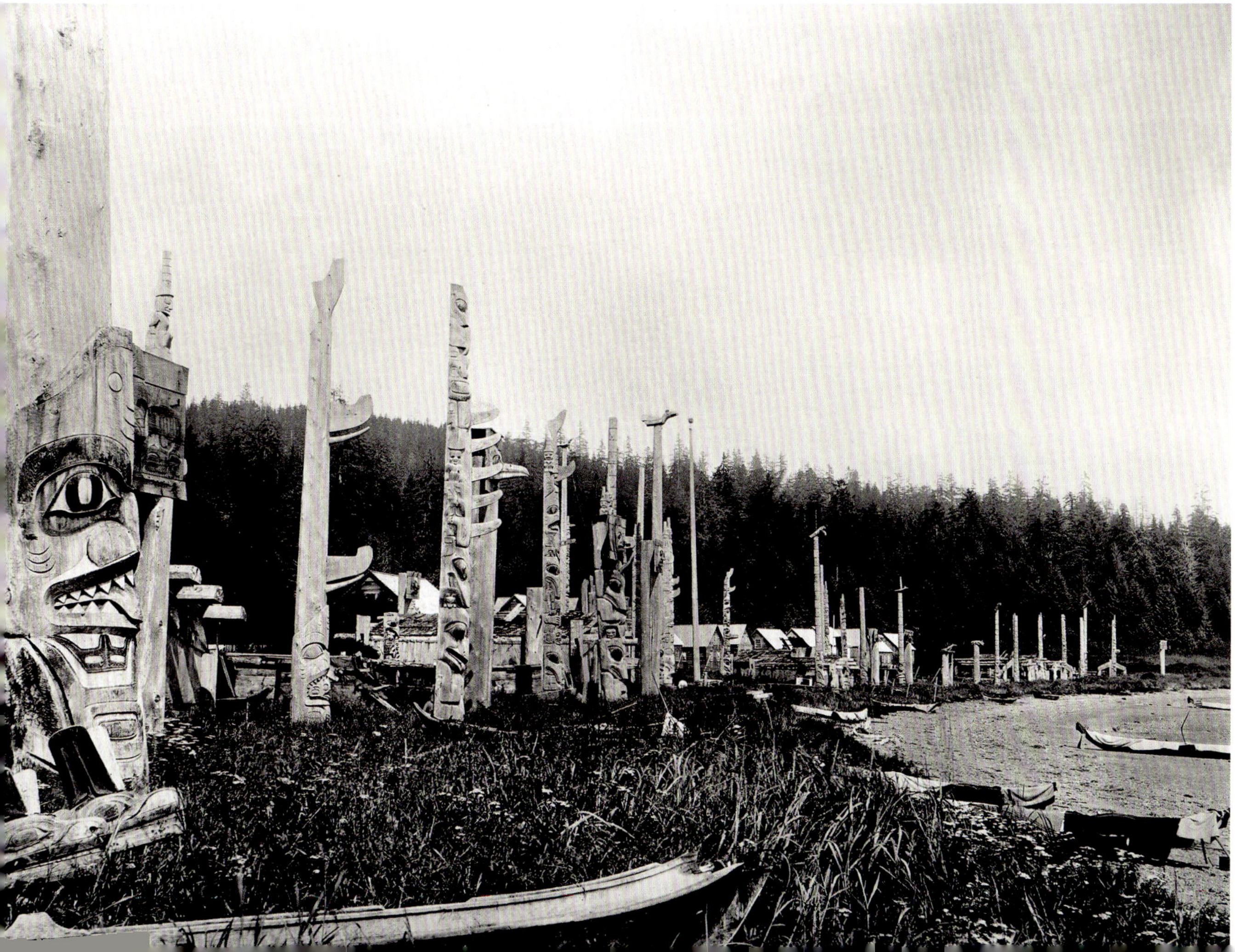

3.33 Two 'Waasg̱uu mandas are visible at the lower left corner in this photograph of Hlg̱aagilda Llnagaay (Skidegate). Photograph by the Maynards, 1884. © The Field Museum, image no. CSA17439.

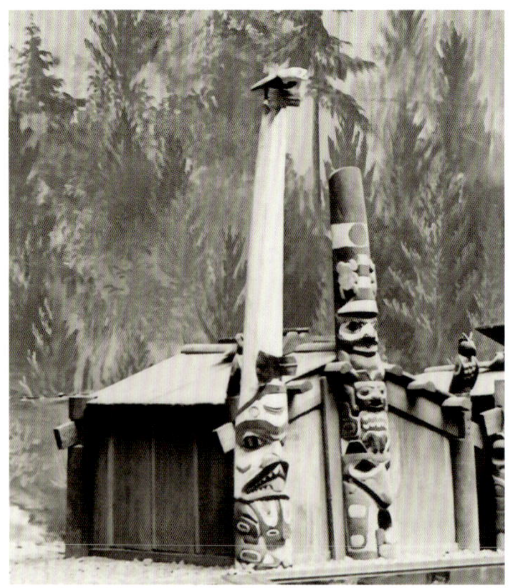

3.34 *above* Detail of figure 3.38, Missing House Model No. 4—Guudguniis Naas, Horned Owl House made by Adam Brown, 1892. 88 cm × 89 cm × 101 cm. Courtesy of the Field Museum, cat. no. 17818, exchanged with the Brooklyn Museum, 1903, cat. no. 05.589.7788.

3.35 *right* Owl figure from a corner post of missing Owl House (see figure 3.34), Field Museum, cat. no. 17818, 14.9 cm h. Brooklyn Museum, by exchange, 1903, cat. no. 05.589.7788. Photograph by the author.

HOUSE MODEL NO. 4 / *Made by Adam Brown (Cowgill)*

House Model No. 4 represents Guudguniis Naas or HlG̱an Naas "Horned Owl House" or "Fin House." Deans called it "Coot Coo Nass, Horned Owl House," and reported that it was made by Adam Brown (Cowgill) (figures 3.34, 3.35). The original house that had been gone for many years in 1892 was owned by a woman from Skedans or Cumshewa who got rich from a ship that was wrecked near her house, according to Deans. The house appears at the far left in Dawson's 1878 photo (see figure 2.2) and O. C. Hastings 1879 photo (figure 3.36), but not in photos taken in the 1880s. This house was at the far southern end of Skidegate. Newcombe recorded the name of the first house on the south side of Skidegate as "Sga'na na'as" [SG̱aana Naas]. He received this information in 1906 from Charles Jefferson of the HlG̱aay.yuu Laanas clan (R6), based on the Dawson photograph. This is the name Swanton listed for his house #17 ("killer-whale house"), belonging to the "Djaxui' sqoa'ladaga-i clan" (Jiiaxwii Sḵaahladasg̱aay, R5) (Swanton 1905a, 286).[36] MacDonald described the southernmost Skidegate house as "Fin House," after Swanton's house #19: "LgAn na'as, from the family of "Lgai-u' la'nas" (HlG̱aay.yuu Laanas, R6)," but his description of the figures on the pole are drawn from Newcombe's description of SG̱aana Naas. Both of these clans had the killer whale as a crest.

Deans describes the figures on the model pole as a whale at the bottom, an owl, and an otter. Judging by his order of figures, one might assume that the humanoid figure at the top is the otter, but this figure wears a hat with sgil flanked by frogs and doesn't resemble an otter. A finlike projection at the top has a circle on a white band that is identified as the moon, crest of the owner of the house, by Deans. The old house frontal pole on the southernmost house in the Dawson photo (see figure 2.2) does have a finlike projection at the top and is most likely the house upon which this model is based. The other figures on the original pole are difficult to discern in Dawson's photo, but the Hasting's photo is much clearer (see figure 3.36). A small human watchman figure sits in front of the fin and is likely represented by the human figure at the top of the model pole. A large figure below the watchman has a down-turned beak or snout and human heads in its ears.[37] On the model pole there is a small owl below the watchman figure as well as two owls on the corner posts (figure 3.35).

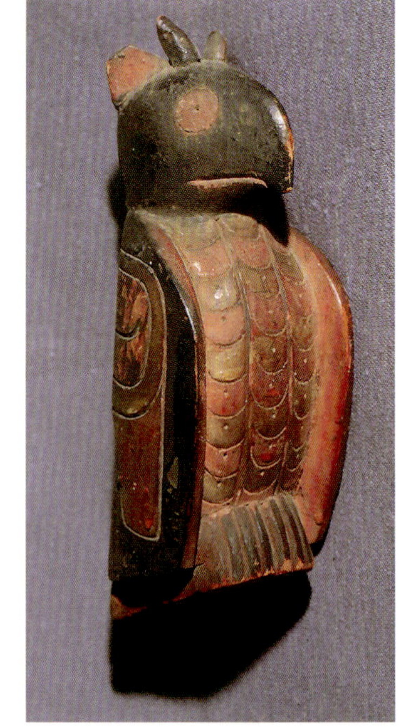

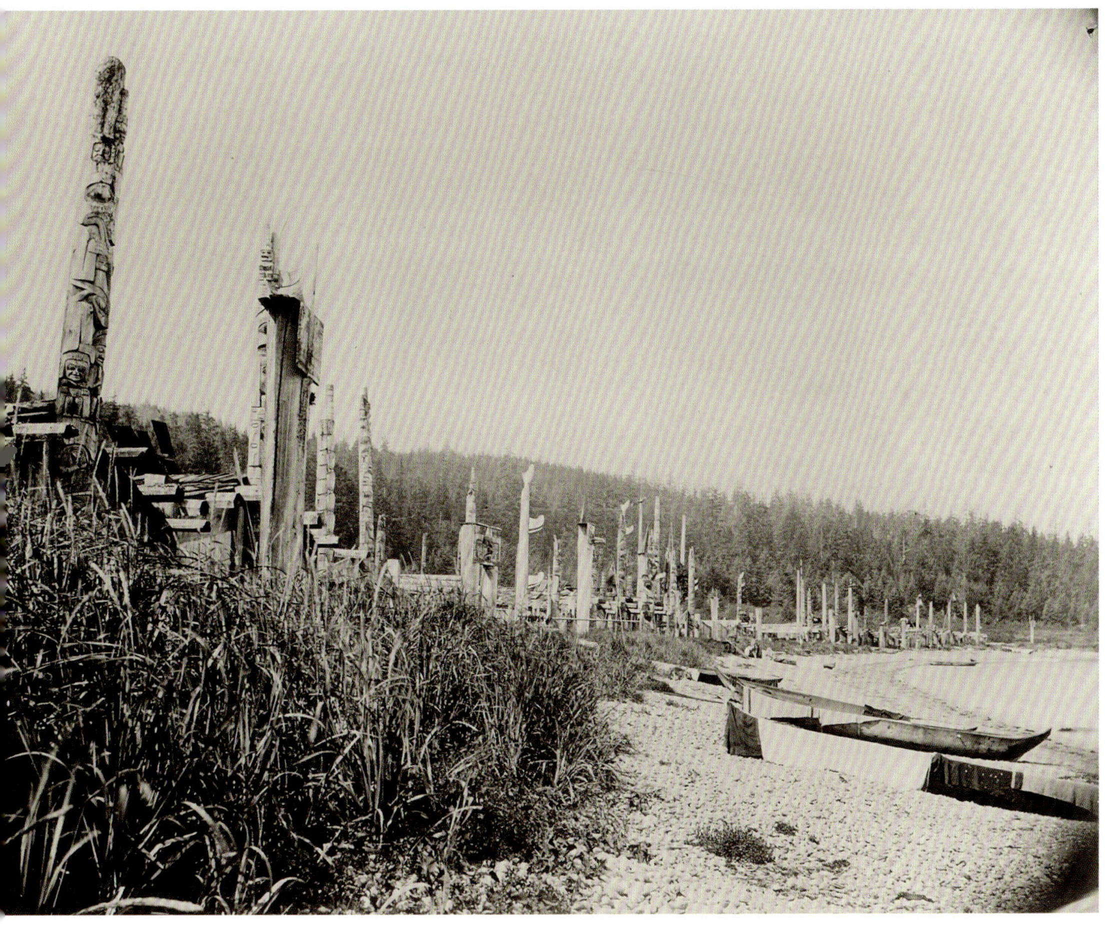

3.36 Hlg̱aagilda (Skidegate) from the south end showing the frontal pole of Guudguniis Naas or Hlg̱an Naas (far left pole). Photograph by O. C. Hastings, 1879. Image PN5535. Courtesy of the Royal BC Museum and Archives.

Could this figure with the downturned beak represent an owl? If so, it must be a supernatural owl, since on the old pole this figure has arms and legs. It holds in its hand a small inverted human head, and a creature with its head downward crouches on its belly. Could this creature be the otter? Below is a small human figure wearing a shaman-like headdress flanked by two other human figures with their legs extending through the ears of the lowest figure. These are identified as Dsoltqanaqati and his brothers by Newcombe.[38] These are not represented on the model pole.

The large figure at the bottom has frogs protruding from its eyes and an extended tongue (identified as "KaindagAng sganawai" [X̱aayda Sg̱aanawaay] by Newcombe [supernatural being killer whale]). Perhaps the two small frogs at the top flanking the hat on the model pole refer to the frogs at the bottom of the old pole. As with all of the model poles, they are rarely direct copies of the originals they are intended to represent. Small figures can become large, and large figures can become small or entirely left out. It is most likely that the woman of this house that Deans mentions was from Hlḵinul Llnagaay (Cumshewa) rather than Ḵ'uuna Llnagaay (Skedans), since the St'awaas Ḵiig̱awaay clan of Cumshewa (E5) are known as the "Screech Owl People" and had the screech owl crest. It would have been her clan crests displayed on the corner posts. Given this, it seems that Deans should probably have named this house model St'aw Naay "Screech Owl House." If Newcombe or MacDonald's information is correct, her husband might have been either R5 or R6 (Skidegate Inlet People or Skidegate Town People), but the moon on the top of the pole, which is not a crest of Hlḵinul Llnagaay clans, gives the clue that perhaps her husband was from K̲'uuna Llnagaay (Skedans). The moon is a crest of the Raven clan G̱aag'yals K̲iiG̱awaay (R4). According to the current Chief Gidansda, Guujaaw, Skedans chiefs often married Cumshewa women (personal communication, July 28, 2017). Barbara Wilson suggested that perhaps this woman might be Jenny, Ninii Nanggaa (E5), the sister of Lluuguud (personal communication, February 10, 2004).[39] She lived in the late nineteenth century, so it could have been an older clan relative of hers.

The source of this woman's wealth is said by Deans to have been a ship that was wrecked near her house in the early nineteenth century. Looking at the historical record, we know that the schooner *Resolution*, the tender of Captain Robert's brig, the *Jefferson*, was attacked at Cumshewa in July 1794 and sunk there. All aboard were killed except for one man who was held captive for a year (Roe 1967). A year later Captain Bishop on the ship *Ruby* and the American vessel *Mercury* returned to Cumshewa to rescue the sailor:

> The ship staid and made good trade there afterwards—and then Sailed in Company with the Mercury to Comswas, to try and Catch that Chief, and redeem the Poor Sailor—this was executed with the desired Success, for on the Evening of their arrival they seized Scatts Eye the Chiefs Brother, his Family, and a son of Comswas. In doing this there was several Lives lost, on the side of the Natives and the Women fought with a degree of Desperation unequalled. Having secured their Prisoners, they demanded the Sailor, whose Existence was denied by everyone for a long time, but at last on a Promise that their lifes [*sic*] should be sacred and Seeing the Humanity of their conquorers [*sic*] in dressing their wound &c one of the Women confessed that he was chained to a tree in the Woods.—The man who owned this Poor Fellow as his slave, was Brother to the only Native that was killed in the attack of the vessel, and when a Division took Place of their Booty, He was decreed to him as a Sacrifice to the manes of his Brother. This Native demanded all the accumulated treasures of Sacctseye [*sic*] to redeem him, and which was Paid the next day, when the Sailor was brought on board the Mercury by two Women in a Canoe. (Roe 1967; Wright 2001b).

From this we learn that Sacctseye (or Skatts Eye), said to be Cumshewa's brother, and his family were captured and ransomed for the enslaved Boston sailor, and he had to pay dearly for his release and that of the sailor slave (Wright 2001b, 77). Also, a Cumshewa man whose brother had been killed during the attack on the *Resolution* had been given the sailor as compensation, and the following year when Skatts Eye and family were taken as hostages to force the sailor's release, this man demanded all of Skatts Eye's wealth, before releasing him. It may be that the woman associated with "Owl House" profited from the sinking of the *Resolution* as well as the ransom of its crew. The story may have been sanitized for Deans's benefit. This is merely speculation on my part, but no other ships are known to have been wrecked off of Cumshewa or Skidegate.

Adam Brown (Cowgill) / *See Genealogy Chart 4*

The maker of both "Owl House" and "Mosquito Hawk House" was Adam Brown. Deans tells us his Haida name was Cowgill (Deans 1893b, 27). He was born in the 1830s. Adam Brown is listed in the 1891 census as fifty-five years old, a fisherman, living in Skidegate with his wife, Lizzie (age fifty-four), described as a cannery hand. He was baptized in Gold Harbour on March 12, 1891, and said to be age fifty-one in that record, which would put his birth somewhere between 1836 and 1840. A man named "Cowgath" (age twenty-five) is listed in the 1881 census, living in House #5, at the opposite end of the village from the houses he carved as models. He was living with an older man named "Keetshantlans (age sixty-five) and a woman named "Kitkonay" (age sixty). She may be Gid qunee, a sister of Q'aaw quunaa and Albert Edward Edenshaw. Since the ages were rarely accurate on these census reports, it is possible that "Cowgath" may be "Cowgill," the same man, although this would put his birth date at 1856. His death date is recorded as June 15, 1892, at age fifty-seven, and he is buried in Skidegate. His gravestone in Skidegate says he was from Hiellen (the village at Tow Hill on the northeast corner of Graham Island). Deans reports that he died a few days after he finished the last model house for him. The Hiellen origin makes sense, given the 1881 census information, since Albert Edward Edenshaw's uncle had a house there and lived there for a time with his family.

GENEALOGY CHART 4

Adam Brown

Peter Brown

Adam Brown
Cowgill
b. ca. 1836 at Hiellen
d. June 15, 1892

Lizzie
b. ca. 1837

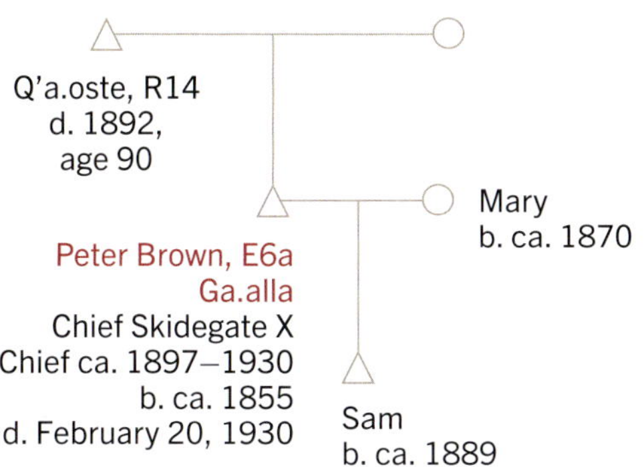

Nothing is known of Adam Brown's clan affiliation. It is possible that he was a relative of Peter Brown (see below), although Brown is a common name among the Haida. No other works of art are known to have been attributed to Adam Brown, which makes these two model houses so interesting.

HOUSE MODEL NO. 22

House Model No. 22, "House of the High Crest," was placed (incorrectly) fifth in the row between House Models Nos. 5 and 6 in the WCE installation (figures 3.37, 3.38).[40] In the village this house was situated differently, between Guudguniis Naas, "Owl" or "Fin" house, and Sgyam Sgwaan Naas, the house with the pole with many coppers, and it has been placed here in the sequence for that reason. It represents the full-size house named Naa sda ahgan g.jiing.ngas (NaastA Angjiwas "House People are ashamed to look at it is so Overpoweringly Great") (see figures 2.2 left behind mortuary pole, 2.5 left).[41] Swanton's identification for this house (his #18, Na s'A'ndjiwa) was translated "house where the people do not care to eat anything because they have so much" of the Hlg̱aay.yuu Laanas (R6) (Swanton 1905a, 286).[42] The Skidegate Haida Immersion Program (SHIP) translated the word Naasta angjiwas as "house—looking away" (SHIP February 6, 2004), and Naa S'anjuu as "House where the people do not care to eat anything because they have so much" (email Septem-

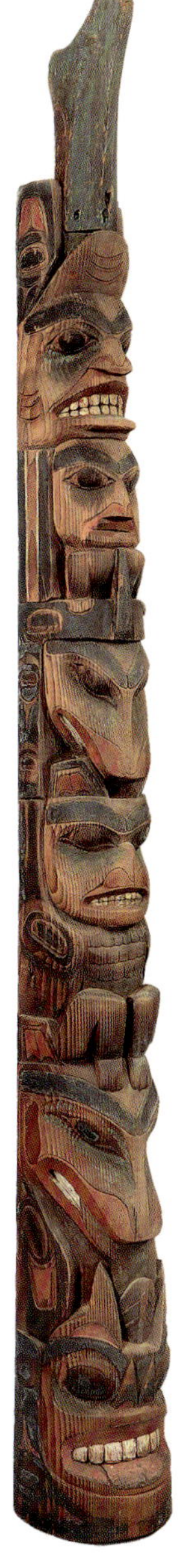

3.37 Frontal pole from House Model No. 22, "House of the High Crest," 1892, 148.6 cm h × 14 cm w × 12.1 cm d. Photograph courtesy of the University of Pennsylvania Museum, cat. no. 29-47-203 (old cat. no. 37.691), purchased from the Field Museum in 1900, originally Field Museum, cat. no. 17814.

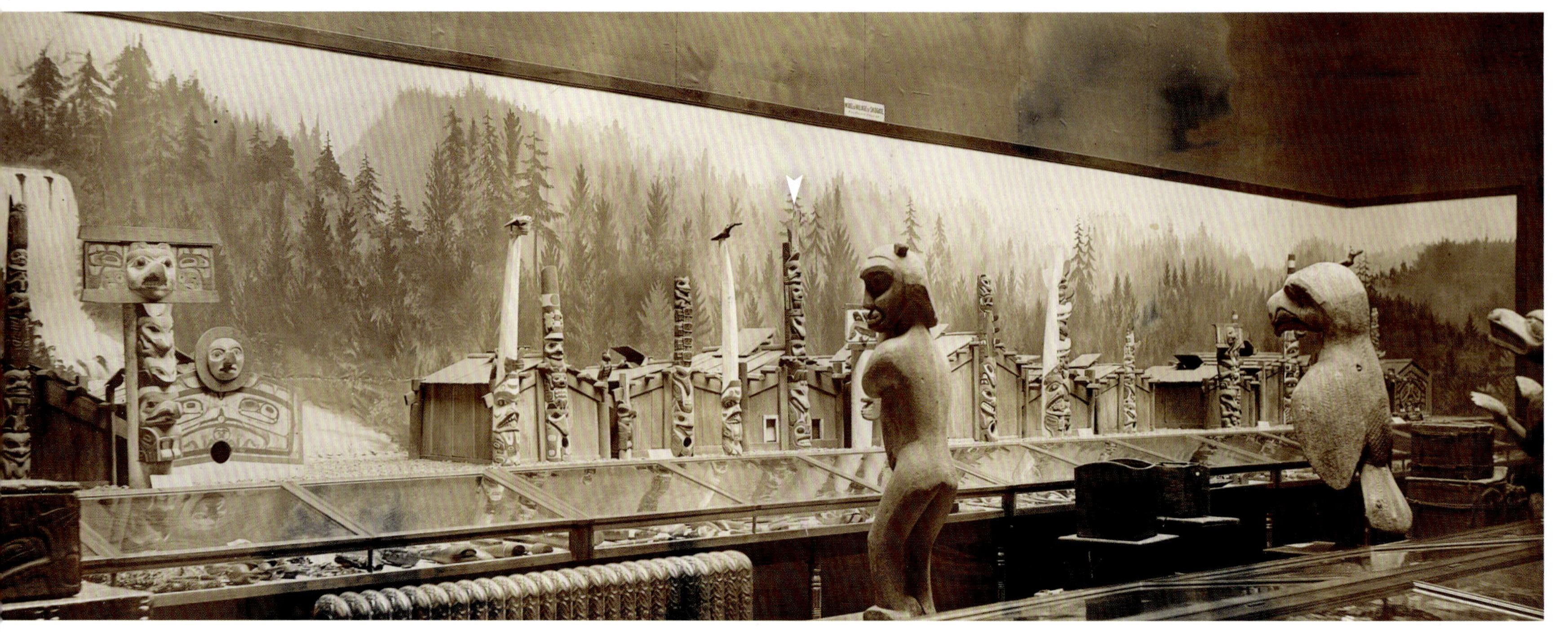

3.38 Some of the World's Columbian Exposition model houses displayed in the Jackson Park Museum, pre-1921. © The Field Museum, image no. CSA8055.

ber 30, 2020). Kathleen Hans translated Naasta agangjiingas as "Stay far away from the house" (personal communication, February 7, 2004).

Deans called the model of this house "House of the High Crest, Nass Tans-a-wie—I have the most stylish house in town." SHIP translates Naa S'iijuu as "the owner had the most stylish house in town" (email September 30, 2020). Deans reports that this house belonged to the first Jefferson, built after the death of the "whaler Captain Jefferson." Newcombe gives the Haida name of this chief as Tlini.[43] John Robson carved another simpler model of this frontal pole for John Swanton (figure 3.39). Based on Robson's information, Swanton gives the house owners' name as Dō'anai "Younger One," and also says the Tsimshian called this chief ı!nē't, likely the same name Newcombe spelled Tlini (Swanton 1901b). The wife of Jefferson was named "SqAnxa.i" or (Skunx̱a) meaning "Clean Woman" according to Newcombe and Swanton, but they give different Eagle clans for her: Naa 'Yuuwans X̱aaydaG̱aay (E6a) and Naa S'aagaas X̱aaydaG̱aay (E6b).[44]

Deans says that the three lowest figures (sculpin, killer whale, owl) belonged to Jefferson, the three above belonged "more or less" to his wife. These he lists as killer whale and boys in a canoe (from a story relating to the owl on the pole), and dogfish, the wife's crest. Deans erroneously identifies Jefferson's wife as the daughter of Skidegate the Great or "Jacks as he used to be called" (Deans 1893b, 52).[45] On the frontal pole of both the original and the model of this house, which is a fairly close copy, there is a dogfish at the top with its tail pointed up. The model lacks the watchmen that flank the dogfish tail. A human figure is below the dogfish, then a whale, owl, and another whale. The figure on the bottom of the original pole is obscured in the photos, but the model has a sculpin at the bottom. All the teeth on the model are painted white.

According to Deans, this model house had an inside house

post that displayed Jefferson's wife's crests, which Deans describes as the same as Skidegate the Great's crests (Deans 1893b, 52). Here Deans's lack of understanding of Haida crests and the matrilineal descent system is revealed, since Haida children have the crests of their mothers, not their fathers. Haida marriage traditions taught that one should marry someone in the opposite moiety (Eagle or Raven), and children were of the mother's clan. If Jefferson was a Raven (R6), his wife most likely would have been an Eagle (either E6a or E6b, as Newcombe and Swanton say).[46] If Jefferson's wife was truly Skidegate the Great's daughter (as Deans wrote), she would have been a Raven, and not had the same crests as her father. However, if Jefferson's wife was Skidegate the Great's sister's daughter, she would have shared his Eagle clan and crests. She is therefore more likely to have been Skidegate's niece or great niece. The figures on this (now missing) inside house post were described by Deans to be Skidegate's crests: the thunderbird (mosquito hawk), killer whale with the bat, an owl, and a killer whale. Skidegate the Great may have lived in the time before the E6 clan split into the Naa 'Yuuwans X̱aaydaG̱aay (E6a) and Naa S'aagaas X̱aaydaG̱aay (E6b). Their crests both included the raven, 'WaasG̱uu, dogfish, weasel, eagle, sculpin, and halibut, but did not include the killer whale (Swanton 1905a, 273).[47] This again contradicts Deans's understanding of the Skidegate crests. Certainly the killer whale would have been Jefferson's own HlG̱aay.yuu Laanas Raven clan crest.

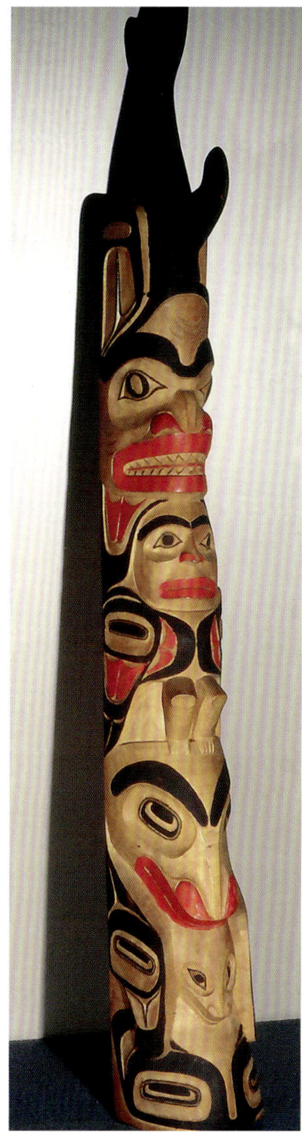

3.39 Model pole based on NaastA Angjiwas, "House people are ashamed to look at it is so overpoweringly great" (Newcombe). Commissioned by John Swanton, 1901, made by John Robson, 84 cm h × 10.5 cm w × 13 cm d. Courtesy of the Division of Anthropology, American Museum of Natural History, cat. no. 16/8751. A handwritten note on the Swanton typescript says: "There is probably some story connected with this pole but it has been forgotten" (Swanton 1901b).

MODEL POLE NOS. 3 AND 4

Flanking Houses 4 and 5 in the WCE display were two dogfish memorial poles, Kaaniihl Q'aa.l (figures 3.40, 3.41, see also figures 3.33 [left] and 3.42 [center]).[48] These are models of two memorial poles that were placed in front of Jefferson's house (discussed above) in Skidegate. Deans tells us that the pole with the eagle on top (figure 3.40), which stood to the left, was raised by the Chief Skidegate, who died during the summer of 1888 or 1889, as a memorial to his sister (or cousin). Newcombe gave the

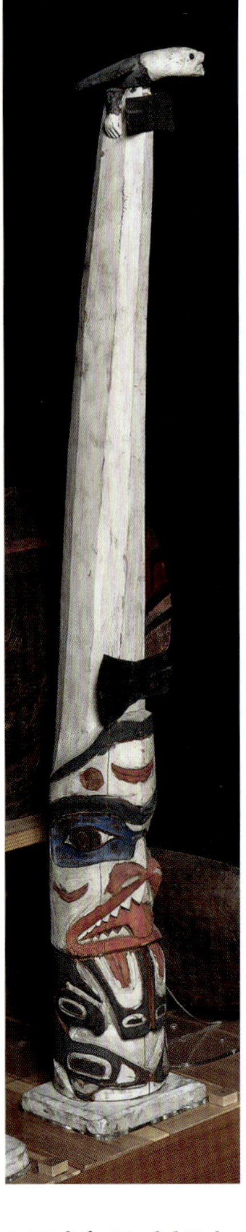

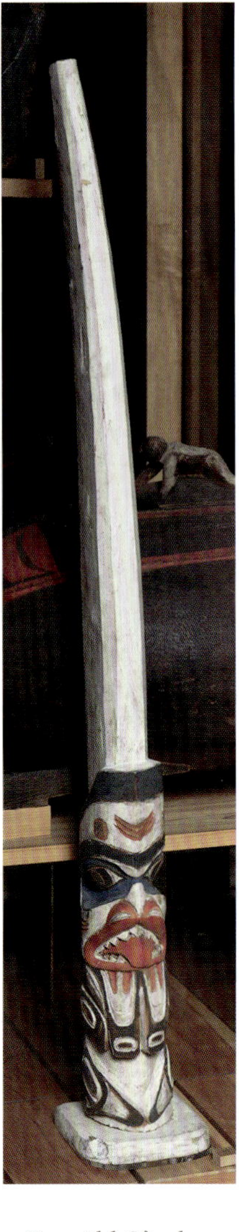

3.40 *left* Model Pole No. 3, Kaaniihl Q'aa.l, Memorial for Kaaniihl, 1892. Courtesy of the Field Museum, cat. no. 17817. Photograph by Gail Specht.

3.41 *right* Model Pole No. 4, Kaaniihl Q'aa.l, Memorial for Kaaniihl, 1892. Courtesy of the Field Museum, cat. no. 17815. Photograph by Gail Specht.

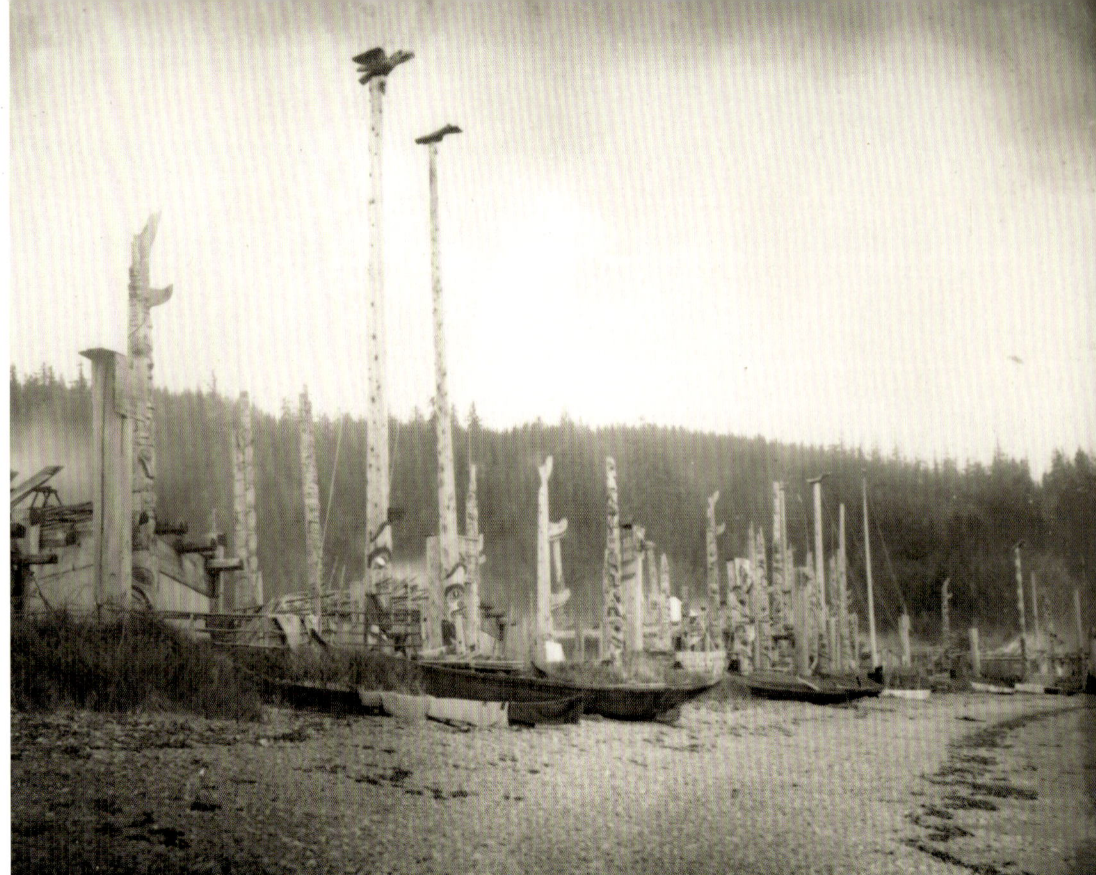

3.42 View of HlGaagilda Llnagaay from the south end. Photograph by the Maynards, 1884. Neg. no. 9078. Courtesy of the Royal BC Museum and Archives.

name of this Chief Skidegate as "Dogankilas."[49] This model pole has a copper attached horizonally above the dogfish. Deans says the dogfish pole to the right (figure 3.41), with a raven on top, was raised as a memorial to the same woman, "Can-hiss-to-Wagia" (Kaaniihl aawga), by this Chief Skidegate's rival and cousin "Nine-sing-wuss" or "Nin-ging wuss" (Nang Jingwas), whom he describes as "a raven of the eagle phratry" (Deans 1893c, 82).[50] James Deans variously describes the woman to whom these poles were a memorial as either a sister or cousin of both of these men, whom he said were related. Exactly how they were related is unclear. We know that Skidegate and his brother Niisdaka.na were of the Naa 'Yuuwans X̱aaydaG̱aay (E6a) clan and Nang Jingwas was Naa S'aagaas X̱aaydaG̱aay (E6b). At some point in the past these two clans separated, and a rivalry developed between them. Deans records a long account of their rivalry, which culminated in their raising these two memorial poles in an attempt to one-up each other (Deans 1893b, 82–85).

Photographs of the village show that the dogfish pole with the eagle on top was raised first, between the 1879 photo taken by Hastings and the 1881 photo taken by

Dossetter (see figures 3.36, 2.5). The pole with the raven on top was raised before the 1884 photo taken by the Maynards (figure 3.42). At that time Paul Nang Jingwas was living in a house eight doors to the north and must be the Nang Jingwas who raised the dogfish memorial with the raven on top. The other pole is said to have been raised by Dogangakillas "younger brother who speaks well" (SHIP February 6, 2004), or "younger brother who has more power than older brother," referred to as Chief Skidegate by Deans.[51]

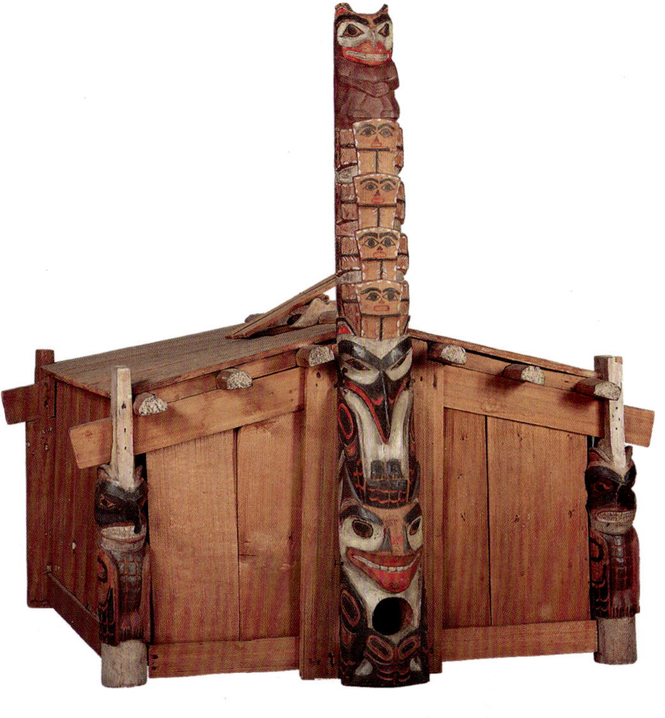

HOUSE MODEL NO. 5 / *Made by Adam Brown (Cowgill)*

House Model No. 5 is Sgyam Sgwaan Naas, "Sparrow Hawk House" (figure 3.43). Deans called it "Scamsum Nass, Mosquito Hawk House," but while Deans's translation of "scamsum" is mosquito hawk, the word "sgyam sgwaan" in X̱aayda Kil actually means "sparrow hawk." It was made by Adam Brown (Cowgill). According to Deans, the original house was built by a Haida man named Jefferson who was given the name Jefferson by a Captain Jefferson, said to be a whaler from Newburyport, Massachusetts, who lived in this house and gave his name to the head of the house

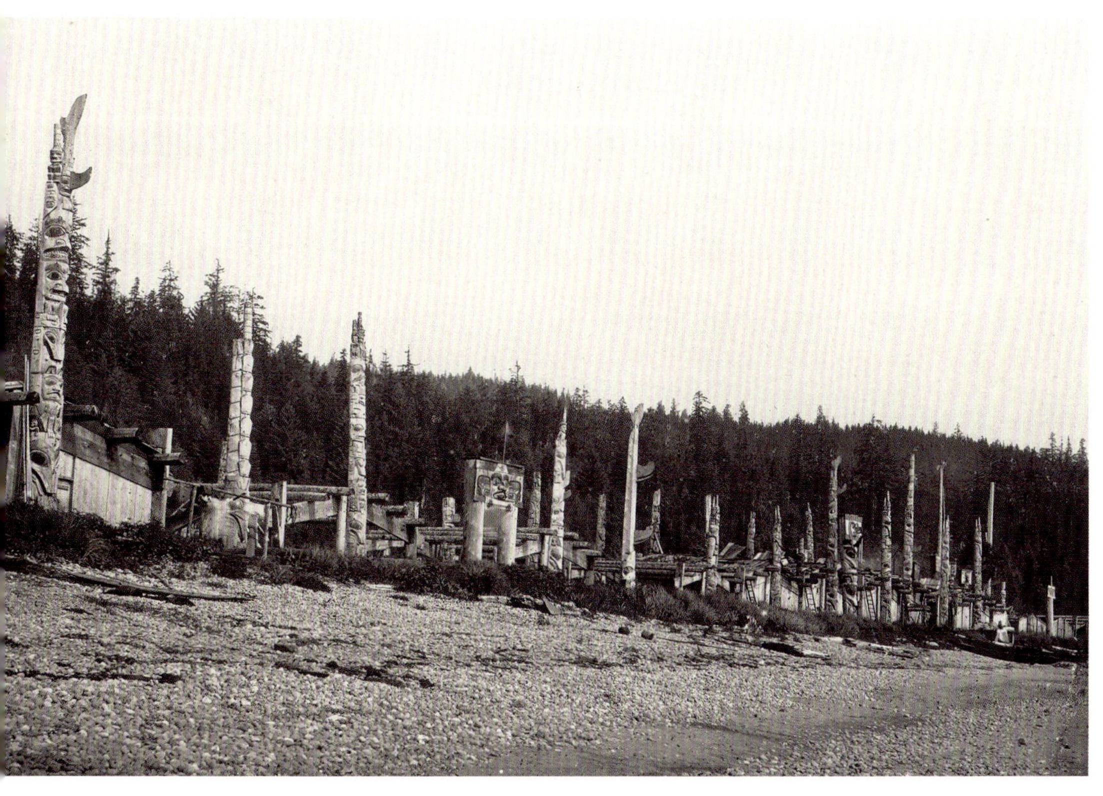

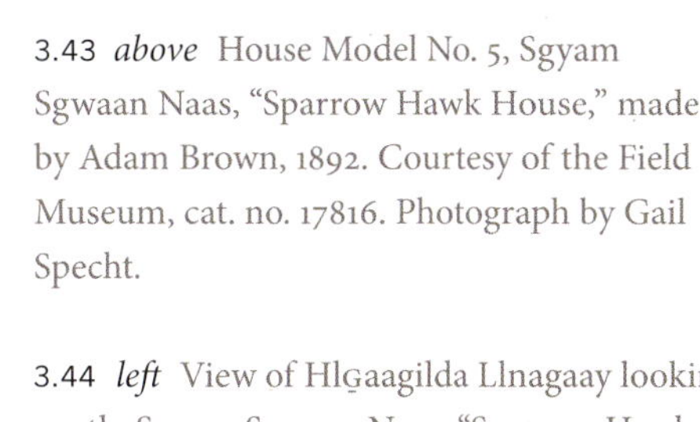

3.43 *above* House Model No. 5, Sgyam Sgwaan Naas, "Sparrow Hawk House," made by Adam Brown, 1892. Courtesy of the Field Museum, cat. no. 17816. Photograph by Gail Specht.

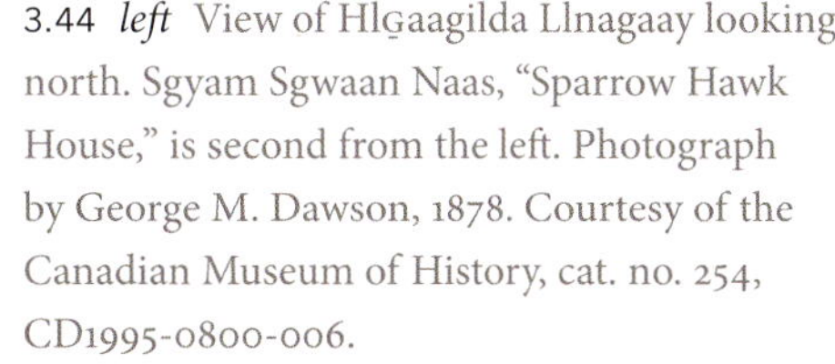

3.44 *left* View of HlG̱aagilda Llnagaay looking north. Sgyam Sgwaan Naas, "Sparrow Hawk House," is second from the left. Photograph by George M. Dawson, 1878. Courtesy of the Canadian Museum of History, cat. no. 254, CD1995-0800-006.

(figure 3.44). This whaler is said by Deans to have died after a few years, ca. 1832, and the Haida man named Jefferson lived during the time of Skidegate the Great. Newcombe in describing the original house for this model received his information from Charles Jefferson, who was of the same clan as the original Jefferson (Hlg̱aay.yuu Laanas, R6).[52]

MacDonald misinterpreted Deans's notes about this man and said: "Mosquito Hawk House was the first house built by C. Jefferson, an American whaler from Newburyport, Massachusetts, who settled at Skidegate in 1832" (MacDonald 1983, 54). An old letter, preserved in a private Skidegate collection, dated 1861 from C.H.H. that recommends the Old Captain Jefferson whom he has known for two years, whose uncle was old Skidegate mentions in olden times: "a man named Jefferson died at QC and gave this his namesake half of his ship & cargo & since then he (this Jefferson) has gone by that name of Jefferson."

Both Deans's account and this 1861 letter indicate that the house was not built by a whaler, but rather by the Haida man with whom the Captain Jefferson came to live, and to whom this Captain Jefferson gave his name and property after his death. A thorough examination of the records of whaling ships and captains that were sailing out of the East Coast that are kept at the New Bedford Whaling Society, however, revealed no whalers nor any ships' captains named Jefferson that can be documented from any maritime archival records from this time.[53] In fact, American whalers were not even frequenting North Pacific waters until after 1835 and did not take shelter at Haida Gwaii until much later than 1832. However, there is evidence that a Haida man was named Jefferson well before 1832. He is mentioned in log of the *Volunteer* (Captain James Barrett) and given a ride June 14, 1817, from Cumshewa to Skidegate, where he disembarked June 27 (Barrett 1817–1821).

Given the lack of evidence for a whaler named Jefferson, it is interesting to note that Captain Robert's brig (mentioned above) was the *Jefferson*, and it was the *Jefferson*'s tender sloop, the *Resolution*, that was sunk at Cumshewa. I would speculate that it is possible that the brig's name *Jefferson* may have been acquired or taken, along with the booty and/or ransom, thus being the source of this Haida Jefferson's wealth and name (Wright 2001b, 69–76). It would make sense that the name of this ship, whose tender was defeated in war, would have legitimately been owned by the victors, as was custom throughout the Pacific Northwest Coast. As with the story of the source of wealth of the woman of "Owl House," the story may have been sanitized for the benefit of outsiders to recommend the character of the Haida Captain Jefferson, and for the benefit of gullible collectors such as Deans.

Deans identified the figures on the pole as a sculpin on the bottom, a raven, and an otter above the twelve coppers that are placed above the raven. Sparrow hawks are placed on the corner posts of the model. The stack of coppers was explained by Deans as Jefferson's solution to filling his pole with symbols of his wealth without offending Chief Skidegate, who would have disapproved of filling the whole pole with crest figures, a privilege Deans reports was reserved for the chief at that time.

Dawson's 1878 photo (figure 3.44) shows the original house frontal pole had no figure at the top, only a stack of six sgil surmounting seven coppers. Behind the front-facing coppers may be eight more coppers on their sides as on the model. There may be more on the opposite side, though this side is obscured in Dossetter's photo (see figure 2.6). A transforming raven with humanoid nostrils on its downturned beak is below the stack of coppers. If there was a sculpin below the Raven at the bottom of the original pole, it is not visible in the Dawson photograph.

HOUSE MODEL NO. 6

There has been confusion about the original house that was the inspiration for House Model No. 6, Táwll Naas or G̱uuajii Naas, "Rainbow House" or "Wolf House." Deans describes the model as "Rainbow House, Cah Towel ah Coot Coo or Wolf House, Chooatz ah Nass" and the figures on the model pole as grizzly bear (lowest), rainbow (human with rainbow around head, body painted black), raven, wolf on top, and wolves on the corner posts. Deans tells us that the original house belonged to the family of the wife of the man who made the model, but he failed to give us the maker's name. We have only a partial view of this missing house from the WCE and Field Museum

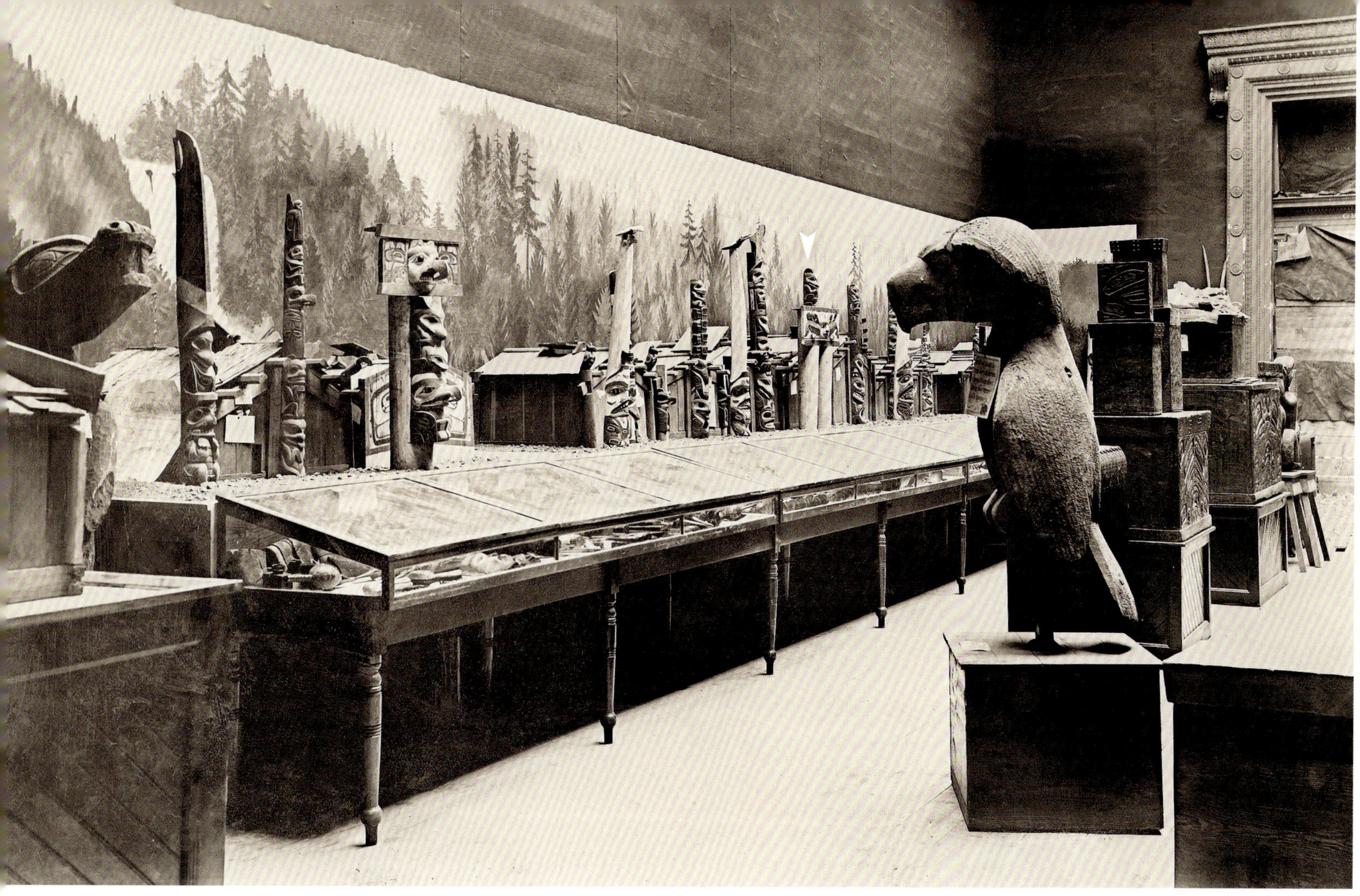

3.45 Some of the World's Columbian Exposition house models displayed at the Jackson Park Museum, pre-1921. © The Field Museum, image no. CSA8076. This photo shows just the top of missing House Model No. 6, Táwll Naas or G̱uuajii Naas, "Rainbow House" or "Wolf House" (Field Museum, cat. no. 17812). It is visible sticking up above the Double Dogfish Mortuary Pole No. 5 in the middle right of the photo.

installations, showing only the top wolf figure and the wolves on the corner posts (figure 3.45), so it is difficult to compare with historical poles in the village (see figure 1.1).

No doubt based on Deans's numbering that places this house just to the right (north) of SG̱yam SG̱waan Naas (House No. 5), MacDonald associates this model with the old house (his #27) "Always Wanting More House," built by Tlinit of the Skidegate Town People (R6) (MacDonald 1983, 53) (figure 3.46) as identified by Newcombe. MacDonald took this information from Newcombe's notes for his house #5, who described it as "Na agAnkilAdlAndas—Always Wanting More, Chief Tlinit" (the first Jefferson) of the HlG̱aay.yuu Laanas clan (R6).[54] Newcombe described the figures on this tall pole as three watchers at the top: SG̱aana (killer whale) with man's face, man's face, SG̱aana, SG̱aaga (shaman). Newcombe's description differs from MacDonald's, who described the figures, perhaps interpreting what he saw in the photograph, as three watchmen at the top, a Ts'aamus (snag), with a man in its mouth and eagle between its fins, a killer whale with a rainbow-person holding on to its dorsal fin, and rainbow (quoting Deans's description of a rainbow), and a whale devouring a seal, and an owl (again quoting Deans's description of an owl). The photographs of the frontal pole of this house as well as Newcombe's description of the figures (which include no wolves) do not match with the model house

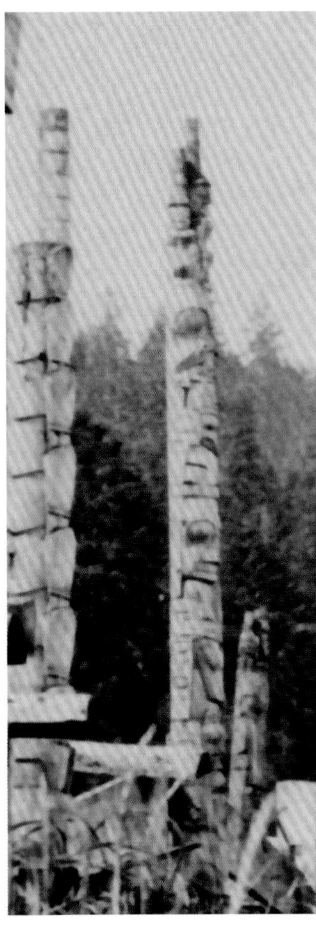

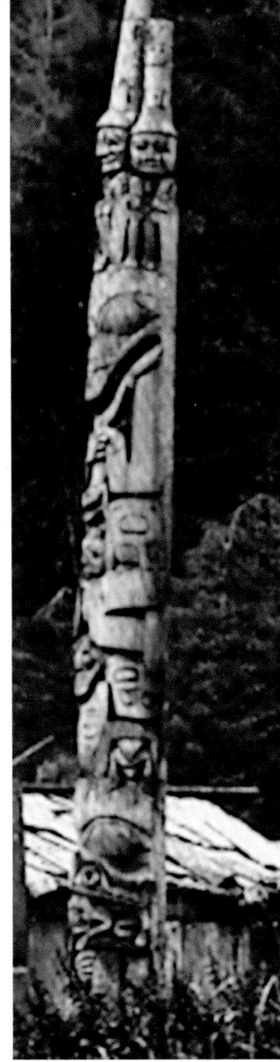

3.46 "Na agAnkilAdlAndas—Always Wanting More" House, seen in the center to the right of the coppers pole in of this detail of O. C. Hasting's photograph of HlG̱aagilda, 1879. Neg. no. PN5535 (see figure 3.36). Courtesy of the Royal BC Museum and Archives. This house might have been the one after which Táwll Naas or G̱uuajii Naas, "Rainbow" or "Wolf" House, was modeled.

3.47 "Mountain House," seen three houses to the right of "Always Wanting More" house in HlG̱aagilda (Skidegate). Photograph by Edward Dossetter, 1881. Detail of American Museum of Natural History Library, Image #42267.

Deans calls "Rainbow or Wolf" house or any other WCE house model. Newcombe's account that old Jefferson owned "Always Wanting More" house (along with Sparrow Hawk House and People are Ashamed to Look at it House), further suggests that the model Wolf/Rainbow house was based on a different house. Since Jefferson is mentioned so prominently with the other two models of his houses, one would think that Deans would have also identified Model No. 6 with Jefferson, if it had been his house. Instead, Deans says only that the model was made by a man whose wife was related to the owners.

The only frontal pole in Skidegate that appears to have a wolf at the top is the one called "Mountain House" by MacDonald (his #24, figure 3.47), which stood three houses to the right (north) of Always Wanting More House. It is described as having a sea wolf at the top and a bearlike figure at the bottom, identified as a snag by MacDonald (1983, 52). Newcombe didn't describe this wolf frontal pole in his notes, and none of the houses on Swanton's list seem to match this one. The model named "Mountain House," by Deans, also obscured in the photos, does not look like this pole (see Mountain House No. 8 below).

For these reasons, "Rainbow House" (No. 6) has been left here in the sequence of Deans's numbering, given the probability that the rainbow figure described by Deans on the model pole, although we can't see it, represents the rainbowlike human figure seen in the photograph of the pole on the house that stood in this position in the village, to the right of SG̱yam SG̱waan Naas.[55]

MODEL POLE NO. 5

This is a model of Skunx̱a or Stathli X̱aad, "Skunx̱a or Stathli's Mortuary Pole," raised for the mother of "a late Chief Skidegate" (figures 3.48, 3.49). It is a double mortuary pole, meaning it has two posts supporting the coffin box and panel above. Deans tells us it was raised by her daughter, who took her name and inherited all her property; this old woman was one of two sisters who had ten of a family. Deans gives her name as "Secon High or Scoon High." This is likely his attempt at spelling Skunx̱a, "Clean," which is the name of Jefferson's wife

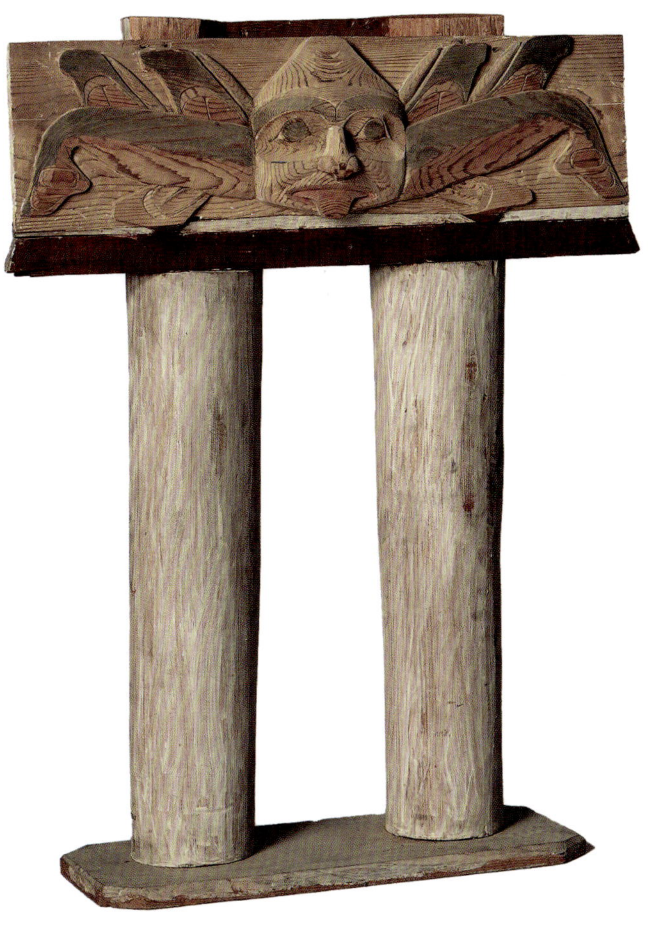

3.48 Model Mortuary Pole No. 5, Skunx̱a or Stathli X̱aad, "Scoon High," 1892, 35.5 × 26.5 in. Courtesy of the Field Museum, cat. no. 17813. Photograph by Gail Specht.

(see House Model No. 22). Newcombe reports the name for this woman as "Hihgayel Hagihas Stathli" ("Wants More Property") of the Naa S'aagaas X̱aaydaG̱aay (E6b).[56]

There are three other known models of this mortuary pole in the American Museum of Natural History (figure 3.50), the Oakland Museum (cat. no. 16.920), and the Royal British Columbia Museum (cat. no. 228). The American Museum of Natural History model was made by John Robson for Swanton. The Oakland model has been attributed to Robson as well. Swanton confirms Newcombe's identification of this woman as being of the Naa S'aagaas X̱aaydaG̱aay (E6b) and gives her name as "sku'nxai (clean)" (Swanton 1901b, 4). MacDonald reports that "Wants More Property" was the mother of the Chief Skidegate, who owned "Dug-Out House" (see below) (MacDonald 1983, 53, 27X).

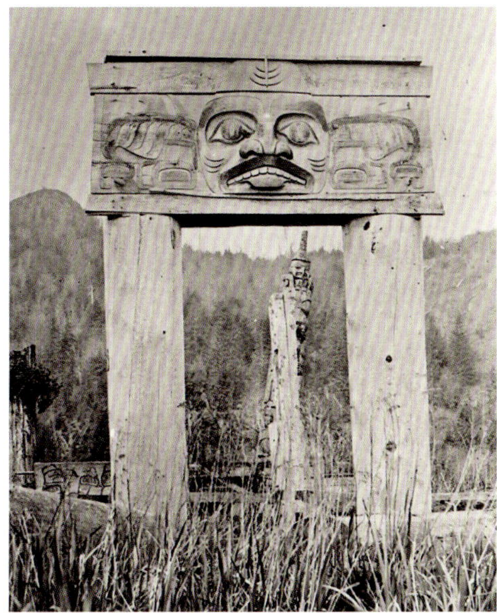

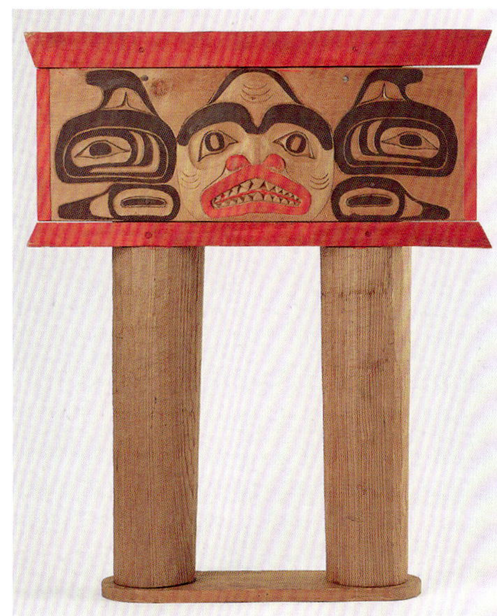

3.49. *left* Skunx̱a double mortuary pole representing a dogfish. Photograph by the Maynards, 1884. Neg. no. PN5795. Courtesy of the Royal BC Museum and Archives. Erected in honor of Skunx̱a, the mother of a Chief Skidegate by her daughter, who held her name and property.

3.50 *right* Model of Skunx̱a double mortuary pole, commissioned by John Swanton from John Robson, 1901, 56.7 cm h × 46.3 cm w × 12 cm d. Courtesy of the Division of Anthropology, American Museum of Natural History, cat. no. 16/8760.

HOUSE MODEL NO. 7 / *Made by Peter Brown (Ga.alla)*

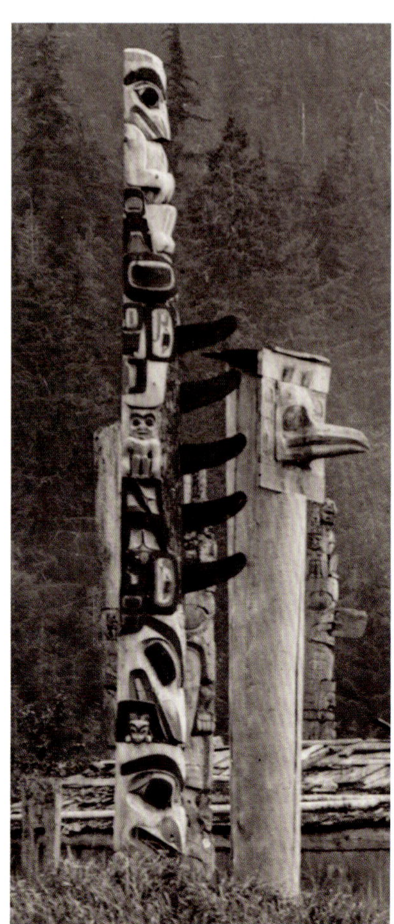

3.52 Detail of figure 2.5, Edward Dossetter photo of Hlg̱aagilda Llnagaay (Skidegate), showing full-size freestanding memorial pole on which frontal pole from Model House No. 7 was based. Erected by Phillip Jackson, Chief Sg̱iidagiids IX, in honor of his wife's uncle (Swanton 1901b). American Museum of Natural History Library, Image #42268.

This model house, Gud K̲wiig̱a X̱iigangs, "House Upon Which the Clouds Make a Noise," is unusual in that the frontal pole is a model of a freestanding memorial pole that was never attached to a house (figures 3.51, 3.52). Deans gave the model's name as "Coot-quee-gay-heegan, Eagles Storm Cloud Wind Sounding House." He identifies the maker as Peter Brown (Galla) and the figures as a brown bear at the bottom, an "Aquillo," a fabulous sort of whale (on this model with four fins), and at the top an eagle, but the typescript was corrected to say "wolf" (Deans 1893b, 29). He points out that the fifth fin was left out for lack of space. Clearly the figure at the top is not an eagle, and most likely is not a wolf either. Both Newcombe and Swanton identify the top figure on the original pole, for which this is a model, as a mountain goat. Newcombe identified the figures on the original memorial pole as a goat at the top, a five-finned whale (K'aag̱waay) and a grizzly bear at the bottom.[57] According to Swanton, who recorded the story of this pole from another model of it made by John Robson (figure 3.53), the pole was put up by Jackson (Chief Sg̱iidagiids) for his wife's uncle after he died. The uncle belonged to G̱aag'yals K̲iig̱awaay (R4) (Swanton 1901b, 3). Newcombe said that this was put up for Skidegate's wife who belonged to the Skedans people.[58] Swanton identifies the figures as a mountain goat on the top, three-finned whale (there are only three fins on the Robson model, but four on the WCE model), and grizzly bear at the bottom (Swanton 1905a, 131–32). Swanton's original notes identify the three-finned whale on the Robson model as a "tca'gan x̱ū'aji [Chaag̱an xuu.ajii] (sea-grizzly bear)" instead (Swanton 1901b, 3).[59]

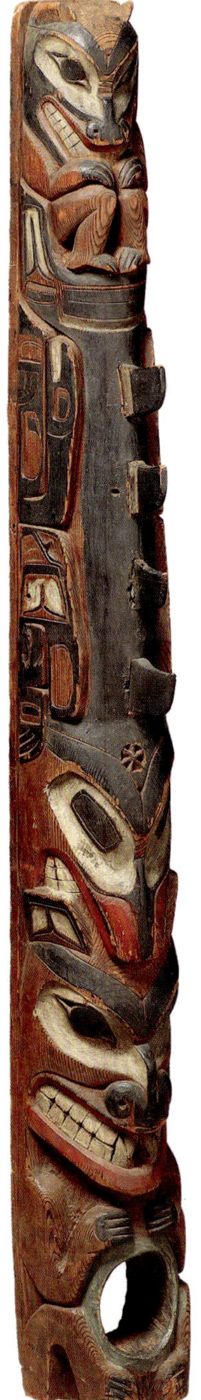

3.51 Frontal Pole from House Model No. 7, Gud K̲wiig̱a X̱iigangs, "House Upon Which the Clouds Make a Noise," made by Peter Brown (Ga.alla), Chief Skidegate IX, 1892, pole: 114.5 cm h × 13 cm w × 10.5 cm d (house missing). Portland Art Museum, Portland, Oregon, cat. no. 46.34, Helen Thurston Ayer Fund Purchase. Photograph courtesy of the Portland Art Museum. Originally Field Museum, cat. no. 17811, purchased by the University of Pennsylvania Museum in 1900, cat. no. 37.685.

The house with which the original memorial pole is associated did have a frontal pole (figure 3.54). This pole has three watchmen at the top, and a bird with a downturned beak below, identified as a raven by Newcombe, and a Sg̱aana (killer whale) at the bottom.

Newcombe's information obtained from Charles Jefferson says this house was owned by Logot (R5).[60] This house was apparently no longer occupied by the time the memorial pole in front was raised in the 1880s. Based on photographic evidence, the memorial pole went up between 1879 and 1881, when Dossetter photographed it.

Ga.alla, Peter Brown / *See Genealogy Chart 4*

It is interesting that the maker of this model memorial–turned–frontal pole (discussed earlier) was Peter Brown, who succeeded Phillip Jackson as Chief Skidegate (see Appendix I, Chronology of the Sg̱iidagiids Town Chiefs). Jackson would have been the one who commissioned the original memorial to his wife's uncle, and probably well known to Peter Brown. Peter Brown (Ga.alla), of the Naa 'Yuuwans X̱aaydag̱aay (E6a), held the town chief position of Chief Skidegate in the early twentieth century, ca. 1897–1930. He was brought from Old Massett to take this town chief position after Phillip Jackson. He is listed in the Old Massett census for 1891 as age thirty-five, a fisherman. His wife was Mary, age twenty-one, a cannery hand. Their son, Sam, was two years old at that time. Peter Brown was baptized in 1894. According to Marius Barbeau, Peter Brown was the son of Sam Q'a.oste, a Kuun Laanas Raven (R14), who died in 1892, age ninety (Barbeau 1916–1954, BF 253.5). According to the government death records, Peter Brown died on February 20, 1930, age seventy-five, at Skidegate (BC Archives Microfilm #B13374). This would make his birth date ca. 1855.

This date of birth differs from that on the gravestone of Chief Skidegate, b. 1843, d. 1930. This may be the Chief Skidegate who was the father of Elizabeth Skidegate (Sterling, Jada iljus). James Young remembered

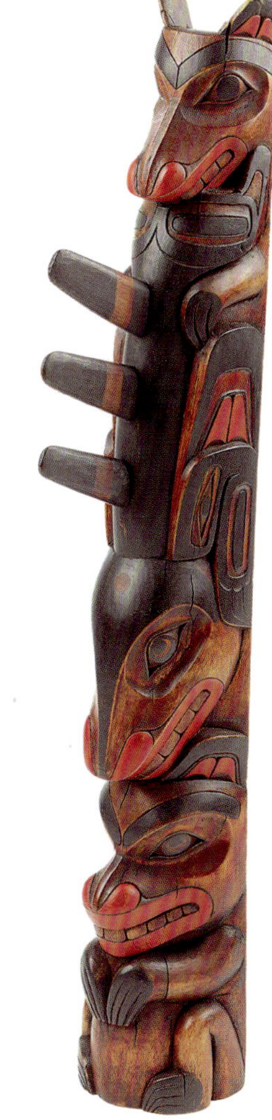

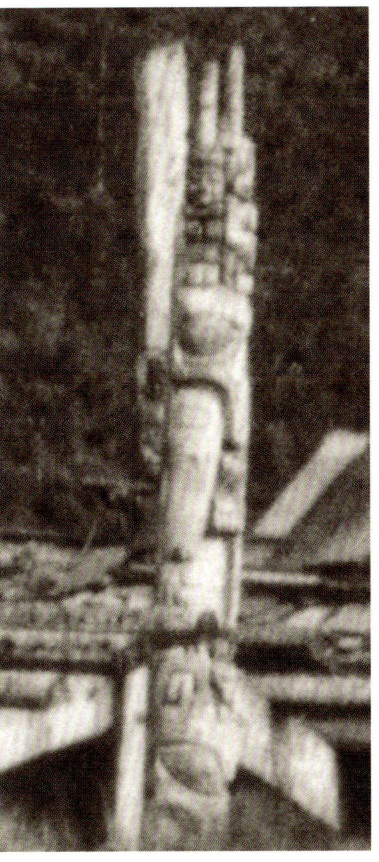

3.53 *left* Model pole commissioned by John Swanton, 1901, made by John Robson, 65 cm h × 9.5 cm w × 14 cm d. American Museum of Natural History, cat. no. 16/8755. Representing the freestanding memorial erected by Phillip Jackson, Chief Skidegate IX, identified by Swanton as a mountain goat at the top (missing the horns), sea grizzly bear in the middle (three-finned whale), and grizzly bear at the bottom (Swanton 1901b).

3.54 *above* Detail of figure 3.44, Dawson photo of Hlg̱aagilda Llnagaay showing the house frontal pole of the "House Upon Which Storm Clouds Make a Noise," which stood behind the pole honoring Phillip's Jackson's wife's uncle. Photograph by George M. Dawson, 1878. Courtesy of the Canadian Museum of History, cat. no. 254, CD1995-0800-006.

that she returned to Skidegate after her father's (Captain Skidegate's) death and put up a gravestone for him, and she died shortly after (James Young, personal communication, February 7, 2004). BC Archives death records say Elizabeth Skidegate died in Skidegate, October 6, 1934, age seventy (BC Archives microfilm # October 6, 1934). This would put her birth ca. 1864, when Peter Brown would have been twenty-one, assuming he was born in 1843 as the gravestone reports. Gravestone #155 in the Skidegate cemetery reads: "In Loving Memory of Chief Skidegate [Galla] b. 1843, d. March 4, 1930 age 87." It is unclear whether this is Peter Brown's gravestone, since his death date is different (February 20, 1930, age seventy-five) (Haida Gwaii Museum n.d.). In some cases the dates that were put on gravestones were the dates that they were made/moved to the cemetery, rather than the actual death date of the deceased. If Elizabeth Skidegate raised this stone shortly before her death in 1934, she may have had the date March 3, 1930, put on it, even though her father died earlier in the year.

HOUSE MODEL NO. 8 / *Made by Phillip Jackson*

3.55. House models displayed at the Jackson Park Museum, pre-1921. See "Mountain House" behind and to the left of Model Pole No. 6 at the right of the photo. © The Field Museum, image no. CSA8095.

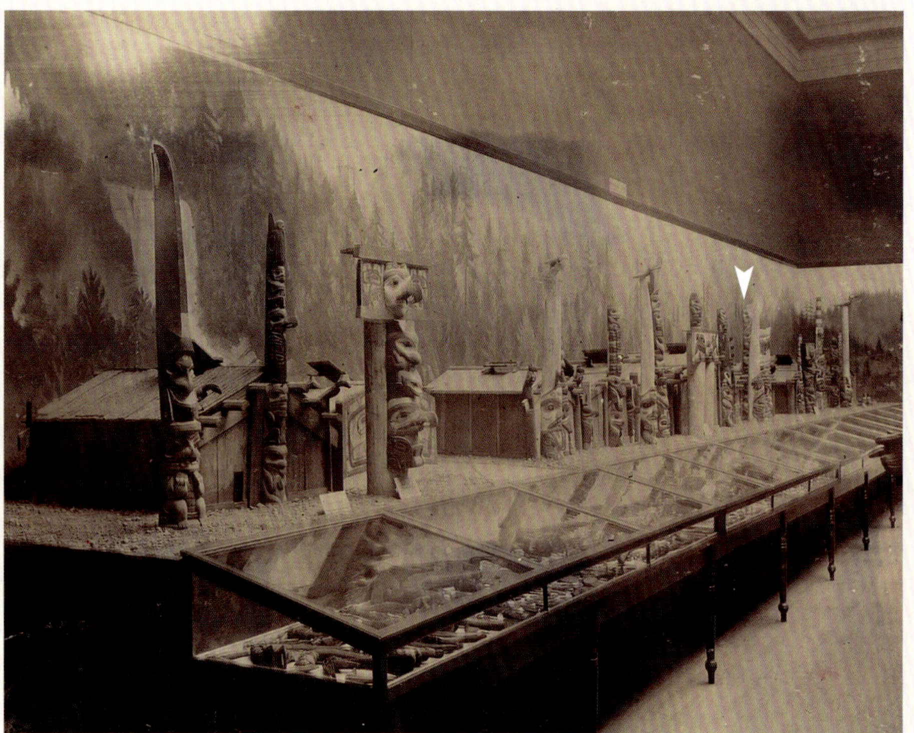

Phillip Jackson, the maker of this model house, Tlldaḡaaw Naas, "Mountain House," was the same person who raised the five-finned killer whale memorial discussed earlier (figure 3.52). Phillip Jackson was Chief Skidegate ca. 1892–1897, of the Naa 'Yuuwans X̱aaydaḡaay (E6a). According to Deans, this model was based on a house belonging to an uncle of his named "Gallah" who was a Raven. The name Ga.alla was an Eagle name, also held by Peter Brown (E6a), so Deans was likely wrong about his clan.

The model is now missing and is known only from Deans's description. He called it "Kelder on Nass, Mountain House" and partial photographs (see figures 3.55, 3.56, center right, hidden behind the two-finned dogfish pole, Model Pole No. 6). Deans describes the figures on the model pole to be a brown bear (crest of Gallah) at the bottom, raven, eagle, and dogfish with another eagle (crests of Gallah's wife) at the top. There is once again some confusion about which was the original house upon which this model was based. The frontal pole that appears to be

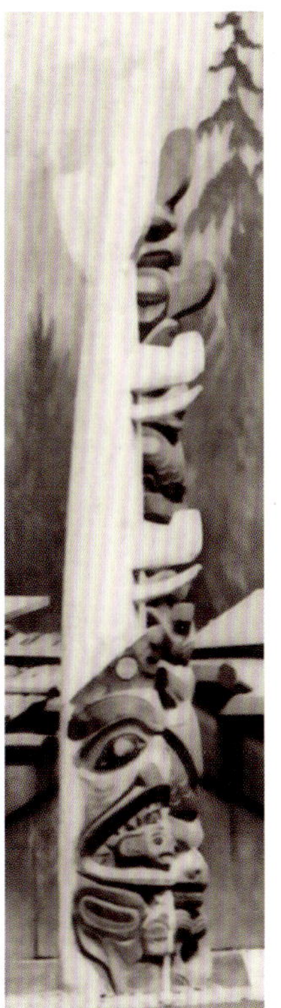

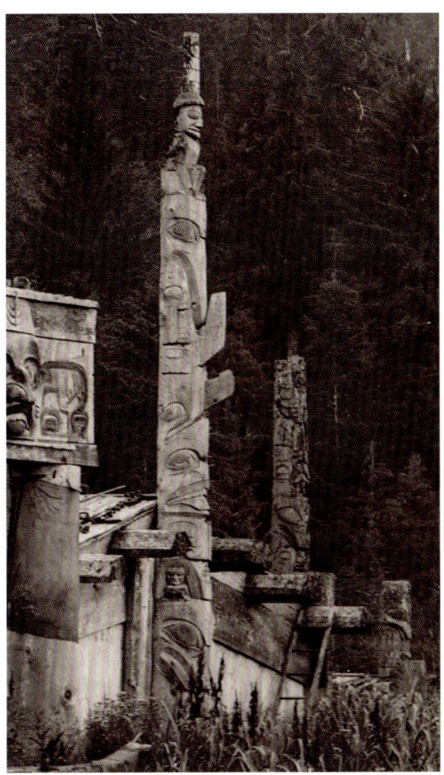

3.56 *above left* Partial view of missing Model House No. 8, Tlldag̱aaw Naas, "Mountain House," made by Phillip Jackson, Chief Skidegate IX, 1892. Behind and to the right of Model Pole No. 6 (detail of figure 3.38). Courtesy of the Field Museum, cat. no. 17809, image no. CSA8055.

3.57 *above right* "Killer Whale House," detail of figure 2.5, photograph by Edward Dossetter, 1881, showing pole in back row (center right). American Museum of Natural History Library, Image #338294.

the closest match to this model (figure 3.57) has a different order of figures, a long beaked raven-like bird topped by a watchman figure at the top, with the dogfish with its tail up below. This house was located to the left/south of the house called "House Upon Which Storm Clouds Make a Noise," so if this is the original house, the order of the models of these two houses was reversed in the WCE installation.

Newcombe's description (his #9) links this house with Swanton's house #17, "killer whale house," the name also given to the house by MacDonald (see figure 3.57) (MacDonald 1983, 53).[61] Swanton described another model of this pole (now missing), made for him by John Robson (figure 3.58), and identifies the owner as Lō'gōt, the same man who owned the house associated with the five-finned whale memorial just discussed. Of the Robson model pole, he says: it "belonged to Lō'gōt ["Wave-Eagle"], chief of the Seaward-Sqoā'ładas (R5), and stood at Skidegate.[62] His wife was of the Rotten-House-People (E6b). The dogfish at the top, with its tail standing up straight and its head brought forward, as well as the raven immediately beneath it, belonged to her; while the killer whale at the bottom, which as its tail folded up below was her husband's crest" (Swanton 1905a, 123).

Newcombe, based on information provided to him in 1906 by Charles Jefferson, reports that this house was erected by Lō'gōt's wife and called Sg̱aana Naas (Killer Whale House). He identifies the figures as a single watcher on top, raven, dogfish, and killer whale at the bottom. Lō'gōt's wife is identified as Naa 'Yuuwans X̱aaydag̱aay (E6a), and Lo'got as a Raven, Jiiaxwii Sk̲aahladasg̱aay (R5).[63] The Deans model of "Mountain House" is said to have a bear at the bottom rather than a killer whale. This figure on the

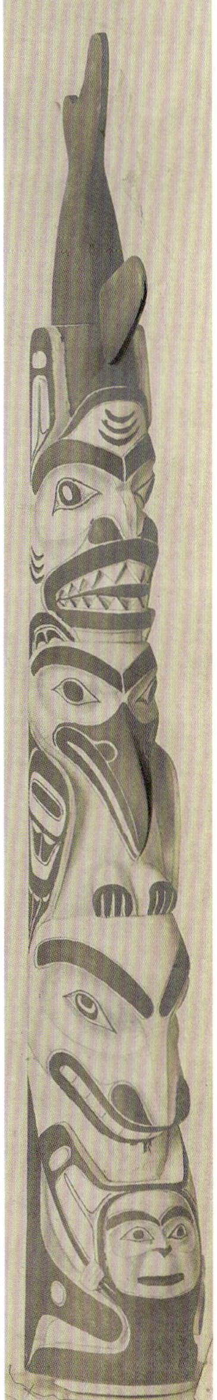

3.58 Model pole commissioned by John Swanton, made by John Robson, 1901. Missing from American Museum of Natural History collection, cat. no. 16/8757. Representing a pole of the Jiiaxwii Skaahladasg̱aay (R5). The chief's name was Lō'gōt and his wife belonged to the Naa S'aagaas X̱aaydag̱aay (Swanton 1901b).

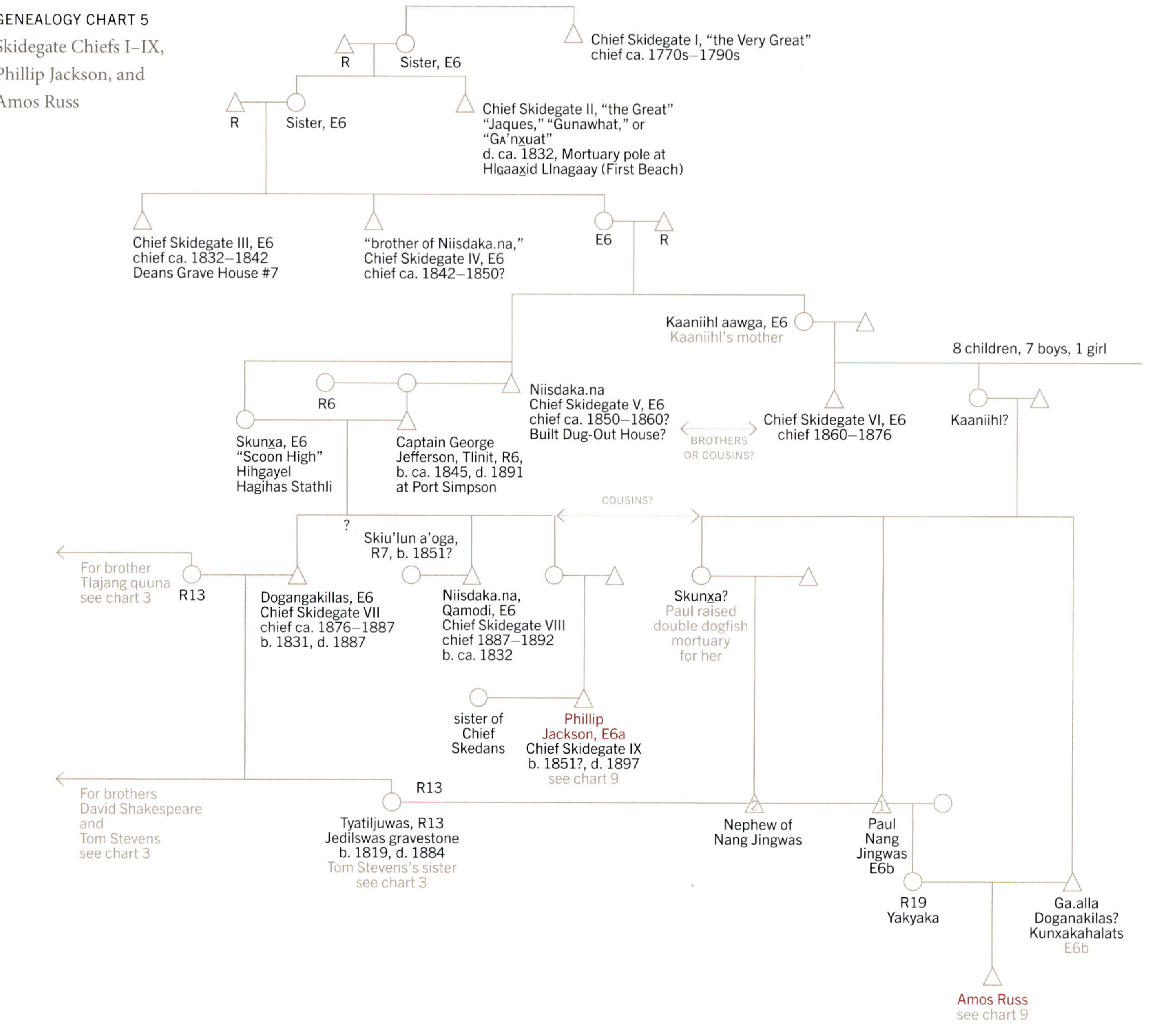

GENEALOGY CHART 5
Skidegate Chiefs I–IX, Phillip Jackson, and Amos Russ

model is obscured in the photos, but the figure at the bottom has a humanoid-like face. The figure on the bottom of the old pole in figure 3.57 appears to have a bearlike ear, unlike the Robson model, which is clearly a whale. Perhaps it was a sea-bear, that combines the features of whales and bear. Swanton places his "Killer Whale House" next to and south of Rotten House. It may be that this Killer Whale House, if it was aligned with Rotten House and immediately to the south, was an older house positioned in the back row of houses behind House in Which People Must Shout to Be Heard. This back row of old houses is only partially visible in the historical photographs, but there is an old pole in the row behind that has a whale on it (head down), but this pole doesn't have a dogfish at the top (see figure 3.57). The Ts'aamus is a crest of the Jiiaxwii SḵahladasG̲aay (R5) (Swanton 1905a, 269), a supernatural being that can take many different forms. Perhaps the figure at the bottom was a Ts'aamus in the form of a sea bear.

Phillip Jackson / *See Genealogy Chart 5*

Deans reports that Phillip Jackson became Chief Skidegate IX in 1893 after the death of the previous chief in the last winter: "On account of Chief Skidegate's death last winter [1892], Jackson has been duly elected chief, so his name is now Skidegate" (Deans 1893b, 89). Phillip Jackson, of the Naa 'Yuuwans X̲aaydaG̲aay (E6a), held the name Chief Skidegate before Peter Brown (1892 through his death in 1897). He was baptized July 12, 1893. His gravestone may be the one that has the inscription: "Skidegate d. 1897 age 56" (see Appendix I, Chronology of the SG̲iidagiids Town Chiefs). He made one model, "Mountain House," which is now missing. It is possible that he also made Model Pole No. 8, Gidansda X̲aad, "Memorial Tomb of Skidance," since he is the one who with his wife raised the full sized X̲aad. Thanks to Newcombe's notes, we know that Phillip Jackson was married not to the "daughter" of Skedans as Deans said, but rather to the sister of Chief Skedans (R4) (see Model Pole No. 8, below.[64] The 1891 census for Skidegate lists Chief Skidegate (Family #371), age forty, living with Moses McKay and his wife Eliza (Sarah Jefferson?). He would have been the Chief Skidegate who died in 1892, although his age here seems too young. The name of Phillip Jackson does not appear in this census.[65]

MODEL POLE NO. 6

K̲alga Jaada Q'aa.l, "Kalga Jaada Memorial Pole," represents a dogfish with its head and pectoral fins at the bottom and the body with two dorsal fins, spines, and tail pointing up. It holds in its mouth a sculpin with its tail coming down below the mouth between the dogfish pectoral fins (figure 3.59). The model obscures the view of House Model No. 8 in the WCE installation photograph (see figure 3.56). According to Deans, it was erected by a woman named "Cannah," [Kaaniihl] wife of a man named Lansing (Moses McKay), in memory of as well as to hold the remains of her grandmother "Call-cah- juil" (K̲alga Jaada, Ice Woman).[66] Moses McKay (R10) was married to Sarah Jefferson (Kaaniihl, Naa 'Yuuwans X̲aaydaG̲aay, E6a). The dogfish with its head at the bottom devours a sculpin, the crest of "Call-cah-juil" (K̲alga Jaad) (Deans 1893b, 87). Henry Moody gave Newcombe the name of this woman as Hitlgayet del ga Hagihas "no one could cross over her" [Gam nan tl'aa la t'algii k̲aa hll.nga gang] (SHIP, September 18, 2007).[67]

The original memorial pole stood in front of "Killer Whale House" discussed above (see figure 3.57). A Maynard photograph of it clearly shows a small sculpin in the mouth of the dogfish (see figure 3.33, left). The model is a very close copy. The story of K̲alga Jaad is an important one in Haida history, going back to the time of

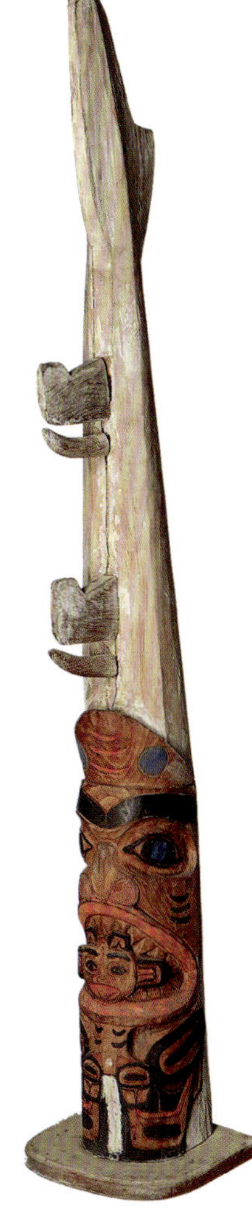

3.59 Model Pole No. 6, Kalga Jaada Q'aa.l, 1892, 54 in. h × 9 in. d. Courtesy of the Field Museum, cat. no. 17810. Photograph by Gail Specht. Full-size pole was erected by a woman named Kaaniihl in honor of her grandmother, K̲alga Jaada (Woman of the Ice) (Deans 1893b, 87). (See Maynard photo, figure 3.33 double finned dogfish, second from left).

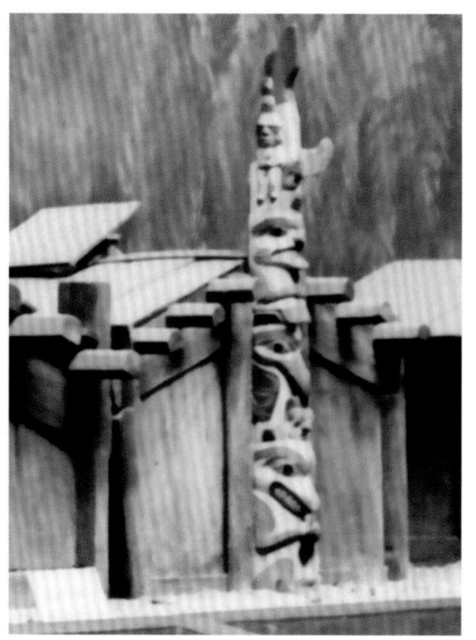

3.60 *above* Missing Model House No. 9, Naa Ǥawdlas, "New House," made by William Dickson (Dixon), 1892 (missing from Brooklyn Museum, cat. no. 05.589.7787, exchanged with the Field Museum, original cat. no. 17808) (detail of figure 3.38). © The Field Museum, image no. CSA 8055.

the ice age. As the climate became colder and colder and the land was covered by ice and snow, the Haida were led by Ḵalga Jaad to the south, where they lived until the climate warmed, when they returned to their Haida Gwaii home (Wilson and Harris 2005, 126; Haida Gwaii Museum 2014, 50). James Deans published this story twice, spelling the name "Calcah Jude" (Deans 1895, 66; Deans 1899b, 3).

HOUSE MODEL NO. 9 / *Made by William Dickson (Dixon)*

William Dickson (Dixon) made "Nah Clechus, New House," spelled Naa Ǥawdlas, based on an old photo of Skidegate "taken 16 years ago," according to Deans in 1893 (figure 3.60). This must have been one of the photos taken in 1878 by George Dawson. This house appears in both the Dawson and Dossetter photos (figures 3.61; see figure 2.5 middle). Unfortunately, the house model is now missing. Deans reports that the original house belonged to some of Jackson's wife's relatives. He describes the figures on the model as a bear or wolf with the doorway in its belly, a raven with an eagle at the tail, dogfish woman at the top, with watchmen, "tuden skeel" (Daajing sgilgaay) at either side of the upraised tail. The original house did not have the door in the frontal pole. Newcombe's notes identify this full-size house as #16, based on the Dawson photograph. According to Newcombe, the house belonged to a recent Chief Skidegate named Doganais or Doganaikilas.[68] "He was Amos Russ's father. His wife was named Yak'yaka' . . . She belonged to the Naikun keowai [R19]. Crests seen are Dogfish followed by raven, the crests of the man and at the bottom is a sgana, the crest of the woman."[69]

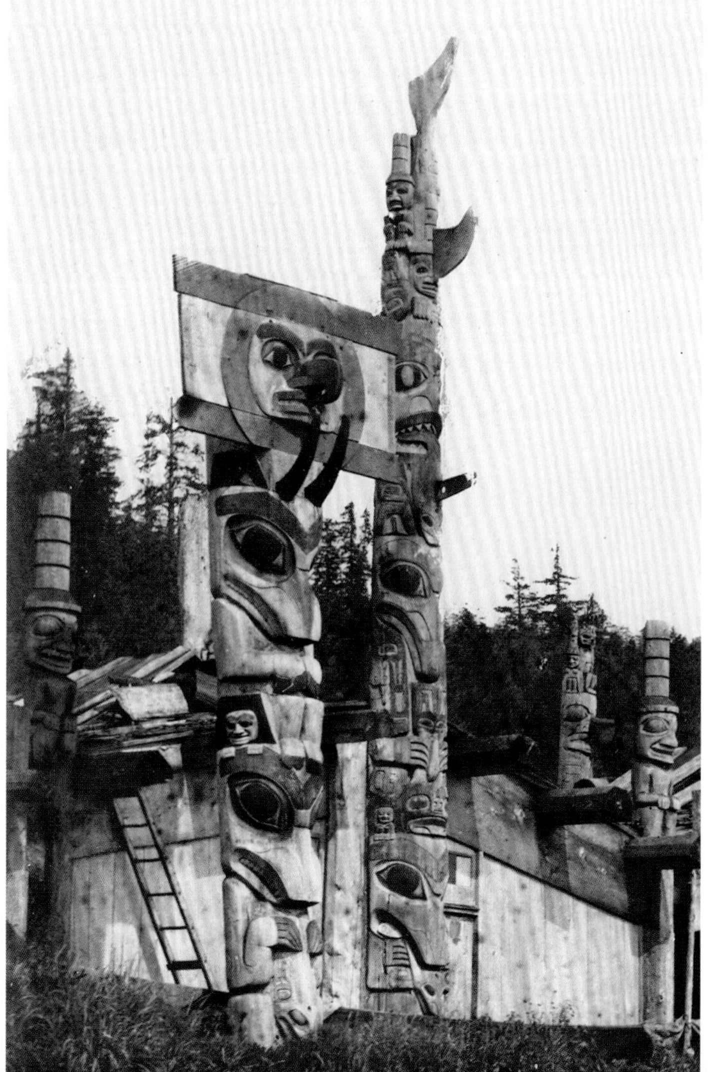

3.61 "House Chiefs Peep at from a Distance (because it is too great to come near)," and Gidansda mortuary pole, detail of photograph by George M. Dawson, 1878. Courtesy of the Canadian Museum of History No. PA37756 (detail of figure 2.3, left).

The photographs of this pole show the bottom figure does not appear to be a whale (SG̱aana) as Newcombe, above, and later MacDonald repeats (MacDonald 1983, 52). It has bearlike ears and arms and legs, holding a seallike figure in its mouth. The original house had human watchmen figures on the corner posts, but the model did not have these. Newcombe does not give a name for this house, but MacDonald calls it "House Chiefs Peep at from a Distance (because it is too great to come near)" (MacDonald 1983, 52). This name was given by Swanton to his house #21 Na'gi ɪ'ʟx-agit k!a'-idᴀngᴀns. A house by this name is said to have stood at Tlell along with its neighbor, Stil na'as "Steel House," both owned by the Naa 'Yuuwans X̱aaydaG̱aay (E6a) (Swanton 1905a, 286).

William Dickson (Dixon) / *See Genealogy Chart 6*

William Dickson (figure 3.62) was listed in the 1891 Skidegate census #380 (age thirty) with his wife, Susan (age twenty-seven), with their children, Simon (age eight) and Maria (age six). His gravestone says: "b. 1866, d. March 10, 1904, married Louisa" (#17). It is unknown how (or if) William Dickson was related to George Dickson, the maker of House Model No. 19. George Dixon (age thirty) is listed in the 1891 census for Skidegate with his wife Mary (age twenty-five) (see below).

William was of the Jiiaxwii Gidin.naay (E11) (Seaward Eagles clan) according to Henry Young (Barbeau 1916–1954, Unpublished Notebooks) who came from the Cape Ball area. William was baptized by the Methodist minister Rev. Crosby on October 5, 1885. Marius Barbeau discusses William Dickson as a carver of argillite shaman figures (Barbeau 1958, 3–4) and argillite platters (Barbeau 1957, 10). However, Barbeau's attributions should be questioned. One of the platters Barbeau attributes to William Dickson has also been attributed to John Robson and is now believed to be by John Cross, based on its style (Barbeau 1957, 11, figure 7; MacDonald 1996, 217, plate 157). An argillite figural shaman group attributed to William Dickson by Barbeau was collected by Rev. Thomas Crosby, said to be a friend to Dickson, but Barbeau goes on to say this carving (NMAI, cat. no.15/4538) was attributed to Thomas "Collison" by Luke Watson and Charlie Gladstone (Barbeau 1957, 4, figure 2). Since the model house is now missing, and the existing photographs don't allow a close examination, it is difficult to say much about the carving style. William Dickson and John Cross were apparently closely related. John Cross's son Robert Cross Sr. was adopted by William and Susan Dixon. Robert married Louisa Smith Dixon and had two sons, Pat Dixon, a well-known twentieth-century argillite carver, and his brother Denny, and a daughter, Molly.

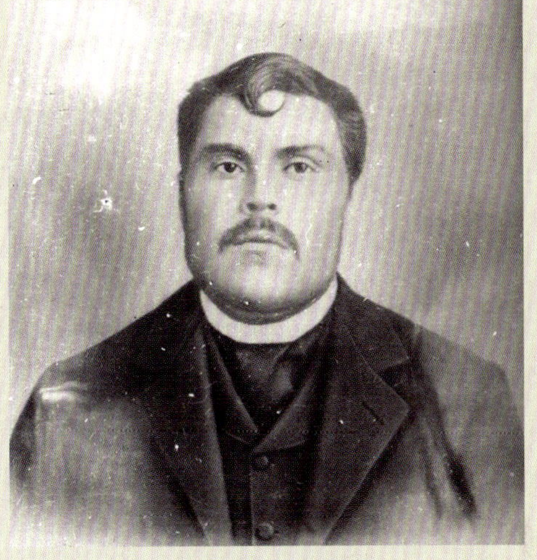

3.62 This is a portrait identified as William Dixon, Ayaai, a Raven of Skidegate by Barbeau. The footnote to the figure says "Old photo of the carver William Dixon shows him wearing a roman collar, like the clergy, to imitate the Rev. Mr. Kirby's costume. This photo was identified as Dixon by Henry Young of Skidegate" (Barbeau 1958, 3, figure 1, fn1). Canadian Museum of History #102048, CD1996-1149-023. Identified in Canadian Museum of History records as "Portrait of a former chief of Skidegate, Marius Barbeau, 1947," I have found no evidence to suggest that William Dixon was a former chief of Skidegate, nor that he was a Raven (see Genealogy Chart 6). In fact, Henry Young identified him to Barbeau as an Eagle (Barbeau 1916–1954, Unpublished Notebooks).

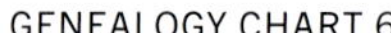

GENEALOGY CHART 6

William Dickson (Dixon), George Dickson (Dixon), and George Young

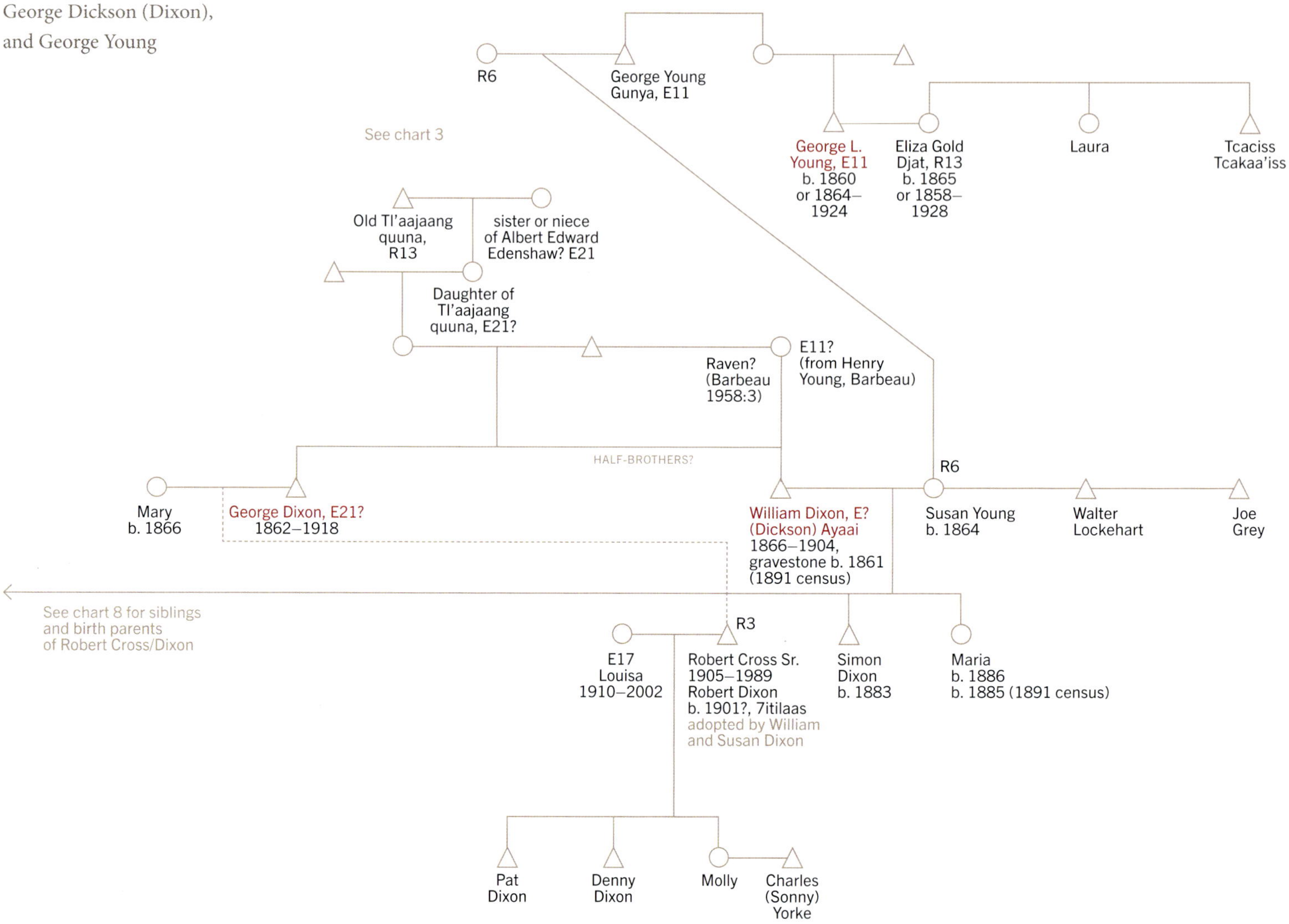

MODEL POLE NO. 8

Gidansda X̱aad, "Gidansda Mortuary Pole," called by Deans "the Memorial tomb of Skidance," stood in front and slightly to the south of the house described above (figures 3.63, 3.64).[70] It had been erected before Dawson's 1878 photo was taken (see figure 3.61). Deans reports that the original pole was raised by the owner of the house it was in front of, a Skidegate man (Phillip Jackson) and his wife, to the memory of her "father" who was "a late chief of the Skedans tribe," suggesting that he had passed away by 1893. According to Newcombe (1906), Phillip Jackson's wife was the sister of Chief Gidansda, and she put up the majority of the money for the raising of the pole, which is recorded by marks cut on the back of the pole, each signifying twenty blankets given away by her, valued at $2.50 per blanket. This pole was raised before its honoree passed

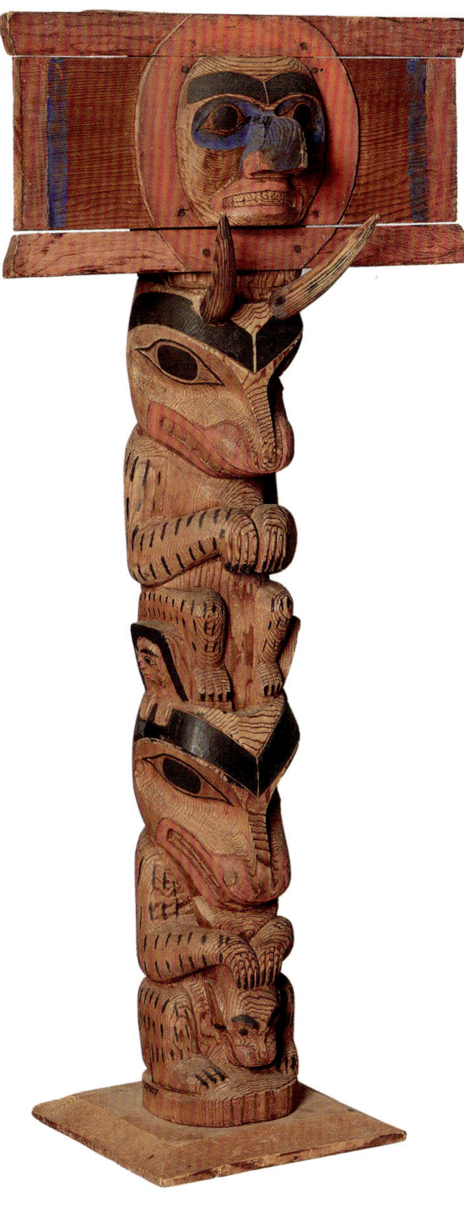

3.63 Model Mortuary Pole No. 8, Gidansda X̱aad, "Gidansda Mortuary Pole," 1892, 34.75 in. × 16.5 in. × 8 in. The full-size pole (see figure 3.61) was erected before 1878 in honor of Chief Skedans (Gidansda) before his death by his sister and her husband, Phillip Jackson (Chief Skidegate IX). Courtesy of the Field Museum, cat. no. 17807. Photograph by Gail Specht.

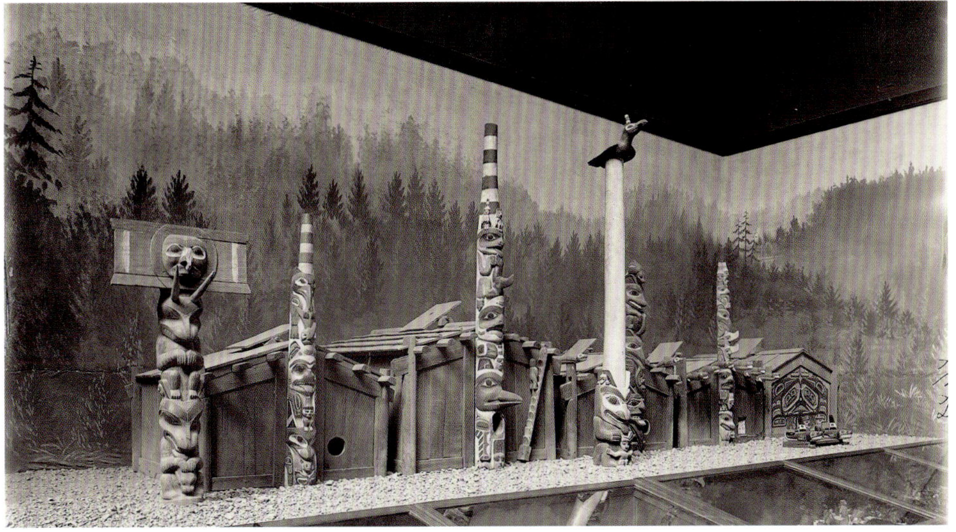

3.64 Jackson Park installation of World's Columbian Exposition poles showing the model of Gidansda X̱aad (cat. no. 17807) displayed at the far left, pre-1921. © The Field Museum, image no. CSA8070.

away, since Newcombe says that Skedans himself was present at the potlatch at its raising.[71] Though this monument is in the form of a mortuary pole, the body of this deceased chief was buried at a later date in the cemetery in Skidegate. Dawson met and described Chief Skedans as a middle-aged man on July 14, 1878 (Cole and Lockner 1993, 39). It would have been this man that mortuary was honoring. The village of Skedans was occupied when Dawson was there in 1878, but shortly afterward the inhabitants moved north to Skidegate.

In 1906, Newcombe reported that this mortuary was erected by the predecessor of the present Chief Skidegate (who was then Peter Brown), who he says was married to *a sister* of Chief Skedans, and that he and his wife wished to do honor to Chief Skedans during his lifetime. He reports that this Skedans was distant from the current Chief Skedans (Henry Moody) by one intermediate chief (the intermediate chief would be Peter Tate). Newcombe corrected Deans in identifying the woman who raised this pole, the wife of Skidegate, as Skedans's sister (not his daughter, as Deans incorrectly says).[72] The figures are a brown bear at the base and mountain goat above, with a moon on the mortuary panel, all crests of the G̱aag'yals K̲iiG̱awaay, "Those Born at Dead Tree Point" (R4).[73] The original Skedans pole was taken to Stanley Park, where it fell and remained next to a replica carved by Mungo Martin. Today a new replica carved by Bill Reid and Werner True stands in this place.

On April 14–15, 2017, a memorial potlatch and headstone raising was held in Skidegate for the late Chief Gidansda, Percy Williams (1930–2015), and a pole in

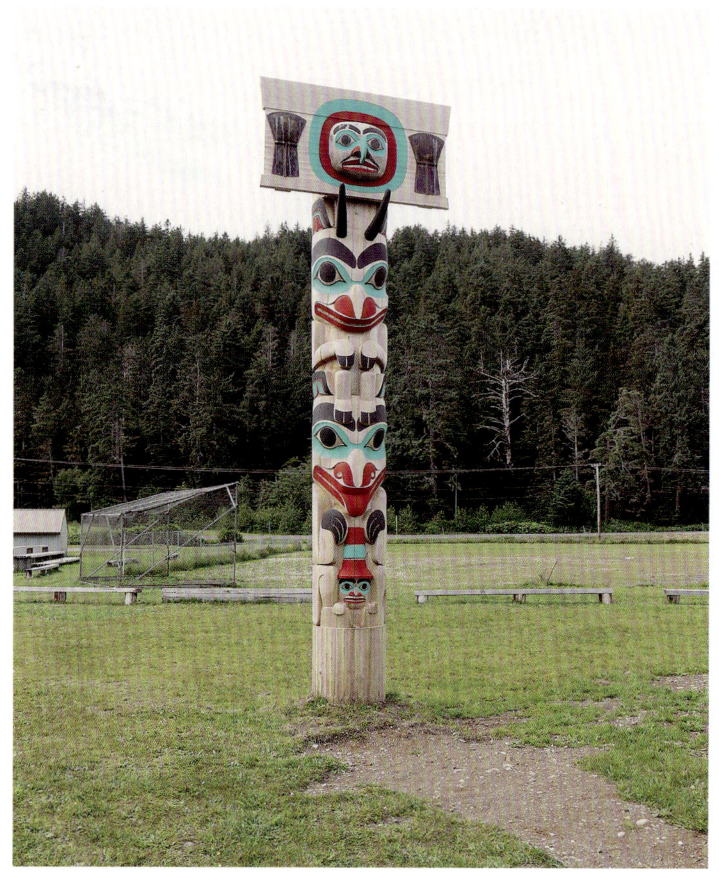

3.65 Gidansda Mortuary Pole, raised in Hlg̱aagilda Llnagaay in honor of Percy Williams, April 15, 2017. Photograph by the author.

his honor was raised on a hill overlooking Skidegate in the playfield outside the George Brown Recreational Centre (figure 3.65). This was followed by the installation ceremony for the new Chief Gidansda (Guujaaw). On this occasion twenty-five new coppers were given out to the Haida Hereditary chiefs, visiting chiefs, and other honored guests. The new pole closely replicates the old Skedans pole that was raised in Skidegate by Phillip Jackson, with the moon on the top panel, a mountain goat below, and a bear at the bottom—all crests of the G̱aag'yals K̲iig̱awaay, Ravens of Skedans. The new pole has two coppers attached on either side of the moon on the top panel, no human figures in the bear's ears, and a human figure wearing a chief's hat being held by the bear at the bottom.

The previous Chiefs Gidansda, in reverse order, were Niis Wes (Ernie Wilson, 1913–2009), James Roy Wilson (1905–1984), Susan Moody Young Williams (1866–1971), George Young (1893–1975), Henry Moody (1872–1945), Peter Tate (1836–1901), and the Gidansda known as "Captain Skedans." A "Captain Skedans" is listed in the 1891 census, age fifty-eight, living in Clew with his brother Peter Tate, age sixty. The Gidansda for whom the old pole was raised would have been his predecessor, likely the Gidansda who met Dawson in 1878.

Poles

In our ways, "the event" is as important as the Pole itself. Raising a pole and opening a House are the highest level of Potlatch.

In the Potlatch, individuals, the House, Coppers and Canoes are given names. Particular individuals are entitled to be tattooed and people are initiated into Dance societies.

It is the chance for the Clan to show the people who they are in relation to Haida Gwaii.

This is the Law-making process followed by payments of debts associated with the event and witnesses gifted, all critical to the economic system which is measured on not how much property is held, but rather by how much is given.

—Chief Gidansda, Guujaaw, May 26, 2022

HOUSE MODEL NO. 12

The missing House Model No. 12, called X̱uuya Naas "Raven House" by Deans, is thought to represent Naa G̱ii iitl'lx̱id Ḵayd Aanagung, "House Chief Peeped at from a distance because it was too great to let them come near" (figure 3.66). According to Deans's numbering system, this model would have been placed between Hliman Naas (No. 11) and Dug-Out House (No. 13) in the WCE installation, but instead the John Cross model house No. 2/21 was placed there (see figure 3.2, left). This was corrected (likely by Boas) in the installation, where the model was placed between G̱awdll Naas (No. 9) and Nang Jingwas Naas (No. 10). In the village the original old house (Newcombe's #17 and MacDonald's #22) on which model No. 12 was based was located immediately to the south/left of Paul Nang Jingwas's house and (to the north/right of) Doganakilas's house (figure 3.67), as in the WCE installation. Deans reports that this house was owned by one of the Chief Skidegates who died in 1888 or 1889 (Deans 1893c, 8). In another account he implies the owner had the name "Nastacana" (Niisdaka.na). He suggests that this man inherited the Chief Skidegate position from his brother, when he died, and the old chief's house was pulled down and a new one erected by Niisdaka.na near to it. Deans reports that this man was Chief Skidegate in 1880 and that he was the sixth in succession to "Skidegate the Great."[74] The figures on the model pole are identified as whale on bottom eating seal, Bright Sunshine, raven with feet on the tail of the dogfish (Deans 1893b, 35–36).

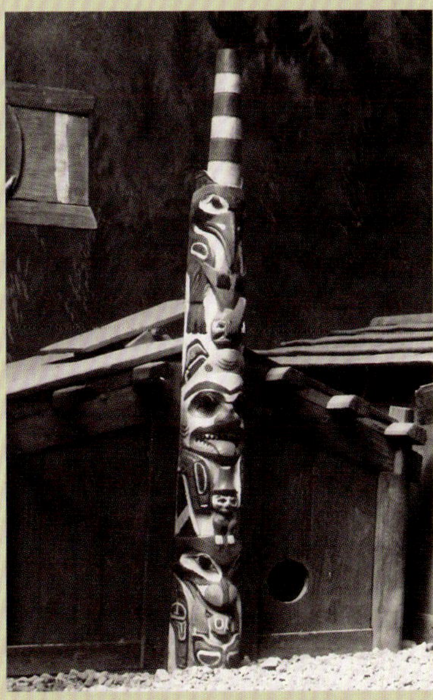

3.66 Missing House Model No. 12, X̱uuya Naas, "Raven House," or Naa G̱ii iitl'lx̱id Ḵayd Aanagung, "House Chief Peeped at from a distance because it was too great to let them come near," 1892. University of Pennsylvania Museum, cat. no. 37.684 (loaned to the Boy Scouts, now missing, originally the Field Museum, cat. no. 17806). Detail of figure 3.64 (left).

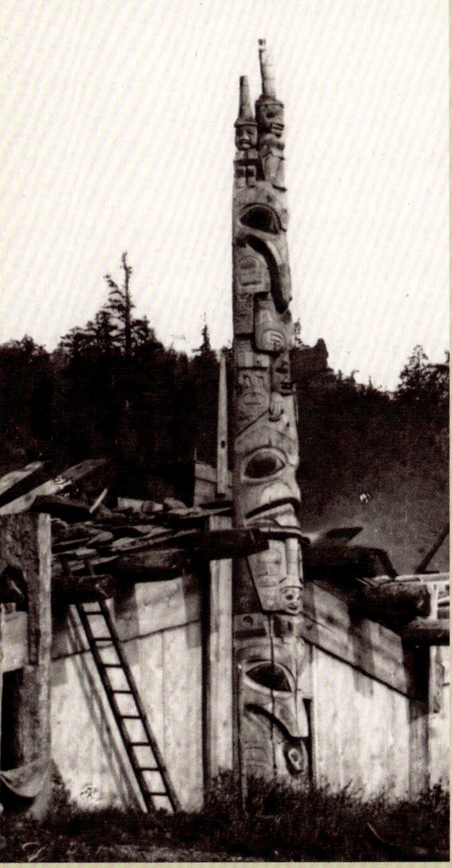

3.67 HlG̱aagilda Llnagaay (Skidegate), 1878. Detail of photograph by George M. Dawson showing Naa G̱ii iitl'lx̱id Ḵayd Aanagung, "House Chief Peeped at from a distance because it was too great to let them come near." Courtesy of the Canadian Museum of History, no. PA37756 (see figure 2.3).

Contradicting Deans, Newcombe identifies the owner of the house (his #17) as Nang Jingwas's brother, the highest chief of the Naa S'aagaas X̱aaydaG̱aay (E6b).[75] He goes on to say that Amos Russ's father was a brother to Nang Jingwas. He gives the name of the house as Nagi itlʌgit kaidʌngans, "the house people are ashamed to look at," spelled today: Naa G̱ii iitl'lx̱id Ḵayd Aanagung, with the translation "House Chief Peeped at from a distance because it was too great to let them come near" (SHIP email September 30, 2020). The wife's name was Queskun unʌnds, "high up in the sky."[76]

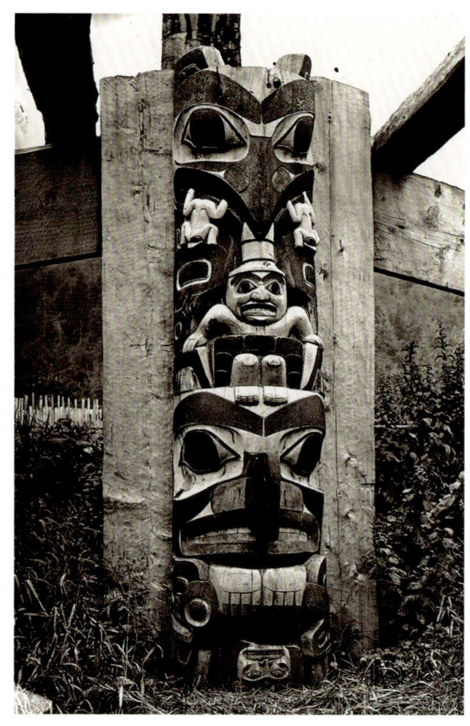

3.68 Inside house post from Naa G̱ii iitl'lx̱id Ḵayd Aanagung, "House Chief Peeped at from a distance because it was too great to let them come near." Royal British Columbia Museum, cat. no. 1. Photograph by Edward Dossetter, 1881. American Museum of Natural History Library, Image #42288.

There was an inside house post in both the original house and the model, which is now missing, described by Deans as having a thunderbird with a raven on top flying away with a man. Newcombe describes the original inside house post, now in Victoria (figure 3.68), and gives the name of the house as "'The house which chiefs peep at from concealment' (feeling their inferiority)," which belonged to the chief "Though younger brother must be obeyed," of the "Rotten House" division of the Eagles of Skidegate (Naa S'aagaas X̱aaydaG̱aay, E6b).[77] This would be Paul Nang Jingwas's brother, Dogangakilas.[78]

When Edward Dossetter photographed the house post in 1881, the wall planks had been removed, but the frame and frontal pole were still standing, and laundry was hung in front of the house. By the time the Maynards photographed this post in 1884, the beams of the house were no longer there. The inside house post was purchased by James Deans in 1892 and is now at the Royal British Columbia Museum. Newcombe said this inside house post was made by "one of the Edenshaws of Massett."[79]

HOUSE MODEL NO. 10

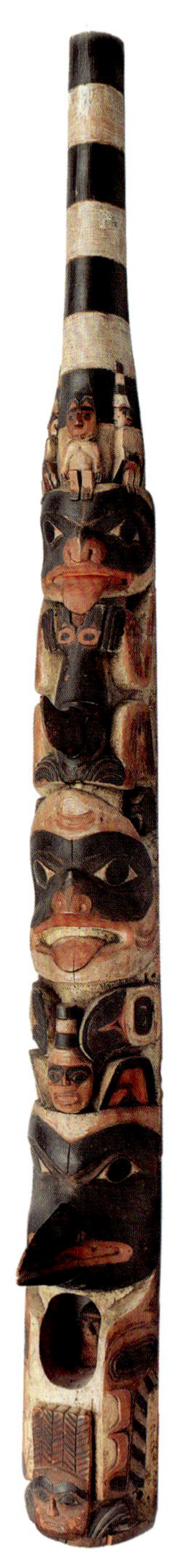

3.69 *right* Frontal pole from House Model No. 10 (house missing), 1892, Iitl'lx̱id Naas or Nang Jingwas Naas, "Chief's House" or "Nang Jingwas' House," 60 in. × 6 in. at base × 9.25 in. at largest nose (152.4 cm × 15.2 cm × 23.5 cm). Brooklyn Museum, cat. no. 05.589.7786, by exchange with the Field Museum, cat. no. 17805. Photograph courtesy of Brooklyn Museum.

This model is a close copy of the original house that belonged to Paul Nang Jingwas (Naa S'aagaas X̱aaydaG̱aay, E6b), even including the ladder that shows on Dossetter's 1881 photograph (figures 3.69, 3.70). A human figure peaks out of the doorway of the model, and another climbs the ladder in the model. Deans called it "Chief's House, Eltga Nui." Today this would be spelled Iitl'lx̱id Naas or Nang Jingwas Naas "Chief's House" or "Nang Jingwas House."

Newton H. Chittenden described "Nin-Ging-wash" as a ranking chief of Skidegate ca. sixty-five years old in 1884, and the richest man in Skidegate. He reported that Nang Jingwas received this name, which means "the long stick," when he erected the frontal pole (Chittenden 1984 [1884], 80–81). Deans repeated this account, adding: "This totem post according to tradition was five fathoms long and cost ten blankets per fathom or in all fifty blankets, each blanket cost by the bale $2.50, or in all independent of house $125" (Deans 1893b, 31).

The figures on the model are a raven with the doorway in its belly (the original

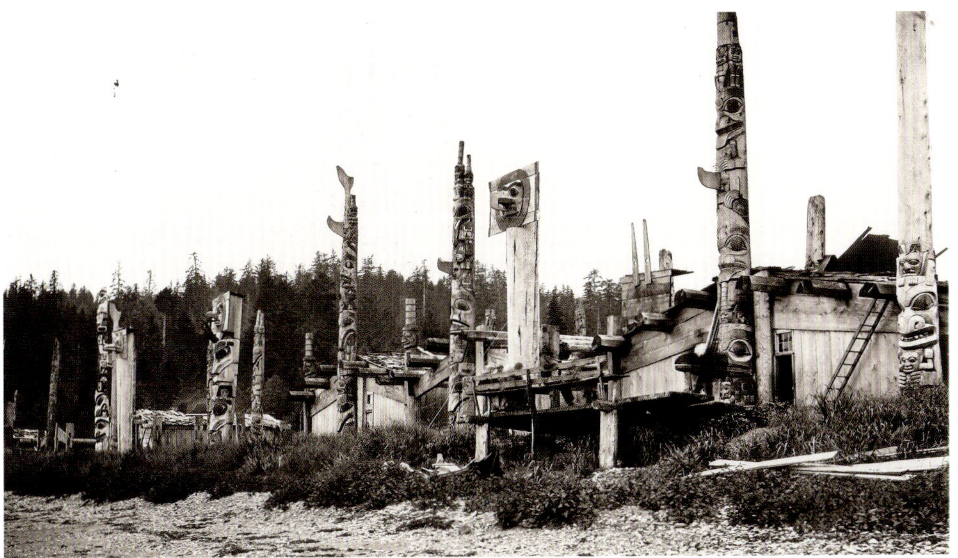

3.70 Paul Nang Jingwas's house in HlG̱aagilda Llnagaay (Skidegate) is on the right in this photograph by Edward Dossetter, 1881. American Museum of Natural History Library, Image #42267 (see also figure 2.6, middle).

house had the door to the side of the pole), a dogfish, bear, and watchmen figures at the top.[80] On the original house frontal pole a small human figure wearing a hat supports the beak of the Raven. Speaking of this figure, Newcombe (his #18) reports: "The latter was put there to shame a son of one of the Edenshaws who 'stole' or induced the Hudson Bay factor at Port Simpson to let him take away, a fine 'copper' left in pledge there by Nang Jingwas for some flour. It was left there for some years. The name of the thief was GinaoAn."[81]

Since Newcombe clearly describes this Ginaawaan as a "son of one of the Edenshaw's," one might assume that this was Charles Edenshaw's son, Robert, whose Haida name was Ginaawaan, but he would have been a small boy, only ten years old at the time Nang Jingwas died in 1888. Since this house was built before it was first photographed in 1878, Robert would not have been born yet. More likely it was the older Ginaawaan, Albert Edward Edenshaw's brother-in-law (Isabella Edenshaw's mother's uncle), and he was incorrectly identified as the son of an Edenshaw. Perhaps this copper was one of the coppers that was attached to the raven-finned memorial pole put up by Ginaawaan in Klinkwan, Alaska. If so, it may have been the one called Mountain-Copper (Ldao t!aos), said to have very little value (Swanton 1905a; see Wright 2001b, 177, 210, 351n43).

John Robson also carved a model of this frontal pole for John Swanton (figure 3.71). Based on Robson's information, Swanton identified the figures on the pole as an eagle in the nest (in the tail of the raven), raven, dogfish woman, and grizzly bear.

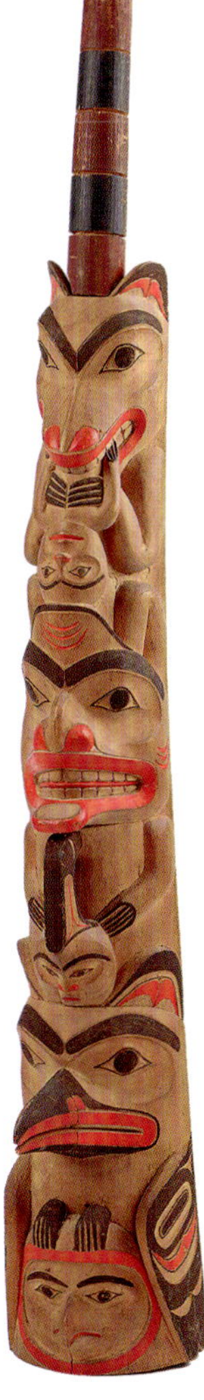

3.71 Model pole commissioned by John Swanton, 1901, made by John Robson, 96.7 cm h × 13.8 cm w × 20 cm d. American Museum of Natural History, cat. no. 16/8748. According to Swanton this represents the house frontal pole belonging to "Nuñ jī'ñwas" [Nang Jingwas] of the Naa S'aagaas X̱aaydaG̱aay (E6b), the grandfather of Amos Russ. His wife's name was "nā'ga să'nłnagaidŭñwas" meaning "in his house there is daylight," of the Naay Kun Ḵiig̱awaay (R13). From the bottom the figures represent grizzly bear, dogfish with labret, raven, and eagle in nest (Swanton 1901b: 1).

He confirms the owner of the pole was Nang Jingwas of the Naa S'aagaas X̱aaydaG̱aay (E6b), the grandfather of Amos Russ.[82] He further identifies Nang Jingwas's wife as nā'ga sa'nłnagaiduñwas "in his house there is daylight," of the Naayii Kun Ḵiig̱awaay (R13) (Swanton 1901a; Swanton 1901b, 123). This would have been his first wife, as his second was said by Chittenden to be the daughter of "Seotsgi" who was Ḵaay'ahl Laanas (E9). Scotsgai's daughter would have been of his wife's clan, Skoa'laadas (R10) (a daughter of Skotsgai was also married to George Young, see George Young in this chapter; MacDonald 1983, 118).[83] Edward Dossetter photographed two men standing in front of this house in 1881 (figure 3.72). Posing as they are in a proprietary manner, it is possible that the one in the uniform is the owner of the house, Paul Nang Jingwas.[84] The man to the right who holds the bowler hat in his hand could possibly his brother, Doganakilas, Amos Russ's father, Ga.alla (Doganakilas?), although there is some disagreement about their identities.[85]

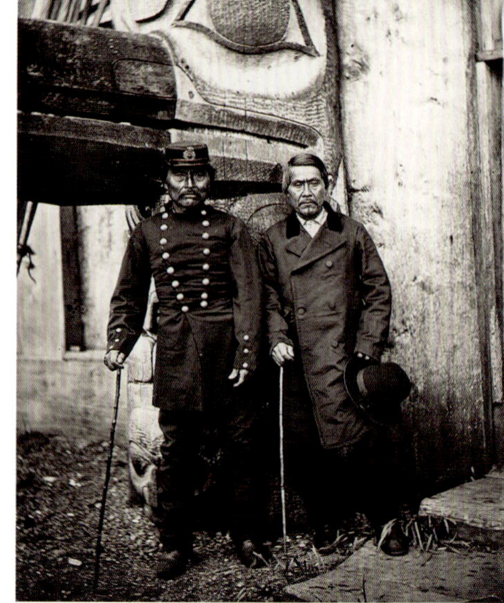

3.72 Two Haida men posing in front of Paul Nang Jingwas's house; their identities are uncertain, but one is likely Paul Nang Jingwas. Photograph by Edward Dossetter, 1881. American Museum of Natural History Library, Image #42263.

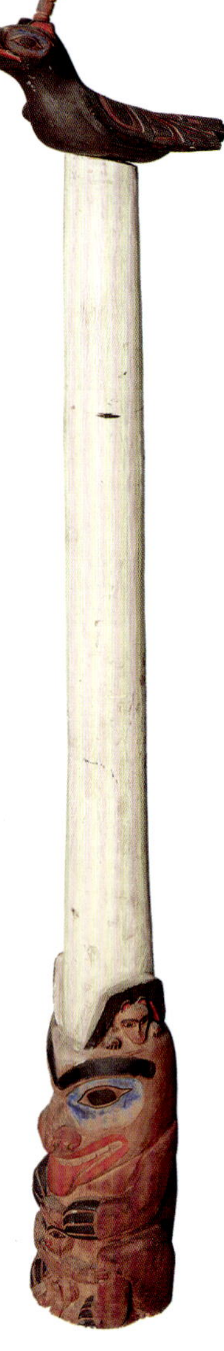

MODEL POLE NO. 9

In front and to the right of Paul Nang Jingwas's house stood a memorial pole that according to Deans was erected by the Chief Skidegate who lived about 1888 in memory of the mother of Chief Skedans (see figure 3.70 far right). It is represented by Model Pole No. 9 (figure 3.73). There is a Raven on top, bear holding a man at bottom. Small bears are in the ears. According to Deans, her name was "Cat-bow-wuss." Chief Gidansda, Percy Williams, said that this name may be Jat-jew-was, meaning "Big Lady" (Percy Williams, personal communication, August 22, 2006), thus the pole might be called Jat-jew-was Q'aa.l or "Jat-jew-was' Memorial Pole." This pole does not appear in Dawson's 1878 photograph of Nang Jingwas's house, so it must have been raised between 1878 and 1881 when Dossetter photographed it.[86]

Deans reports that this type of memorial pole was called "Tillell," now spelled Tl'laal, the word for fireweed (*Epilobium*), because like the plant it was long and slender (Deans 1883b, 89).

3.73 *left* Model Memorial Pole No. 9, Jat-jew-was X̱'aad, "Jat-jew-was' Memorial Pole," Chief Skedan's Mother's Memorial Pole, 160 cm h × 36.8 cm d. Courtesy of the Field Museum, cat. no. 17804. Photograph by Gail Specht.

HOUSE MODEL NO. 11 / *Made by Moses McKay (Lansing)*

Deans was uncertain how to translate the Haida name of this now missing model that he called "Nuh Hlimun Nuus or Nah Thlimmen Nass," which he interpreted as House of the Dolphins (or "walrus" he wasn't sure which), sometimes called Whale House (figure 3.74; Deans 1893c, 7; Deans 1893b, 32). Perhaps he based this interpretation on the dolphin-like figures on the corner posts, although he himself identifies them as whales (see below). The spelling of the Haida name that Deans uses for this house is very similar to the name of a house known in T'aanuu Llnagaay, "Plenty of Tliman Hides in This House," or Hllman Naas "Elk-blanket (skin) House." This word was used frequently in eighteenth-century fur traders' journals to mean the heavy elk hides traded from the Columbia River to the northern tribes for use as armor, so this name would indicate the owner was wealthy.[87] Swanton lists a house in Skidegate (his #20) named "ŁimA'n na'as," interpreted as "ŁîmA'n-blanket house," which he describes as having occupied the place where Amos Russ's house stood in 1901 and belonged to the Naa S'aagaas X̱aaydaG̱aay (E6b) (Swanton 1905a, 286). This most likely is the original house of which Deans's House No. 11 is a model.

Deans recounts two stories about the figures on the pole, which include raven (as woman) with a broken beak at the bottom, in the middle raven with a halibut (part of the broken beak story), and 'WaasG̱uu with a whale was at the top. Deans points out that the 'WaasG̱uu should have several whales in its tail and mouth, and the carver decided to put whales on the corner posts, as he couldn't fit them all on the pole. The two circular doors on this model had swinging closures inside, which Deans instructed should always be placed with the painted side out (Deans 1893c). No old houses that closely resemble this model could be found in the photographs. Deans positioned this model house to the left of the John Cross House Model (no. 2/21) and to the right of Model No. 10, Paul Nang Jingwas's house. The house in this position in the village, located to the immediate right of Nang Jingwas's house, was identified by Newcombe as a house owned by "Eldjiwas" (figure 3.75 left).[88] Newcombe identifies this Eldjiwas [Iljuuwaas] as being of the "Lanatsagas," Laana Tsaadas (E7). According to Swanton (1905a, 274), they lived with the "Gîtîngī'djats" (E6c) at K'il, inside Sandspit point, which they owned.

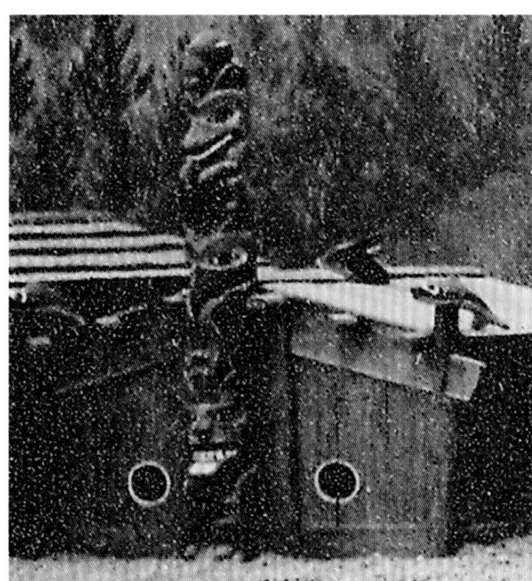

3.74 Missing House Model No. 11, Hllman Naas, "Elk-blanket (skin) House," called by Deans "Nuh Hlimun Nuus or Nah Thlimmen Nass, House of Dolphins," made by Moses McKay (Lansing), 1892. The Field Museum, cat. no. 17803. Purchased by the University of Pennsylvania Museum, 1900, cat. no. 37.688.

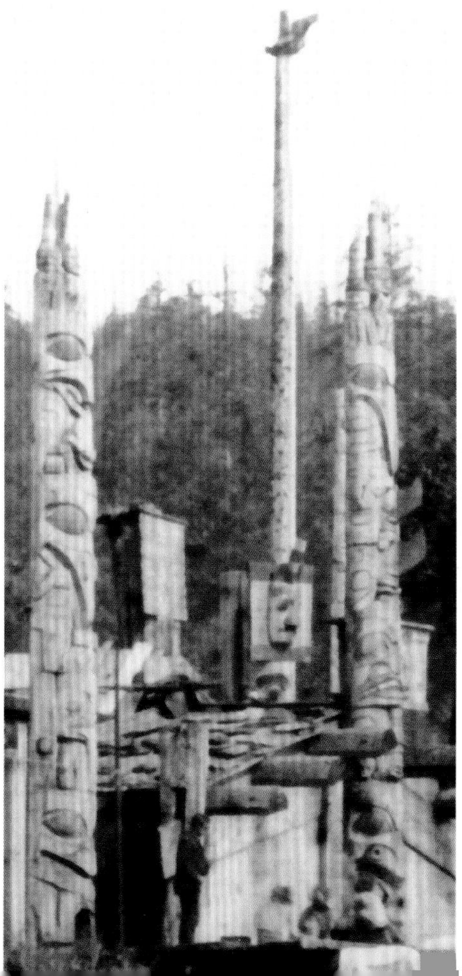

3.75 Detail of George Dawson's photo of HlG̱aagilda Llnagaay (Skidegate), 1878 (see figure 2.3) showing Iljuuwaas's House (left) and Naa Gudgiikyagangs "People call to each other in it" (right).

According to Newcombe, on this old pole the eagle at the top and the raven were the man's crests, and a killer whale at the bottom was the wife's crest, who belonged to the same people as Josephine Gladstone's mother—the Raven clan K'aadaas Gaa K̲'iiG̲awaay (R3).[89] A newer house farther north in the village belonged to Daniel Iljuuwaas, identified as belonging to the E11 clan (see House Model No. 16). It seems unlikely that Newcombe would have described the wife of the Iljuuwaas, who was the owner of this house (the house to the right of Nang Jingwas's house), as "belonging to the same people as Josephine Gladstone's mother," if this Iljuuwaas *was* Daniel Iljuuwaas, since Josephine Gladstone's mother *was* the wife of Daniel Iljuuwaas. He may have been confused about this, unless there were two different men named Iljuuwaas with houses in Skidegate.[90]

A handwritten note says that this pole was smashed when it was taken down for Newcombe in 1897. The original pole of this house differs from the model (No. 11) in having an eagle at the top rather than a 'WaasG̲uu. The figure at the bottom is bearlike with a dorsal fin extending up behind a humanoid figure on its head, perhaps a sea grizzly, as MacDonald suggests, or a 'WaasG̲uu as Deans reports. MacDonald (1983, 50) also identifies the humanoid figure as a mouse with an extended tongue and a mountain spirit at the tip of the tongue. These don't appear on the model pole.

> The Laana Tsaadas (E7) clan recently held the first clan feast in over 150 years. After several generations of cultural dormancy, my brother Jesse and I, as eldest grandchildren of the Matriarch, Evelyn Crosby, felt it was imperative to step up and say: despite all odds, hawanuu adlaan t'alang iijang "WE ARE STILL HERE"!
>
> —Kaalga Jaad Erin Brillon, July 19, 2022

Moses McKay (Lansing) / *See Genealogy Chart 7*

Moses McKay made the model of Hllman Naas (above). He was said to be the sole survivor of the "Seaward Sqoa'ladas," Sgwaahlaadaas (R10) of Ts'aahl Llnagaay (Swanton 1905b, 80, 131). He is also called Lansing by Deans, Swanton, and Newcombe (see note 3.66) and is listed (age thirty-five) in the 1891 census for Skidegate, living with Chief Skidegate (age forty) (Family #371) and Eliza McKay (age thirty-three) and James McKay (age fifteen). Moses was baptized November 26, 1893, and died January 8, 1910, at age sixty-five (b. 1845). It is unclear whether this Eliza was Moses's wife or whether she was also known as Sarah, but Moses was also married to Sarah Jefferson (E6a), and they adopted James McKay, from Sarah's sister, Anne Jefferson, who was the mother of Ed and Louie Collinson. Moses McKay's wife, Sarah Jefferson, must have been the woman who raised the memorial K̲alga Jaada Q'aa.l (Model Pole No. 6). Moses McKay worked as a consultant to Charles Newcombe when he visited Skidegate, helping to identify the owners of poles that Newcombe wished to purchase.

HOUSE MODEL "NO. 2," ACTUALLY NO. 21 / *Made by Niislant, John Cross*

This is likely a model of Naa Gudgiikyagangs, "People call to each other in it" (figure 3.75 right). In the Field Museum catalog this model house (figure 3.76) was called Deans's Model No. "2," but it was misnumbered, since according to Deans's description, House Model No. 2 fits the model of the SG̲ang Gwaay house (see figure 3.13), now in Vienna (Deans 1893b, vol. 38, folder 3, pp. 20–21).[91] There was no House Model No. 21 on Deans's long list (Deans 1893b, vol. 38, folder 3, p. 50), but this model was placed between Iljuuwaas's Hllman Naas, "House of Dolphins" (No. 11), and Dug-Out House (No. 13) in the WCE installation.[92]

The model matches the original pole of the house that stood between Iljuuwaas's Hllman Naas and Dug-Out House in the village. The distinctive double-finned dogfish shows clearly in photographs by both Dawson (figure 3.75) and Dossetter (see

GENEALOGY CHART 7

Moses McKay (Lansing)

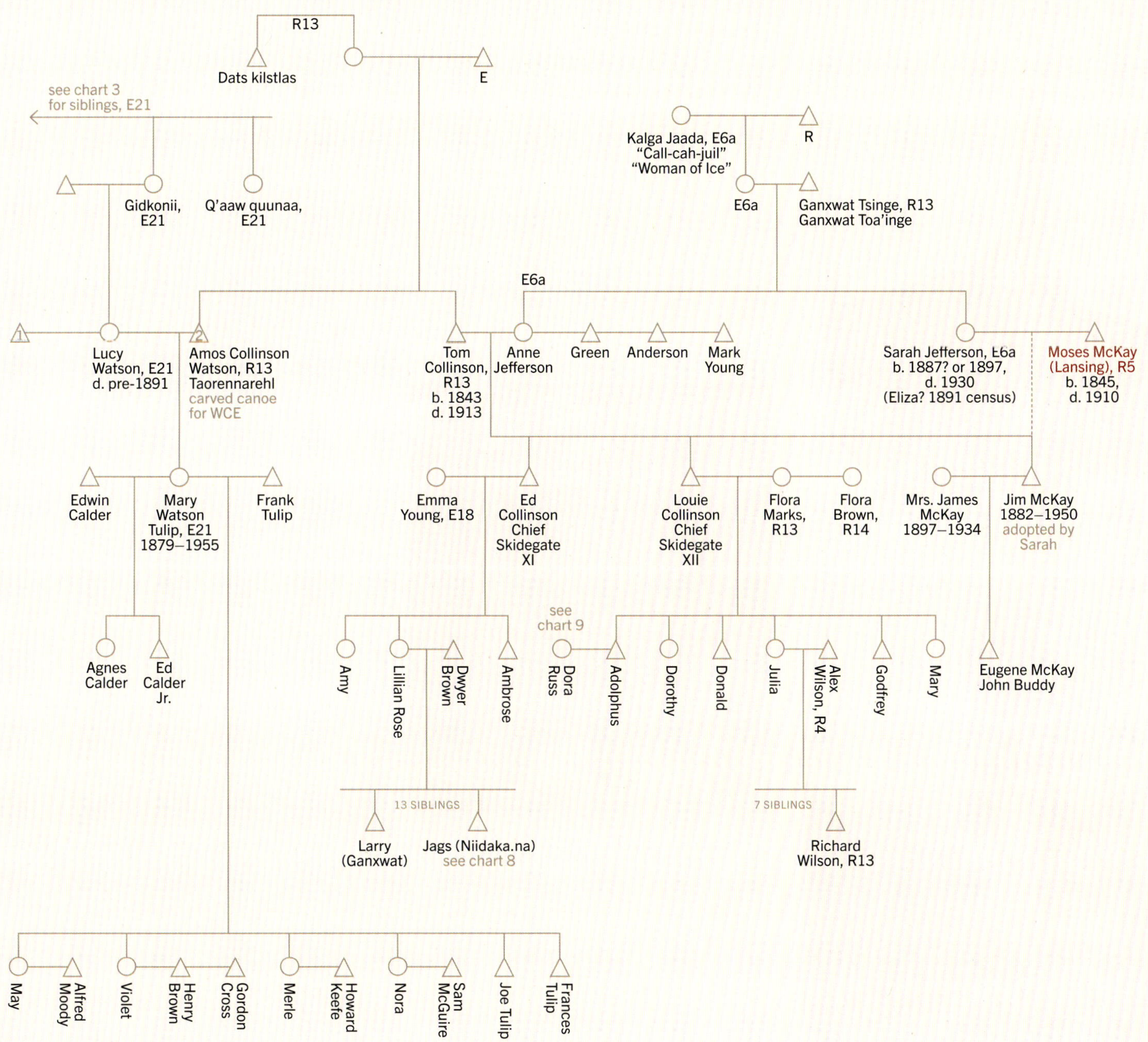

3.76 House Model No. "2" really No. 21, Naa Gudgiikyagangs, "People call to each other in it," 1892, made by Niislant, John Cross, 110 cm × 11 cm × 13 cm. Courtesy of the Field Museum, cat. no. 17802. Photograph by Gail Specht.

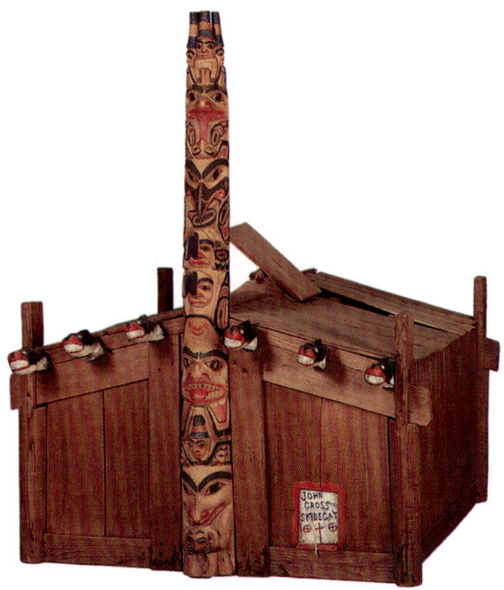

figure 2.6 to the left of the flag pole). Swanton (his #14) gives the house name as "Nā'ga gutgi L! kia'gans, people call to each other in it," so-called because it was too large to make one's self heard across the inside without raising the voice, belonging to the Naa 'Yuuwans X̱aaydaG̱aay (E6a) (Swanton 1905a, 286).[93] Newcombe says this was Nestaqana's (Niisdaka.na) house (his #20), named "Na gutgitl kaigAns," translated: "it is so large that when people inside want to speak to each other they are obliged to shout," now spelled Naa Gudgiikyagangs and translated "People call to each other in it" (SHIP email September 30, 2020). According to Newcombe, when young, this chief had the name Qamoti, and when he died, his name was raised to G.ula kaitlgat or "Grease-dish inlaid with abalone." His wife's name was ItldigAwa.i and was from a Skedans family. She also used the name Qamoti and was a great chief woman in her own right.[94]

Inside the original full-size house there was a house post that was collected by James Deans in 1892 (figure 3.77). Newcombe identifies the figures on this inside house post as raven with a broken beak at the top, and whale below. Inside this model house there is no house post, but there are a shaman figure holding a rattle, and smaller male and female figures flanking him (figure 3.78). In the corner a plain plank hangs from the roof beam, simulating a box drum. These figures are inside a model house that has a closed door, perhaps suggesting this is a private ceremony. This small door is painted white and hangs on a cotton string. It has the name "John Cross Skidegate" painted in black at the top and a cross with flanking circles with crosses inside painted in red below the name. This is the only model house that has the maker's name written on it. No one at the WCE would have been able to see inside, given the way the models were set back on the platform on the display, so why were these figures made? John Cross may not have known that the people viewing the houses would be kept that far away and not able to open the front door or the smoke hole flap to look inside. Shamans were arrested and

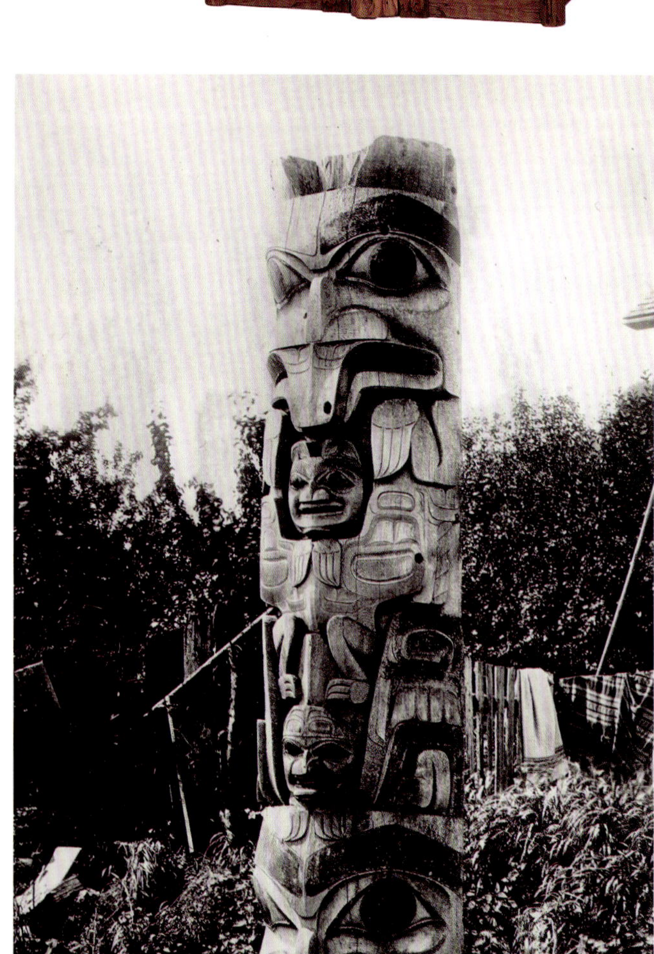

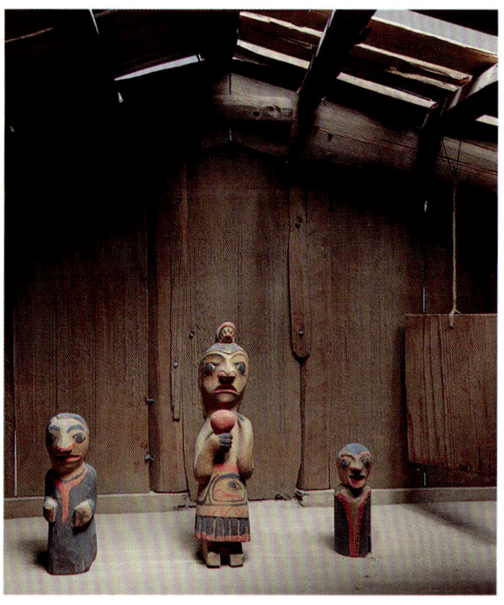

3.77 *left* Inside house post from Naa Gudgiikyagangs. Royal British Columbia Museum, cat. no. 2. © The Field Museum, image no. CSA17452.

3.78 *above* Interior of House Model "No. 2" really No. 21, showing a shaman with round rattle and two small flanking figures, 1892, made by John Cross. Courtesy of the Field Museum, cat. no. 17802. Photograph by Gail Specht.

punished if they were caught doing their work during this time. Their hair was forcibly cut off to remove the spiritual power that resided there.[95] Ironically, at this same time, shamans would earn money by posing with their regalia.[96] Cross's inclusion of the shaman practicing inside the house but hidden from view by a door with a cross is perhaps meant to reflect this social irony. Of course, the cross was a symbol of John Cross's name.

Niislant, John Cross / *See Genealogy Chart 8*

Of all the house model artists, Niislant (John Cross) is among the best known (figure 3.79). He had a distinctive style of carving and has been described as "one of the most prolific jewelers of the time" (Bunn-Marcuse 2007, 88–97; see also Holm 1981, 192–93). There has been some confusion about his clan, but his grandson, Billy Stevens, reported that he was of the of the Naa 'Yuuwans X̱aaydaG̱aay (E6a) (Billy Stevens, personal communication, February 9, 2004).[97] Arthur Moody told Barbeau that Cross had lived for ten years at Xaayna Llnagaay on Maude Island before moving to HlG̱aagilda and that he lived there with his "uncle Dan."[98] His first wife was Fanny Iljuuwaas (variously spelled Ellsworth, Ellguwaas, etc.), the half-sister of Josephine Iljuuwaas Gladstone. They were both of the K'aadaas Gaa K̲'iiG̱awaay (R3). Fanny preceded him in death on November 24, 1918 (BC Archives Microfilm #13363). They had eight children, including Hazel Stevens (d. 2000), the mother of Billy Stevens (d. 2007).[99]

Cross later married Annie, Ike Hans's mother. Two of his sons, Raymond and Gordon, were raised by their aunt Josephine Gladstone. Rae and Gordon were interviewed by Marius Barbeau in 1947. They described their father as a Sea Sculpin who was famous as a warrior who fought in the last battle with the Hlawak Tlingit. They reported that he was a crack shot, a sniper, and a seal hunter as well as an artist and a storyteller. He made his gun sight out of a gold piece. They said he earned his living from his carving and carved until he died (Barbeau 1916–1954, box 314, folder 11). He died at age eighty-five on February 2, 1939, at Skidegate (BC Archives Microfilm #B13374).

Perhaps recognizing his considerable carving skill, Deans commissioned John Cross to make three of the model houses

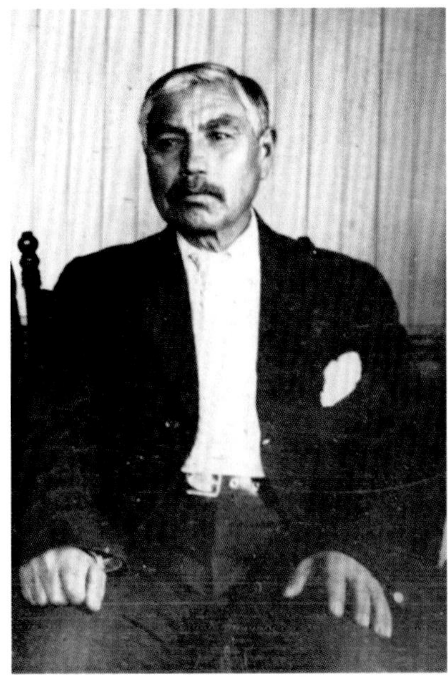

3.79 Niislant, John Cross, ca. 1910. Photograph from Hazel Stevens. Courtesy of the Haida Gwaii Museum at K̲ay Llnagaay, Skidegate, BC, Canada, Image Ph 05459.

"People call to each other in it" (No. "2," really No. 21), which has his name on the door, "Food House" (No. 14) and "Copper House" (No. 26), both now unfortunately missing (see below). He worked in wood as well as argillite, silver, and gold and he also did tattooing.[100] Bill Holm pointed out that nineteen of the twenty-seven tattoo designs published by Swanton (each identified by artist) were made for him in crayon by John Cross (Holm 1981, 192–93; Swanton 1905b, plates XX 1–7, 9–11, 13–17, and XXI 2, 4, 6, 10). The original drawings are in the American Museum of Natural History Anthropological Archives (figure 3.80). These drawings help to attribute other two-dimensional designs by Cross. The formline ovoid of the eye socket is consistently unbroken, with a formline-U appended to the ovoid in the cheek area, with the formline of the lower jaw attached to the U. Secondary Us often flare at the base and taper at the top, eyelid lines are often constricted in his two-dimensional designs. As described by Holm, his "flat designs are almost frantic in their dynamic action." Unfilled spaces around the main design on platters were often filled with U-forms based on the edge of the platter with double secondary Us inside (figure 3.81). Stylized faces inside ovoids often had long eyebrows with a central hump and upturned forward end (see Holm 1981, 192–93). The model of Naa Gudgiikyagangs gives us an

3.80 *right* Drawing of five-finned whale in crayon on paper, made by John Cross for John Swanton 1901. 20.3 cm × 28 cm. Courtesy of the American Museum of Natural History, Anthropological Archives Z/24 F (see Swanton 1905b, plate XX 17).

3.81 *below* Argillite platter with five-finned whale design attributed to John Cross. Florida Museum of Natural History, cat. no. P-1200. Photograph by Jeff Gage.

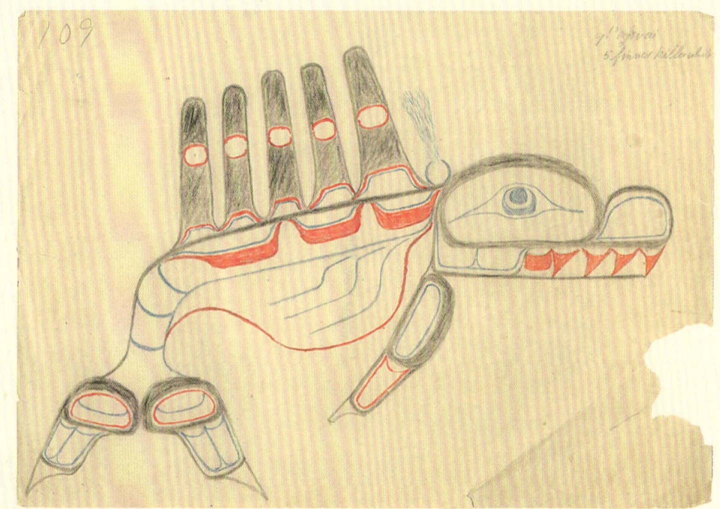

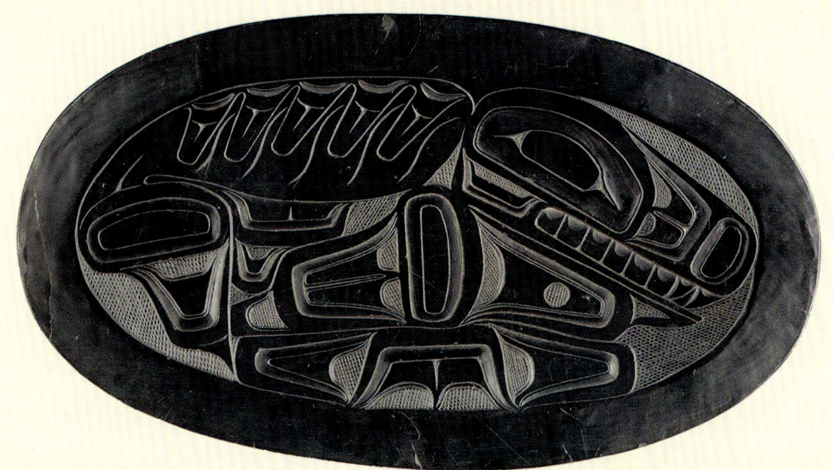

example of how Cross's two-dimensional design was applied to his three-dimensional sculpture. Note the upturned forward end of the eyebrow of the dogfish, secondary double Us with flaring bases and constricted eyelid lines. Naa Gudgiikya-gangs is the only model house that has the artist's name displayed, but Cross signed his name on at least two other pieces, an argillite pipe (Museum of Vancouver, cat. no. AA2337) and a silver bracelet (Royal British Columbia Museum, cat. no. 13064; Bunn-Marcuse 2007, 91). This helps us to attribute many other pieces to him.

Figures that were frequently depicted by Cross on his carvings include the 'Waasg̱uu, and the five-finned whale. As mentioned earlier (see William Dickson in this chapter and note 3.14), his work has often been misattributed to other artists such as George Smith, William Dixon, and John Robson. Drew and Wilson attribute an argillite platter that has a 'Waasg̱uu and naw (octopus) design to William Dixon (Canadian Museum of History, cat. no. VII B 1420) (Drew and Wilson 1980, 206). This was no doubt based on Barbeau's earlier attribution (Barbeau 1957, 10–11). George MacDonald later attributed this platter to John Robson (MacDonald 1996, 216); however, the flaring U-forms, unbroken eye socket ovoid, and jumbled quality of the design signal Cross's style, discussed in much more length by Kathryn Bunn-Marcuse (2007, 88–97).

GENEALOGY CHART 8

John Cross and Daniel Iljuuwaas

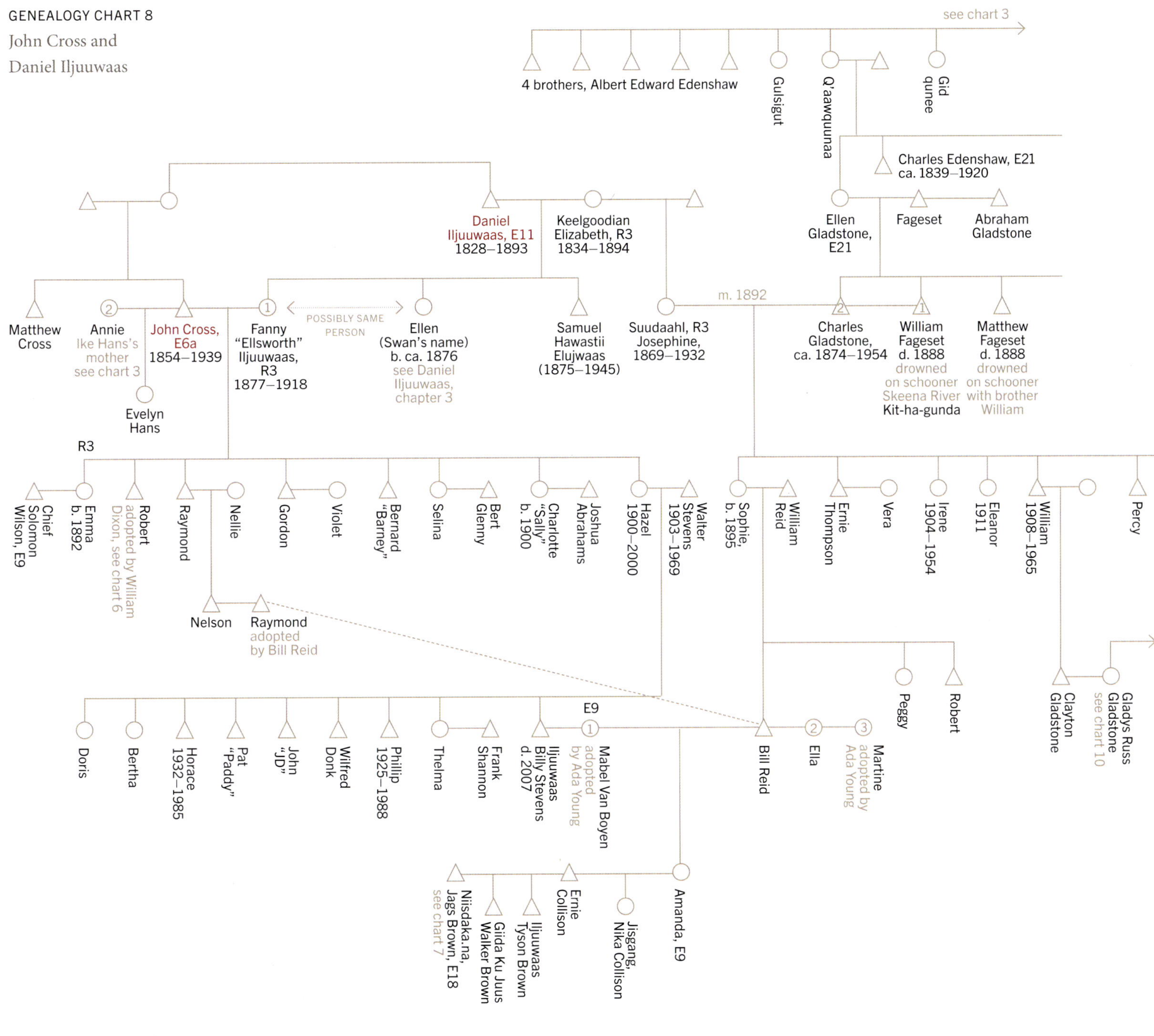

MODEL POLE NO. 10

In front and to the left of "Dug-Out House" stood Skiu'lun awG̱a X̱aad, "Skiu'lun's Mother's Mortuary Pole," that was one of the last old poles standing in Skidegate (figure 3.82; also see figures 2.6 and 3.87 left). It was taken down in 1958 and sent to the Museum of Vancouver. It was repatriated to the Haida Nation in 2019. The model pole was positioned to the right of "Dug-Out House" in the WCE installation and was sent to Vienna after the fair, never having been cataloged by the Field Museum (figures 3.83, 3.86). According to Deans: "Skidegat the present chief, 1892, erected this Suthlingun to receive the remains of his wife in the event of her death, and if she died away from home and was buried there, it showed her husband's respect for her. She died at home and was buried in the graveyard at the village" (Deans 1893b, 1893c, 90). He goes on to say the figures are a man holding a whale, and the Ts'aamus, and that this Chief Skidegate died in December 1892. John Robson also carved a model of this post, now at the American Museum of Natural History in New York (figure 3.84). Swanton's notes record that pole as: "A memorial post set up to a chief's wife, who was the last of the Qo'ganas family. One of her names was Skiu'lun a'oga ("skiu'lun's mother")." He identifies the figures as "Tce'm'as" (Ts'aamus, snag), and "sga'na lqa'na sq!asti'ñ" (two-finned killer whale, SG̱aana K'uunans), both as crests of the wife (Qugaangaas, R7) (Swanton 1901b, 4).

3.82 Skiu'lun awG̱a X̱aad, P. J. Ryan postcard, 1920s. Image PN5583. Courtesy of the Royal BC Museum and Archives.

Newcombe reports that this mortuary was erected for "the wife of one of the Skidegates. She belonged to the Qogangas or sea-otter family of the Ravens R7, which used the killer, tcᴀmaos & rainbow as crests. Of these the two first are seen on the Xat" (figure 3.87 left).[101] Because of this clan affiliation, the pole has been referred to as the Sea Otter Pole (notes with photo at the Haida Gwaii Museum, Canadian Museum of History, Neg. No. 96–30). It is interesting that Swanton says that the two-finned killer whale was a crest of the wife's clan (Qugaangaas, R7) in his description of Robson's model of this pole, but in his listing of clans and crests in his published work, he lists just the killer whale, not specifying a two-finned killer whale, as their crest (Swanton 1905b, 269).[102]

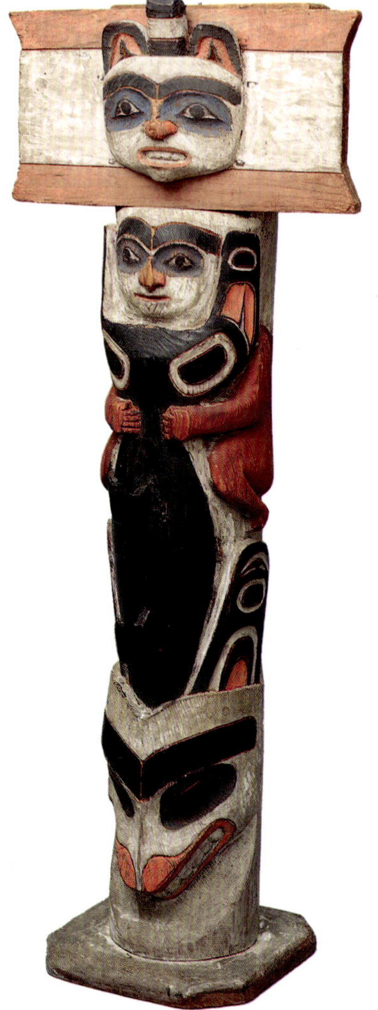

3.83 Model Mortuary Pole No. 10, Skiu'lun awG̱a X̱aad, Deans: "Skiu'lun's Mother's Mortuary Pole," 1892. Never cataloged at the Field Museum but sent by them to the Ethnographic Museum in Austria (now the KHM-Museumsverband, Weltmuseum, Vienna), cat. no. MVK VO_51762 (see figure 3.86 right). Courtesy KHM-Museumsverband, Weltmuseum, Vienna.

An older X̱aad stood to the right (north) of this pole and slightly behind (see figure 3.87, 3.90). It had a grizzly bear on the top panel, a whale with a prominent blow hole at the top, and a sea bear below. This older pole was also said to have been for a wife of one of the Skidegates.[103] No model was made of this pole for the WCE.

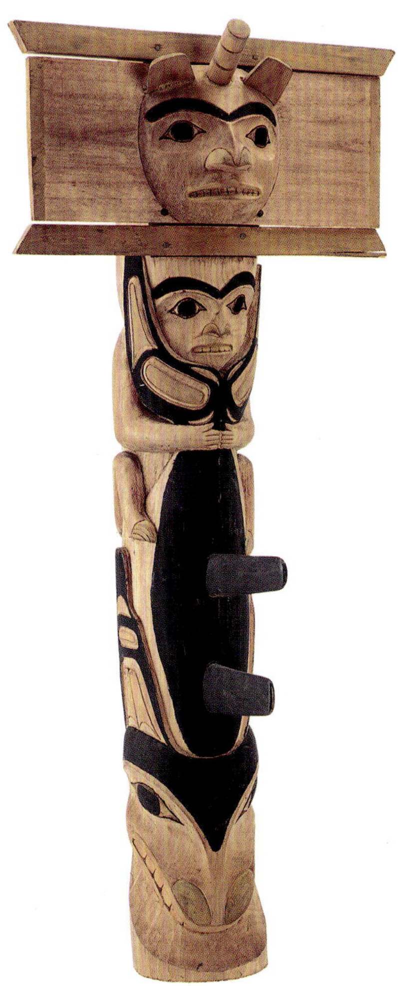

3.84 *above* Model Skiu'lun awg̱a X̱aad, Commissioned by John Swanton, 1901, made by John Robson. 66 cm h × 26 cm w. American Museum of Natural History, cat. no. 16/8759. Photograph by Denis Finnin.

HOUSE MODEL NO. 13

House Model No. 13 was called "Tau gu Cuntle, Dug-Out House" by Deans (figures 3.85, 3.86). This would be spelled Daa.a Guu Ḵaahll in X̱aayda Kil, translated "House Pit/Hole Walk Out." According to Deans, this is a model of the house of the Chief Skidegate who was an invalid 1892: "It is the present chief's house and is habitable although not constantly occupied by him. Being an invalid he generally lives in some of his peoples' houses where their wives see to his wants" (Deans 1893b, 7–38). This would be the Chief Skidegate, Qamoti, who died in October 21, 1892.[104] The name "Dug-Out House" refers to the excavated interior (daa.a, spelled by deans dau, taw, or tau). The right to construct excavated houses was an inherited privilege of certain chiefs. The model is made of yellow cedar and fully painted on the front with a chest-like "double-eye" formline design. On the left side is a more configurative design of a whale with a small dorsal fin, perhaps a baleen whale, while on the right side is a Sg̱aana, killer whale, with the tall dorsal fin bent down across the body.

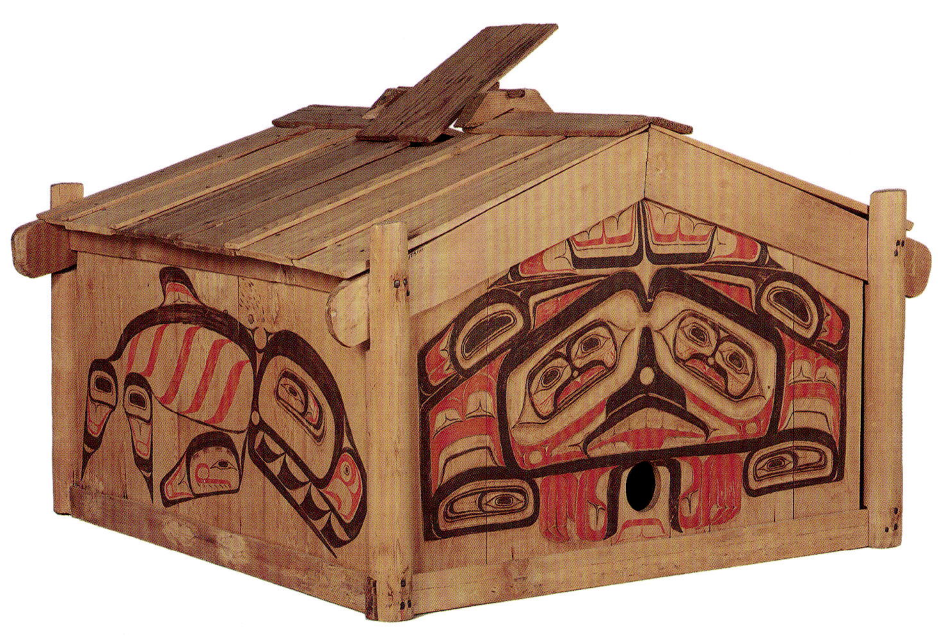

3.85 *right* House Model No. 13, Naa S'aagas, "Rotten House" or Dug-Out House, Daa.a Guu Ḵaahll, "House Pit/Hole Walk Out," 1892, 59.7 cm h x 36.5 cm w × 86.4 cm d. Courtesy of the Field Museum, cat. no.17800. Photograph by Gail Specht.

3.86 Detail of figure 3.2, photograph of World's Columbian Exposition installation showing Dug-Out House and Skiu'lun awG̱a X̱aad. Field Museum, cat. no. 17800, and KHM-Museumsverband, Weltmuseum, Vienna, cat. no. MVK VO 51762.

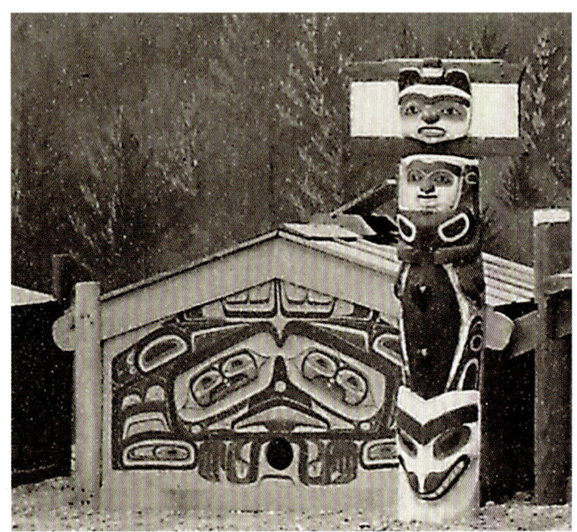

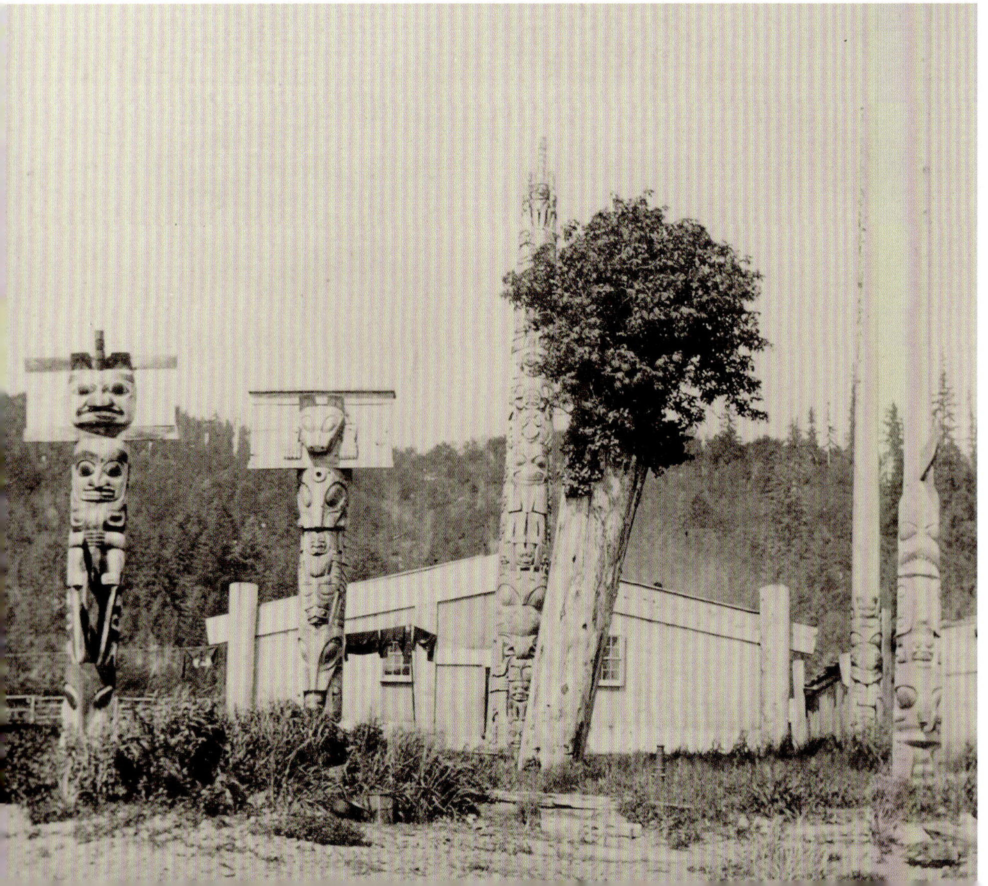

Strangely, Deans described the chestlike design on the front of the house as representing an "Auchwillo" or five-finned whale (K'aaG̱waay), said to the be chief of the SG̱aanas. He pointed out that the five-finned whale was not a crest of any of the Skidegate chiefs and speculated that it may have been used here to signify that he was a greater chief (who could use others' crests) (see House Model No. 7, note 59). In fact, I would argue that the design on the front of the house shows no features that could represent a five-finned whale. Chest front designs such as this one are sometimes identified as representing the wealth giver from under the sea (Gonakadeit in Tlingit or K̲umugwe' in Kwakwa̱la). This supernatural being is represented in a number of ways throughout the Northwest Coast—from a sea monster to a humanoid face on a chest or house front. Swanton calls this house (his #16) "Na saga's" ("Rotten House") after the clan name Naa S'aagaas X̱aaydaG̱aay (E6b). A tall frontal pole apparently belonged to an earlier house on this site, as it stands slightly out from the front of the house. The first photo to clearly show this house dates to 1879 (figure 3.87). A photo taken two years later by Dossetter in 1881 shows how the house was set back from the other front row houses (see figure 2.6). By this time there were no painted panels visible.[105]

No maker's name was recorded for this house model. The style of painting on the front of the house shows a consistency in the unusual placement of the C-shaped reliefs in the ovoids, extending them down to the base of the inner-ovoid, leaving only a thin line there. Some features might look superficially similar to Zacherias Nicholas's style—the knuckles on the fingers, the back-swept formline at the corner of the mouth in the inner ovoids on the front—but the wavering formlines and irregular ovoids on the house front are those of a less skilled designer and would counter this similarity. The whale designs on the sides, however, look like these may by a different artist who had a steadier hand. The dashing in the eye in the pectoral fin

3.87 Dug-Out House in HlG̱aagilda Llnagaay (Skidegate). Photograph by O. C. Hastings, 1879. Image PN5585. Courtesy of the Royal BC Museum and Archives.

joints is an interesting feature that might link this artist to other pieces. In particular, this stylized face motif with dashing in the eye socket is found on the plain sides of some bentwood boxes. The smooth tapering of the formlines, the proportions of the ovoids, the elegant beaked-head secondary design in the baleen whale's snout, and the overall composition of the whales on the sides surpass the design on the front of the house, suggesting two different hands at work.

MODEL POLE NO. 16

Model Pole No. 16, TcidshaAd X̱aad, "TcidshaAd's Mortuary Pole," should have been placed in front of "Dug-Out House" in the WCE installation but instead was positioned much farther to the right in front of "Eagle People's House" (House Model No. 25) and "Food House" (House Model No. 14), according to the installation numbers (figure 3.88). No photo is known of this portion of the installation. On his list Deans describes this pole as having been raised by Alfred Power to his friend who was of the G̱aahllns Kun people and identifies the figures as a "Mosquito hawk" and a five-finned whale (Deans 1893b, 93). However, the upper figure on this model pole is clearly a dogfish, not a five-finned whale (as Newcombe's handwritten note in the margin of this list points out).

Deans's description doesn't fit this model, and the only other model with a five-finned whale is House Model No. 7, which he describes elsewhere (see House Model No. 7). Model Pole No. 16 is most likely a model of the memorial seen to the far right in the photo of "Dug-Out House" (see figure 3.87). A handwritten note by Newcombe describes this as a memorial pole erected by C. Jefferson to the memory of his first wife of the Na Yuans (Naa 'Yuuwans X̱aaydaG̱aay E6a). However, "?nasagas?" is written in above this, so there is a question as to whether she was E6a or E6b. Newcombe points out that the name TcidshaAd, was an old Tsimshian name that he identifies as belonging to the Nasagas (Naa S'aagaas X̱aaydaG̱aay, E6b), but in either case, this suggests that C. Jefferson would have been of a Raven clan, if his wife was an Eagle.[106]

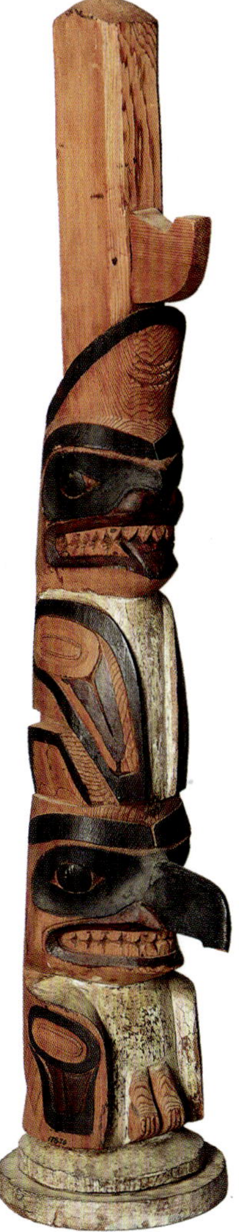

3.88 Model Pole No. 16, TcidshaAd X̱aad, "TcidshaAd's Mortuary Pole," C. Jefferson's wife's Memorial Pole, 1892, 97.8 cm × 15.2 cm. Erected in honor of TcidshaAd (E6b or E6a), first wife of C. Jefferson (Newcombe 1900–1911, Add. Mss. 1077, vol. 55, folder 10, "Skidegate Houses and Totem Poles, C. Jefferson, J. Wesley, A. Russ informants," Memorial Pole #21). Courtesy of the Field Museum, cat. no. 17830. Photograph by Gail Specht.

HOUSE MODEL NO. 15 / *Made by Amos Russ (Gedansd)*

This model, now missing, was omitted from Deans's longer list of houses (he lost his notes) but is included on his short list as "Chief's House," which belonged to the last Chief Skidegate who died suddenly in 1888 or 1889 (Deans 1893b, 39, 1893c, 10–11). The Field Museum catalog describes the model as has having white tops on the front corner posts and red around the doorway (figure 3.89).[107] The figures on the pole match a house that was located just to the north/right of "Dug-Out House" (figure 3.90), identified by Newcombe (from C. Jefferson) as Chief Skidegate's house,

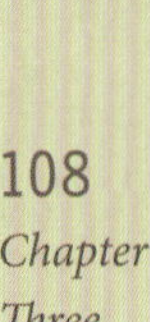

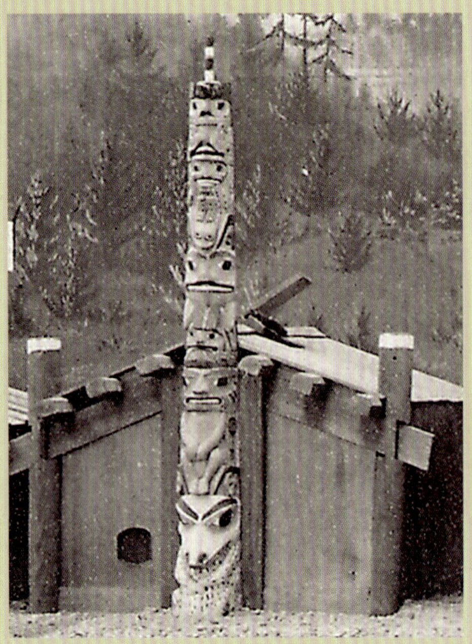

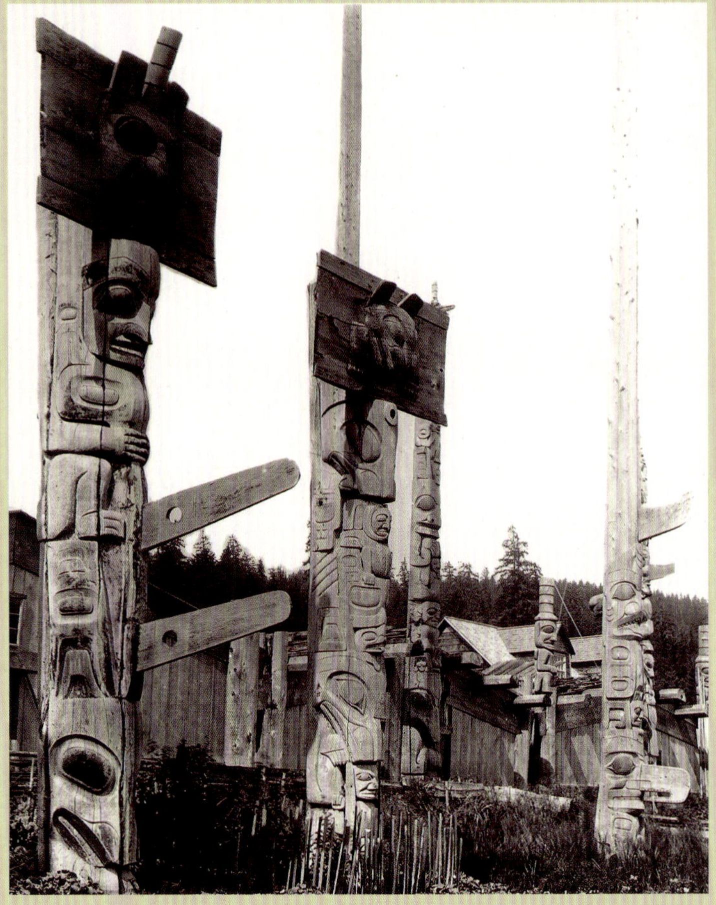

3.89 *above* Detail of figure 3.2, Missing House Model No. 15, Daa.a Guu K̲anhlln (literally House Pit Lean On) “House better than the ones that have house-holes” or Daa.a Guu K̲aahll “House pit walk out,” made by Amos Russ, 1892. Field Museum, cat. no. 17827. Purchased by the University of Pennsylvania Museum, cat. no. 37.692.

3.90 *right* “Shining House,” third pole from the left behind the mortuary pole panel. Photograph possibly by the Maynards, 1884. Image G-02207. Courtesy of the Royal BC Museum and Archives.

“dagul-kundl.”[108] He translates this name “house bellying up over the central pit,” indicating this was a chief’s house, since excavated house pits were inherited privileges. He links it with Swanton’s #13, “Da’agu qᴀ’nłin,” which Swanton translates “House better than [the ones that have] house-holes,” belonging to the Naa ’Yuuwans X̲aaydaG̲aay (E6a) (Swanton 1905a, 286). Newcombe’s translation of the name makes more sense than Swanton’s, since we know that this house had an excavated house pit, just as “Dug-Out House” did, next door (Percy Williams, personal communication, 2006).[109] SHIP translates the name Daa.a Guu K̲anhlln as “House better than the ones that have house-holes (literally ‘house pit lean on’)” (SHIP September 30, 2020).

Newcombe identified the figures on the frontal pole as a raven at the top with a three-ringed hat, two whales below (these are obscured in the photograph, see figure 3.90), a woman doctor with puffin beak rattles, another small whale, ’WaasG̲uu, a slave, and grizzly bear at the bottom (crest of the wife). His wife is identified as “Djat iʟjus.” She belonged to the Naayii Kun K̲iiG̲awaay (R13). Another model of this house frontal pole was made by John Robson for John Swanton in 1901 (figure 3.91). It is much

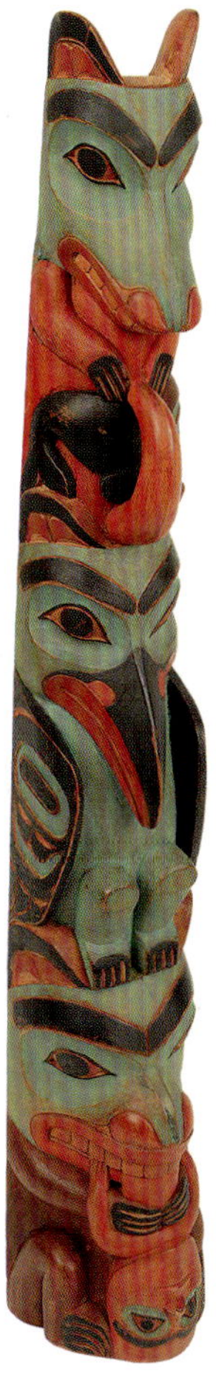

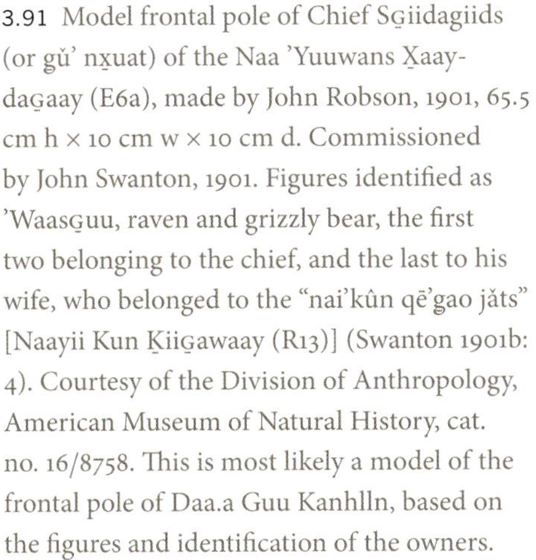

3.91 Model frontal pole of Chief SG̱iidagiids (or gŭ’ nx̱uat) of the Naa ’Yuuwans X̱aay-daG̱aay (E6a), made by John Robson, 1901, 65.5 cm h × 10 cm w × 10 cm d. Commissioned by John Swanton, 1901. Figures identified as ’WaasG̱uu, raven and grizzly bear, the first two belonging to the chief, and the last to his wife, who belonged to the “nai’kûn qē’gao jăts” [Naayii Kun K̲iiG̱awaay (R13)] (Swanton 1901b: 4). Courtesy of the Division of Anthropology, American Museum of Natural History, cat. no. 16/8758. This is most likely a model of the frontal pole of Daa.a Guu Kanhlln, based on the figures and identification of the owners.

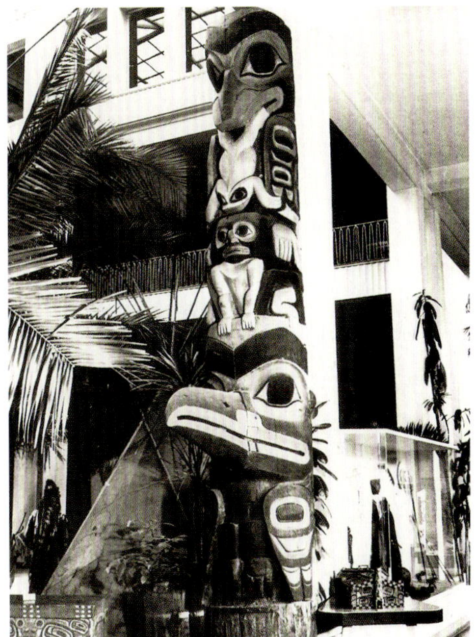

3.92 Inside House Post of Daa.a Guu Kanhlln, “House better than the ones that have house-holes,” or Xaahl TayG̱aaw, “Shining Sitting There House,” attributed to Albert Edward Edenshaw, 4.85 m h. Courtesy of the Übersee-Museum, Bremen, Germany, acquired by Hugo Schauinsland, 1896–97 (see Wright 2001b, figure 4.39).

simpler than Amos Russ’s model, reversing the order of the raven and ’WaasG̱uu, with the bear still at the bottom.

At the back of this house was the inside house post that is now at the Übersee Museum in Bremen (figure 3.92). MacDonald incorrectly reported that this inside house post was originally in Dug-Out House (House No. 13, see note 3.105) (MacDonald 1983, 49). Newcombe says that this inside house post was actually in the house next door, represented in the House Model No. 15, Daa.a G̱uu Kanhlln.[110] It is unknown whether the model house had a model interior house post, since the house is now missing, but Deans doesn’t mention one.

The owner of this house was apparently the Chief Skidegate who preceded the owner of “Dug-Out House,” and may have been raised as early as the 1840s. Both the original frontal pole of this house and the inside house post were attributed to “Chief Edenshaw”: “The two poles were both made by Chief Edensaw so often mentioned by Drs Boas and Swanton as an artist and narrator of Haida stories. He is still alive, getting high prices for his slate and silver work and is considered to be the most influential man of his tribe.”[111]

The inside house post was purchased by the director of the Übersee Museum, Hugo Schauinsland, during a trip to British Columbia in 1896–97. Newcombe’s comment dates after the purchase of this pole, and he was quoted by von J. Weissenborn, who published an article in 1908 saying that “an elder chief named Edenshaw who had carved these poles in his youth still lives” (Weissenborn 1908). The old Chief Albert Edward Edenshaw (ca. 1812–1894), the maternal uncle of Charles Edenshaw (ca. 1839–1920), had passed away by this time, so Newcombe and Weissenborn were clearly referring to Charles Edenshaw as the carver here. However, since the original house poles likely date to the 1840s, I have speculated that more likely it was Albert Edward Edenshaw who carved the poles, possibly assisted by his very young nephew (Wright 2001b, 216–19). This attribution was also based on the style of the carving. The ’WaasG̱uu figures would have been familiar to Albert Edward Edenshaw, as they were on his house frontal pole at K'yuusda as well (Wright 2001b, 143, figure 3.29).

In his report on the Bremen inside house post, Newcombe describes the figures on the inside house post as an eagle with a downturned beak at the top, a frog in its mouth, and a human figure crouching on the head of a raven at the base. It stood in the center of the village, on ground formerly occupied by a chief of the closely allied family called the Yaku Gitanee (E8b).[112]

Amos Russ (Gidansd) / *See Genealogy Chart 9*

Amos Russ (Gidansd, b. 1850 (or 49?)–1934), was the son of "Yak'yaka,'" (Naayii Kun K̲iiG̲awaay, R13), who was the daughter of Paul Nang Jingwas. His father was Dogangakillas/ Ga.ala.[113] He has been known more for his early conversion to Christianity and his role as a community leader than for his artistry. According to his son-in-law's biographer, at about the age of sixteen, while visiting Victoria, Russ attended Methodist revival meetings and was baptized by the Rev. Russ, who gave him the name Amos Russ. He is said to have argued with his grandfather, Nang Jingwas, who asked him to renounce his new religion. Refusing, he is said to have cut down his totem poles, cutting them up for fire wood (Morley 1967, 28–30). It is unclear which Skidegate poles these may have been. Russ has been credited with bringing the first Christian missionary, George Robinson, to Skidegate in 1883 (Van den Brink 1974, 78–79). James G. Swan also described Robinson as a missionary when he met him in 1883 (see Swan's journal quoted below under Daniel Iljuuwaas). However, Robinson was not ordained and had been a teacher in Fort Simpson before Amos Russ brought him to Skidegate. A Tsimshian teacher, Edward Mathers had been sent by Rev. Collison to Skidegate six years earlier in 1877 with his wife and family and constructed a mission house at Skidegate. He had received Christian instruction from the Anglicans at Metlakatla. The first ordained Methodist missionary to arrive in Skidegate was Mr. G. F. Hopkins in June 1884 (Collison 1981, 123–24).[114]

The Methodist missionary, Thomas Crosby, had come to Port Simpson in Tsimshian territory on the mainland in 1874 (Bolt 1992, 54), but the Methodists had been actively converting Native people living near Victoria in the 1860s. It was reportedly in Victoria that a Skidegate man named "Gidanst" was converted and took the missionary's name, Amos Russ.[115] It has also been said that Russ attempted to bring Rev. Collison to Skidegate while the Anglican was still in Port Simpson in 1875, when Collison was committed to the mission in Metlakatla and later Old Massett (Morley 1967, 29–30). However, Rev. Collison himself reported that it was Nang Jingwas who visited him in Port Simpson and was the spokesperson for the group of Skidegate Haidas, who objected to the Tsimshian teacher Collison had sent, asking for a white teacher instead. When no funds for this were available, they went to Fort Simpson, where they succeeded in getting the Methodist missionary to move to Skidegate in 1884 (Collison 1981, 123–24). Given Rev. Collison's account, perhaps by this time Russ and Nang Jingwas were no longer in disagreement.

Amos Russ was first married to a Tsimshian woman but later married Jaadahl Sing.G̲ang.na (Agnes Hubbs) in 1877 (Neylan 2003, 304) (figure 3.93). She had previously (as a young girl) been married to Chief Stilthda in Old Massett. After the death of Stilthda in 1877, she went to Port Simpson and attended the Thomas Crosby School for Girls, where Amos Russ met her and married her the same year. They had eleven children. In his later life, Russ was a band councilor and argued for Haida land claims before the McKenna-McBride commission in 1913 (Foster and Harvey 2018).

Memories of Amos and Agnes Russ

I am one of the great-grandchildren of Gidansd (Amos Russ) and Jaad Aahl Sing.G̲ang.nga (Lady of the Dawn Agnes Russ). I will share some family history related to the lives of my great-grandparents in Skidegate. They lived through a time of great cultural change among the Haida. Amos (R13 Naaykun K̲iiG̲awaay) was the grandson of Nang Jingwas (E6b Naa S'aagaas X̲aaydaG̲aay), the ranking Chief in Skidegate in the 1880s (b. ca. 1814, d. 1886 [Wright 2001b, 220]). Amos had been identified as Chief Nang Jingwas' possible successor, despite being the opposite moiety. Agnes (R20, Taas Laanas) was born in Old Kasaan, Alaska, while her family was visiting at the home of her maternal uncle, Chief Skowal (R20). She grew up as the only child in the household of her grandparents Chief Weah (E14) and Jaad Ḵingee Ḵongaawas (R20) in Massett. Close family members recalled that she was covered with tattoos over most of her body. She was married at a young age to a young Massett Chief who died soon after.[116] Amos was baptized as a Christian in the 1860s which led to estrangement from his grandfather in Skidegate. Amos and Agnes married in Fort Simpson on November 10, 1879 where Agnes, also recently baptized, had been attending the Crosby School for Girls. They moved to Skidegate about 1883 with their first two children. This would have been shortly after the earliest photos of Skidegate Village. Both Amos and Agnes were ravens and it was taboo at the time to marry within the same moiety. As a result, when they returned to Skidegate, Agnes was adopted as an eagle by Paul Nang Jingwas (E6b). It was reported that good money was paid for the adoption.

Amos worked as a Native constable during his time on the mainland. One of his more dangerous assignments was to arrest a Nisga'a at his village in the Nass. Amos was a key figure in establishing the churches in HlG̱aagilda (Skidegate), Xaayna (Maude Island), and New Kloo (Ḵ'aadasG̱uu Llnagaay, Louise Island) and led their construction. Grace Stevens (b. 1885, d. 1973), Amos and Agnes's third child, recalled that Amos had many jobs including interpreting for the missionaries, owning a water-powered mill and making furniture, building frame houses, trapping, fishing dogfish for the oilery at Skidegate Landing, fishing for salmon on the Skeena (while Agnes worked in the cannery), and serving as the first Chief Councillor for Skidegate. She also recalled sailing by canoe as a young girl from Skidegate to the Skeena. Their eldest son Billy Russ followed in Amos' footsteps as the second Chief Councillor for Skidegate. Amos built one of the first frame houses in Skidegate. A granddaughter, Alberta Brown (b. 1913, d. 1997) recalled carrying chum salmon on the long way from their net in the river to their cabin on the Deena River in Skidegate Inlet. Agnes told her a story about visiting Frederick Island as a child (where R20 had resided) and going out by canoe hunting sea otter. She recalled the human-like cry of the sea otter as it was being killed. Her daughter Grace was told that as a young girl that Agnes had a baby sea otter as a pet. Another grandson, Vernon Jones (b. 1918, d. 1994), recalled a boat trip from Skidegate to Frederick Island with Amos and Agnes as a young man.

I potlatched in 2009 as Chief Nang Jingwas of the Naa S'aagaas X̱aaydaG̱aay Skidegate Gidins (E6b). Nang Jingwas means "the one standing tall" which has been attributed to a tall house pole that he raised. Nang Jingwas became the head chief in Skidegate after successfully competing with Chief Skidegate in raising a memorial totem pole for a cousin who had died. I succeeded Chief Skidegate Dempsey Collinson (E6a, b. 1928 d. 2008) as the head of our clan. Uncle Dempsey was the maternal grandson of Amos and Agnes Russ and the paternal grandson of Louie Collinson (Chief Skidegate XII).
—Nang Jingwas, Russ Jones, December 30, 2020

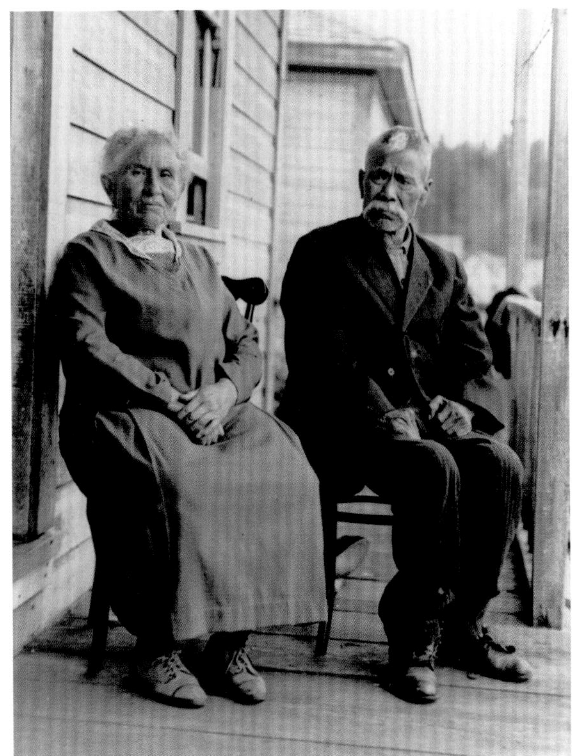

3.93 Agnes and Amos Russ. Photograph courtesy of Russ Jones.

GENEALOGY CHART 9

Amos Russ

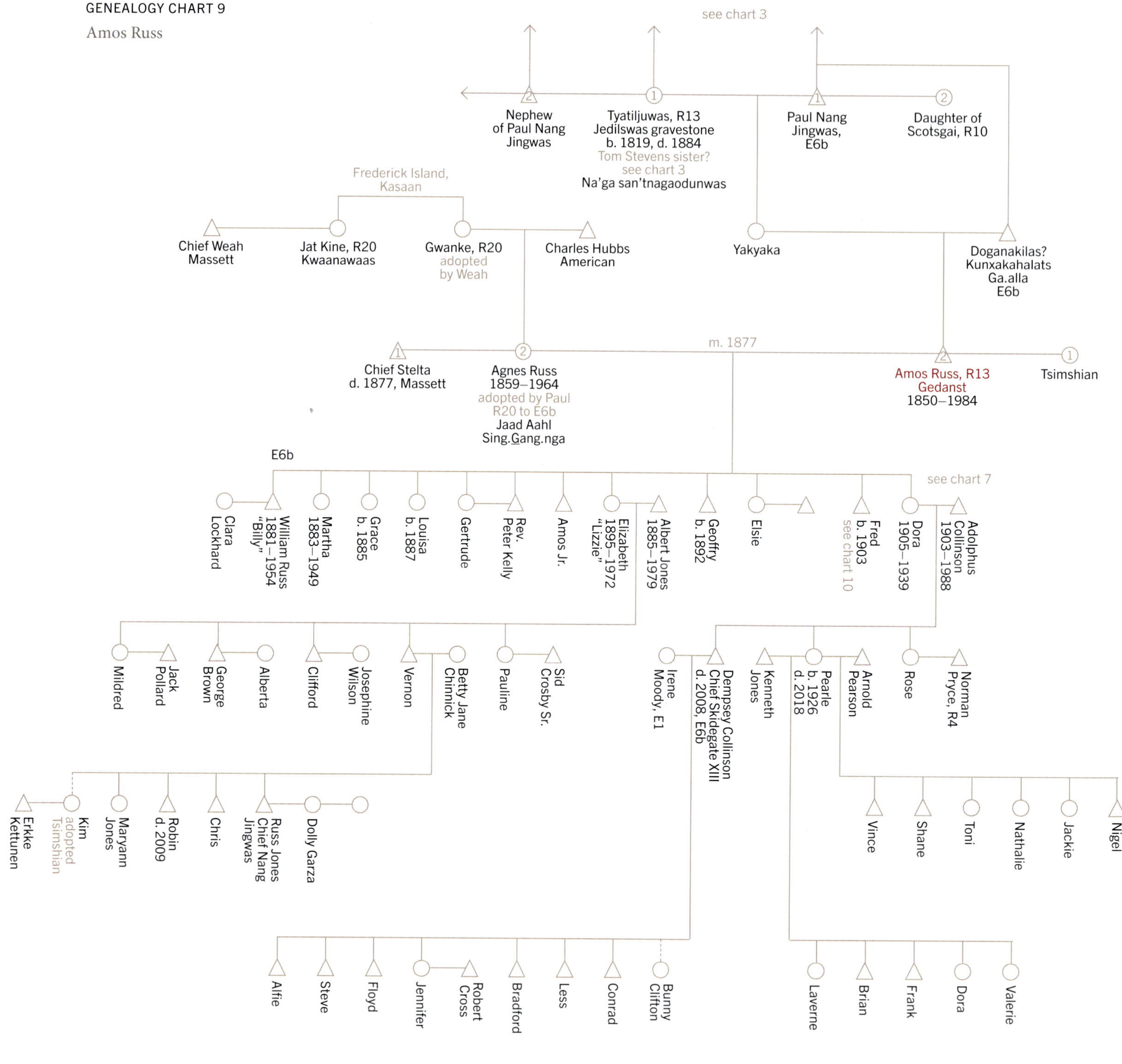

HOUSE MODEL NO. 16 / *Made by Daniel Iljuuwaas*

Deans called this model “Nah ga deelans, Thunder & Lightning House” (figure 3.94). Today this would be spelled Naa G̱a Hiilangs, “Thunder Storm House.” He reports that both the original house and the model were made by Daniel Iljuuwaas, “Elzuwuss,” and the frontal pole alone was still standing in 1892. According to Billy Stevens, the great-grandson of Daniel Iljuuwaas, he built this new house when he moved up from Church Creek to Skidegate sometime in the 1870s (Billy Stevens, personal communication, February 9, 2004). Given the newness of this house, the model of it should not have qualified for the commission of model houses for the WCE, since it was built after Boas’s desired late date of 1864. Clearly that wasn’t an issue for Daniel Iljuuwaas, so he was able to make a very close copy of his own full-size pole.

The original house looked new in 1878 (figure 3.95) as well as in the 1881 photograph (figure 3.96). The house was positioned immediately to the right/north of Daa.a Guu Ḵunhlln Naas (House Model No. 15) in both the village and the WCE installation. It is distinguished by having watchmen figures on the corner posts of both the model and the original house (figure 3.97). Deans describes these figures as having high hats with blue and white rings (Field Museum catalog). On the frontal pole there is a whale-like figure at the base holding a woman, said by Deans to be “Nuch Nah Simgate’s [Nanasimget’s] wife.” A human figure, dogfish, raven, and three watchmen are above. The roof of the model had six “bands” running parallel to the house beams, which Deans explains were a method for keeping the roof covering from blowing away (Deans 1893c, 11–12; 1893b, 39–40). These small planks are visible in the photo of the missing model (figure 3.94).

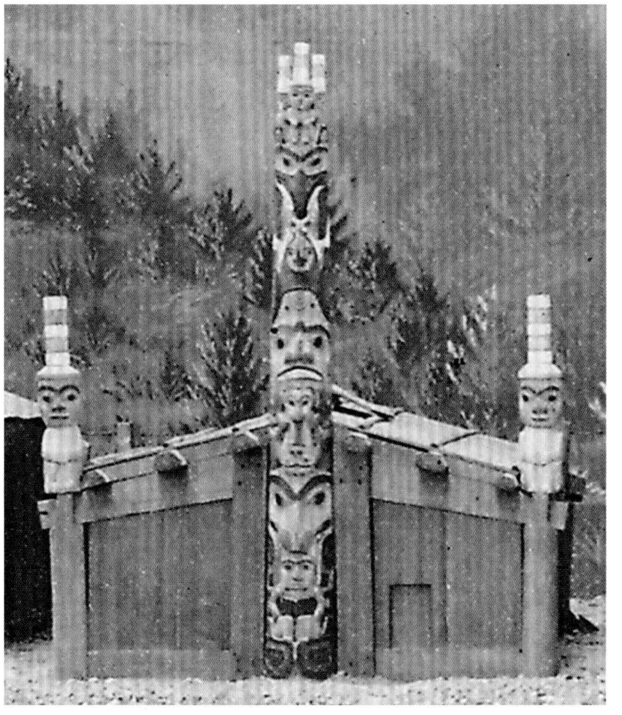

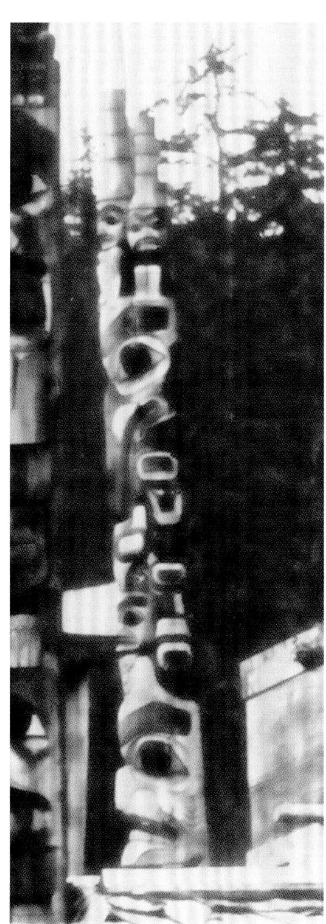

3.94 *above* Detail of figure 3.2 (center left), missing House Model no. 16, Naa G̱a Hiilangs “Thunder Storm House,” made by Daniel Iljuuwaas, 1892. Field Museum, cat. no. 17833, given to Marshall Field Co.

3.95 *middle* Detail of figure 2.3, Dawson’s 1878 photograph of HlG̱aagilda Llnagaay (Skidegate) showing Thunder and Lightning House. Canadian Museum of History, Library and Archives of Canada PA37756.

3.96 *bottom* Detail of figure 2.6, Dossetter’s 1881 photograph of HlG̱aagilda Llnagaay (Skidegate) showing Thunder and Lightning House.

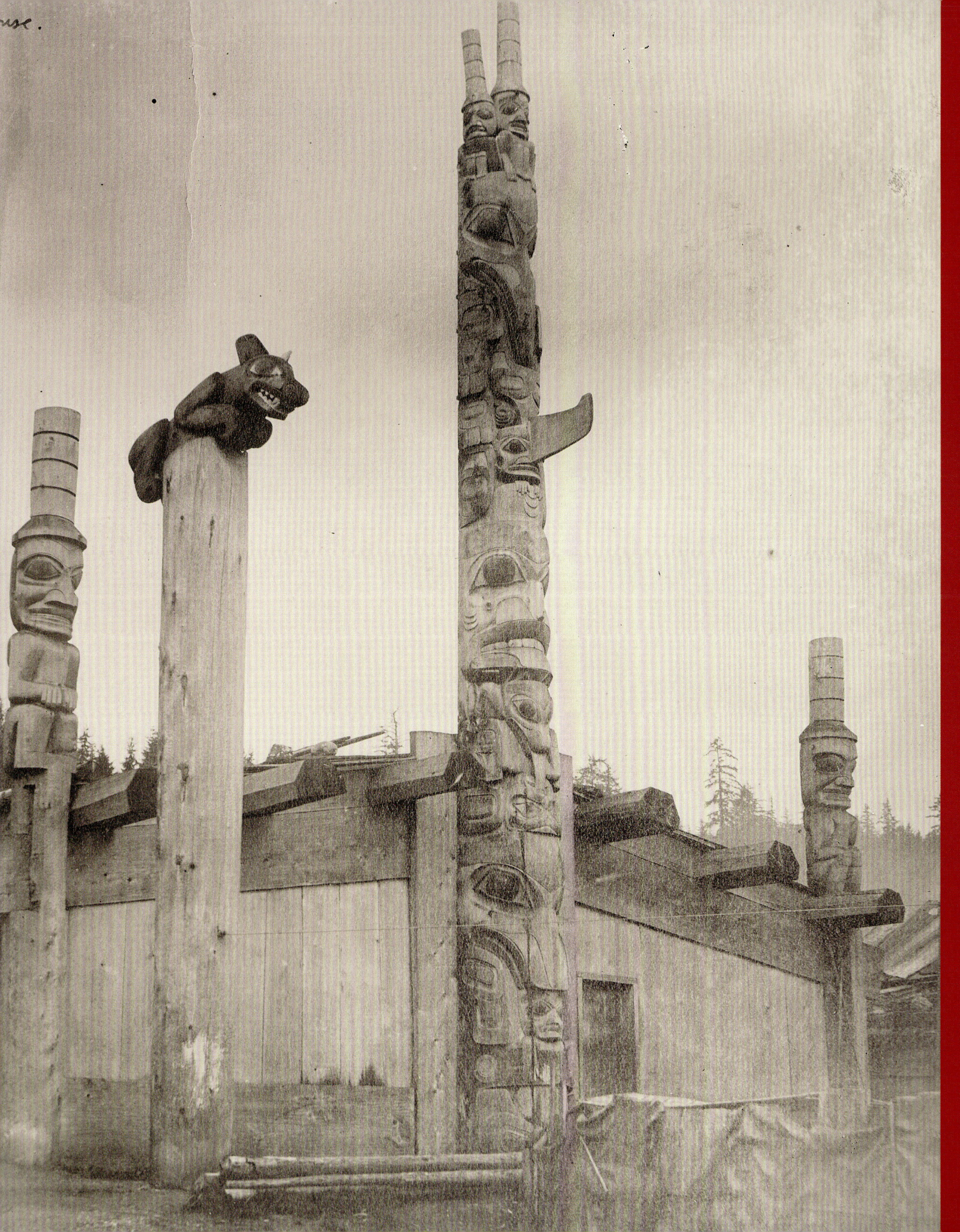

3.97 Naa Ǥa Hiilangs. Photograph by the Maynards, [1884?]. Image PN5796. Courtesy of the Royal BC Museum and Archives.

Swanton (his #8) lists a house named "Na gut hi'lans (house upon which the thunder roars)," belonging to the family "Djax̱ui' gîtînā'-i" (Jiiaxwii Gidin.naay, E11), which is likely the one on which this Model No. 16 is based.

A second model house, also made by Daniel Iljuuwaas for James Deans, but not sent to the world's fair, is said to represent "one of his houses." It has a woman with a labret and a rainbow headdress instead of a dogfish in the middle (figure 3.98). The rainbow was a crest of Daniel's wife, Keelgoodian (Elizabeth), who was of the K'aadaas Gaa K̲'iiG̲awaay (R3). This house was collected at the same time as the WCE house models but sold by Deans to the Provincial Museum in Victoria (now the Royal British Columbia Museum). The raven near the top of this RBCM model has birds coming out of its nostrils, similar the house frontal pole on the other Iljuuwaas house at the south end of the village. This confirms the connection between Daniel Iljuuwaas and the house that Model No. 11 was based on (see House Model No. 11; see figure 3.75).

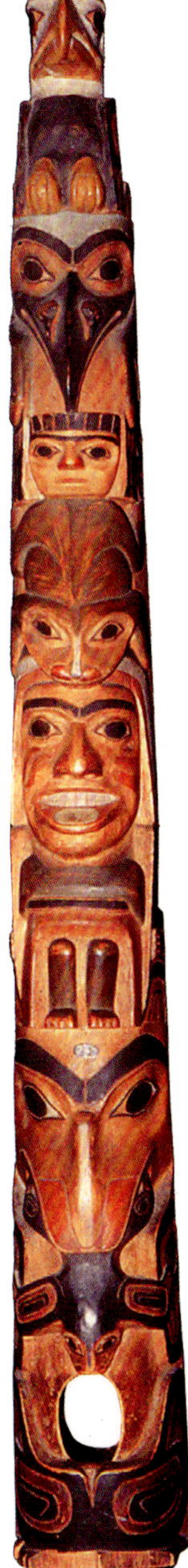

3.98 Second model of Iljuuwaas's house (frontal pole only shown). Made by Daniel Iljuuwaas for James Deans, 1892. Cat. no. 232. Courtesy of the Royal BC Museum and Archives.

Daniel Iljuuwaas (anglicized as Ellsworth or Ellswarsh) / *See Genealogy Chart 8*

Daniel Iljuuwaas, said to be of the Seaward Eagles, Jiiaxwii Gidin.naay (E11), moved to Skidegate from Church Creek (K̲'aadasG̲u Llnagaay), and was originally from T'aanuu Llnagaay. The 1881 Skidegate census (house #8) reports that "Iljuwas" (age forty-five) was living with his wife, Keelgoodlian (age forty-two), and daughter Shoodatle (age seventeen) and son Shadyoo (age seven). It is believed that the later names of this family are Daniel Iljuuwaas, his wife (Elizabeth), a daughter Suudaahl (Josephine), and son (Sam Hawastii). Another younger daughter, "Ellen," mentioned as being about seven years old in Swan's journal, would have been about five years old at this time, but, curiously, she is not listed in the census (Swan n.d. [1883], August 27, 1883, 54). It may be that this young girl was given the name Ellen by Swan, who may have had difficulty pronouncing her Haida name, since his own daughter, born in 1845, had the name Ellen (McDonald 1972, 11).[117] The only place we find the name Ellen in the Iljuuwaas family is in Swan's journal.

This family had visited James G. Swan in Port Townsend two years before Swan visited Daniel Iljuuwaas's house in August 1883, when he was traveling around Haida Gwaii, collecting objects for the Smithsonian Institution (see the introduction). During this visit Swan stayed with Alexander McGregor at the oil works (dogfish oil). His journal of that year reports:

> Tuesday, August, 28th. 1883. Showers all day and evening. Rev. Mr. Robinson the Methodist Missionary came from Skidegate village this morning with Ellswarsh and wife, Sam, his dumd [*sic*] boy and Ellen his youngest girl a child of about seven years.[118] They were very glad to see me. Two years ago this family with an elder daughter Soodatl were in Port Townsend and occupied a room near my office where

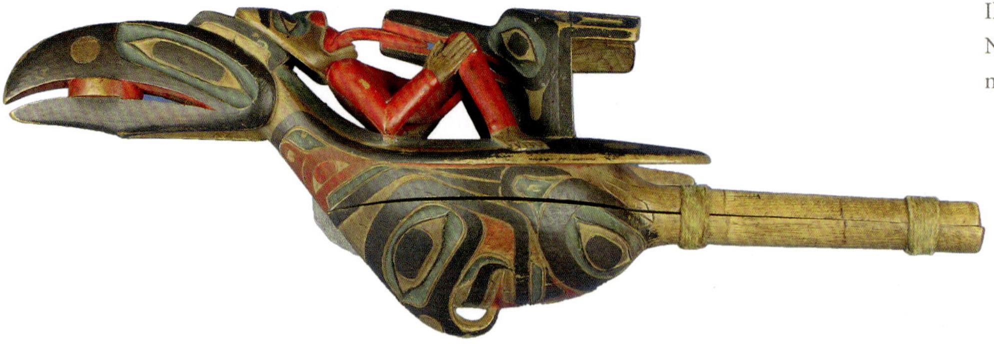

3.99 Raven rattle, made by Daniel Iljuuwaas. Purchased by James G. Swan from Daniel Iljuuwaas, August 1883. National Museum of Natural History, Smithsonian Institution, cat. no. 89079.

> Ellswarsh worked making silver bracelets and other articles of jewelry. The children were very fond of me and came to my office every day and they had not forgotten the kind treatment they recieved [*sic*] from me. I bought a pair of silver bracelets of Ellswarsh and a dance rattle.
>
> Mr. Robinson told me he should leave for Fort Simpson tomorrow and kindly offered to take letters. Ellswarsh invited me to go to his house at Skidegate village where he had some things to show me.
>
> AUGUST 29th. 1883. -& 30th. I remained in my quarters buying curiosities of the Indians. Ellshwarsh's daughter Soodatl and her husband Kit-ha-gunda, or William came to see me and brought some stone carvings which I purchased. (Swan 1883a, 54)

Unfortunately it has not been possible to identify which of the argillite carvings purchased by Swan on this trip were made by Suudaahl's first husband, William/Kit-ha-gunda, or the two silver bracelets made by Daniel Iljuuwaas. The Swan collection at the National Museum of Natural History does include a raven rattle that was identified by Swan as having been made by "Ellsworth a Skidegate carver" (figure 3.99) as well as a "dancing dress," an appliquéd tunic, with a dogfish on the front and a 'WaasG̱uu on the back, that was owned by Ellswarsh and worn by him on ceremonial occasions (Smithsonian Swan collection archives, Box R, no. 25, #199, cat. no. E89194–0). There is also a box drum collected from Iljuuwaas with a 'WaasG̱uu on one side and a humanoid bird with a salmon in its body on the other (figures 3.100a,b). These crests are most often associated with other clans (the 'WaasG̱uu with E6 and E8b, and the dogfish with E3, E4, E6, E7 and R10, R17, and R19). Daniel Iljuuwaas, however, was of the Seaward Eagles, Jiiaxwii Gidin.naay (E11), and Swanton explained that in addition to raven, sculpin, beaver, and frog, the 'WaasG̱uu was used by the E11 clan only after the death of "Yestaqa'na," Niisdaka.na, when his family permitted them to use it. Swanton doesn't mention the dogfish as being used by E11 (Swanton 1905a, 114–15, 274), but this was also a crest used by the E6a clan and might have come to Daniel Iljuuwaas with the 'WaasG̱uu crest.[119]

Swan also purchased a headdress that belonged to Suudaahl, which, according to Swan, shows her likeness at age twelve (figure 3.101). Walker Brown, Daniel Iljuuwaas's great-great-grandson, believes that it is possible that Daniel Iljuuwaas also carved the headdress frontlet (Pringle 2015). A studio photograph, taken of Suudaahl while she was in Port Townsend, shows her similarity to the carving (see figure 3.102). Interestingly, a note by James G. Swan written on the back of this photograph says that Suudaahl gifted his own daughter, Ellen, some ermine skins: "Queen Charlotte Islands, picture of Soodatl, daughter of Ellsmarsh [*sic*] of Skidegate, BC. The girl who sent the ermine skins to Ellen M. Swan of Boston. Taken in June 1862 [*sic*].[120] Soodatl is now married and lives in Skidegate in her father's

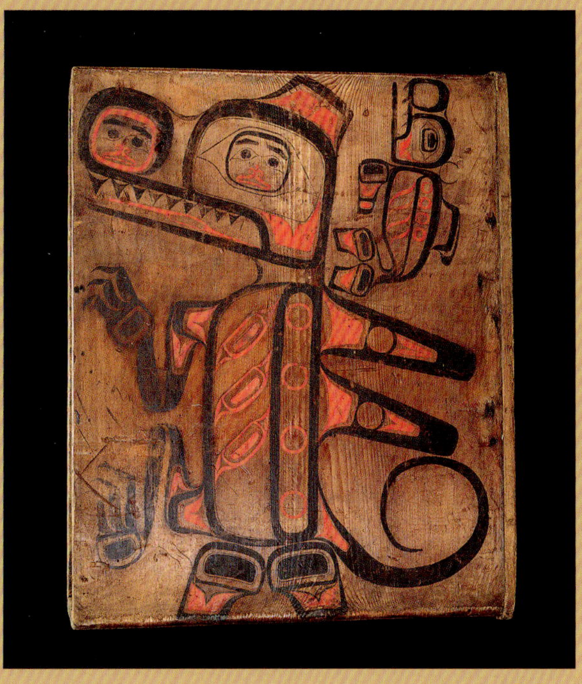

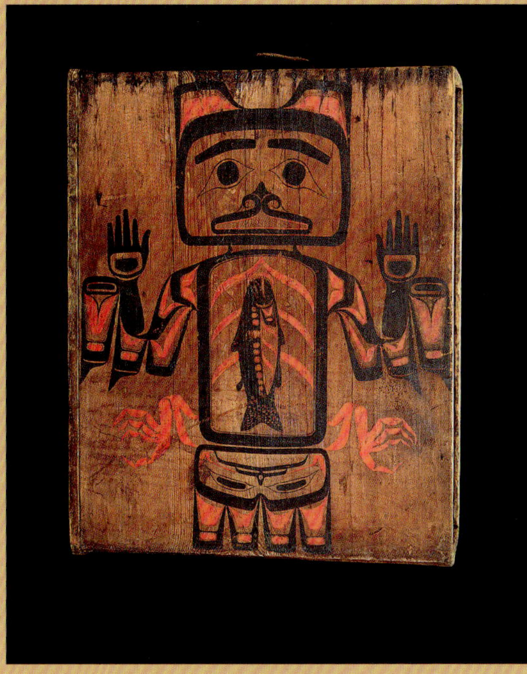

3.100 A & B Box drum, collected by James G. Swan from Daniel Iljuuwaas, 1893. (a) ’WaasG̱uu (sea wolf) with small whale; (b) humanoid bird with fish in belly. National Museum of Natural History, Smithsonian Institution, cat. no. E89141-0.

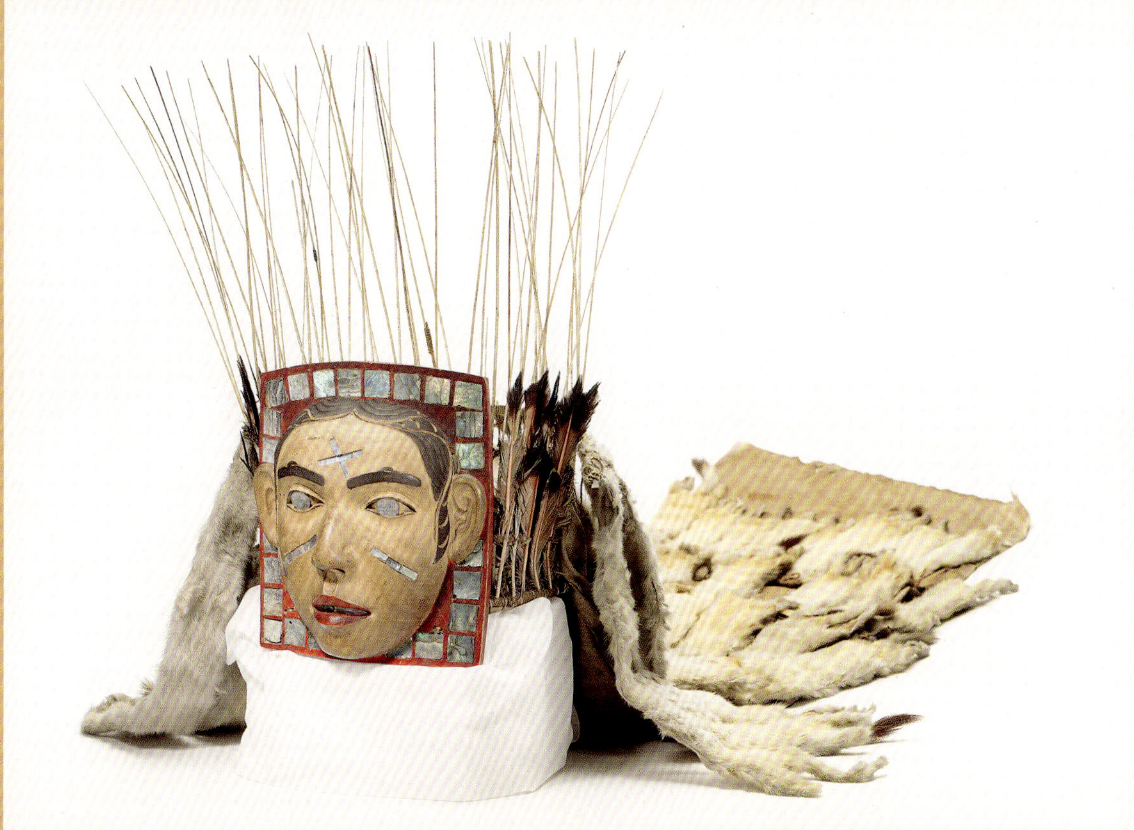

3.101 Headdress with carved wooden portrait frontlet with abalone inlay, sea lion whisker and flicker feather crown, and ermine skin trailer, 143 cm l. Belonged to daughter of Daniel Iljuuwaas, Suudaahl, also known as Josephine Gladstone, showing her portrait at age twelve. Purchased by James G. Swan from Suudaahl, August 1883. National Museum of Natural History, Smithsonian Institution, cat. no. 89186-0.

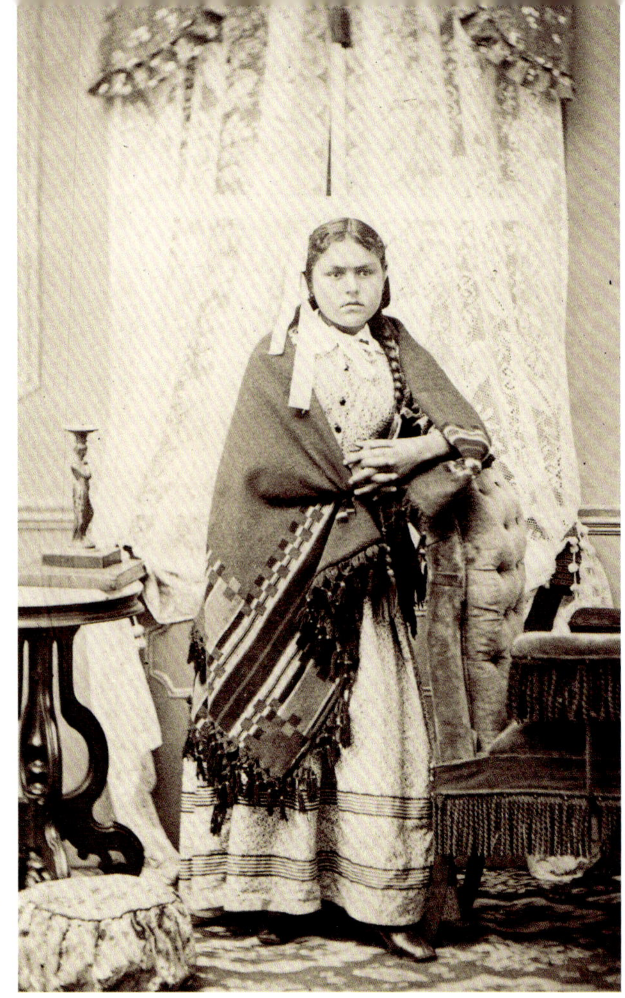

3.102 Suudaahl. Photograph most likely by O. C. Hastings, June 1882, Port Townsend. University of Washington Libraries, neg. no. NA630 (Collection no. 564: Aa-46). See note 3.120.

house. James G. Swan, Port Townsend, W.T. November 26th, 1883" (UW Libraries, Special Collections, online catalog, NA630).

Hazel Stevens, Daniel Iljuuwaas's granddaughter, told her son Billy Stevens that her mother's stepsister Josephine had the name Suudaahl (b. 1869, d. 1932) and was also called Sahl Nanaay by the family, and she danced at the opening celebration of his house, a young girl at the time.[121] She danced on the beach in welcome.[122] She said that Iljuuwaas rented this house out for potlatches (Billy Stevens, personal communication, February 9, 2004).[123] She might have worn this headdress at the time. This confirms that his house was built in the 1870s. Josephine was later married to Charles Gladstone (in 1892), who was the nephew of Charles Edenshaw. Billy Stephens did not know about any other husband of Josephine, but the William, Kit-ha-gunda, to whom she was married when Swan visited in 1883, was apparently Charles Gladstone's older brother, William Fageset, who drowned with another brother on a schooner at the Skeena River in 1888 (Walker Brown, email to author, April 2007).

The second Skidegate census report in 1891 (Family #369) lists three people from the family: Daniel Samuel (age twenty-nine), Illsworth Fanny (age seventeen), and Illsworth Martha (age thirty-five), both listed as lodgers (L). This census doesn't list a husband, but Daniel would have been about fifty-five years old and was still alive, since he carved a house model the following year. Daniel Ellsworth is believed to have died in 1893 and may have simply been away when the census was taken. The age of twenty-nine seems wrong for Sam, but this must be Daniel's son Sam.[124] Also listed is a younger daughter, Fanny (who became the wife of John Cross, see above). John Cross (age thirty) is listed in the 1891 census (Family #368), living with a family immediately adjacent to the Iljuuwaas family. Her age suggests that this Fanny, age seventeen, may be the "Ellen" described by Swan (see above), and Fanny and "Ellen" were the same person. Josephine (not found on the 1891 census) married Charles Gladstone in 1892. Gladstone, age twenty-three, was living as a single lodger with Thomas Collinson's family (Family #406) in 1891. Their marriage record reports that Daniel Ellsworth was Josephine's stepfather, and Elizabeth Ellsworth was her mother (BC Archive microfilm #B11367). It is unlikely

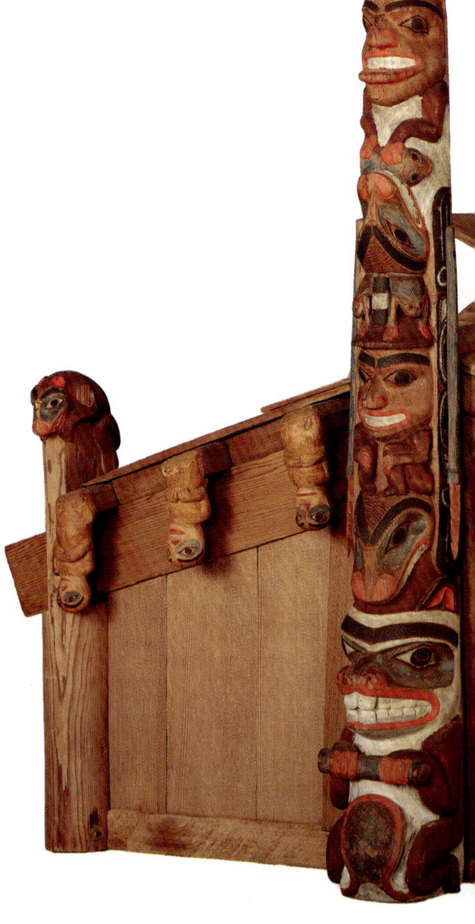

that the Martha in the census was another name for Elizabeth, since if Elizabeth was the first wife of Daniel, she would have been fifty-two at this time, not thirty-five.

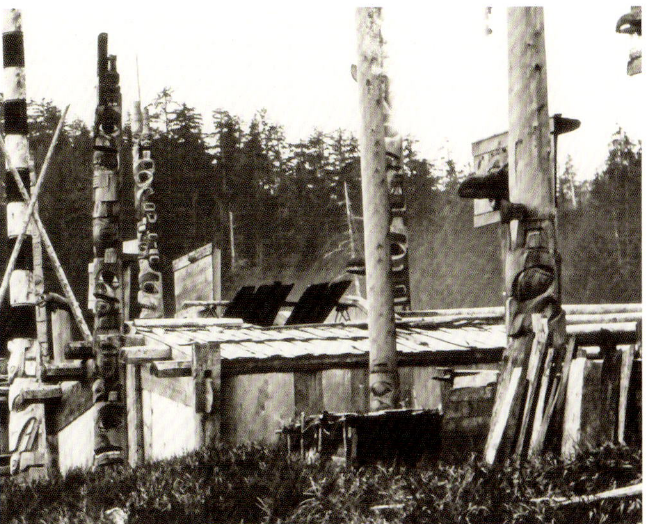

3.104 Detail of figure 2.6, Tl'aajaang quuna's house in HlG̱aagilda Llnagaay (Skidegate). Photograph by Edward Dossetter, 1881.

HOUSE MODEL NO. 18

There is no description of House Model No. 18 (figure 3.103) on Deans's lists, but this number was written in the margin by C. F. Newcombe on Deans's two lists, indicating this is where the model should be (Deans 1893c, 13; 1893b, 44). In its place is a description of the full-size house that belonged to Tl'aajaang quuna, "Clads-an-Coona," which stood forward toward the beach from the other houses in Skidegate (figure 3.104). This house, named Naa G̱a Gayhlas, "House of the Waves" (spelled "Nah-ra-Kieth las" by Deans), marked the division between the Skidegate Eagles' houses to the south and the Naay Kun K̲iiG̱awaay (Those Born at Rose Spit) houses on the northern (right) side of the village.[125] The entire full-size Skidegate house was purchased by James Deans from Tom Stevens (who then had the name Tl'aajaang quuna), shipped to Chicago for the WCE, and installed at South Pond (see figures 1.1, 1.3). The frontal pole is now installed in the foyer of the Field Museum (figure 3.105, left).

Deans described the full-size Skidegate pole as having a brown bear eating a boy at the bottom, a sort of shellfish that lives in the sand that the Haidas call "Coon," a killer whale bearing away Nanasimget's ("Nach noo Simgat's") wife, and the fin of the whale between two "images" on top (Deans 1893c, 13). Newcombe, recorded Tom Stevens's information, which lists the figures on this full-size pole as a grizzly bear at the bottom, Ts'aamus (snag), and a SG̱aana (killer whale) with its dorsal fin between two watchmen at the top.[126]

This Skidegate house pole does not resemble the House Model No. 18 in any way. Deans's report explains the name of the house referred back to another house, Tl'aajaang quuna's original House of Waves that was built in the village of G̱aahllns Kun Llnagaay or "High Point Town." He explains that the house was destroyed five times by tidal waves and always rebuilt. After the fifth rebuilding, the town was attacked by the Tongass Tlingit. After this, Tl'aajaang quuna decided to rebuild his house at a different site that Deans spelled "Kie" on a flat point near Skidegate. He had a dream that this house had several men with their heads down and their hair waving in the wind. He built this house according to his dream with six figures attached to the beams hanging upside down with hair attached. It is this "Kie" house that is represented in the model according to Deans.[127]

3.103 House Model No. 18, Naa G̱a Gayhlas "House of the Waves," 1892. Courtesy of the Field Museum, cat. no. 17834. Photograph by Gail Specht.

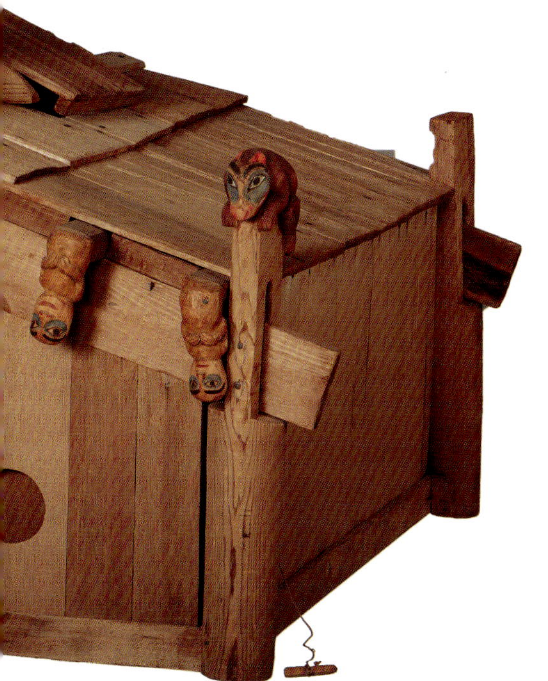

The WCE model of this "six heads" house (see figure 3.103) has a beaver placed at the bottom. Above the beaver is a double-headed creature with teeth, one head faces down and the other up. On its back crouches a human figure wearing a hat with frogs on it. At either side are harpoons with serrated points attached as separate pieces over clawed appendages with formline designs. This unusual figure may represent the 'WaasG̱uu skin being worn by the young man, the son-in-law of the female shaman in the 'WaasG̱uu story. At the top this woman wears a labret and has a bear cub on her head. In her hands is what appears to be a small whale also held in the teeth of the 'WaasG̱uu figure. Bears are placed on the corner posts, and human figures hang upside down from the six beams.

John Robson carved a model pole for Swanton in 1901 said to be Tl'aajaang quuna's frontal pole (figure 3.106). This model does not resemble the pole sent to Chicago except perhaps in the bear at the bottom. It includes a bear with two cubs and a frog at the bottom, with a beaver in the middle, and an eagle at the top. The beaver and small bears on Robson's pole are the only similarities to the six-heads model pole. Swanton's description of the model pole obtained from Robson translates the name Tl'aajaang quuna as "greatest one who throws back the waters hurled against him" and his wife's name was "ī'lga jăt kîlk! ī'gůs," "chief woman whose voice is sharp, i.e., if she says anything it hurts someone or has effect," of the Staastas clan (E21). He explains that the eagle and beaver are Staastas crests, while the bear was Tl'aajaang quuna's (Swanton 1901b, 2 #7).[128] Swanton lists the Skidegate version of this house (his #9) as "Na'ga ga'ilas, house to which the tide comes" (Swanton 1905a, 286).

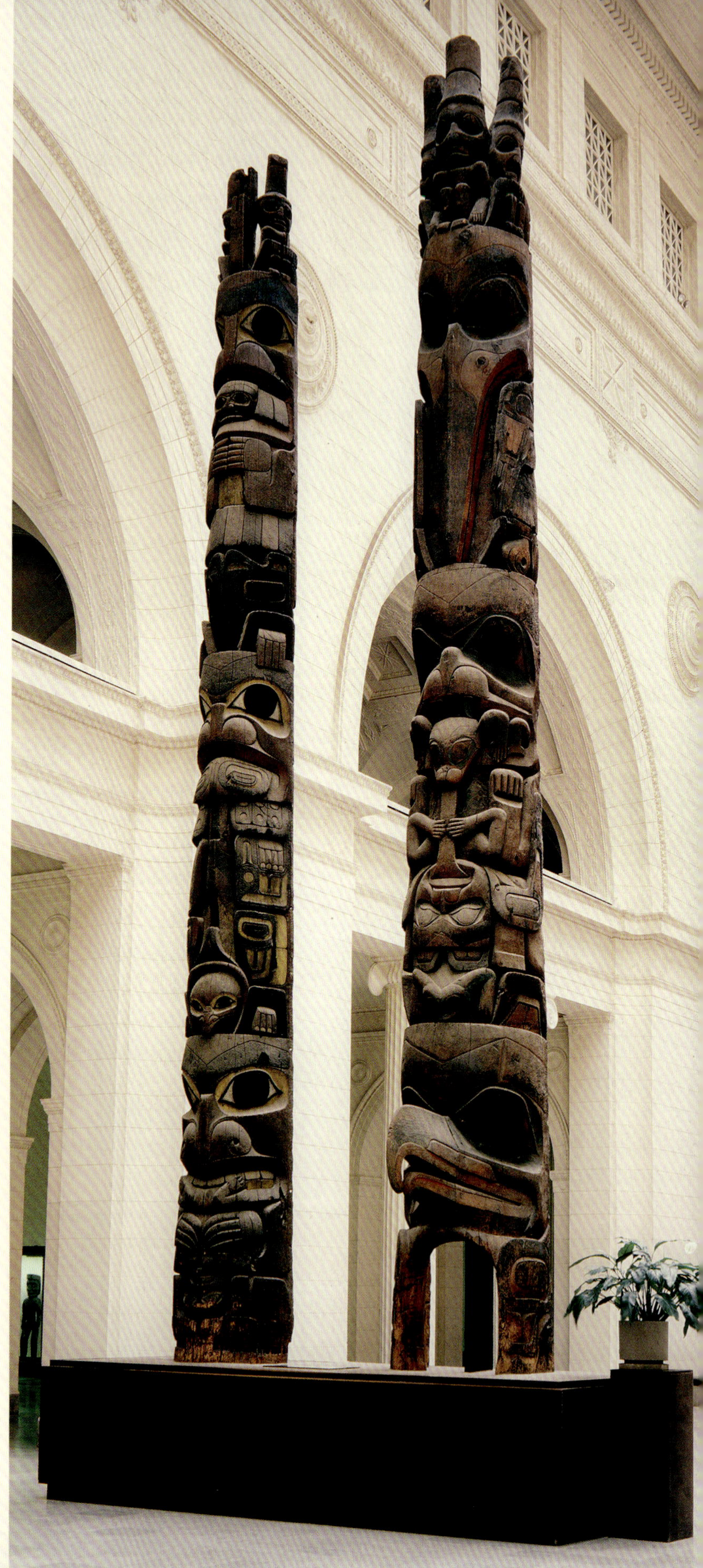

3.105 Two Haida poles currently displayed in the foyer of the Field Museum, previously installed in 1893 at the World's Columbian Exposition (see figure 1.1, left). House fontal pole from Xaayna Llnagaay, "House Where People Always Want to Go" (right) (MacDonald 1983, 64, House 5), possibly made by Zacherias Nicholas (see Zacherias Nicholas biography above). Field Museum, cat. no. 19339, gift of Edward E. Ayer. Tl'aajaang quuna's house frontal pole (left), HlG̱aagilda Llnagaay (Skidegate), 42 ft. h. Field Museum, cat. no. 17999. Purchased by James Deans from Tom Stevens, Tl'aajaang quuna, 1892. © The Field Museum, image no. A108441.

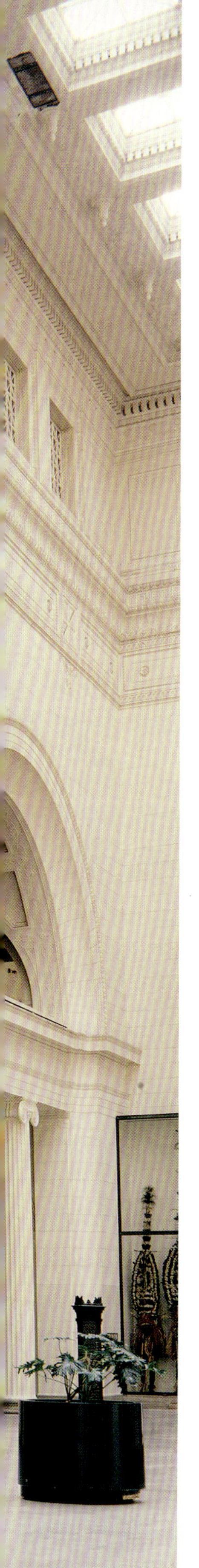

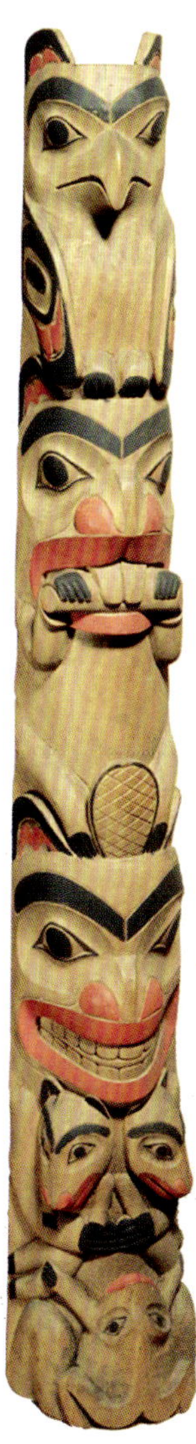

3.106 Model pole, made by John Robson, 75.3 cm h × 10.7 cm w × 9 cm d. Commissioned by John Swanton, 1901. Said to be the pole of Tl'aajaang quuna, named after Cape Ball chief "'greatest one who throws back'; the waters hurled against him." He was married to "ī'lga jăt kîlk! ī'gŭs," "chief woman whose voice is sharp" of the Staastas clan (E21) (Swanton 1901b: 2). American Museum of Natural History, cat. no. 16/8754. Photograph by Bill Holm.

If Robson's information about the clan of Tl'aajaang quuna's wife is correct, then Deans was wrong when he said that the old Tl'aajaang quuna at Cape Ball was married to a "daughter" of Edenshaw. Deans misunderstood the Haida matrilineal clan and exogamous marriage systems where Eagles usually marry Ravens. We know that Gwaayguu 7anhlan (7IDANsuu), Albert Edward Edenshaw's wives and daughters were a Yahgu Laanaas Ravens (R19), so it is more likely that this Tl'aajaang quuna may have been married to Edenshaw's sister or niece (E21).[129] Gwaayguu 7anhlan was born ca. 1812 at G̱aahllns Kun Llnagaay, the village near Cape Ball. It was some time after his birth, when the sea cut away much of the land here in the tidal waves mentioned above, and the village was attacked by the Tongass people sometime before 1840. After this time Edenshaw moved north, and his sisters' families moved south (see Wright 2001b, 111–12). It was also at this time that the older Tl'aajaang quuna built the house with six heads on the beams at "Kie." Deans was likely wrong again when he said that the man from whom he bought the Skidegate house (Tom Stevens) was the grandson of the old Tl'aajaang quuna.

Deans says of the older Tl'aajaang quuna:

> The man from whom I bought the old house was it appears the grandson of this Clads an Coona [who built the six-head house]. This chief married a daughter of Edensaw, then Chief of Hiellen near Nai Coon. This wife belonged to the bear crest. After their marriage their new house took the name of Choo Chooats a nass, and the people Chooats a nass hadry, Bears House people. Afterward on the grandfather's death a son inherited the name and property. By these means he obtained a higher rank among his people, this enabled him to marry a chief's daughter. This he did by taking to wife one of the Edensaw family. After his marriage he wished to build a new house. To enable him to do so a large number of the family relatives contributed a quantity of blankets and food. When he built this house he put also the six men with their heads down, on the end of the rafters. By so doing he took in addition to his other names that of Cadgo Cloo-unal (or six heads). Since the family came to Skidegat this branch has retained the name

of Kuthlano. Today there are fifteen branches of this family, ten at least of them have houses in Skidegat. The person from whom I bought the house has lately taken the family name or [*sic*] Clads an Coona, he it seems was brought up by his mother's brother. This uncle whose name at first was Hung daas and who afterwards became Clads an Coona. When this uncle died a few years ago he inherited the family name and his uncle's property excepting that of Cadgo-Cloounal (six heads) this seems to have gone to another branch of the family. The person from whom I bought the house had also for his first wife a daughter of the Edensaw. She helped largely to build this house. By inheriting the family name, property, and by his connection he was entitled to a tuden skeel of two heads. (Deans 1893b, 44–45)

Deans contradicts himself here, first saying that the grandfather gave his crests to his son and further down saying that Tom Stevens inherited the house and names from his uncle, his mother's brother. Deans also says here that the old Tl'aajaang quuna's wife was of the bear crest, but we know that the bear was Tl'aajaang quuna's crest, not a Staastas crest. It is possible that the name passed between different lineages.[130] Certainly Deans's account is confusing the information that he was given by Tom Stevens and the maker of the house model. The maker of the model house was not identified by Deans, but since the full-size Skidegate house was purchased from Tom Stevens who held the name Tl'aajaang quuna in 1892, it is possible that he also made both this model and the model memorial pole for his maternal uncle Hungo Dass (see below).

MODEL POLE NO. 11

In Deans's list of model poles, he reports that this memorial pole, "Hungo Dass' Xat" (Hungo Dass Q'aa.l) was erected by Tl'aajaang quuna (Tom Stevens) "in memory of his friend Hungo Dass," but in the quoted account of Tl'aajaang quuna's full-size pole (see above), he explains that Hungo Dass was another name of his maternal uncle who raised him, and from whom he inherited the name Tl'aajaang quuna (figure 3.107). The original of this memorial pole with a raven at the top stood to the south of Tl'aajaang quuna's house (see figure. 3.104, left). The photographic record shows that it was erected between 1878 and 1881. Deans identifies the figures on the model pole as a sG̱aana, but Newcombe's margin notes corrects this to be a 'WaasG̱uu. On a different list Newcombe describes this figure as a sea bear.[131] Tl'aajaang quuna's Naayii Kun K̲iiG̱awaay crests do not include the 'WaasG̱uu but do include the grizzly bear and killer whale (Swanton 1905a, 270).

At the end of Deans's account of the Order of House Models, House No. 18, he adds: "The long hat (memorial column) made by Clads an Coona should be placed on right corner of this house. In the village it stood about six feet away from the house.

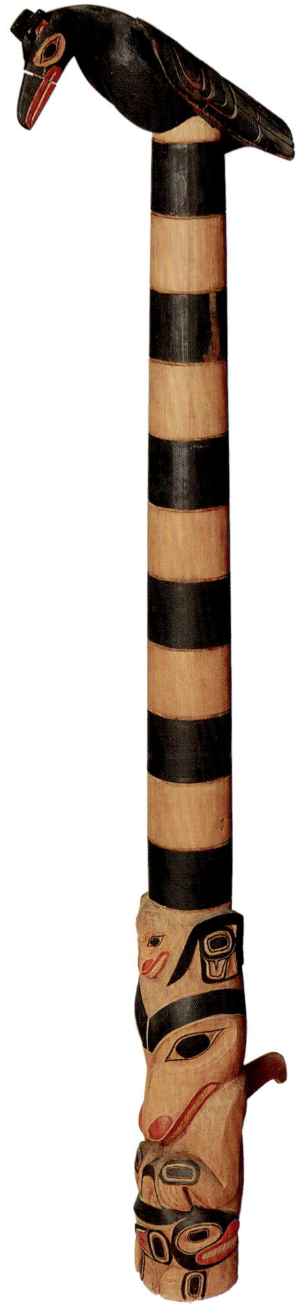

3.107 Model Pole No. 11, Hungo Dass Q'aa.l, "Hungo Dass Memorial Pole," made by Tom Stevens, Tl'aajaang quuna, 1892, 64.5 in. × 12.5 in. (missing one of two fins on back). Courtesy of the Field Museum, cat. no. 17842. Photograph by Gail Specht.

This hut [*sic*] is no. 8 or 9 in report of memorial columns" (Deans 1893c, 13–14). Deans must have been referring here to the Hungo Daas memorial (Model Pole No. 11), not Model Pole Nos. 8 or 9, as he seems to be guessing at the number. Model Pole Nos. 8 and 9 were made for Gidansda and his mother, and the original poles for these models were located much farther to the left (south) of Tl'aajaang quunas's house. The Hungo Daas memorial was erected very near the south corner of Tl'aajaang quuna's house in the village (see figure 3.104), so it seems that Deans must have meant to say to place the model pole at the left rather than the right corner of the model house. In fact, it was placed in front of the centered grave house in the model village (see figure 3.2), two houses to the left of Tl'aajaang quuna's house. All this is just to point out that if this is the pole Deans was referring to, he clearly identifies its maker as Tl'aajaang quuna, Tom Stevens. This is the only freestanding model pole in the set that has a documented maker.

Tom Stevens may have made at least three of the models for the WCE, House Model Nos. 18 and 20 and Model Pole No. 11. The open, centered, and unconstricted treatment of the eyelid lines seems similar between the Hungo Daas pole and the House of Waves frontal pole, suggesting they might have had the same maker. If so, why didn't Deans list Tom Stevens as the maker of House No. 18? Unfortunately the frontal pole of House Model No. 20 is missing, so a close stylistic examination is not possible, but it does seem possible that these all represent Stevens's work.

3.108 Model House No. 19, Saahna Gud Xaay Naas, "Relaxing at the House in the Sun," Deans's "House of Contentment," made by George Dickson (Dixon), 1892, 91 cm × 88 cm × 93 cm. Exchanged with the Brooklyn Museum, cat. no. 05.589.7791, originally the Field Museum, cat. no. 17832. Photograph courtesy of Brooklyn Museum.

HOUSE MODEL NO. 19 / *Made by George Dickson (Dixon)*

Deans reports that the original house that this model was based on was built by Tom Stevens, but the model was made by George Dickson (see below). Deans listed this model as Seen-ah-coot-kai-nai or Seen-ah-Cootkie, the "House of Contentment," numerically between Tl'aajaang quuna's Naa G̱a Gayhlas, "House of the Waves," and "Box House," next in the northward direction (figure 3.108; see figure 3.2). This is correct in the sequence of Skidegate houses, although there was one house between them for which no model was made (MacDonald 1983, 46, house 11). I have therefore placed it here in the sequence, but Deans again contradicts himself when he says that this is the model of a house that was "farthest west in the part of Skidegat known as Cathlins Coon lannas hadry," a description that he also gave to House Model No. 18 (Deans 1893b, 44, 46). In the WCE installation Deans's numerical order wasn't followed, and "House of Contentment" was placed to the left of Tl'aajaang quuna's Naa G̱a Gayhlas, "House of the Waves," perhaps in response to Deans's comment that it would be "west" (left/south) of the other Cape Ball houses.

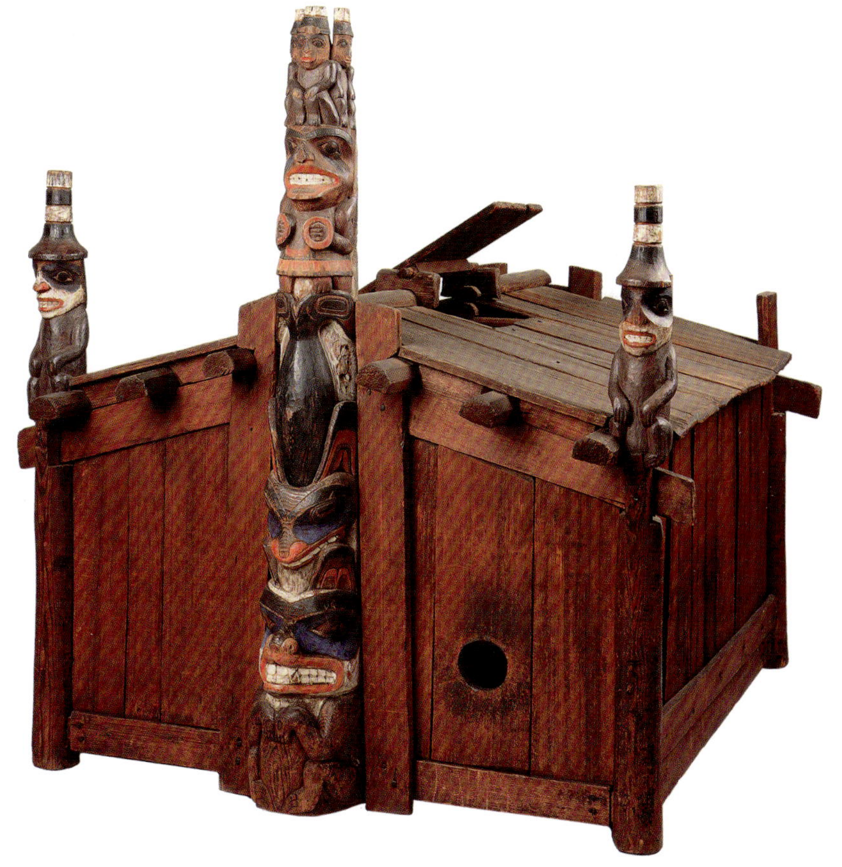

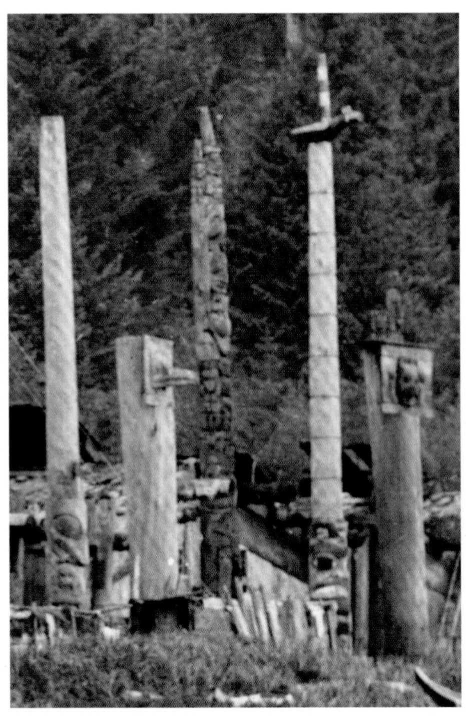

3.109 Detail of figure 2.5, showing the north end of HlG̱aagilda Llnagaay (Skidegate), see in the center the old house after which the "House of Contentment" model may have been made. Photograph by Edward Dossetter, 1881. Image #42268. American Museum of Natural History Library.

The figures on this model pole are identified as a 'WaasG̱uu at the bottom, whale, and female shaman, with three watchmen at the top and one watchman on each corner post (Deans 1893b, 46–47), but the lowest figure on this model is clearly a beaver with large incisors and a flat cross-hatched tail (figure 3.108). It is the whale and the female shaman above that are part of the 'WaasG̱uu story, not the beaver at the bottom. Deans tells the 'WaasG̱uu story in conjunction with this model and says that the head only of the 'WaasG̱uu is shown with the whale on its back, seeing the whale as both a 'WaasG̱uu and whale.

The old house had a tall pole (figure 3.109, center) and was located two to the north/right of Tl'aajaang quuna's house in the village. The figures do include watchmen at the top, a whale head facing up, a human figure, and another whalelike head facing down, perhaps representing the 'WaasG̱uu. Several small figures are below on the tall pole and at the base is a large bearlike figure—or could it be a beaver? In either case, it is probable that MacDonald was correct in associating this model with the house to the north of Tl'aajaang quuna's house, giving it Deans's name, "House of Contentment," but he was incorrect that the owner was Daniel Iljuuwaas (MacDonald 1983, 47, house #10).[132] Deans does not identify this as Iljuuwaas's house; rather, he says that it was built by Tl'aajaang quuna. Neither Newcombe nor Swanton mention a house by this name (Swanton 1905a, 286). SHIP suggested that Deans's spelling of the house name "Seen-ah-coot-kai-nai or Seen-ah-Cootkie" might be the Haida phrase "Saahna gud xaay naay" as "relaxing at the house in the sun" (SHIP February 11, 2004), also not similar to any of Swanton's house names.

It is very interesting that the lowest figure on the "House of Contentment" model is a beaver, like the one on the Tl'aajaang quuna House Model No. 18. Also on Model No. 18 the double-headed 'WaasG̱uu figure with the human figure wearing a hat on its back, flanked by harpoons at either side, resembles the whalelike figures with a human figure between toward the top of the house to the right of Tom Stevens's house, Naa G̱a Gayhlas (see figure 3.109). It is likely that House Model No. 18 was inspired in part by the pole on this house to the north of Naa G̱a Gayhlas, not Naa G̱a Gayhlas. The beaver at the base is a crest of the Staastas (E21) clan, identified by both Deans and Swanton with Tl'aajaang quuna's wife. In front of this house was a memorial pole with a beaver at the base and a raven at the top. No model of this memorial pole was made. It is said to have been erected by Tl'aajaang quuna for one of his wives, "ga.agit, 'branches'" of the Staastas Eagles (see figure 3.109; MacDonald 1983, 46, 10M [M is MacDonald's code for memorial pole]).[133] This supports, as Deans reports, that this house belonged to Tl'aajaang quuna, rather than to Daniel Iljuuwaas.

George Dixon (Dickson) / *See Genealogy Chart 6*

George Dixon's name was spelled "Dickson" by Deans and also in the 1911 census but spelled "Dixon" on his gravestone, census, and death record. His birth may have been in 1856, 1861, or 1862. The government death record lists his death at Alliford Bay, BC, on August 6, 1918, but his gravestone at Skidegate reads: "George Dixon, b. 1862, d. Aug. 7, 1918, age 56 years." In 1891 he (age thirty) and his wife, Mary (age twenty-five), are listed in the census for Skidegate. In 1911 they are also listed in the Skidegate census (ages fifty-five and forty-five), but this time with an adopted son, Robert, age seven. This is likely John Cross's son Robert Cross Sr., who had been adopted by one of his uncles named Dixon (see section on "William Dixon," above). By this time William Dixon had passed away. Robert was still living with Mary Dixon, according to the 1921 Skidegate census, listed as twenty years old.

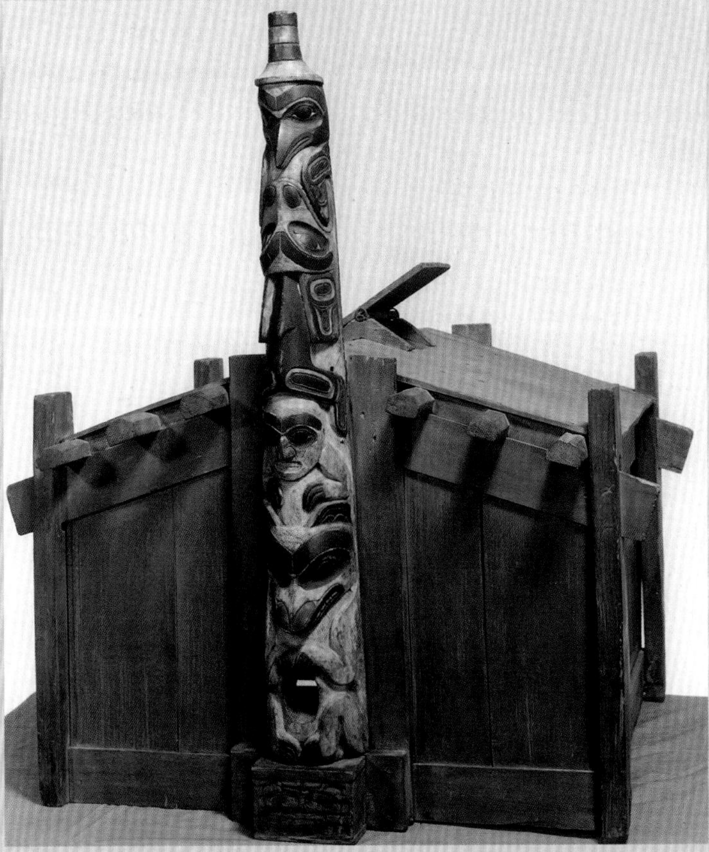

3.110 House Model No. 20, G̱uuda Naas "Box House," made by Tom Stevens, Tl'aajaang quuna, 1892, 76.5 cm × 101 cm × 86 cm, exchanged with the Brooklyn Museum, cat. no. 05.589.7792 (missing the frontal pole, only the house remains), originally the Field Museum, cat. no. 17837. Photograph courtesy of the Brooklyn Museum, neg. no. BMA/AAPA photo.

Since George Dixon made a model of a house belonging to Tom Stevens (Tl'aajaang quuna), they may have been closely related. James Deans reports that George Dickson's grandmother was a daughter of the old Tl'aajaang quuna (likely speaking of the uncle of Tom Stevens who had that name—see Genealogy Chart 3), and her mother was a daughter of the Massett Chief Edenshaw. This cannot be correct, since Tl'aajaang quuna's daughter would have been an Eagle (E21) given Tl'aajaang quuna (R13) was married to a Staastas Eagle (E21). But Edenshaw's daughter would have been a Raven (R19). As discussed earlier, Old Tl'aajaang quuna's wife was probably Edenshaw's sister or a niece (sister's daughter—see the discussion for House Model No. 18). It is most likely that this is another example of Deans's confusion about Haida genealogy, and that these women were aunts or great-aunts rather than grandmother and great-grandmothers.[134] So, Deans's information is not helpful in determining George Dixon's clan. If his maternal grandmother was Tl'aajaang quuna's daughter, he would have been an Eagle (E21). However, if his great-grandmother was Edenshaw's daughter, he may have been a Raven, relating him to both E21 and R19 clans. There is some suggestion that George Dixon was a brother or half-brother to another of the house model artists, William Dixon, whom we know to have been an Eagle (see discussion on William Dixon, earlier in this chapter). Since they shared the name Dixon, they may have shared a father, with different Eagle mothers.

HOUSE MODEL NO. 20 / *Made by Tom Stevens (Tl'aajaang quuna)*

Deans called this model "Cootah Nass, Box House," spelled today G̱uuda Naas (figure 3.110). Deans identified the maker of this model house as the present "Clads an Coona," Tl'aajaang quuna, Tom Stevens, in 1892. The figures on the model pole are identified as brown bear, fisherman named Skulsit, whale, and raven at the top. The name of the house, he points out, comes from the box placed at the base of the frontal pole, which has a design of the Ts'aamus (snag) on it (Deans 1893b, 49). The Ts'aamus is represented in an abstract formline design on the model box at the base of the model pole (figure 3.110)

MacDonald suggests that the original house was also owned by Tl'aajaang quuna (his #8) and was located to the north of Tl'aajaang quuna's two other houses. James G. Swan sketched this house when he visited Skidegate in 1883 (figure 3.111). He labeled the figures as a "Tchimos" (Ts'aamus, snag) at the top, dragonfly [Mamats'iik'ay], "Thlkama" [Hlk̲yama] kelp, "KooKooltakook" centipede, mouse [Kaagan], and "Hoorts" [Xuu.ajii] bear at the bottom (Miles 2003, 126). There are also two watchmen on either side of a small bearlike figure on the head of the Ts'aamus. The kelp figure is visible in the Maynards's photograph of this pole (see figure 2.10—the pole to the right of the double mortuary pole, center left), and there was a doorway through the belly of the bear at the bottom visible in Dawson's photo (see figure 2.2, to the left of the double mortuary pole, center right). This bear holds a human figure upside-down in its mouth. There does not appear to be a box at the base of the old pole, but there was a step up to the doorway. The model lacks the dragonfly, kelp, centipede, and mouse, and has a whale instead, with a raven filling the position of watchman at the top. The placement of the Ts'aamus on the box at the base of the pole of the model suggests that this model is indeed meant to represent the old pole that had a Ts'aamus at the top. Tom Stevens chose to use a raven instead at the top, which represents his crest. Why he chose to replace the dragonfly with a whale is unknown. The dragonfly became a crest of the Yaku Gitanee (E8b) after they moved to Skidegate (Swanton 1905a, 274). The pole was apparently no longer standing in 1892 when the model was made (see Newcombe photo, RBCM E22-II/15, ca. 1895).

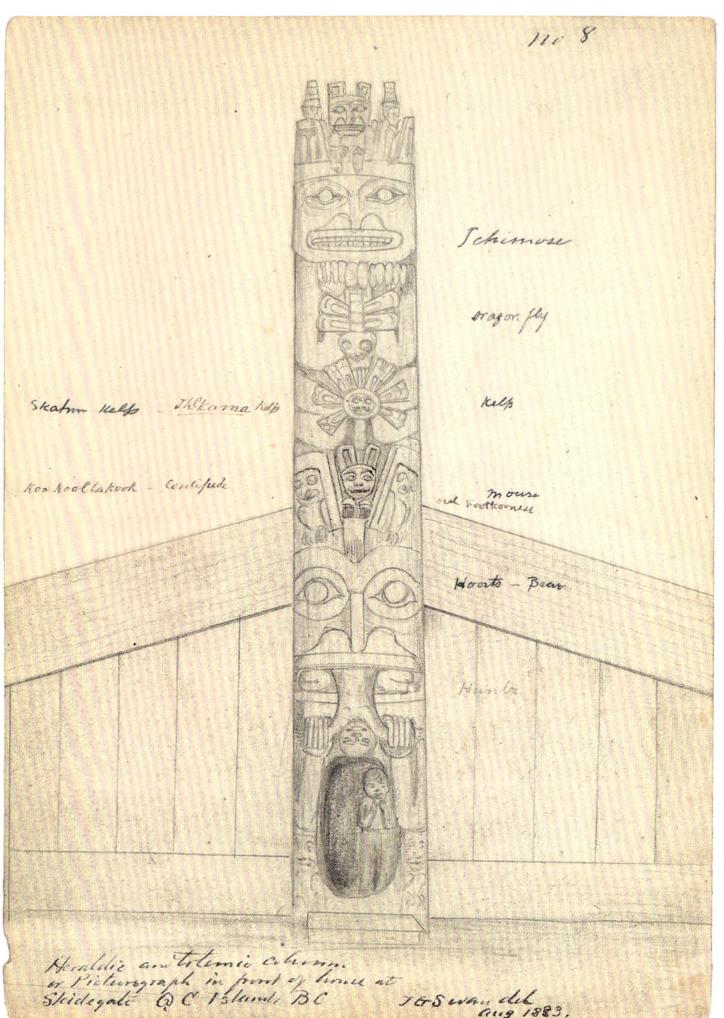

3.111 Drawing by James G. Swan entitled: "Heraldic and totemic column or Picturograph in front of house at Skidegate QC Island, BC," August 1883, 25.4 cm × 18 cm. This is Swan's drawing of "Box House" that includes his written notes identifying the figures. Franz R. and Kathryn M. Stenzel Collection of Western American Art. Yale Collection of Western Americana, Beinecke Rare Book and Manuscript Library, Image ID 1013436 (see Miles 2003, 126).

Tom Stevens (Tl'aajaang quuna) / *See Genealogy Chart 3*

Tom Stevens (b. ca. 1837, d. 1902) held the name Tl'aajaang quuna, of Those Born at Rose Spit, Naayii Kun K̲iiG̲awaay (R13). He owned the Great Splashing of Waves house in Skidegate that he sold to James Deans and was installed at the WCE. We know that he was married to a woman named Isabella (E11/E6a). After the death of Tom Stevens in 1902, Isabella married Zacherias (see House Model No. 3, above in this chapter). However, he also had an earlier wife. Deans says: "The person from whom I bought the house [referring to the large house sent to the WCE] had also for his first wife a daughter of the Edensaw. She helped largely to build this house" (Deans 1893b, 45). As discussed above, Tom Stevens, being a Raven (R13), would most likely have married Eagle women. It may be that his first wife was the widow of his maternal uncle, the Old Tl'aajaang quuna, namd "Ga agit, 'Branches.'"

Tom Stevens's family had originally come from the village at Cape Ball, G̱aahllns Kun Llnagaay, and according to Deans, he was raised by his maternal uncle, who had the name Hungo Daas before he became Tl'aajaang quuna. Tl'aajaang quuna then was passed to Tom Stevens. Albert Edward Edenshaw (7IDANsuu) also came from that village but moved north, while his sisters moved south to Skidegate in the nineteenth century. If he was married before Isabella, no children by this first marriage are known. He had several children with Isabella, including Fanny Blackstone, who married Henry Young. He was apparently the brother of Skilduunaas, David Shakespeare, and his sister was married to Amos Russ's father (see Genealogy Chart 3).

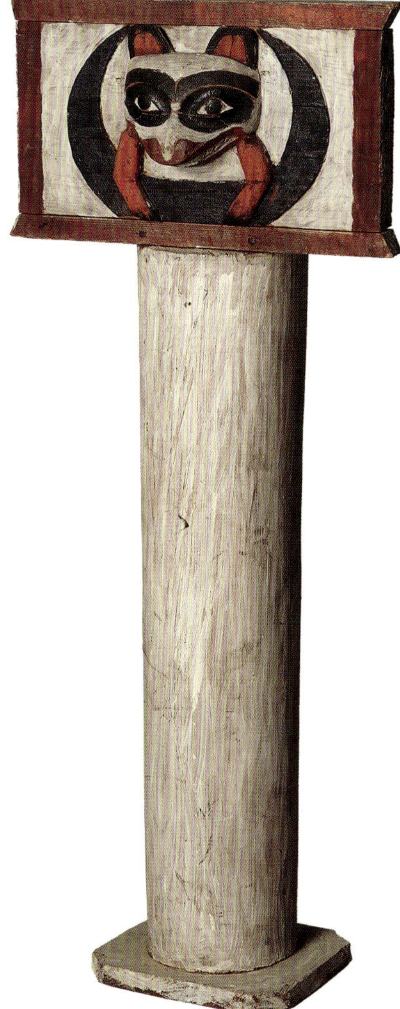

3.112 Model Mortuary Pole No. 14, Tl'aajaang quuna Sahlln GyaaG̱ang, "Tl'aajaang quuna's Mortuary Pole," 1892, 37.5 × 15 in. Courtesy of the Field Museum, cat. no. 17841. Photograph by Gail Specht.

MODEL POLE NO. 14

Deans reports this is a model of the mortuary pole, "Claads-an Coona's Suthlingun" now spelled Tl'aajaang quuna Sahlln GyaaG̱ang, raised for the old Tl'aajaang quuna, Tom Stevens's uncle, who died ca. 1862 (Deans 1893b, 92). It has a bear in a nest on the panel (figure 3.112). Newcombe confirms this, with information from Charles Jefferson and John Wesley, saying it was for the first Tl'aajaang quuna (R13). He lists this pole next to the memorial pole for Tl'aajaang quuna's wife named "Ga agit, 'Branches'" who belonged to the Eagles of the Staastas division (see above).[135] The model of Tl'aajaang quuna's mortuary pole was placed in the WCE installation in front of "Box House" and it is most likely a model of the mortuary pole that appears to the left in Maynards's photo (see figure 2.10) and to the right in Dossetter's photo (see figure 3.109).

HOUSE MODEL NO. 23

Naa G̱a Ḵayhlas, "Tray House," called by Deans "Nah Keetah or Nuh ru Kiethta, House of Dishes," was said to have belonged to "Weenuts" [WiiG̱anad], uncle to John Dellseugas (Bone Belly) [Dalskujas] (figures 3.113a, 3.113b).[136] The figures on the model are identified as a bear holding a boy at the bottom, raven with the moon in his beak, a beaver holding a stick, and an eagle on top. Frogs were placed on the projecting beams and on the platform in front of the house model. According to Deans, the

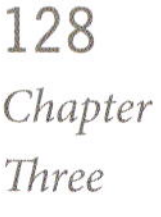

3.113 A & B House Model No. 23, Naa G̱a Ḵayhlas, “Tray House,” Deans’s “House of Dishes,” 1892. Courtesy of the Field Museum, cat. no. 17822. Photographs by Gail Specht (house and pole were photographed separately when pole was on exhibit).

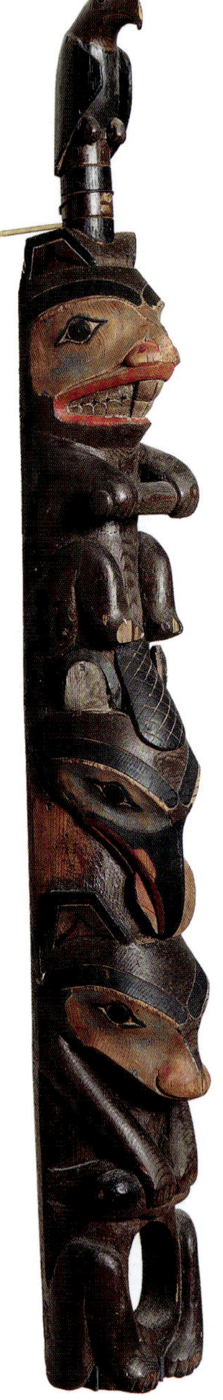

wife of “Weenuts” was a Raven related to Chief Skedans (G̱aag’yals Ḵiig̱awaay, R4). Deans notes that the house on which this model was based belonged to the “Cathlins Point,” G̱aahllns Kun (Cape Ball) Eagle people, but gives no name to the model maker (Deans 1893b, 54–55).

MacDonald uses Deans’s name “House of Dishes” (his #7) for the house that stood between “Box House” and “Grizzly Bear’s Mouth House.” However, the figures on the model pole don’t match the photo of this original house frontal pole that has a dorsal fin flanked by watchmen at top (and a snag below, according to MacDonald [1983, 46]). If indeed this model is from a house at the north end of the village, perhaps it could be a model of a different house located to the north of Grizzly Bear’s Mouth House, called “Grizzly Bear House” by MacDonald (his #4; see figure 2.10, middle and right). This pole had a beaver at the top and a bear with a man at the bottom, and there were bears on the six projecting house beams. However, these bears on the beams more closely resemble “Eagle Peoples House” (see Model No. 25 below).

Swanton lists the chief’s name “Wi’nats” [Wiig̱anad] as belonging to the Jiiaxwii Gidin.naay—“Seaward Eagles” (E11), a Rose Spit clan that has both beaver and frog as crests (Swanton 1905a, 274). There is some reason to believe that a person with this name (also spelled Waekus, Wakus, Weenitz, Weynatz) was an argillite carver and silversmith who working in Victoria in the 1860s (see Wright 1985, 2–3; Bunn-Marcuse 1998, 82–83; Bunn-Marcuse 2007, 17; Bunn-Marcuse and Collison 2018, 273–75). In Robert Brown’s report to the Royal Geographical Society in London he spoke of

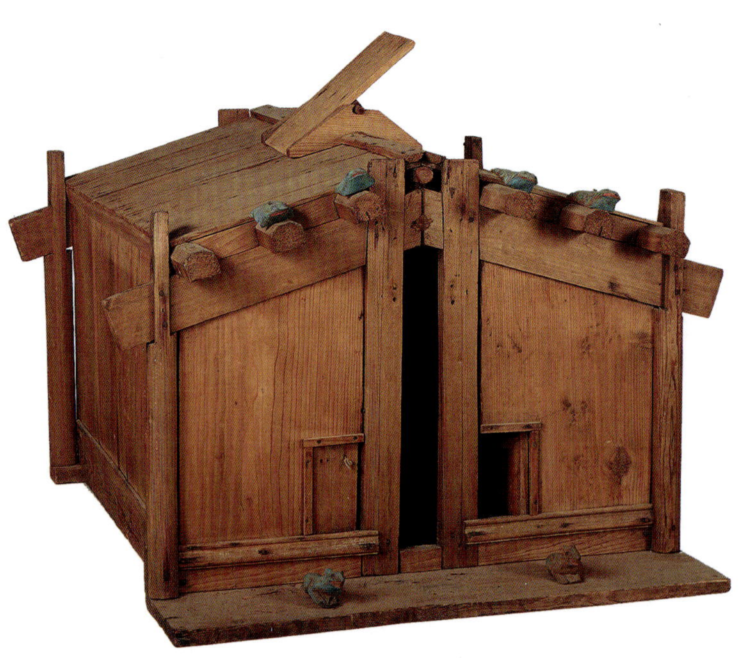

his visit to Victoria in 1866: "A man called Waekus made out of gold coin a pair of bracelets, for the wife of the English Admiral on the Station, of such beautiful design and execution, that they were universally admired. The same man afterwards designed the cast-iron railing now ornamenting the balcony of the Bank of British Columbia, in Victoria. He could scratch a fair portrait on ivory, and I have seen a bust of Shakespeare executed by him in slate from an engraving" (Brown 1868–1869, 389). Sophia Cracroft described this railing earlier in 1861: "This over, we said good bye to that excellent man Mr. Dundas, and went on under the guidance of the Bp & Mr. Good, sent by the Governor for the purpose, to an iron foundry over the bridge & near the native Indian village, in order to see some very remarkable carvings by an Indian in wood, for castings. They are admirable—copied from drawings, & shew wonderful power of imitation" (Cracroft 1974, 79).

Frederick Dally, a photographer who lived in Victoria during this time, photographed this man and commissioned him to make two bracelets for him.[137] However, he didn't know his name:

> When the Bank of British Columbia in Government Street, Victoria required some cast iron railing for ornamentation of the front of the first storey, they employed a clever carver belonging to the Hydah tribe living on the Queen Charlotte's Island to carve in wood the desired pattern to be cast from; this same Indian was renowned for his beautiful carved work in the making of silver bracelets, so before I left the Colony, I gave him a small bag of silver coins being Mexican and Peruvian coins of various values in a number of 50 telling him to make a pair of bracelets with the design of a cully-cully [bird] on them, that is all that I told him about the pattern, I never asked for his name nor where he lived, and that I would give him half the number that was in the bag for his work. In course of time having long since forgotten all about the circumstance, he came to me one day with the most beautiful pair of carved silver bracelets that I had ever seen, with the American eagle engraved on them, the pattern taken from the American half dollar. His portrait may be seen in one of the Album's lower left hand corner, a ring through the septum of his nose.
>
> An Indian boy that had taken great interest in his work of making the bracelets looked with covetious [*sic*] eyes upon them and was resolved to become possessed of them, so one Saturday night, after he had seen the finishing of the same, he quarreled with his friend because he would not give them up which he could not do as he had already delivered them up to me, which was not known to the boy who then gave him a stab in the back with a shoemaker's knife and placed him on the sacking of his bed without any kind of covering, where his life blood slowly ebbed away and formed a puddle underneath, this I saw when my friend D. Jones came on the Sunday morning to tell me of his fate. (Augaitis et al. 2006, 106; Dally n.d.)

The date of this death was not recorded, although it would have been before Dally left Victoria in 1870.[138] *The British Columnist*, April 26, 1874, confirms he had died before 1870. This article also links the name spelled "Wakus" to "Weenitz":

> "A Savage Artist," Victoria, April 23, Editor—On looking over the Family Herald for Feb. 19, 1870, No. 1400, vol. XXVII, p. 686, I was surprised to find in a notice of a (then) recent meeting of the Geographical Society that "A Hyday Indian named Wakus" made the design of the cast iron railing now on the balcony of the Bank of British Columbia, Victoria. The Heralds's statement is quite correct. The skillful redman was named Weenitz. He was a native of Queen Charlotte Island and in the early days of the gold rush was noted for the fidelity with which he carved the likeness of persons on bone or ivory. He was also clever as a worker in metals, producing gold and silver ornaments from coins, exquisitely chased and finished. Specimens of his handiwork are still extent [*sic*] in many households, but we believe that poor Weenitz died some years ago.

Curiously, there is also a report in the *British Columnist* telling of his amputation in 1862: "AMPUTATED.—Weynatz, the Hydah Indian who was such a proficient carver, and who made the design for the railing of the balcony of the Bank of British Columbia, severly [*sic*] injured his arm yesterday by the explosion of a pistol. He was conveyed to the Royal Hospital, where in the course of the day the hand was amputated by Dr. Trimble. He is now doing well" (*British Columnist* 1862). This report combined with Dally's would suggest that he continued carving after this amputation, making him an even more remarkable artist, since Dally's reports would have followed the amputation report in time. This spelling of the name "Weynatz," which was later spelled "Weenitz" and "Waekus," may in fact be the name Wiiganad that Swanton spelled "Wi'nats," since the Haida pronunciation includes a g pronounced at the back of the throat, which to a non-Haida speaker might have either been missed or heard as a "k."

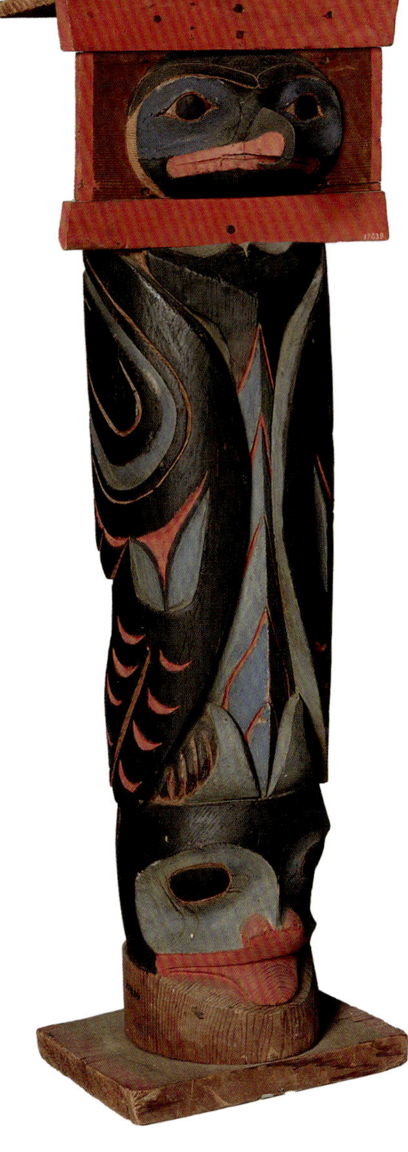

3.114 Model Mortuary Pole No. 13, Wiiganad Sahlln Gyaagang, "Wiiganad's Mortuary Pole," 1892, 29.5 in. × 10.25 in. × 8.5 in. Courtesy of the Field Museum, cat. no. 17839. Photograph by Gail Specht.

This artist had long been dead by the time the House Model No. 23 was carved in 1892. No silver bracelets made by him can be firmly documented, although it is possible that one now at the Royal British Columbia Museum (cat. no. 13535) might be by his hand (Bunn-Marcuse and Collison 2018, 273–74, figure 2). A portrait of a Victoria politician, said to be Amor de Cosmos, founder of the *Daily British Colonist* and the second premier of British Columbia, was said "by family lore" to have been made by Waekus ca. 1860. This figure is also now in the collection of the Royal British Columbia Museum (Bunn-Marcuse 2007, 17; Bunn-Marcuse et al. 2018, 274, figure 3). Whether or not James Deans had ever heard of this artist in Victoria or taken note of the Bank of British Columbia railing, he did not connect him with this house model. It would be interesting to know if the owner of the original house was in fact the Victoria carver or another Wiiganad entirely, since we know the name was held by several people, including two women (see below).

MODEL POLE NO. 13

Wiiganad Sahlln Gyaagang, "Wiiganad's Mortuary Pole," shows a raven's head on the mortuary panel, with the wings folded around the post and a sculpin at the base (figure 3.114). According to Deans: "This model was raised to the memory of Wee-nuts, wife of a man named Hlalls. Who had it raised to her memory. . . . When this post was raised it was intended at death to put her body into it, but it was put in the graveyard, owing to the march of improvement. She took the name of Weenuts from a man by that name from whom she acquired it by heritage as well as purchase. She also got all his effects." Deans's suggested label for this post was: "Erected by Klalls of the Cathlins Coon hadry to the memory of his wife, Weenuts, who [wadlehon?] Getaga Cahie (eat up a whole sculpin) from her getting all Weenuts belongings" (Deans 1893b, 92).

Newcombe's margin notes point out that "Weenuts" is a man's name, but Deans explained how the name came to this woman. There are two mortuary posts that show in the photographs of Skidegate that have bird's beaks projecting from the panel in this manner that stood to the right of Tl'aajaang quuna's house. One of these had a carved bird's body with ovoid wing joints clearly carved on the post (figure 3.115)

(MacDonald 1983, 47, #12X). This must be the original after which this model was carved.[139] Deans says that this post had more coloring than any other in the village. Sidney Crosby became WiiG̱anad, the hereditary chief of the Naa 'Yuuwans X̱aay-daG̱aay (E6a), at a Skidegate potlatch held on June 20, 2011.

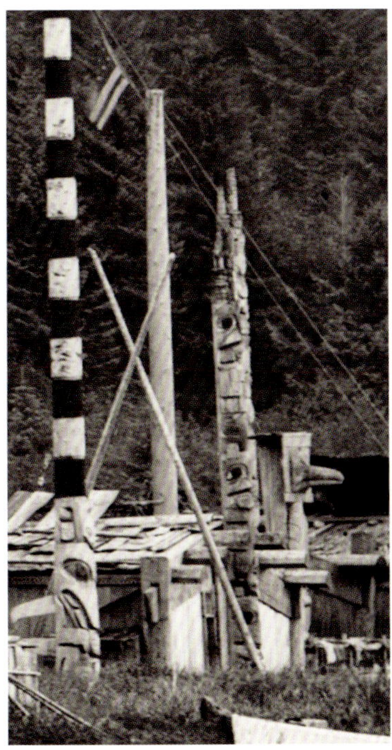

3.115 *above* Detail of figure 2.5, HlG̱aagilda Llnagaay (Skidegate) showing the WiiG̱anad mortuary pole at right. Photograph by Edward Dossetter, 1881.

HOUSE MODEL NO. 24 / *Made by John Robson (Gyaawhllns) and David Shakespeare (Skilduunaas)*

Xuuajii X̱iihlii Naas, "Grizzly Bear Mouth House," had a fully painted front, carved in low relief, depicting a grizzly bear's head and front legs (figures 3.116, 3.117).[140] Portraits of Judge Pemberton of the Victoria police court and George Smith, town clerk, both wearing hats, were placed on the corner posts. Deans identifies the two figures on the model as being Pemberton with the top hat, and Smith with the smaller cap, differentiated to show their relative status. Deans also reports that the original house was built by "Goatlins" first saying he was the grandfather of the parties who built this model, and later that he was an uncle of one of the parties (Deans 1893b, 58).[141] We know that John Robson's Haida name was Gyaawhllns, and since he inherited this name from the owner of this house, he would have been his maternal uncle, both of the Naayii Kun Ḵiig̱awaay (R13).

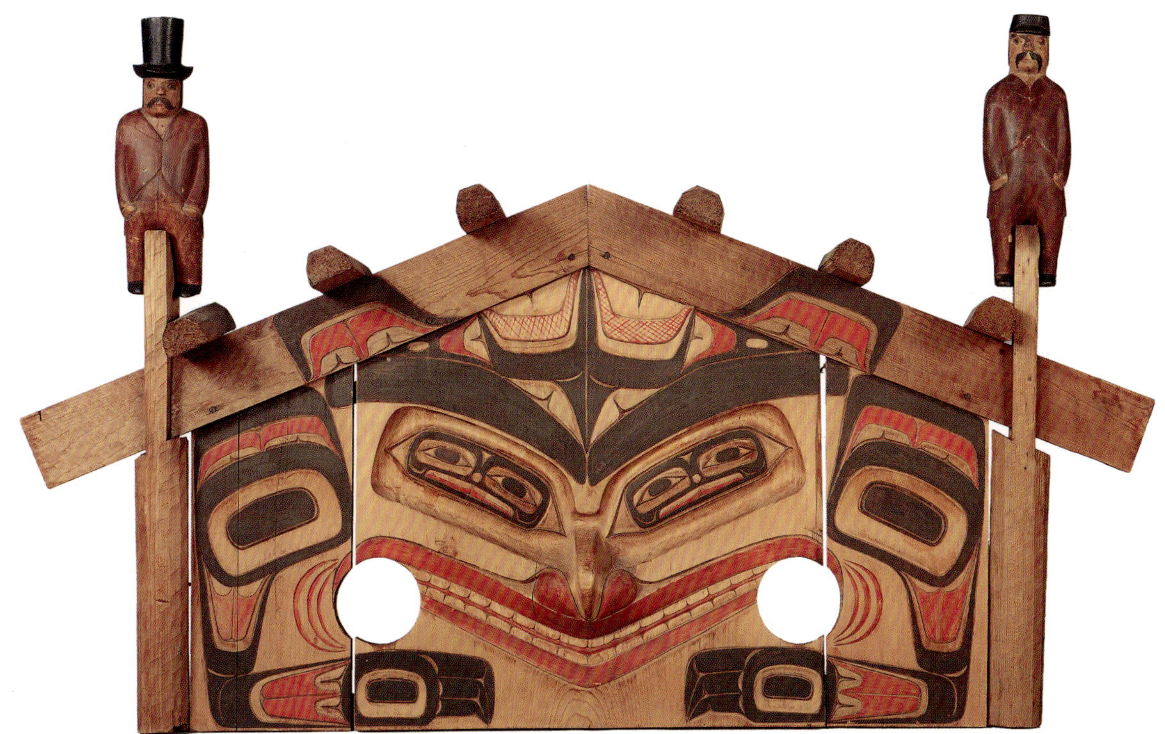

3.116 *right* Model House No. 24, Xuuajii X̱iihlii Naas, "Grizzly Bear Mouth House," made by Gyaawhllns, John Robson, and Skilduunaas, David Shakespeare, 1892, 54 cm h × 111 cm w (21.25 in. h × 43.7 in. w). Courtesy of the Field Museum, cat. no. 17990 (façade and corner figures only remain, no inside figures). Photograph by Gail Specht.

3.117 Detail of figure 2.10, HlG̱aagilda Llnagaay (Skidegate) showing Grizzly Bear's Mouth House. Photograph by the Maynards, 1884. Canadian Museum of History, Library and Archives of Canada, PA 71-3087 (see figure 2.10 for full view).

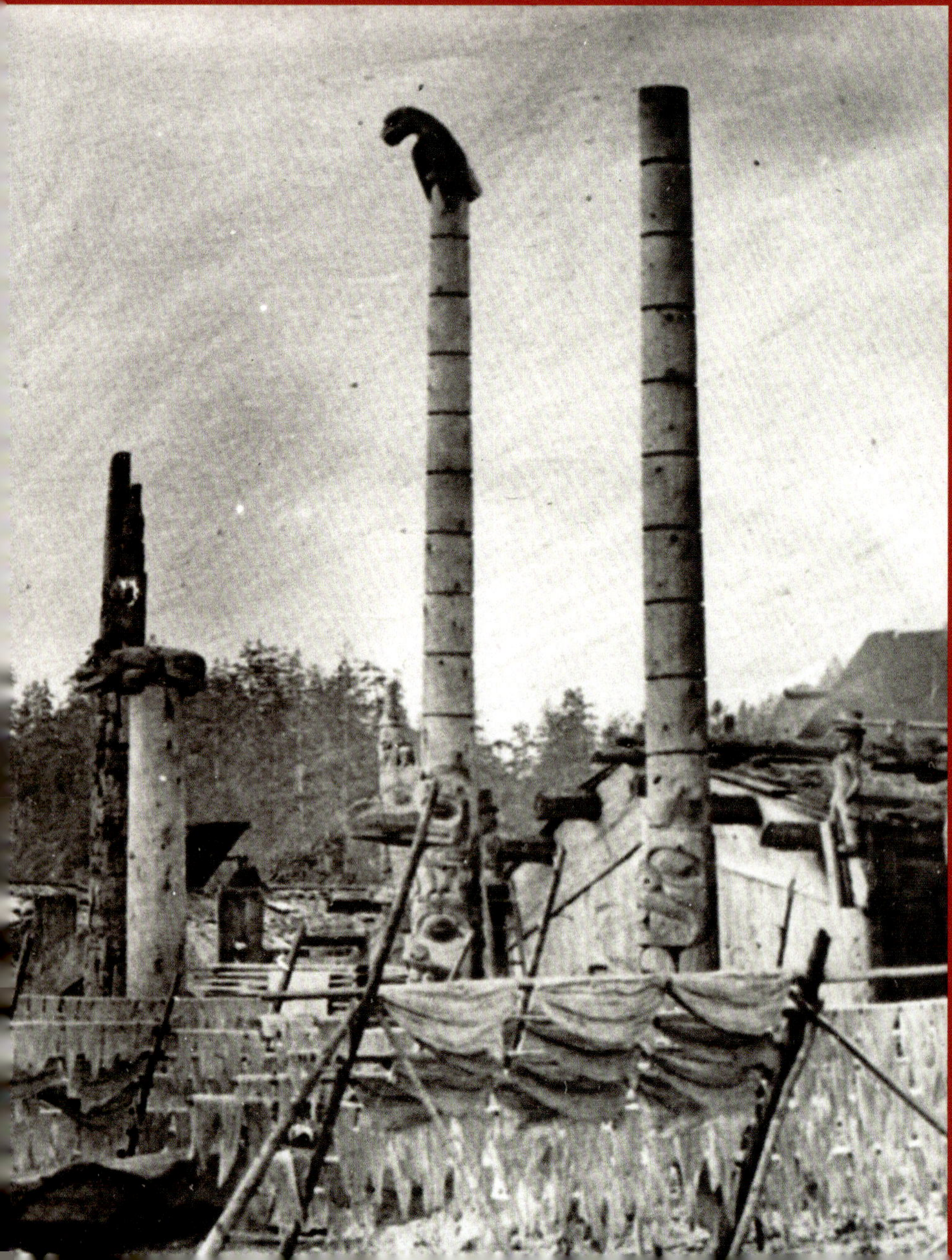

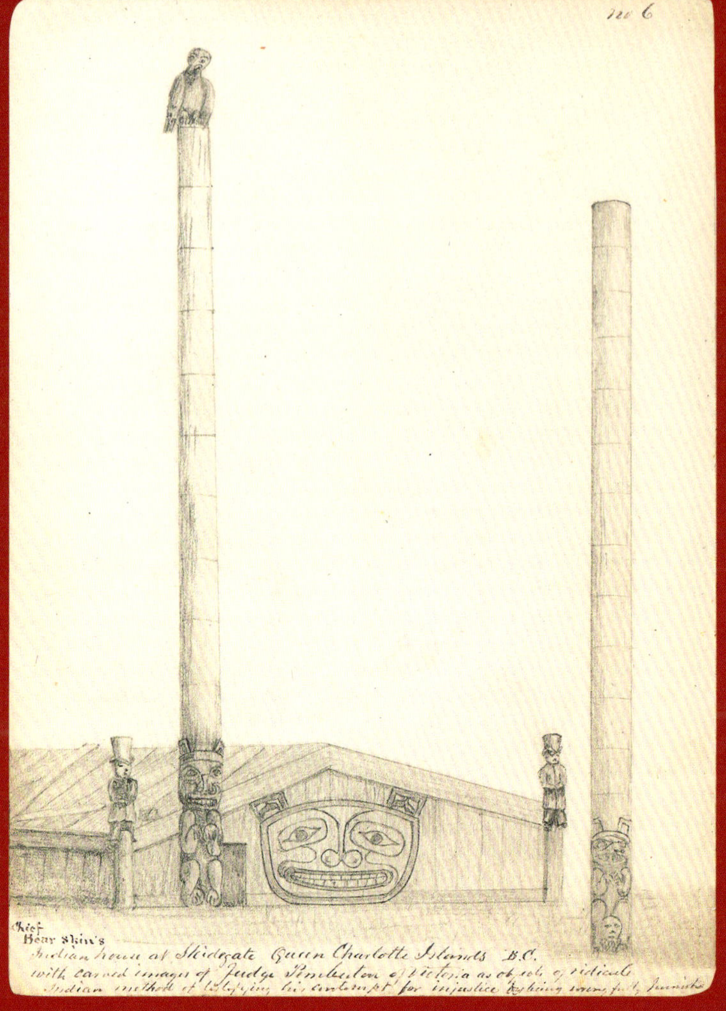

3.118 Drawing by James G. Swan entitled: "Chief Bear Skin's Indian House at Skidegate Queen Charlotte Islands, B.C. with carved images of Judge Pemberton of Victoria as objects of ridicule, Indian method of displaying his contempt for injustice by being exempt from his jurisdiction," August 1883, 25.4 cm × 18.1 cm. Franz R. and Kathryn M. Stenzel Collection of Western American Art. Yale Collection of Western Americana, Beinecke Rare Book and Manuscript Library, Image ID 1013469 (see Miles 2003, 127).

According to Deans, sometime in the early 1870s the owner of this house was jailed briefly in Victoria for being drunk and disorderly and released after the payment of a fifty dollar fine. To save face, regain his status, and ridicule these men, upon his return to Skidegate, he had the effigies for the Victoria officials put on his corner posts (Deans 1893b, 56–57). These ridicule figures can be seen in both Dawson's 1878 photo (see figure 2.2 far right) and the Maynards's 1884 photograph of the house (see figure 3.117). The carving of "ridicule" figures was an established custom on the Northwest Coast.

Swanton lists this house (his #5) as "Xu'adji xeli'" ("grisly-bear mouth") Family Naayii Kun K̲iiG̲awaay (R13). James G. Swan identified the owner of this house as "Chief Bear Skin" on his sketch of the house in 1883 (figure 3.118): "Chief Bear Skin's Indian House at Skidegate Queen Charlotte Islands, B.C. with carved images of Judge Pemberton of Victoria as objects of ridicule, Indian method of testifying his contempt for injustice by being exempt from his jurisdiction" (Miles 2003, 127).

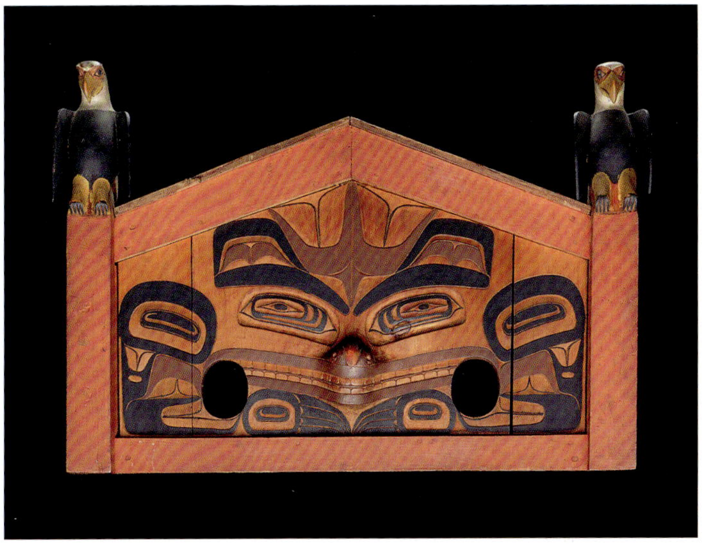

3.119 Model of Grizzly Bear's Mouth House, attributed to John Robson (the Canadian Museum of History attributes this model to both Robson and David Shakespeare), 66 cm h × 70 cm l × 48 cm w. Acquired at Skidegate before 1900 for the Lord Bossom Collection. Courtesy of the Canadian Museum of History No. VII B 1556.

The Swan drawing has a single rectangular door to the left of the bear's head, rather than the two oval doors that are visible in Dawson's photograph and used on the four models that were made of this house. It also shows only the bear's head not the shoulder joints, front legs, and claws as on the models. The house front is obscured by the rack of drying fish in the Maynard photo, so it is difficult to see the bear design (see figure 3.117). John Robson made a second model of this house that is now in the Canadian Museum of History (figure 3.119). On this model eagles are placed on the corner posts, and the bear's ears are shown squeezed below the gable planks as in the Swan drawing. Two argillite models of this house were carved by Charles Edenshaw (see Wright 2001b, 248–49, figures 5.16 and 5.17; Wright and Augaitis 2013, 162–65, figures 186, 187). These have sea lions carved on the roof and formline designs on the sides as well as the bear on the front. One has the bear's ears on the gable planks, and the other does not. Deans points out that the inherited right to display or wear bears' ears, Taan gyuu, "Tan Gue," was a high privilege (Deans 1893b, vol. 38, folder 3, p. 56).

Swan collected an appliquéd dancing shirt from "Chief Bear Skin" when he was in Skidegate in 1883 (figure 3.120). His notes say that he acquired it for twenty-five dollars and it was "difficult to obtain." It displays the bear crest of Gyaawhllns.

Unfortunately, only the house front and corner post figures from the WCE model remain at the Field Museum, and the rest of the house and a group of figures depict-

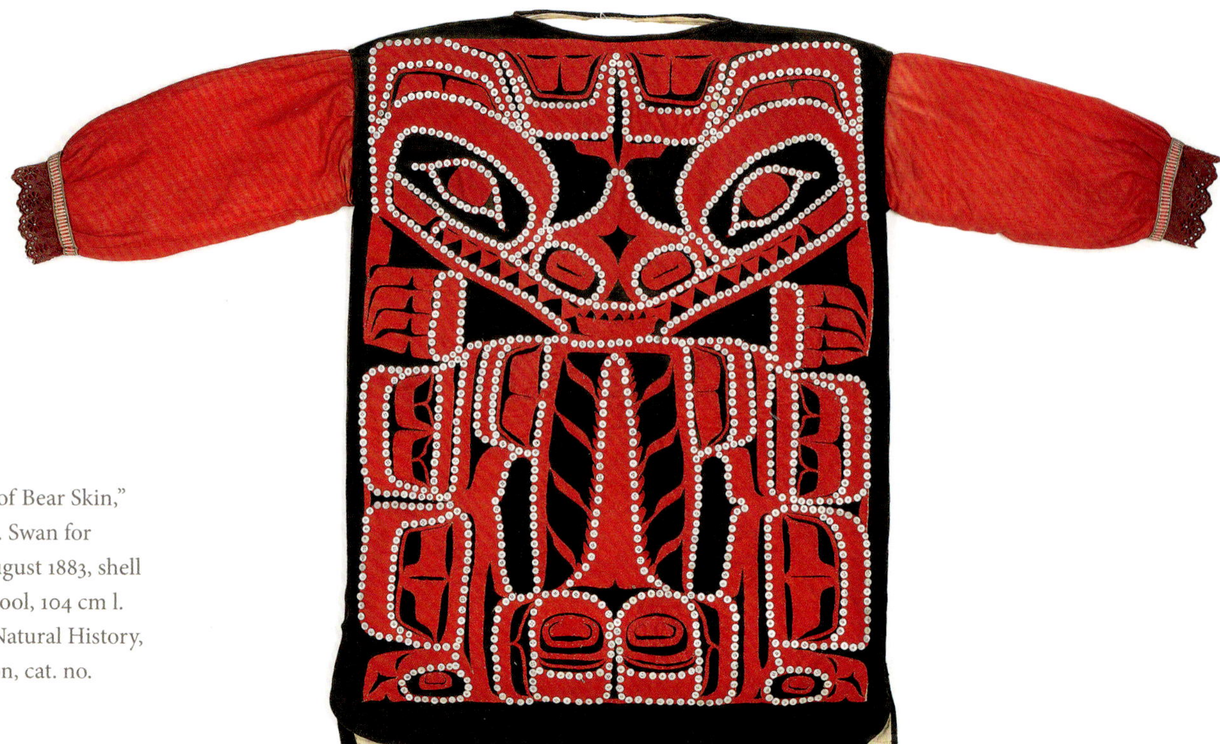

3.120 "Dancing Shirt of Bear Skin," purchased by James G. Swan for twenty-five dollars, August 1883, shell buttons, cotton, and wool, 104 cm l. National Museum of Natural History, Smithsonian Institution, cat. no. E129984-0.

ing a girl's puberty ritual that were inside are missing. Deans described the girl's puberty ritual that was enacted by the figures inside:

> Inside of the house is the model of a Lall [Taag̱uunah], that is when a girl reaches a certain time in her life she is kept behind the curtains, as it were, for a month or six weeks or until the return of the event, when her friends make presents to their chief and the rest of the tribe, and she gets a name and is at liberty to marry. The girl is shown as looking behind a wall on which is painted a Cahie or sculpin [K'aal], which is the name she is given. This used to be the great event in her life and was known and spoken of by young and old. The place of her confinement is generally made by hanging blankets over a rope in a corner of the house. None has had to undergo this ordeal for about three years I believe (Deans 1893b, vol. 38, folder 3, p. 57).

Deans reported that the first menstrual seclusion that was traditional among the Haida women had not been done since 1889, but we know that the practice was continued into the twentieth century, though kept hidden from the Christian missionaries.[142]

MODEL POLE NO. 15 / *Figure 3.121*

Directly in front of Grizzly Bear's Mouth House were two beaver poles with small bears between their ears, erected in honor of women of this family, both of which were carved as models for Deans (figure 3.121). These are also shown in Swan's sketch of "Bear Skin's" house (see figure 3.118). Deans reports that one of these poles was erected by Tl'aajaang quuna to the memory of his wife "Ellgie Towei (Chief's Wife)." Deans translated "Ellgie Towei" as "Chief's Wife," but the Haida word for "chief" is Iitl'lx̱aayda, Itl'lG̱as, or Kilslaay, and the word for "wife" is JaaG̱a. This woman may have been Albert Edward Edenshaw's sister, named ""ī'lga jăt kîlk! ī'gŭs," "Chief woman whose voice is sharp" (Staastas, E21). It is possible that "Ellgie" was Deans's spelling of "Llgaay." "Llgaay gwii sdiihlda" means balance (restoring balance). "Towei" may be Taaxwii, which means friend.[143] The model of this pole has a raven with a copper in its beak at the top. Deans goes on to say: "The raven at the top with the tan [copper] in its mouth shows her to have been a good and thrifty wife, bringing peace and plenty to her family." The original pole stood to the right/north and was missing the bird on top when it was first photographed by Dawson in 1878 (see figure 2.2, far right). At that time there was only one beaver pole in front of this house. The model memorial pole was positioned just to the right of "Grizzly Bear's Mouth House" at the WCE as it was in the village (see figure 3.117, right), though it falls outside of the photograph of the installation (see figure 3.2).

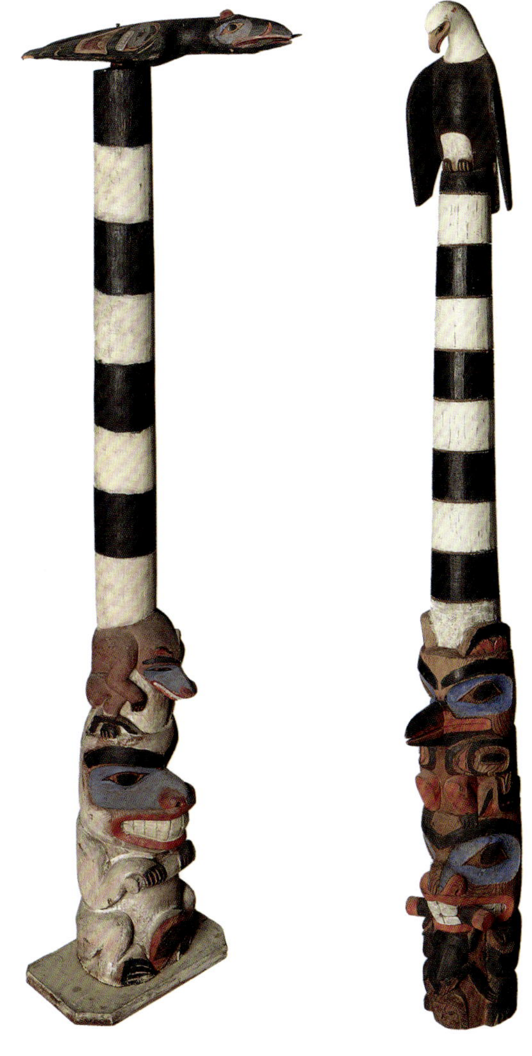

MODEL POLE NO. 17 / *Attributed to Gyaawhllns, John Robson*

A newer memorial pole appears in the 1881 Dossetter photos in front at the left/south corner of "Grizzly Bear's Mouth House" (see figure 2.5, far right). Deans reports of the model of this pole, "This Hat was erected years ago more as a mark of respect for his wife, by one of the Cathlina Coon folks named John Robson. . . . As soon as she dies it is the intention of her people to cut it down, then she will have a costly marble monument in the graveyard" (figure 3.122) (Deans 1893b, 93). This pole has an eagle at the top, a raven, and a beaver with a frog on its chest at the base. Newcombe confirms this pole was put up by John Robson and gives his wife's name as "Klakona" of the Staastas (figure 3.123, left). This woman, Q'aaw quunaa, was Charles Edenshaw's mother, and Albert Edward Edenshaw's sister. She died in 1896. Robson died in 1924 at the age of seventy-eight.

Newcombe referred to this pole as the "Amos Russ Monument," but it is unclear why, since Robson would have been alive when he wrote this.[144] Since both Q'aaw quunaa's crests (eagle and beaver) and Robson's crest (raven) appear on the pole, it may be that Robson raised the pole to honor his wife on the occasion of his marriage to her. Robson was Charles Edenshaw's stepfather, although he was seven years younger

3.121 *left* Model Pole No. 15, ī'lga jăt kîlk! ī'gŭs Q'aa.l, "ī'lga jăt kîlk! ī'gŭs's Memorial Pole," 1892, 60.5 in. × 14.75 in. × 12 in. Courtesy of the Field Museum, cat. no. 17840. Photograph by Gail Specht.

3.122 *right* Model Pole No. 17, Q'aaw quunaa GyaaG̱ang, "Q'aaw quunaa's Memorial Pole," attributed to John Robson, 1892, 62 in. × 6 in. × 9 in. Courtesy of the Field Museum, cat. no. 17838. Photograph by Gail Specht.

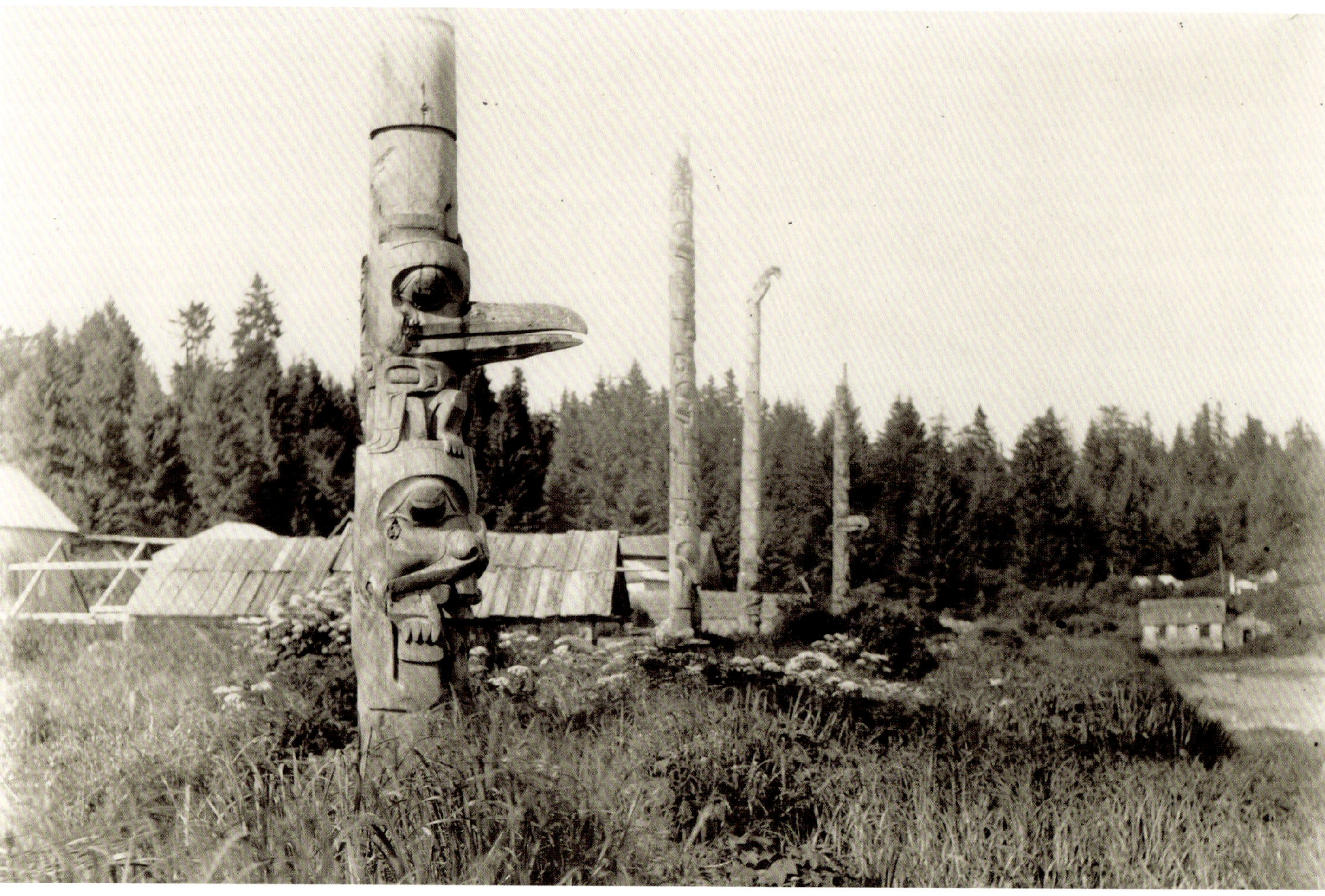

3.123 Q'aaw quuna's pole in the foreground with the frontal pole from "Fort House" to the right, followed by Jane Shakespeare's beaver pole (the last old pole standing in the village), and to the far right, "House to Which the High Tide Comes," the house farthest north in the village whose frontal pole was purchased by C. F. Newcombe and sent to Melbourne, Australia (see figures 3.134 and 3.135). Photograph by C. F. Newcombe, [1897?]. Image PN18. Courtesy of the Royal BC Museum and Archives.

than Charles (see Wright 2001b, 249). Though Deans doesn't say so, John Robson most likely carved this model of the pole, based on its style. He also carved another model of the same pole that is much larger (RBCM, cat. no. 231).

A third beaver memorial pole with an eagle on top was located up the beach to the north (figure 3.123, second pole from the left, to the right of Q'aaw quunaa's pole).[145] This was the last old pole that remained standing in Skidegate through the twentieth century. There was no model of this pole in the WCE installation; however, James Deans did collect a model of this pole that he did not send to Chicago, but instead sold it to the museum in Victoria (figure 3.124). According to the family, the full-size pole was raised by Skilduunaas (David Shakespeare) in honor of his wife, Klaaskost, Jane Shakespeare (ca. 1834–1904) of the Staastas (E21) clan. It stood on the site of the Tulip house, later in front of the old Skidegate Band Council office (now Elders of HlG̲aagilda X̲aayda Kil Naay) until the winter of 1989 when it blew down in a winter storm (figure 3.125). It is now on display at the Haida Gwaii Museum at K̲ay Llnagaay.[146]

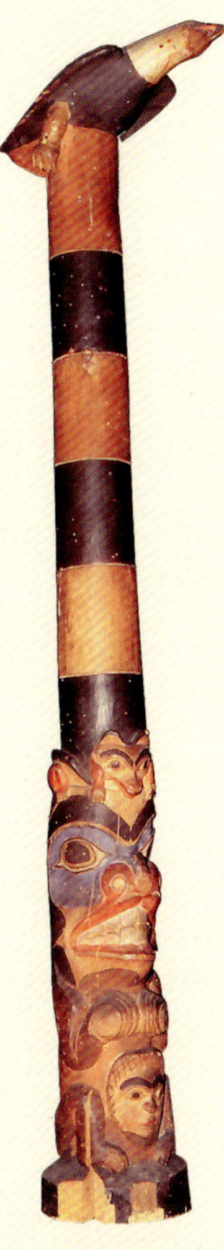

3.124 *above* Model of pole raised in honor of Klaaskost, Jane, by her husband, David Skilduunaas (Shakespeare). This model was not sent to the World's Columbian Exposition but sold by Deans to the Provincial Museum (now the Royal British Columbia Museum) in Victoria. Cat. no. 230. Courtesy of the Royal BC Museum and Archives. Photograph by the author.

3.125 *right* Last standing nineteenth-century pole in HlG̱aagilda Llnagaay (Skidegate), raised by Skilduunaas, David Shakespeare, in honor of his wife, Klaaskost, Jane. Image PN541. Courtesy of the Royal BC Museum and Archives.

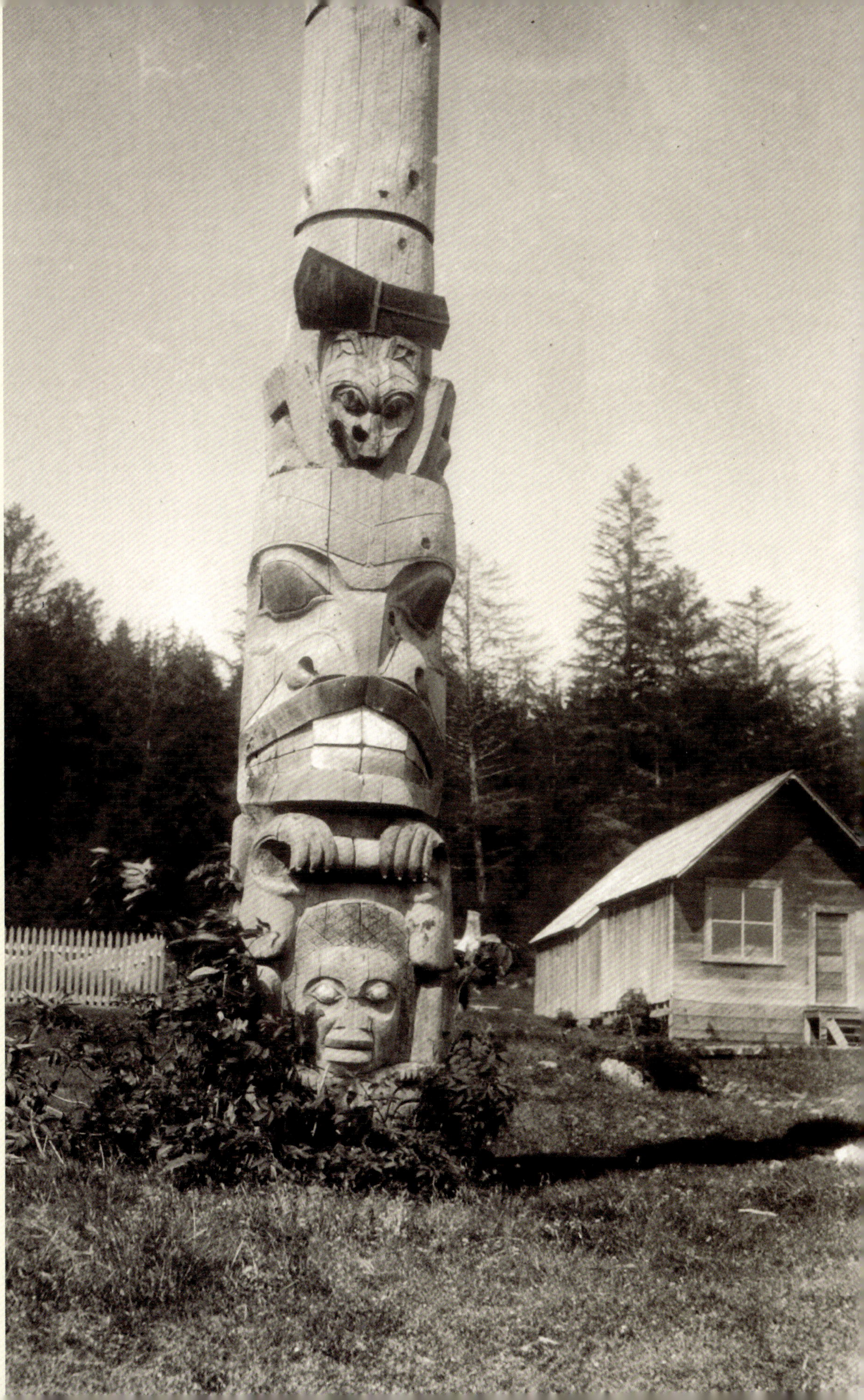

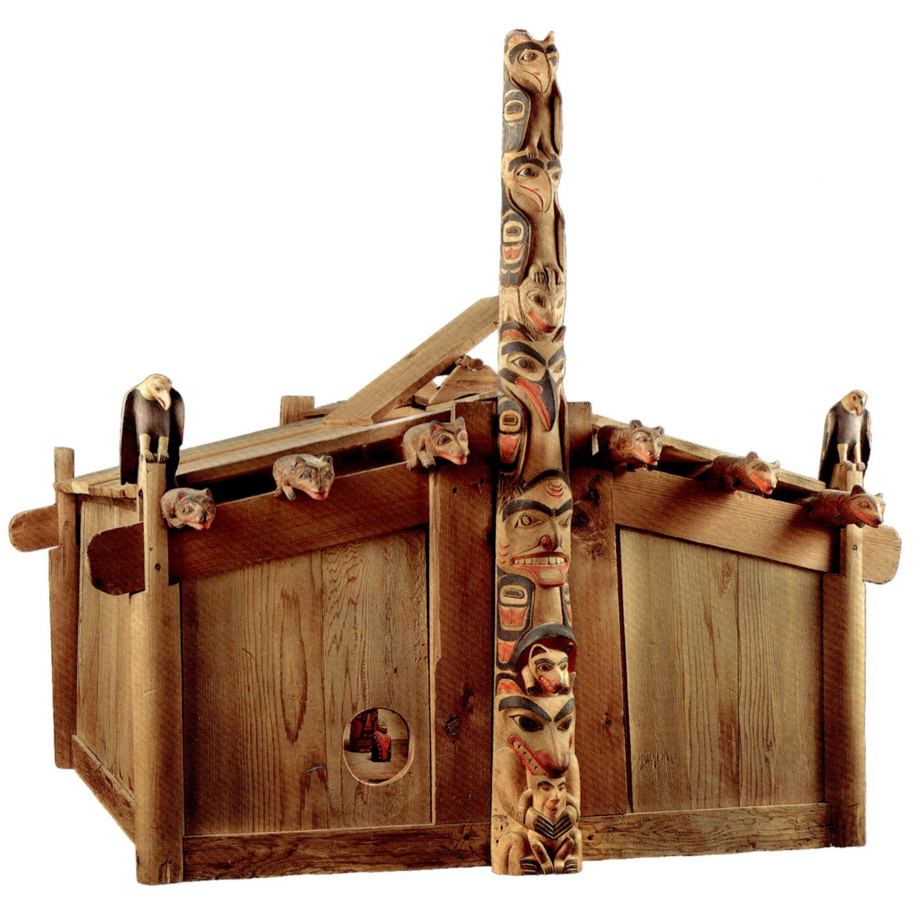

HOUSE MODEL NO. 25 / *Made by John Robson (Gyaawhllns) and David Shakespeare (Skilduunaas)*

This model was made by both John Robson and David Skilduunaas (Shakespeare) (figures 3.126, 3.127). Deans gave two names for the house: "Eagle People's House, Coot nass hadry" (G̲uud Naas X̲aayda means "Eagle house people") or an earlier name: "Taw Shin nass, "Food Island House people" (Taasin naas means "saying you're going to eat house"—SHIP February 11, 2004). The model house has six brown bears on roof beams and eagles on corner posts. The figures on the pole are a small human figure in the arms of a bear, young bear in a nest, dogfish woman, a raven and two eagles stacked at the top. As with the "Grizzly Bear's Mouth House" model, Robson and Skilduunaas placed figures inside. Deans identifies the scene as a "Skagga" (SG̲aaga) or shaman's dance, although no shaman figure is seen. There are ten small figures and two larger figures, one a chief wearing a headdress (figure 3.127). A box drum with an eagle design is suspended from the ceiling and another tall figure with red facial paint and a striped robe wearing no headdress stands near the box drum in the corner (not visible in figure 3.127).

Because of the bears on the roof beams, it is assumed that this is a model of the house that stood immediately to the right of "Grizzly Bear's Mouth House" in the village, which had bears on the roof beams, the only such house in Skidegate (figure 3.128). Newcombe called this Grizzly Bear House, "Huadji naas"

3.126 *above* Model House No. 25, Xuuajii Naas, "Grizzly Bear House" or G̲uud Naas X̲aayda, "Eagle house people," Deans called it "Eagle People's House, Coot nass hadry," made by John Robson and David Skilduunaas, 1892, 98 cm × 53 cm (house), 38.6 in. × 20.9 in. (93 cm × 10 cm × 7 cm) (pole). © The Field Museum, image no. A114844d_013, cat. no. 17836. Photographer John Weinstein.

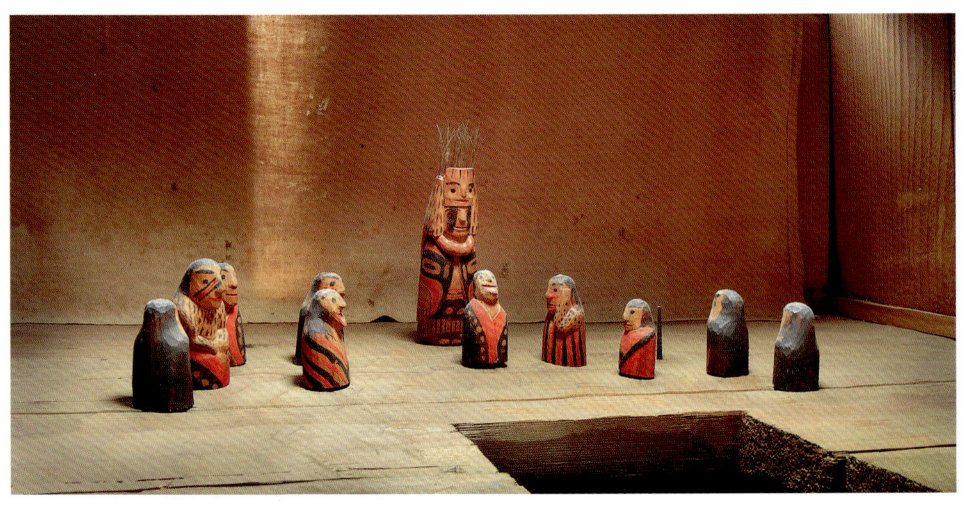

3.127 *right* Interior view of Model House No. 25, Xuuajii Naas, "Grizzly Bear House" or G̲uud Naas X̲aayda, "Eagle house people," showing a large chief figure wearing a headdress, neck ring, and robe, with ten smaller figures wearing robes. Made by John Robson and David Skilduunaas. © The Field Museum, image no. A114844d_021, cat. no. 17836. Photograph by John Weinstein.

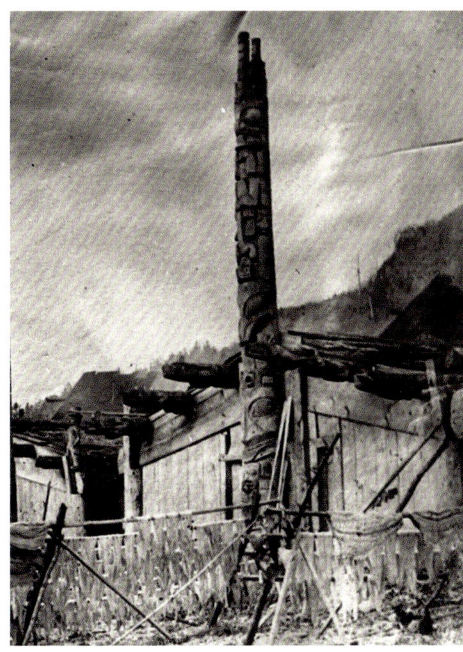

3.128 Detail of figure 2.10, "Grizzly Bear House," in Hlg̱aagilda Llnagaay (Skidegate). Photograph by the Maynards, 1884. Library and Archives of Canada, #71-3087.

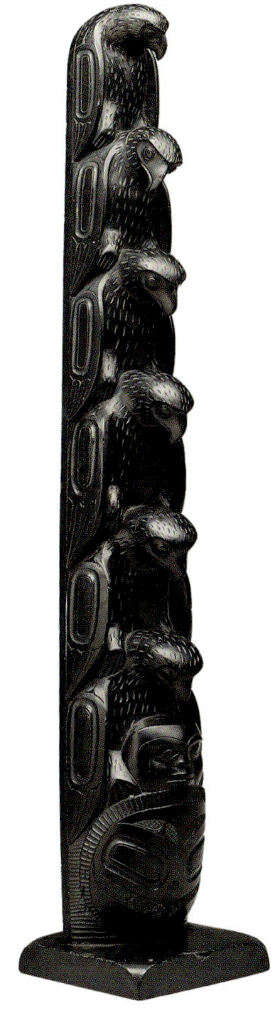

(Xuuajii Naas), and said it belonged to one of the Tl'aajaang quunas, pointing out the six large beams of the roof terminated in grizzlies, and the crests on the pole are at bottom sea-bear, then killer whale (the man's) and beaver and eagle (the wife's). Swanton also listed this house name (his #6) as Xu'adji na'as (Xuuajii Naas). So, the figures on the model pole are different from the ones on this house.

Based on its installation number (written on the back of the model), it was positioned two houses to the right of "Grizzly Bear's Mouth House," and just to the right of "Food House" (Model No. 14) in the WCE installation. There is no killer whale or beaver on the WCE pole, and the model includes a dogfish woman, not seen on the old house. Also different are the stacked eagles at the top of this model pole. It seems likely that Robson was being inventive, combining the bear beams with a story pole. These eagles are similar to two other eagle pole models that were made by Robson (figures 3.129, 3.130) that tell a story that is recounted by Deans of a boy who left his village and encountered an eagle town where he put on the eagle skin and was able to fly and capture whales. The king of the eagles warned to beware of the "Ah Seak," a large clamlike creature (Sḵaw). Of course, the boy when flying about found such a creature and had to touch it and was pulled down. One by one, the other eagles came and tried to pull him up but were also pulled down, until all the eagles were pulled

3.129 *above left* Eagle Story model pole, argillite, attributed to John Robson, 52.7 cm × 10.5 cm × 9.5 cm. Denver Art Museum Collection. Purchased from Julius Carlebach, 1959.296. Photography © Denver Art Museum (formerly National Museum of the American Indian, cat. no. 1610). According to Barbeau, this pole was collected by the Victoria dealer Landserg at Skidegate ca. 1884. He mistakenly attributed it to Charles Edenshaw (Barbeau 1953, 375, 409, figure 293).

3.130 *above right* Eagle Story model pole, attributed to John Robson, acquired 1928. Photograph courtesy of the Royal Ontario Museum © ROM, cat. no. HN838, Image ROM2016_15179_1.

under. The mother eagle came by and recued them, bringing them back to life (Deans 1893b, 59–60).

Gyaawhllns, John Robson / *See Genealogy Chart 3*

Gyaawhllns (b. ca. 1846, d. 1924), John Robson (figure 3.131), was of the Naayii Kun K̲iiG̲awaay (R13, Those Born at Rose Spit). He married Q'aaw quunaa (b. ca. 1826, d. 1896), who was Charles Edenshaw's mother, after the death of Charles's father, and so John Robson became Charles Edenshaw's stepfather, although he was at least seven years younger than Charles and at least twenty years younger than Q'aaw quunaa. This follows the Haida tradition of widows marrying their husband's nephew or brother, although it is unclear exactly how Robson was related to Edenshaw's father (see Wright 2001b, 249–53). The name Gyaawhllns came to him presumably from his uncle of the same name when he also inherited Xuuajii X̲iihlii Naas from him.[147] As mentioned earlier, Deans reports that the original house was built by "Goatlins," first saying he was the grandfather of both John Robson and David Shakespeare, and later that he was an uncle of one of the parties (Deans 1893b, 58). He was more likely an uncle of the Naay Kun K̲iiG̲awaay, as chiefly names and houses were passed down to matrilineal nephews by Haida tradition. It would have been the uncle of Robson who was the one called "Chief Bear Skin" by James G. Swan in 1883, referring to the owner of Xuuajii X̲iihlii Naas, and whose appliquéd tunic with bear design he purchased (see figure 3.120). John Robson may have been the one who sold the tunic to Swan, since his uncle would have passed away by this time.

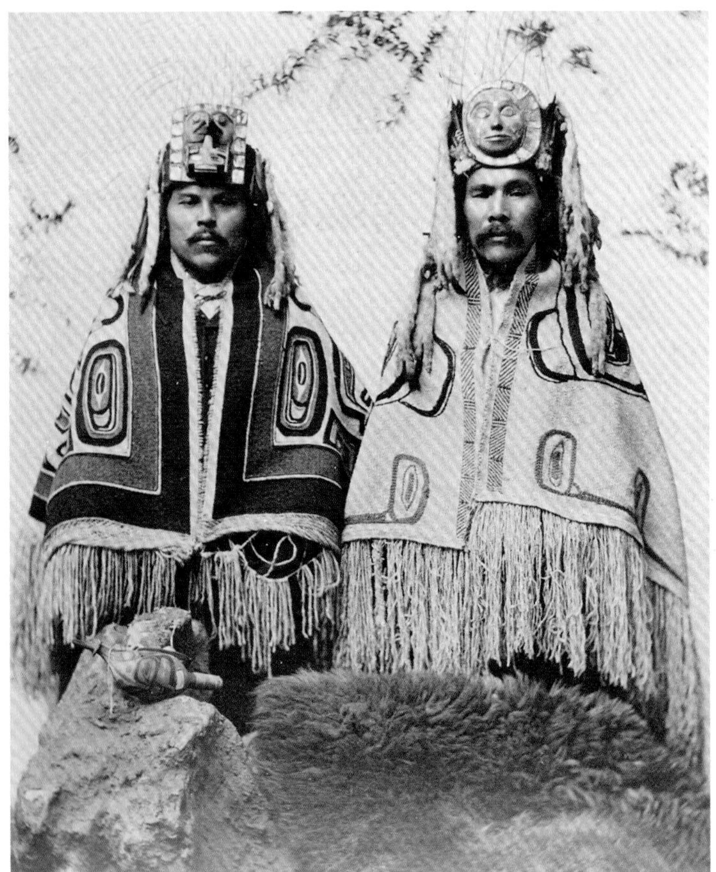

3.131 (Right) Gyaawhllns, John Robson, (left) Nunsdins, Tom Price, in regalia borrowed from Charles F. Newcombe. Photograph taken in Fleming Photographers' studio on Government Street, Victoria, BC, October 1901. Image PN5304. Courtesy of the Royal BC Museum and Archives.

Robson had the name Gyaawhllns in 1881, when the census reports he (Gaotlans, age thirty) was living in house #3 (presumed to be Xuuajii X̲iihlii Naas) with Q'aaw quunaa (age fifty-five, listed as Tlgadsat, referring to one of her other names, 7itl'gajaad ga t'a.aas [see Wright 2001b, 249] and three other people, Tlenow (sixteen-year-old male), Towosgutuungkass (fourteen-year-old girl), and Tloonance (sixty-year-old man). Ten years later the census reports the Christian name, John Robson (age forty-eight), living together with his wife "Clachoonna, age 52" (Q'aaw quunnaa) and a son named John, age twenty, perhaps the son named Tlenow ten years earlier.[148]

Robson and his wife were both baptized in 1893 and Q'aaw quunnaa took the name Martha at that time. That same year

James G. Swan collected an argillite chest that has the name "CAOWTLINS" written in large capital letters on the lid.[149] This chest, which records the name we presume to be of the maker, matches the large body of work attributed to John Robson. A second argillite carving also has the name "Caotlins" carved on the edge (NMAI 14/2211, see Wright and Augaitis 2013, 183, figure 208). A longer version of the name, Gwaiskunagiatlens, was recorded by Newcombe. At the same time, Swan collected a model house that appears to be in the same style (see figure I.15). This model may be of Xuuajii Naas (Grizzly Bear House) based on the bears on the house beams. Robson and Skilduunaas also carved a model of this house for Deans (see figure 3.126). The models have very different frontal poles and are similar only in the bears' heads on the projecting roof beams, a feature that only one house in Skidegate had. Robson's connection with this house, called Eagle House (G̱uud Naas) by Deans, is indicated by two other model poles, one wood and one argillite, that illustrate the story of the eagles who were pulled down into the sea by a giant clam, as told above. On the WCE model (Xuuajii Naas, No. 25) the two eagles at the top of the pole reference this story (see Wright 2001b, 259–60).[150] However, the full-size G̱uud Naas had no eagles. It may be that the eagles were drawn from the frontal pole on Fort House, the next house to the north of G̱uud Naas (see MacDonald 1983, 44, plate 34).

Robson must have been influenced by Edenshaw, as their carving styles are very similar, and Robson's work was often mistaken for Edenshaw's. However, Edenshaw lived in Massett and Robson lived in Skidegate, and there is no evidence that Robson and Edenshaw worked together on any poles.[151] Because John Swanton commissioned a large number of model poles from both Edenshaw and Robson, and identified them by artist, their carving styles have been well documented and can be differentiated.[152] This 1901 commission came almost ten years after the WCE commission and gave Robson an opportunity to carve several of the model poles that had been included in the earlier WCE village but made by other artists. They have been illustrated earlier for comparison with the WCE models (see figures 3.39, 3.50, 3.53, 3.58, 3.71, 3.84, 3.91, and 3.106). Also illustrated for comparison are his model of Xuuajii X̱iihlii Naas (Grizzly Bear's Mouth House), three beaver pole models, and two model eagle poles (see figures 3.119, 3.122, 3.124, 3.129, and 3.130).

Between 1902 and 1911, Robson made several drawings on paper for Charles Newcombe. Two sets of these are now at the Field Museum (FM 79790, fifteen drawings accessioned October 10, 1902, and FM 19986, eight drawings accessioned October 6, 1905), and another set is at the Royal British Columbia Museum (cat. nos. 16538–16596). Robson sent ten handwritten letters to Newcombe dated between 1902–1911 that recount his efforts to be paid by Newcombe at a rate of from fifty cents to one dollar per drawing. These letters also reveal that he had remarried and this wife died of cancer on October 22, 1911 (see Wright 2001b, 264–65, figures 5.28 and 5.29; Newcombe 1900–1911, vol. 5, file 124).

Skilduunaas, David Shakespeare / *See Genealogy Chart 3*

Skilduunaas, David Shakespeare, of the Naay Kun ḴiiG̱awaay (R13), Those Born at Rose Spit, was married to Klaaskost (Jane) the daughter of Gulsigut, Staastas (E21). Gulsigut was the sister of Albert Edward Edenshaw. Their Haida names appear in the 1881 census in Skidegate, living in House #1, Family 2, as Skildoana (male, twenty-five years old) and Tlasgoost (female, forty-two years old).[153] Skilduunaas was baptized with the name David Shakespeare in 1888 (said to be age fifty-one then). Klaastkost was baptized with the name Jane at the same time "age 58" in 1888. Her death record says b. 1834–d.1904, age seventy. As with many Christian names given at baptism, the name "Shakespeare" was likely chosen because it sounded vaguely the same to the minister's ear as the Haida name and was a famous English name. His Haida name has variously been spelled Skaoskea, Skowskeay (Barbeau 1916–1954, box B20, B-F-257.7). The 1891 Skidegate census lists David Shakespeare (male, twenty-eight) and Jane Shakespeare (female, twenty-six) living in House #407, near the Robsons in House #405. Four years later, he drowned at Cape Ball on April 13, 1895, at "age 40." Clearly many of the ages in the census reports were guesses, as Skilduunaas's birth date ranges from 1837 (1888 baptism) to 1863 (1891 census).

Skilduunaas was the brother of Tl'aajaang quuna (Tom Stevens), who was the owner of Naa G̱a Gayhlas, "House to Which the High Tide Comes," Dlaay.yii Naas, "House of Contentment," and the maker of the model of G̱uuda Naas, "Box House" (No. 20). As discussed above, Tom Stevens was the first husband of Isabella, who married Zacherias Nicholas after Stevens's death (see Genealogy Chart 3). The exact relationship between Skilduunaas and Robson is not known, but both were Naay Kun Ḵiig̱awaay, clan brothers. Based on their collaboration on the two poles in the model village, it is likely that they often worked together. Skilduunaas is said to have raised the memorial to his wife, Jane, the last standing old pole in Skidegate (see figure 3.125). Given that he drowned in 1895, well before Jane died in 1904, this pole would have been raised to honor his wife before her death in the same way that Robson raised an honoring pole for Q'aaw quunaa (see figures 3.122 and 3.123).

Aside from this full-size pole and the two model houses made for the WCE, little else has been attributed to his hand. Marius Barbeau recorded a few objects that may have been carved by him (1916–1954, box B.20, File B-F-257.2), but did not mention him in his book on Haida carvers (Barbeau 1957). Barbeau's information came from Henry Young [Gidgii dlaay.yas], who called him "David Six Beer" also saying "his Indian name was Tságái" of Maud Island (Barbeau 1916–1954, box B20, B-F-257.1).[154] Henry Young also attributed a 'Waasg̱uu dish variously numbered 89385 and 89387, saying "it's like the carving of John Robison and David Shakespeare, from Cape Ball village," also a killer whale dish (8) by David Shakespeare or John Robson (Barbeau 1916–1954, box B20, B-F-257.2). In addition, Barbeau's notes list a totem pole in the Aaronson collection with a "Witch Doctor, Thunderbird, Finback Whale," as the work of Skowskeay, David Seexbeer or Shakespeare (Barbeau 1916–1954, box B20, B-F-257.7).

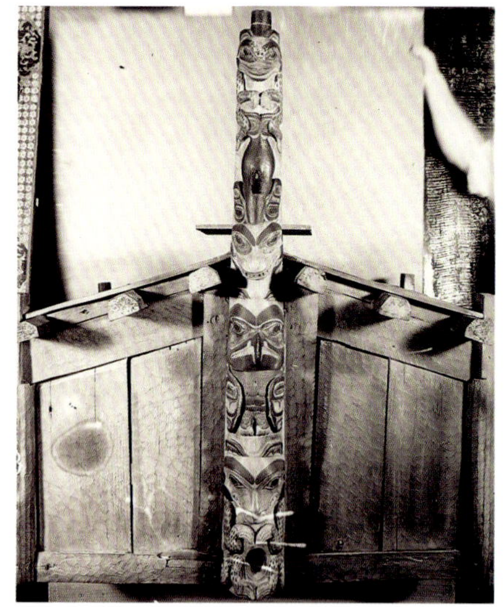

3.132 Model House No. 14, Naa G̱a Gayhlas, "House to which the tide comes" or Taawt'a Gaay Naas, "Food Box House," made by John Cross, 1892, Brooklyn Museum, cat. no. 05.589.7790 (missing—exchanged from the Field Museum, cat. no. 17828). Photograph courtesy of the Brooklyn Museum.

HOUSE MODEL NO. 14 / *Made by Niislant, John Cross*

This model house was most likely installed to the right of "Grizzly Bear's Mouth House" (No. 24) in the WCE installation, according to the installation numbers, but it doesn't show in the installation photo since the photo ends at Grizzly Bear's Mouth House (figures 3.132, 3.133). Deans reports that he wasn't certain of the name "Taw go Nass" or Food House (Taawt'a Gaay Naas means "Food Box House") but that the original house had been gone for many years by 1892 and was located near the center of the village. He describes the figures as an otter at the top, finback whale, eagle, and brown bear at the bottom (Deans 1893c, 9–10; Deans 1893b, 38–39).[155] It is

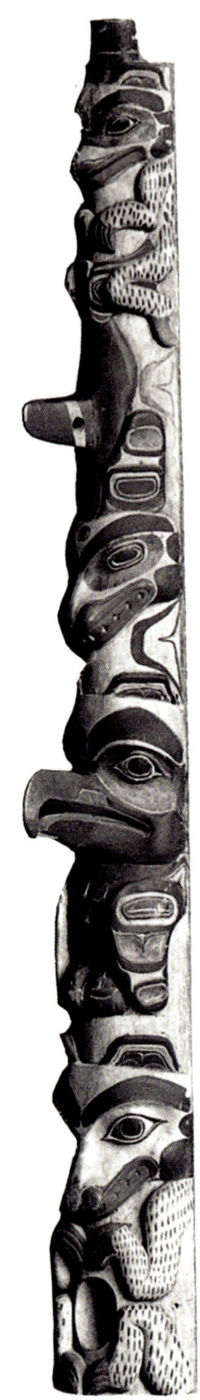

3.133 Frontal pole from missing Model House No. 14, Naa G̱a Gayhlas, "House to which the tide comes" or Taawt'a Gaay Naas, "Food Box House," made by John Cross, 1892. Field Museum cat. no. 17828, Brooklyn Museum, by exchange, 05.589.7790. © The Field Museum, image no. CSA16652.

3.134 Frontal pole from Naa Ga Gayhlas, "High-Tide-House," at north end of HlGaagilda Llnagaay (Skidegate). Purchased from Amos Watson by C. F. Newcombe in 1911, now in the National Museum in Melbourne, Australia. J. P. Ryan postcard. Image PN5224. Courtesy of the Royal BC Museum and Archives.

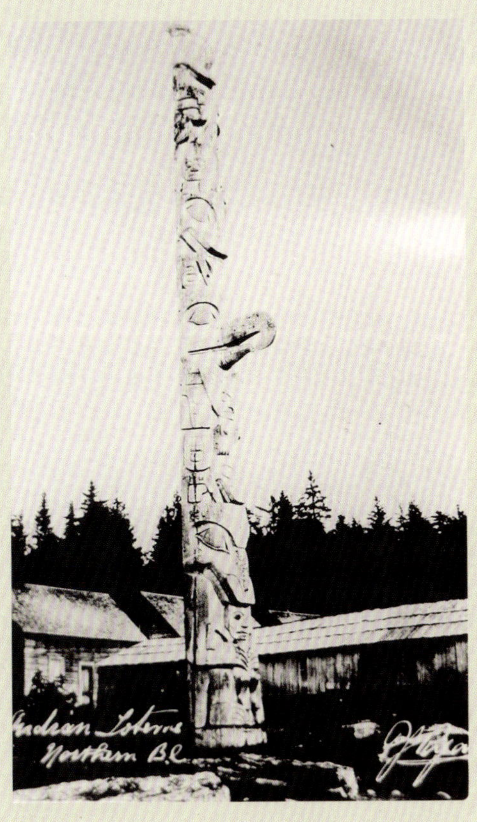

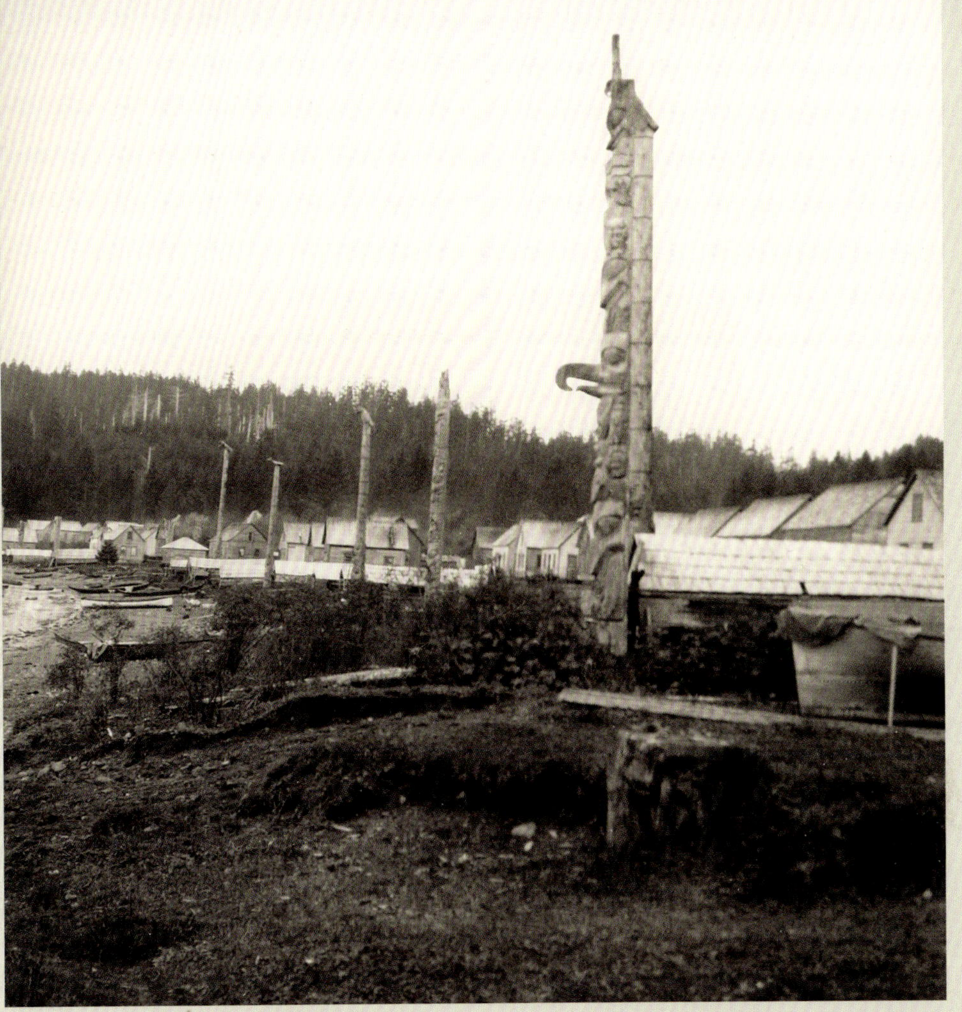

3.135 View from the north of HlGaagilda Llnagaay (Skidegate) looking south, showing a view of the frontal pole of Naa Ga Gayhlas, "High-tide-house" and behind it the pole raised in honor of Klaaskost, Jane Shakespeare, by her husband, Skilduunaas, David Shakespeare (see figure 3.125). Image PN354. Courtesy of the Royal BC Museum and Archives. Photograph by Carmichael, 1907.

likely that Deans's name "Food Box House" was not the Haida name for the original house, given his own uncertainty. No frontal poles with figures that match this model are known from the center part of Skidegate, but a house at the far north/right of the village does have very similar figures that match this model (figures 3.134, 3.135). For this reason it has been placed here in the discussion.

The frontal pole from the north end house was purchased from Amos Watson by Newcombe in 1911 and is now in the National Museum in Melbourne, Australia (figures 3.134, 3.135). Based on the information supplied by Amos Watson, Newcombe identified the name of the last house at the north end of Skidegate as Naga gaitlas (Naa Ga Gayhlas), "High-tide-house," owner: Daji kilstlas (R13), wife's name: Hazanat (E21).[156] This was erected by Dats kilstlas, "like a small bird in good humour." He was of the Naayii Kun KiiGawaay (R13). His wife was of the Staastas (E21), the same clan as the Edenshaws. The house came to be owned by Amos Watson himself. His uncle was the original owner of the name Dats (or Daji) kilstlas. According to Watson, Daji kilstlas belonged to K'yuusda and was a constant companion of the first (Albert Edward) Edensaw known to fame. The crests on the pole were identified in a letter by James Sterling (Amos Watson's son) to Newcombe, January 28, 1911, as a brown bear, eagle, finback whale, and frog on top.[157] This matches Deans's identifications, except for the top figure, called an otter by Deans.

In his 1911 diary Newcombe reported that the pole "stood in front of house in which Charlie Edenshaw was born."[158] According to Sterling, his mother, the wife of the owner of this pole, Amos Watson, was a sister to Chief Albert Edward Edenshaw.[159] However, we know Amos Watson's wife was Lucy Watson, the mother of James Sterling and Mary Watson. Lucy was the daughter of Gidkonii, who was Albert Edenshaw's sister (Wright 2001b, 115).

MacDonald says the two easternmost (northern) houses in Skidegate (his #1A and 1B) had identical frontal poles, and that the one now in Melbourne was with house #1A (farther to the south), but based on Newcombe's 1911 photograph, which shows the Robson's beaver pole behind and to the south of the Melbourne pole, it is likely that the pole was associated with 1B, the northernmost house, as Newcombe reported (not 1A as shown on the map) (MacDonald 1983, 38, 44).[160] This missing model house was made by John Cross, and fortunately there are black-and-white photographs showing both a frontal view with the pole attached to the house (see figure 3.132) and a three-quarter view of just the pole showing the formline details on the side (see figure 3.133). These fit well with the style we know as John Cross's (compare House Model No. "2"/21) with formline Us that flair at the base. Compare the bears at the base with their elongated noses and the deepest part of the eye socket at the edge of the lower eyelid line.

HOUSE MODEL NO. 26 / *Made by John Cross (Niislant)*

Deans describes this model as "Tau Schoass, Copper House," a house that formerly stood in the G̱aahllns Kun, "Cathlins Coon," part of the town. T'aaG̱uu Naas means "Ceremonial Copper House" (see figures 3.3, 3.137).[161] The figures are identified as a bear eating boy at the bottom, a sea otter, a raven, and a whale with its tail around a woman's neck at the top. The model house is now missing, and the only photograph of it is taken from the side where it can just be made out to be second to the last next to the last house, "Cah Guintt," installed in the Skidegate village (figure 3.137). Unfortunately this one surviving photograph shows only the top figures of the whale's tail and the woman's face, but so faintly that it is difficult to assess Cross's carving style, although the ovoid and attached Us forming the flukes of the whale's tail resemble those on the dogfish tail of House Model No. "2"/21.

No houses with this name were described by either Swanton or Newcombe, and it is unclear of which house this might be a model. In Boas's manuscript titled "The Exhibits from the North Pacific Coast," he lists "Copper House" as No. 15 and places it between "Food House" and "Thunderstorm House" (see House Model Nos. 14 and 16). However, his description of the figures on the pole don't match "Copper House": "The figures on the heraldic column represent from below upward: the wolf, the sculpin, the raven, and the bear whose tongue is held by a bird. On the top of the column are the heirs of the chief" (Boas 1893b, 110). On a separate document Boas lists his No. 15 as "Hoiah Nas" Raven House, with the pole figures: wolf, raven, bear (Boas 1893a, 128). Neither of these descriptions match "Raven House" Model No. 15.

MODEL POLE NO. 18

This model, Galla X̱aad, "Galla's Mortuary Pole," is similar to Tl'aajaang quuna's mortuary pole, Model Pole No. 14, with a bear on the panel, but in this case the three-dimensional head of the bear is flanked by formlines depicting the body of the bear (figure 3.136). The bear's ears extend up onto what would have been the lid of the mortuary chest, a feature that Deans called "Tan Gue" (Taan gyuu). According to Deans: "This is a model of the tomb of Haidra Galla a nobleman of the Cathlins Coon hadry a Illth-Cah-geetla lannas or point of the waves people at the town of Skidegate" (Deans 1893b, 94). This would be the G̱aahllns Kun X̱aaydaG̱aay from Cape Ball living in Skidegate, HlG̱aagilda ("Ilth-Cah-geeetla"). If Deans is correct, this must be a different Ga.alla, "Galla," than Amos Russ's father, who was married to Tom Stevens's sister, since he was of the Naa S'aagaas X̱aaydaG̱aay (E6b) (see Model Memorial Pole No. 11).[162]

Because Deans placed this mortuary model between "Copper House" No. 26 and "Cah Guintt" No. 27 at the extreme right end of the village, it might be possible that it represents the old mortuary pole that shows in Dawson's and the Maynards' photographs in this position (see figures 2.2, 3.33). There are no three-dimensional carvings visible on this pole, but it may be that the design was only painted.[163]

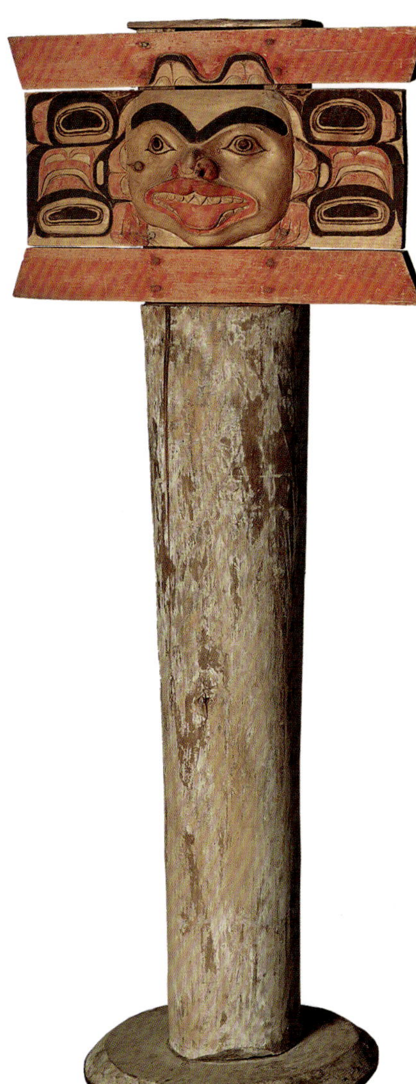

3.136 Model Mortuary Pole No. 18, Galla X̱aad, "Galla's Mortuary Pole," 1892, 96.5 cm × 39.4 cm. Courtesy of the Field Museum, cat. no. 17831. Photograph by Gail Specht.

HOUSE MODEL NO. 27 / *Made by George Young*

The name given to this house by James Deans is "Cah guintt, so named from the boxes which held the sun, moon and stars" (figures 3.137, 3.138). This term was not recognized as being a Haida language word by SHIP (personal communication, 2006). Deans identified the figures as an eagle at the top, "tutl Carbush" (connected with a raven and box of daylight story), and a raven at bottom. "tutle carbush" was also not recognized as being in the Haida language by SHIP.[164] There is a bald eagle at the top, a raven, a woman holding a small child, and raven with the sun in its beak at the bottom.

This model was made by George Young (see Genealogy Chart 6). As with "Copper House," there is no clear indication of which full-size house this models. Boas lists this model as the last house in the village, "No. 25. Name unknown." On the column is seen the bear holding the sun; an unidentified being called TutCabish, and the eagle (Boas 1893b, 113). This was the last model house in the Skidegate village installation, but it does not match that northernmost house in the village (see Model No. 14). The model house was traded by the Field Museum to the University of Pennsylvania Museum and went missing from there after 1920. Subsequently the model pole from this house found its way into the private collection of Miguel Covarrubias. It was then acquired by the dealer Julius Carlbach, who sold it to James Economos. It was auctioned at Sotheby's Paris auction, June 11, 2008, and, fortunately, before the auction it was recognized by Bill Holm as being one of the missing house models, who suggested to Sotheby's that they contact me (the author). The original Field Museum catalog number and WCE installation number written on the back, as well as a comparison with the photograph of the house installed at the extreme right end

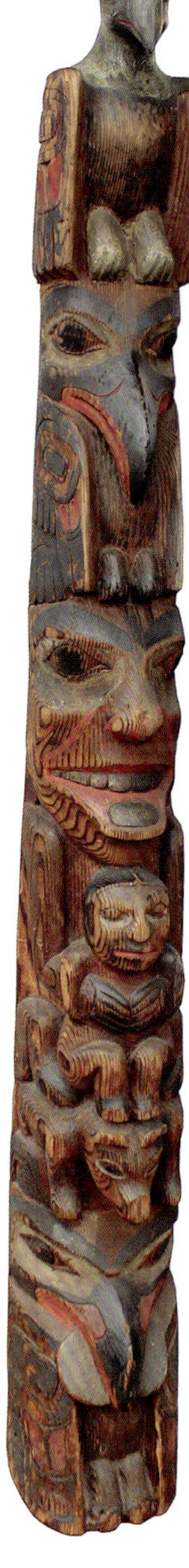

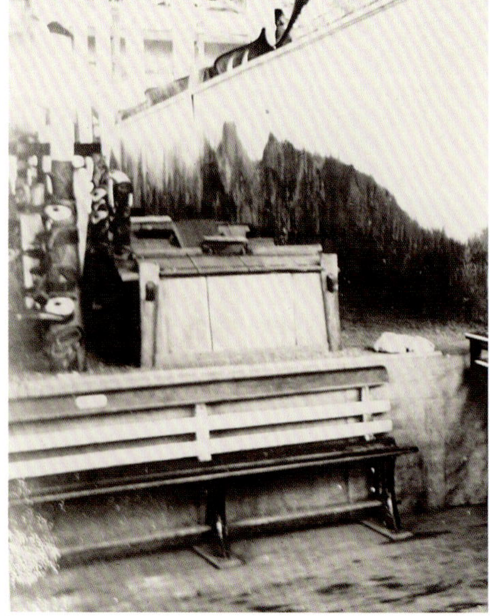

3.137 *above* Detail of figure 3.3, view of the right end of the World's Columbian Exposition installation of Skidegate house models showing the model of Millas Q'aa.l to the left, "Food Box House," between and "Cah Guintt," the last house model in the installation to the right. Courtesy of the Peabody Museum of Archaeology and Ethnology, Harvard University 93-1-10/100266.1.33.

3.138 *left* House Model No. 27, Deans: "Cah Guintt," made by George Young, 1892, 95.3 cm × 11.3 cm × 8.9 cm. The Field Museum, cat. no. 17835, purchased by the University of Pennsylvania Museum in 1900, cat. no. 37.687, missing after 1920. Subsequently the model pole from this house found its way into the private collection of Miguel Covarrubias. It was then acquired by the dealer Julius Carlebach, who sold it to James Economos. It was auctioned at Sotheby's Paris auction, June 11, 2008. The frontal pole is now in a private collection in Vancouver, BC.

of the WCE installation, confirm the identity of the formerly missing pole. It is now in a private collection in Vancouver, BC.

George Young / *See Genealogy Chart 6*

There were at least three George Youngs (all of different clans) who were living in Skidegate in the late nineteenth century. Unfortunately, Deans tells us nothing about the George Young who made House Model No. 27. Based on the evidence, however, it is most likely that the maker of the "Cah guintt" was the George Young who was well known as a carver. This George Young (also known as Gunyaa) (b. ca. 1864, d. February 27, 1924, age sixty) was married to Eliza Gold "djat" (jaada means "woman" in x̱aayda kil) (1858–1928) (Haida Gwaii Museum, Clans of Skidegate). He is listed in the 1891 census living in Skidegate, age twenty-five (b. 1866?), with his wife Eliza (age twenty) and daughter Flora (age three). Eliza (R13) was the sister of the man who reportedly was the first to discover gold in Haida Gwaii (thus her name—Richard Wilson, personal communication, 2006). According to Newcombe, she was the daughter of Chief Skotsgai of Kaisun and Chaatl.[165] There is a George L. Young listed in the 1921 Skidegate census (age sixty-one, b. ca. 1860), along with his wife Eliza (age fifty-six, b. ca. 1865). This must be the same George Young, although the birth dates differ (as they often do on census reports). This George L. Young may have been E11. We know that he was a carver because of his published death notice in the March 11, 1924, *Province Vancouver*, which describes him as "one of the best carvers of totems from the jadite rock found in the neighborhood," meaning argillite.

Another George Young Sr. was Luuguud "Wave Eagle" of the Jiiaxwii Sḵaahladasg̱aay "Down the inlet (seaward) sgwaahlaadaas" (R5) (Swanton 1905b, 269). The name Luuguud apparently moved between clans, as a third George Young, Llguud "The Eagle" (E5), was one of Cumshewa's chiefs (Barbara Wilson, personal communication, 2006). This Llguud's brother Sampson had a son named George W. Young. His mother was Henry Moody's sister Susan of the G̱aag'yals Ḵiig̱awaay (R4). This fourth George Young (R4) was much younger (born the year of the WCE) and became Chief Skedans (the son of Susan and Sampson Young) (b. March 6, 1893, d. 1975, baptized four months 1893).

Barbeau wrote extensively about George Gunya, whom he described as being an argillite flute carver, based on information provided to him by his daughter, Mrs. Susan Young/Dickson/Lockhart/Grey. If Susan Grey's father was George Young, we can deduce that this George Young and George Gunya are the same man. However, since Susan was born ca. 1864, her father could not have been George L. Young, born ca. 1860, discussed above.[166] Barbeau says that the so-called flute carving Gunya was born ca. 1850 and died ca. 1880 (Barbeau 1957, 9), which would have been long before both the house model commissions for the WCE and Susan's birth. Barbeau and Susan must have been referring in this case to George L. Young's uncle, also named George Young. They would have shared the name Gunya. It is the older uncle who would have been the father of Susan Grey/Dickson/Lockhart to whom she refers in her interview with Barbeau (see Genealogy Chart 6). Gunya is described as being the "owner" of the argillite quarry, and Barbeau goes on to erroneously attribute many early nineteenth-century argillite flutes as well as two Kwakwa̱ka̱'wakw whistles to his hand (Barbeau 1957, 2–9; Wright 1977, 18–19).

HOUSE MODEL NO. 17 / *Made by Phillip Pearson*

This is the only WCE model house for which we have no photograph, and no clear indication of the identity of an original house after which it was modeled. It was called by Deans "Nah Heeldans, House of the Shaking or Earthquake House." Naa Hildangs means "Shaking House" and Tllga Hildang Naas, "Earthquake House." It had the installation number 45, which would place it as the last house of the WCE installation, but it doesn't appear on the right-end photo (see figure 3.137). It must have been one of the house models that was displayed elsewhere in the anthropology building along with the SG̱ang gwaay model house (No. 2) and the Tsimshian and Nuxalk model houses (see figure 3.5). These house models were placed in a display that was three rows over from the entrance to the South Seas and New South Wales exhibits. This means that the extra Haida house models were placed on the back side of the painted Skidegate village backdrop. Figure 3.5 shows them near some carved figures that were likely part of the Edward E. Ayers collection that was displayed in this area (see the Anthropology Building floor plan figure 3.4).

Deans reports the figures on this model frontal pole as a bear holding frog in its mouth at the top, a hawk holding man by the feet with head downward, a 'WaasG̱uu with an owl, and a "Keel-Coon-ue (a Sea-Lion-like Whale slave)." He reports the original house was the last of the houses before the Naayii Kun portion of the village, which would place it somewhere to the north of Daniel Iljuuwaas's house, and south of Tl'aajaang quuna's house. This House Model No. 17 fits in that position between Deans's house model Nos. 16 and 18. The only old house with a frontal pole in this position shows in both Dawson's and Dossetter's photographs of the village (see figures 2.3 far right and 2.5 to the left of the striped pole at the right). MacDonald (1983, 47) calls this house "Grizzly Bear House" (his #13), owned by Tom Collinson (R13). Newcombe identified Tom Collinson's wife as Doas of the Naa S'aagaas X̱aaydaG̱aay and the figures on the pole as a dogfish eating a fish at the top, a raven, and below SG̱aana and sea bear at the bottom.[167] This doesn't match with Deans, who reports the owner of the house to be "Quill-ance" who belonged to the Eagle 'WaasG̱uu crest and his wife "Gwah-Nutt" who belonged to the Raven brown bear crest. Deans's notes imply that this man was from SG̱ang gwaay as was the maker of the model, Phillip Pearson. The figures on the model pole also don't match the dogfish and raven figures on the pole of the old house in this position in the village.

None of Swanton's Skidegate house names is similar to "House Shaking" or "Earthquake House," but there is a house on his Skidegate list called "Na kiina'ns, House Making a Noise," his #7, now spelled Naa Kii.ngangs (SHIP email September 30, 2020). This house is placed next to Grizzly Bear House (see Appendix II, Swanton's Skidegate House List), but Swanton's list often doesn't fit the sequence of houses in the village. MacDonald gives this name to his house #7 that is the house

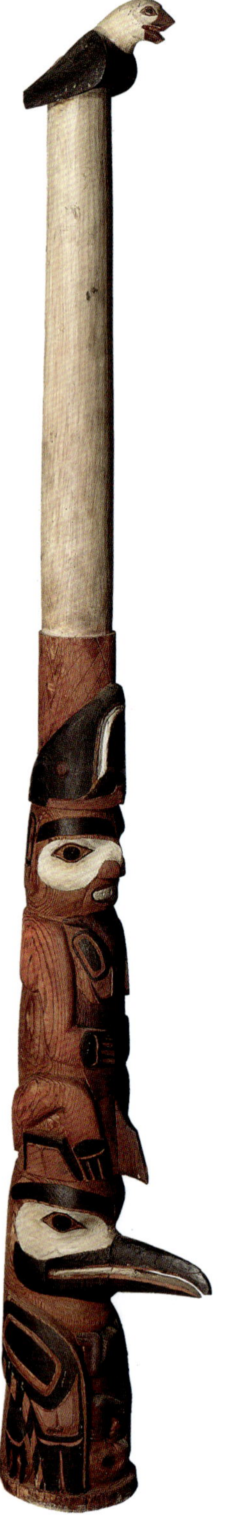

3.139 Model Pole No. 19, Millas Q'aa.l, "Millas' Memorial Pole," 1892, 164.5 cm × 26.7 cm. Courtesy of the Field Museum, cat. no. 17843. Photograph by Gail Specht.

to the south/left of Grizzly Bear's Mouth House. This house had a small pole with a watchman on top but it is difficult to see in the photographs. There was a "House that is always Shaking" at SG̱ang Gwaay (MacDonald's House #6), which apparently did not have a frontal pole, and this was said to also be the name of the Tsimshian chief Tsebassa's house at Kitkatla (MacDonald 1983, 107). Deans describes one of the figures on the model pole as a Keel-Coon-ue (a sea lion–like whale slave) and tells the story of "Keel-Coonuck" that originates at Kitkatla. In it a supernatural whale kidnaps four men and keeps them for a year before releasing them when their friends came looking for them. Since the maker of the model house, Phillip Pearson, is said by Deans to be from SG̱ang Gwaay Llnagaay (Ninstints), this may explain the inclusion of this story on the pole. However, it doesn't help to identify the house in Skidegate.

Phillip Pearson / *See Genealogy Chart 10*

Unfortunately, since Phillip's model house is missing, and no photograph of it survives, Deans's description of it is all we have left to inform us about his work. Phillip Pearson is listed (age twenty-eight, b. ca. 1863) in the 1891 census for Gold Harbour (Family #340), as is his wife, "Lucey" (age twenty-five), and their sons, Timothy (age three) and Peter (age one). He was baptized 1895, age thirty, putting another birthday ca. 1865. His wife "Lucy" was baptized in 1895 at age twenty-two. Their daughter, Mary, married Luke Watson, and their son, Timothy, married Rebecca Wesley (R4a). Luke Watson was the nephew of George Smith (R10a). So Phillip Pearson's son-in-law was the nephew of George Smith, the brother of Peter Smith, the maker of House Model No. 1, bringing the artists who carved model houses for Deans full circle (see Genealogy Chart 1).

We do know from Deans that Phillip Pearson was from SG̱ang Gwaay, and we believe he was from a Raven clan, as his wife was apparently an Eagle (E9) (Haida Gwaii Museum, Clans of Skidegate). K̲aay'ahl Laanas clan history gives the name Laadawga as the mother of Mary Pearson, and her father's name as "Paleface." It is unknown whether this was a nickname for Phillip Pearson. Her brother Timothy Pearson was adopted into this clan. By the time of Dawson's 1878 visit, the people of SG̱ang Gwaay had moved north, although the village was used as a camp by families in later years and, as with all Haida villages, was never "abandoned." The two SG̱ang Gwaay carvers who made models for Deans, Zacherias Nicholas and Phillip Pearson, had perhaps moved north more than ten years before the WCE.

GENEALOGY CHART 10

Phillip Pearson

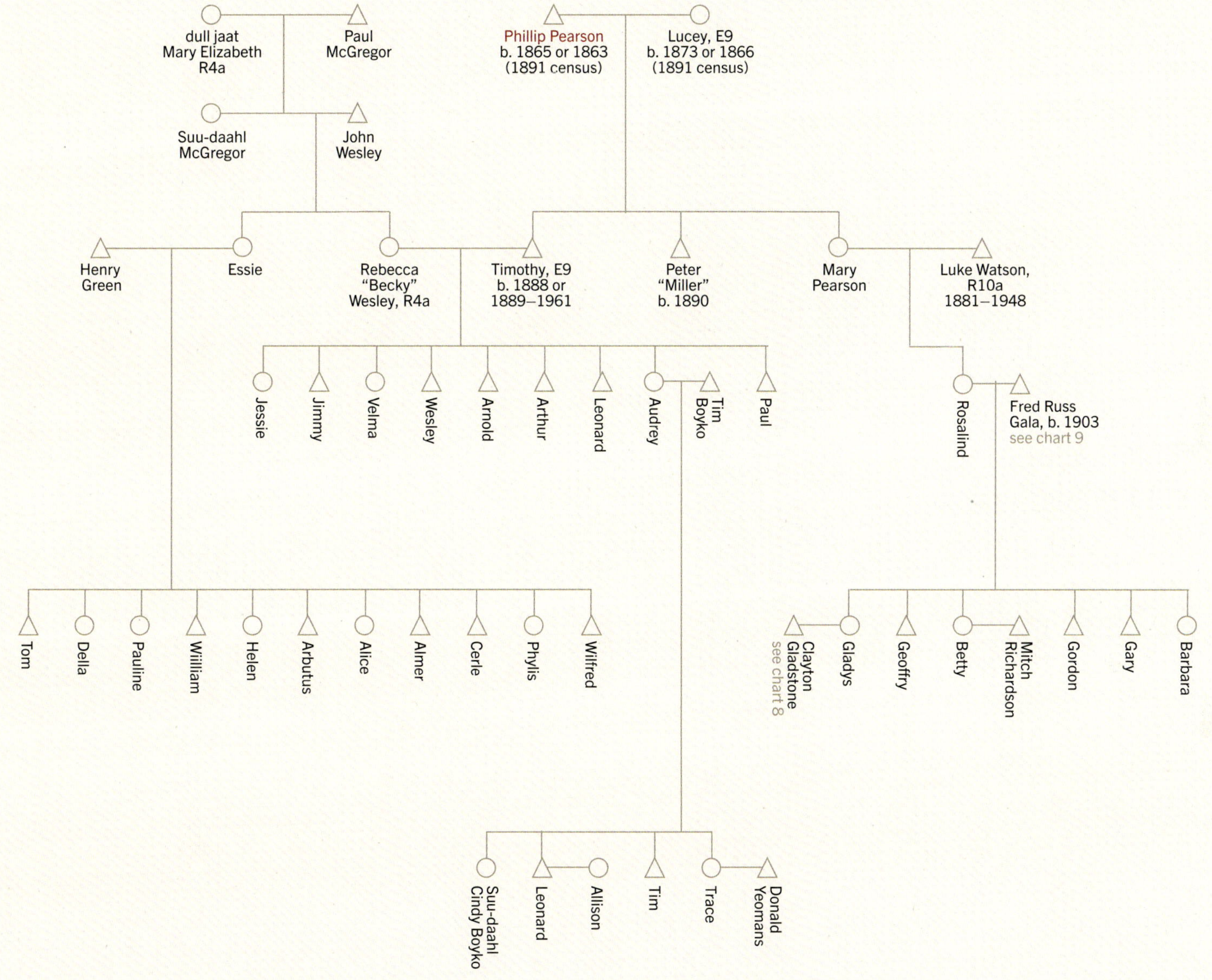

3.140 North end of HlG̱aagilda Llnagaay (Skidegate), view of Millas pole near the cemetery, August 1911. Image PN1388. Courtesy of the Royal BC Museum and Archives.

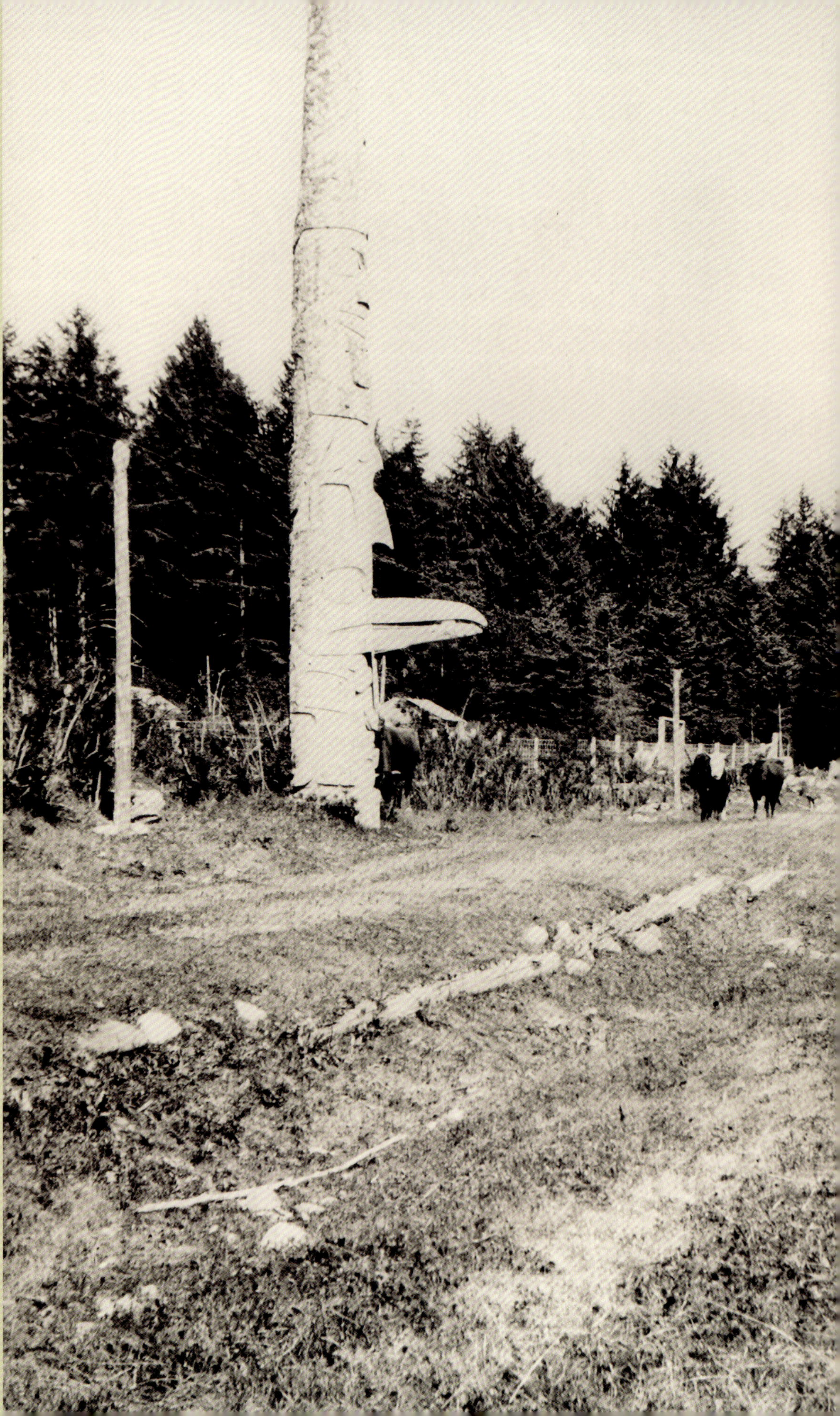

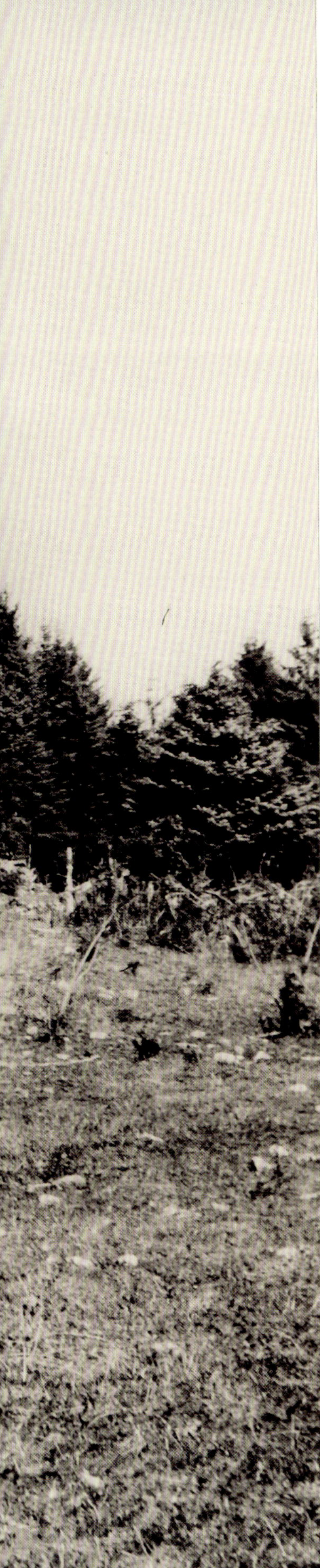

MODEL POLE NO. 19

Millas Q'aa.l, "Millas' Memorial Pole," was the last pole installed in the Skidegate village and is seen in the photo of the right end of the WCE installation (figures 3.137, 3.139).[168] Its installation number (44) confirms its placement in front and to the right of "Cah Guintt." The full-size memorial pole that this modeled was far to the right/north of the last house in the village near the present cemetery (figure 3.140). It was described by Deans as a memorial erected for "a young man named Millas, who died about 1882, by a brother of his who died shortly after, leaving an aged father and mother who in 1893 still live."[169] Newcombe wrote in his diary of 1911 that this pole was created by the mother.[170] Millas (and his brother) were said to be from "Illth-Cah-Geetla" HlG̱aagilda Llnagaay (Skidegate). The pole includes figures that tell the story of a boy who turned into a salmon and was discovered by his father in a net wearing a copper necklace. The boy was brought back to life by the father. A raven at the base of the pole has a frog between its wings with its head facing down. The salmon/boy is above, and an eagle is at the top (Deans 1893b, 94–95). The depiction of the salmon with its tail and pectoral fins on the chest of the boy, with the head of the salmon extending above the head of the boy resembles the depiction of this same story on the model house collected by James G. Swan in 1883 (see figure 1.12). However, on the model house the boy's arms extend up around the head of the salmon, where on the model pole the arms are down with the hands holding the salmon to his chest as on the full-size pole. This brings us full circle from this book's introduction.

GRAVE HOUSE MODEL NO. 7

One last house model was most likely exhibited separately from the model village, as it does not appear in any of the photographs (figure 3.141). Deans identifies it as "Suthling-un Nah of Skidegat the Second," the grave house of the second Chief Skidegate (today spelled SG̱iidagiids Saahlln Naas, "Grave House of SG̱iidagiids"), who lived about 1840 (Deans 1893b, 88). Deans says that this Skidegate was the "son of the Great or First Skidegate"; however, he would most likely have been his nephew, and according to MacDonald's numbering system, he would have been Skidegate III (see Appendix I, Chronology of the SG̱iidagiids Town Chiefs). The model grave house does have the installation number A17 written on back, however, which suggests that it was originally intended to go between House Model Nos. 16 and 19, where the other model grave house was placed in the installation. It may be that there simply was not enough room for both of them there. A small shed roof house does appear at the north end next to the last house in the village in Dawson's photograph (see

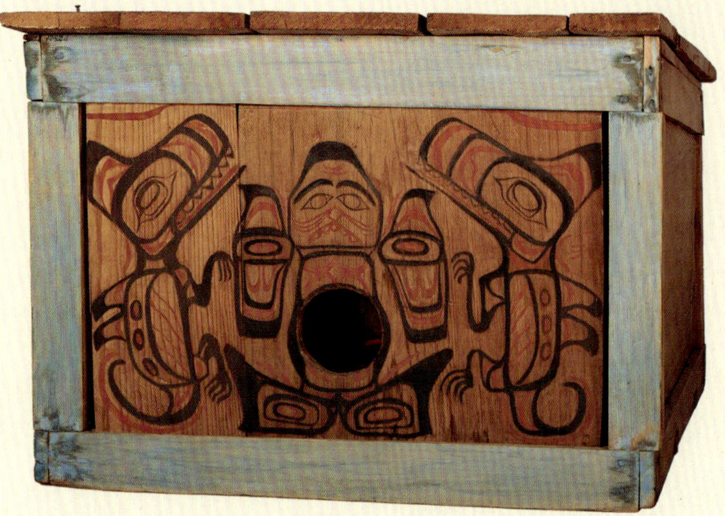

3.141 Model Grave House No. 7, SG̱iidagiids Saahlln Naas, "Grave House of SG̱iidagiids." Deans calls this the "Suthling-un Nah of Skidegat the Second" (this would be Skidegate III, according to MacDonald's numbering system [see Appendix I, Chronology of the SG̱iidagiids Town Chiefs]), 1892. Courtesy of the Field Museum, cat. no. 17824. Photograph by Gail Specht.

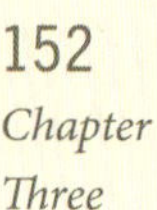

figure 2.2), which MacDonald (1983, 44, 1B MH) identifies as a mortuary house. This is most likely a different mortuary house, given its location, far from the Eagle side of the village. Deans reports that the original grave house of this Skidegate was destroyed in the summer of 1889, when the bones were reburied in the graveyard.

A dogfish is painted around the circular door, flanked by two 'WaasG̱uu. Inside this model is a 'WaasG̱uu manda with a model coffin with painted ravens resting on its back. On top of the coffin is a small button blanket and cedar bark headring. There are also two plain coffins, which are painted red and are on either side, inside this model grave house.

Conclusion

It's amazing how the years fly by. It seems like yesterday when we used to be walking through them village sites observing . . . what must have happened there hundreds of years ago. I always maintained I was born a hundred years too late. I would have loved that kind of a life I think. When I was fishing just till recently, I made it a point, whether I caught fish or not, to go down into that beautiful southern country to see how our ancestors used to live and how well we lived when we were growing up. It didn't matter that I was missing out on a productive day of fishing. It was more rewarding to go ashore, go up in the hills behind Skedans when the sun's setting and look down on the village site and wonder what happened there hundreds of years ago.

—Chief Gidansda, Percy Williams (1930–2015), August 22, 2006

The unique contribution of seventeen Haida carvers who worked in the last decade of the nineteenth century can be appreciated in many ways. As with the generations of their ancestors who preceded them, when commissioned to create a new pole (whether a model or full-size), they didn't just copy the old poles. While they were asked to carve a model of the village as it looked in 1864, what they produced reflected the village as they knew it. They carved what they knew and what they wanted to carve. This included models of many gyaaG̱ang. ngaay that had not yet been raised in 1864, which was fourteen years before the first photographs were taken of the village, and before the influx of Haida families who migrated from the southern, western, and northern villages into HlG̱aagilda after smallpox had devastated their populations.

Migrations and population change had been occurring in Haida Gwaii for many hundreds of years, going back to the time of Nang Kilslas, "The one whose voice is obeyed." New villages were established, and old villages were left for new populations to inhabit. In the north, Haida families migrated into old Tlingit villages that had been left by their northern Tlingit neighbors and created the Kaigani. But in the period of time immediately preceding the commission of this model village, the intensity and urgency of migration had been increased due to extreme population loss. People from both west coast and southern villages moved east and north to HlG̱aagilda Llnagaay, HlG̱aax̱id Llnagaay, Ḵay Llnagaay, and Xaayna Llnagaay. By the end of the nineteenth century the Haida had moved together into two major villages, G̱aw Tlagée (Old Massett) in the north and HlG̱aagilda Llnagaay (Skidegate) in the south. The model village made for the World's Columbian Exposition in 1892 reflects this change, contrary to the wishes of Boas and Putnam, who wanted a model dating to 1864. The eight oldest houses located in the back row of the village and hidden from the photographers were not represented.

Six older houses occupied by Raven men with their Eagle wives were situated at the far left/south end of the village (Nos. 4, 22, 5, 6, 7, 8). Some of these Raven families were from the Jiiaxwii Sk̲aahladasG̱aay and HlG̱aay.yuu Laanas clans (R5 and R6), dating back to a time when the village was a Raven village (see chapter 2). Eight houses owned by Eagle families occupied the most desirable center of the village in front of the oldest houses that were behind them. Of these, three to the south were owned by Naa S'aagaas X̱aaydaG̱aay (E6b) (Nos. 9, 12, 10), with the older Iljuuwaas's Jiiaxwii Gidin.naay (E11) Hllman Naas (No. 11) separating their houses from three Naa 'Yuuwans X̱aaydaG̱aay (E6a) houses (Nos. 21, 13, 15). The last Eagle house, Naa G̱a Hiilangs (No. 16), was owned by the younger Daniel Iljuuwaas (E11), this house and pole being perhaps the last new ones to be raised in the nineteenth century in HlG̱aagilda Llnagaay. This house also marked the end of the Eagle houses. Three new Raven houses belonging to immigrants from the north, the families of Tl'aajaang quuna (R13)—Naa G̱a Gayhlas, Dlaay.yii Naas, and G̱uuda Naas (Nos. 18, 19, 20)—were erected at the north/right end, closest to the center of the village, followed by five more owned by people of the same Naay Kun K̲iiG̱awaay clan (R13), many of whom were married to Staastas women (E21) (Nos. 23, 24, 25, 14, 26). The final two houses (Nos. 27 and 17) are not well documented, but these were all on the right/north side of the village, erected by the most recent arrivals from the north.

It is clear from the range in quality of the models Deans collected that he did not hire only the best carvers in the village. In fact, carvers living in Skidegate and known to be very skilled, such as Tom Price (Chief Nang Sdins), were not included. It is unknown why this might have been; perhaps he declined an offer or was otherwise occupied. It was most likely not because his home village was SG̱ang Gwaay, as at least two other carvers hired were from this village, including Zacherias Nicholas. We only know the identity of one of the four carvers who made model mortuary poles, and in this case, the mortuary pole (No. 1) for the Eagle Chief SG̱iidagiids "the Great," attributed to Zacherias Nicholas, the carver was someone of the opposite Raven moiety, as was the tradition for full-size mortuary poles. In most cases the carvers made models of houses with which they were familiar or in which they had lived (Nos. 1, 2, 16, 18, 20, 24). One of the carvers, Phillip Jackson, was Chief Skidegate at the time of the commission, and one, Peter Brown, succeeded him as Chief Skidegate in 1897 (see Appendix I, Chronology of the SG̱iidagiids Town Chiefs).

While the makers of the model houses and poles were all men, the role of Haida women in the history that these models record cannot be minimized. Of the fifteen freestanding WCE pole models collected by Deans, representing poles that stood in the village of HlG̱aagilda proper, ten are memorials or mortuaries honoring women (Pole Nos. 3, 4, 5, 6, 9, 10, 13, 15, 16, 17).[1] Two of these model poles represent poles that were also erected (paid for) by women (Nos. 5, 6). Two poles honoring men were likely largely paid for by women (Nos. 8, 19). Two poles honoring Kaaniihl (Nos. 3, 4) were raised as part of a rivalry between the two leading Eagle clans in the village. Two poles were raised by women in honor of their awG̱a and nanaay (mother and grandmother) (Nos. 5, 6). Two poles were raised in honor of chief's wives (Nos. 9, 10). Four were raised by a husband in honor of his JaaG̱a (wife) (Nos. 13, 15, 16, 17). Two model houses represent houses either owned or built by women (Nos. 4, 8). In addition to this, perhaps surprisingly, a woman's Laal, private puberty seclusion ritual, was represented in one of the house models (No. 24).

The large number of poles in honor of or erected by women reflects the strength of the matrilineal Haida society as recorded in the houses and poles in the village. The carvers preserved the physical evidence of the history of the village in these model houses and poles, from the oldest families to the south to the newest arrivals to the north, from the rivalries within clans to the intermarriages between them. These family histories were shared with Deans, Newcombe, and Swanton, who sometimes recorded them incorrectly. By comparing their various records with the knowledge shared by the Skidegate community, it is hoped that some errors have been corrected, or at least pointed out in this book.

During the years since I started the research for this book in 2001, many of the Haida elders who generously shared their knowledge with us have passed away. I am grateful to have been able to start this work during a time when they were still with us. As it comes to a conclusion, I know that much more work remains to be carried on by the Haida people who value their histories and culture so much. Many questions remain to be answered about the model houses and the artists who made them, and I know that some that have gone missing will no doubt be rediscovered. Hopefully this book will help in that quest.

Haawa to the many people who helped with this effort. We are grateful to the nineteenth-century Haida artists for documenting their villages in 1892 with such care and for sharing what they knew with James Deans and other collectors. Although Deans made errors in the records he kept, we are grateful to him as well for the record, though flawed, that has survived at the Field Museum. While this book may have corrected some old errors, no doubt it still contains some new ones, and if so, I take full responsibility for any errors and look forward to having future Haida researchers correct them. These little houses and poles hold a lot of information that is yet to be put together. As Barbara Wilson says, it's like a library:

> My Haida name is Kii'iljuus, my English name is Barbara Wilson. I'm the eldest sister of the next in line to be Chief Cumshewa. And as the eldest sister, I'm actually his only sister, I only have a cousin, she's my second cousin. We are the last females of our age; we're the matriarchs of our clan. . . . And so this education we talk about it extends to people my own age, because we grew up in a time when our parents told us to leave the old ways behind, to move on because we had to survive in a white man's world. And so, as I learn stuff, you know, I pass it on to my cousin, and she hopefully passes it on to her children, and I pass it on to mine and my brothers, and we spend a lot of time self-educating ourselves. And given the time we grew up, you know, we grew up in residential schools and we, it was a major turning point for all of us, I think, in Skidegate. You know, where we were busy becoming white men. And somebody put the brakes on. And, you know, that's probably the most delightful thing is somebody put the brakes on and said *whoa, you know. We can't do this. We gotta hold onto who we are.* And now, here we are you know, it's what 20–30 years later, and our kids dance, our women weave and make clothing, and our men carve and tell stories, and it's just like, it's like one of those . . . you know how they talk about Snow White. Somebody kissed her. Somebody kissed the Haida nation and we woke up. That's what it's like you know. I'm overwhelmed when I think of how grateful I am to those people who hung on to bits and pieces, so that we could start putting the puzzle back together again. . . .
>
> And so, I look at those little houses, or the pictures of those little houses, and I've read what Deans was talking about when he was gathering them and what his thoughts were about the exhibit for Chicago. It was Chicago, yeah. And I think wow, you know. There is so much we don't know because of all those people that passed away. You know . . . it's like having a library. Burke Museum. You have your, you have your books of knowledge, you have your manuscripts that have been published and those are the old people. You have your manuscripts that are drafts. Those are people like me, younger people. And then you have the little stories and everything, those are our teenagers and our young people. And then we have a fire. And the library burns and out of 20,000 books that are in various stages, less than 500, less than 600 survive. And here we are today trying to put the library back together again. You know. And I think about that, and I think wow. What a chore. Not a chore negatively, but, what a huge undertaking to try and put all of that back together again. Because the diseases took it away, that was the fire. The diseases were the fire. The smallpox, the influenza, the dysentery, the measles, the mumps. Tuberculosis, you know, all those things. That's the fire. You know, and then here we are with little sparks and we're trying to get everything back together again.
>
> —Kii'iljuus, Barbara Wilson, matriarch of the St'awaas K̲iiG̲awaay (E5), August 24, 2006

APPENDIX I / Chronology of the SG̱iidagiids Town Chiefs

A chronological list of Skidegate chiefs with the Roman numerals I through IX was first published by George MacDonald with no specific names (MacDonald 1893: 40).[1] His list was based largely on the notes of James Deans, who was the first to attempt to describe the sequence of the Skidegate Town Chiefs (Deans 1893b, 1893c). Deans didn't supply a list but mentions some of the Chief Skidegates by number or sequence (starting with Skidegate the Great as I and leaving out Skidegate the "very great"), although his numbers are not consistent. MacDonald's list ends with Skidegate IX (1898–1902). The following list extends the sequence through the twentieth century and presents what is currently known of the identity of these people as well as questions that remain about them. I have changed some of MacDonald's dates to reflect what we know now.

SKIDEGATE I "THE VERY GREAT"—(unknown birth and death dates). Perhaps met by George Dixon in 1787 and said to be an old man at the time. This name was recorded by both Hoskins (Skediates) and Ingraham (Skuttkiss) in 1791 (see Wright 2001b: 36, 44, 50–51, 77, 340). See Genealogy Chart 5.

SKIDEGATE II "THE GREAT"—(unknown birth date, died ca. 1832, assumed to be E6). His other names were "Jacque" and "Gunwhat" (see Deans Model Pole #1). See also George Dawson's account of his grave post (Cole and Lockner: 482). See Genealogy Chart 5.

SKIDEGATE III—(called the second by Deans)—(unknown birth or death dates, chief ca. 1832–42, assumed to be E6). According to Deans, Grave House No. 7 was for this man whom he calls the second Chief Skidegate (MacDonald's III) (see Deans Model Grave House #12, note 3.33). See Genealogy Chart 5.

SKIDEGATE IV—(called "the third, brother of Niisdaka.na" by Deans)—(chief ca. 1842–1850?, E6a). See Genealogy Chart 5.

SKIDEGATE V—NIISDAKA.NA (chief ca. 1850–60?). James Prevost's 1853 letter describes "Nestaqana" as chief during the 1852 Susan Sturgis affair (see Wright 2001b: 160–61, 216–19). MacDonald says Skidegate V built Dug-Out House (his #18) in the mid-nineteenth century (see House Model No. 13). See Genealogy Chart 5.

SKIDEGATE VI—(chief ca. 1860–76?). This would have been the Chief Skidegate who camped on Burnaby Island with GitK̲un of T'aanuu when Francis Poole was mining for copper in Skinkuttle Inlet, August 1862 (see Poole 1872). See Genealogy Chart 5.

SKIDEGATE VII—DOGANGAKILLAS (chief ca. 1876–1887, E6a). This Chief Skidegate has two headstones. He was born in 1831 and died November 22, 1887, at age fifty-six, and "he was cut down without the slightest warning." This must be the Chief Skidegate referred to by James Deans in the description of House Model No. 15—Chief's House or Shining House—made by Amos Russ, "house belonged to Chief Skidegate who died suddenly in 1888 or 89." According to Deans, a Chief Skidegate raised (with his brother, Niisdaka.na) the first of the dogfish poles "sometime in the sixties" in honor of Kaaniihl (Deans 1893b: 84). However, photographic evidence confirms the first dogfish pole was raised ca. 1880 (see Model Poles Nos. 3 and 4), which would have been during the time of Skidegate VII. Newcombe gave the name of this Chief Skidegate as "Dogankilas" (Newcombe 1900–1911: Add. Mss. 1077, vol. 43, folder 4, Notes on totem poles at Skidegate–Dawson photography; see also MacDonald 1983: 54). He may have raised the memorial pole for Jat-jew-was (see Model Pole No. 9). See Genealogy Chart 5.

SKIDEGATE VIII—NIISDAKA.NA (chief ca. 1887–1892, E6a). This Chief Skidegate has three headstones. He was born in 1832 and died October 21, 1892, aged almost sixty. He was baptized April 2, 1892. Skidegate (chief, age forty) is listed in 1891 census living with Moses McKay (age thirty-five), his wife Eliza (age thirty-three), and son (adopted) James (age fifteen). Perhaps this was the brother of Dogangakillas (Niisdaka.na mentioned above). Newcombe says Niisdaka.na owned Na gutgitl kaigAns, "People call to each other in it" (see House Model No. "2" /21). His name in youth was Qamodi and after his death received the name G.ula kaitlgat [Ga.alla] "Grease dish inlaid with abalone" (Newcombe 1900–1911: Add. Mss. 1077, vol. 55, folder 10, Skidegate Village Houses and Poles, Victoria, BC. October 1906, House #20). He was married to ItldigAwa.i, also known as Skiu'lun a'oga ("skiu'lun's mother") of the Qugaangaas (R7), for whom he erected the mortuary pole (see Model Mortuary Pole No 10). This Skidegate was an invalid in 1892 when Deans collected the house models and occasionally lived in Dug-Out House (see House Model No. 13). See Genealogy Chart 5.

SKIDEGATE IX—Phillip Jackson (E6a) (chief 1892–1897). He was a nephew of Ga.alla (G.ula, Skidegate VIII). He was baptized in 1893. He has one headstone that says "Skidegate d. 1897 age 56," so he would have been born ca. 1841. Deans (1893) says Phillip Jackson became chief in 1892—"On account of the chief Skidegat's [*sic*] death last winter, Jackson has been duly elected chief, so his name is now Skidegate" (Deans 1893b: 89). He erected a five-finned whale memorial pole in honor of his wife's uncle (see figures 3.52, 3.53), as well as (with his wife) the memorial pole for Chief Skedans (see Model Pole No. 8). In 1892 he carved House Model No. 8 "Mountain House." See Genealogy Chart 5.

SKIDEGATE X—Peter Brown (E6a) (chief ca. 1897–1930). He died February 20, 1930, age seventy-five, so he would have been born ca. 1855. Peter Brown is listed in the Massett 1891 Census, age thirty-five (fisherman), wife Mary, age twenty-one (cannery hand), son Samuel, age two. Barbeau says Sam Q'a.oste (R14, d. 1892) was the father of Peter Brown (B. F. 256.54, 257.1, 253.5). When Chief Skidegate (Phillip Jackson) died, Ed Collinson and his younger brother Louis were both too young to accept the chieftainship. It was decided to call a relative, Peter Brown, as stand-in for Ed and Louis. Peter Brown carved House Model No. 7 (see figure 3.51). See Genealogy Chart 4.

SKIDEGATE XI—Ed Collinson (E6a) (chief from early 1930s to 1960). He was born 1877, died 1960. When Peter Brown died, the chieftainship went to Ed. Jags Brown relates that when Ed was born in 1877, there was a ceremony to designate him as the next chief. He was carried into the house on a copper (Jags Brown, personal communication, March 9, 2022). See Genealogy Chart 7.

SKIDEGATE XII—Louis Collinson (E6a) (chief 1960– 1970). Brother of Ed Collinson, Louis was born 1881, died 1970. He was well known as an argillite carver. Barbeau says Louis's brother was Amos Watson, but actually Amos Watson was his (and Ed's) paternal uncle (see Barbeau 1957: 118). See Genealogy Chart 7.

SKIDEGATE XIII—Clarence (Dempsey) Collinson (E6b) (chief 1973–2008). He was born September 9, 1928, and died March 2, 2008, age seventy-nine. At a potlatch in 1973, the town chiefship moved to Dempsey Collinson of the Naa S'aagaas X̱aaydaG̱aay, See Genealogy Chart 9.

APPENDIX II / Swanton's Skidegate House List

NOTE This list is from Swanton 1905a: 286. The underlined g and x̲ represent Swanton's g or x with a dot.

Łgagî'lda or Łgai-ū' (Skidegate), from the east [north] end. Informant, Edward, of the Daiyū' ał lā'nas (R 8).[1]

1. ———. *Family:* Djax̲ui' gîtînā'-i (E11).

2. ———. *Family:* Djax̲ui' gîtînā'-i (E11).

3. ———. *Family:* Na yū'ans xā'idAga-i (E6a).

4. ———. *Family:* Djax̲ui' sqoā'ładaga-i (R5).

5. X̲ū'adji xełī' ("Grisly-bear mouth"). *Family:* Nā-iku'n qē'gawa-i (R13).

6. X̲ū'adji na'as ("Grisly-bear house"). According to another Skidegate man, this should be X̲ū'adji Lxol. He said that the above name was used by Skedans, and they would not adopt it for fear of offending him. *Family:* Nā-iku'n qē'gawa-i (R13).

7. Na kīīña'ns ("house making a noise"). *Family:* Djax̲ui' gîtînā-i (E11).

8. Na gut hī'lāns ("house upon which the thunder roars"). *Family:* Djax̲ui' gîtînā'-i (E11).

9. Nā'ga gā'-iłas ("house upon which the tide comes"). *Family:* Nā-iku'n qē'gawa-i (R13).

10. G̲ālgā nā-i ("dark house"). *Family:* Djax̲ui' gîtînā'-i (E11).

11. Na qea'ndi gūdAña ("house people want to see all the time"). Daiyū' ał lā'nas (R8).

12. Q!e-u'xa qā'ala ("house people never pass by"). *Family:* Djax̲ui' sqoā'ładaga-i (R5).

13. Dā'agu qA'nłin ("house better than [the ones that have] house holes"). *Family:* Na yū'Ans xā'-idAga-i (E6a).

14. Nā'ga gutgi L! kia'gans ("people call to each other in it"), so called because it was too large to make one's self heard across the inside without raising the voice. *Family:* Na yū'Ans xā'-idAga-i (E6a).

15. X̲Ał tā'-igo ("shining house"). *Family:* Na yū'Ans xā'-idAga-i (E6a).

16. Na sagā's ("rotten house"). *Family:* Na sagā's xā'-idAga-i (E6b).

17. Sgā'na na'as ("killer whale house"). *Family:* Djax̲ui' sqoā'ładaga-i (R5).

18. Na s'A'ndjiwa ("house where the people do not care to eat anything [because they have so much]"). Łgai-ū lā'nas (R6).

19. ŁgAn na'as ("fin house"). Łgai-ū lā'nas (R6).

20. ŁimA'n na'as ("łimA'n-blanket house"). This was in advance of the others in front of the place where Amos Russ's house now stands. *Family:* Na sagā's xā'-idAga-i (E6b).

21. Nā'gi ī'ʟxagit k!ā'-idᴀñgᴀns ("house chiefs peeped at from a distance [because it was too great to let them come near]"). This stood at Tele'l, and was owned, together with No. 22, by the chiefs of Skidegate. *Family:* Na yū'ᴀns xā'-idᴀga-i (E6a).

22. Stīl na'as ("steel house"). This stood at Tele'l, and was owned, together with No. 21, by the chiefs of Skidegate. *Family:* Na yū'ᴀns xā'-idᴀga-i (E6a).

I obtained the names of two additional houses, which, however, were not contemporaneous with those named above.

Da'gi q!ā'yiña. *Family:* Na yū'ᴀns xā'-idᴀga-i (E6a).

Ldᴀga'o na'as ("mountain house"), a Skidegate house-name.

NOTES

INTRODUCTION

1. According to granddaughter Gladys Vandal, Henry Young had two other names: Gid Gajuus and Taaguus (author's personal communication with Vandal, August 2018).

2. The X̱aayda Kil (Haida language) glossary published by the Skidegate Haida Immersion Program (SHIP) in 2016 has been used for the preferred spellings in this book. Old spellings used by Deans, Newcombe, and Swanton are used when quoting them or referring to their work. To avoid confusion in the following references, I use "SHIP" when referring to unpublished emails or informal meetings, and the bibliographic reference "Elders of HlG̱aagilda X̱aayda Kil Naay 2016" when citing the published glossary.

3. In 2010 the British Columbia provincial government officially restored the Haida name for their home, Haida Gwaii, which had come to be known as the Queen Charlotte Islands after the 1787 visit by George Dixon, who named them after his ship, the *Queen Charlotte*, which had been named for the wife of the British King, George III.

4. The potlatch, the most important ceremony throughout the Northwest Coast, was made illegal by the Canadian government in 1884. For the Haida the potlatch ('Waahl-g̱ahl) is the essential celebration that must accompany the raising of a new house and pole and the validation of an inherited name and other important privileges. It was not until 1951 that the anti-potlatch law was dropped from the Indian Act in Canada (Cole and Chaikin 1990).

5. In the papers of A. W. Vowell, Indian Superintendent for British Columbia, a Department of Indian Affairs of British Columbia, Kwawkewlth Agency, invoice dated August 28, 1893, lists a model of a Nimkish village purchased for twelve dollars for display at the WCE by the Canadian government. It is unknown if or where this may have been displayed at the fair, and the current location of this model is unknown (Vowell 1892, 133).

6. Two recent books examine the history of model poles: one as part of a larger study of totem poles as a whole (Jonaitis and Glass 2010), and one an exhibition catalog (Hall and Glascock 2011).

7. Jonaitis and Glass (2010) report that in the twentieth century several examples of the internal cultural use of models include a 1922 Nuxalk memorial potlatch where mourners carried model totem poles representing the crests of the deceased chief; John Scow's father-in-law sent several model houses to Gwa'yasdam's village as a transfer of privileges; and Sam Henderson carved a model pole for George Hunt as a marriage transfer of crest prerogatives in Fort Rupert, BC. It was also mistakenly reported that the Ḵadjisdu.ax̱ch' models were made when a house was being transported from Old Wrangell to Klukwan. In fact, it was the artist himself who was being transported and made the maquettes in advance of carving the full-size posts (Glass and Jonaitis 2010, in Hall and Glascock 2011, 18–19fn2).

8. An eagle figure said to be a model of a figure from a totem pole that stood in front of a house in Fort Simpson was purchased there by Vincent Colyer, an artist and Board of Indian commissioner. It was accessioned into the Smithsonian in 1872 (cat. no. E11374).

9. The poles now in the Smithsonian collections include one Tlingit pole (E54297), two Tsimshian poles (E23549, E23550), a Kwakwa̱ka̱'wakw pole (E54295), and one Makah house post (E54301).

10. The flood story was depicted on three poles in Haida Gwaii, the original pole belonged to Chief Kaxius in Skedans. He gifted the right to depict this story to both Chief GitK̲un in Tanu and Chief Weah in Massett (MacDonald 1983, 93). We know that GitK̲un and his brother Geneskeles were visitors to Swan in Port Townsend in 1873, and it is possible this model was acquired from them.

11. The National Museum of Natural History archive records report that this photograph (MN-2962) is incorrectly dated 1903 on the back (it was published in USNM Report 1903) and gives it a date of 1879. If our speculations about the model houses in the photo are correct: the Tsimshian model house to the far right in the back row is known to have been sent to Paris in 1885, and another Haida house known to have been sent to Paris in 1883 does not show here, so it may be this photo dates to around 1884 (author's personal communication with Felicia Pickering, NMNH Collection Manager, February 2018).

12. This house front was said by Crosby to have been made by the oldest man in the village, who was then blind. Unfortunately, Crosby did not supply his name (see Swan letter to Baird, SM Anthropological archives, referenced in Cole 1985, 30, 318fn43).

13. This Haida house model was loaned to the Museo Nacional de Antropologia in Mexico City in 1964 and returned in 2012.

14. This Tsimshian model retains the original Smithsonian number written on the base (20863), and we know from the Smithsonian records that Swan collected it at Fort Simpson in 1875 and Spencer Baird sent it to the Trocadero Museum in 1885 (Walsh 2002) (Musee du Quai Branly, Paris, cat. no. 71.1885.78.47). We know the Smithsonian did two major exchanges with the Trocadero Museum: one dated 1883 of approximately eighty-five objects (including five model houses), and one in 1885 of six hundred objects, which included the Tsimshian model house.

15. This model is unusual in having the roof boards painted with formline designs. Only one other wooden model house has this treatment (AMNH 16.1/1164), and its frontal pole may also be by John Robson (see Glass 2011, 186–89).

16. These include three Tlingit house models (the two collected by Swan and one collected by J. J. McLean in 1881, cat. no. SM E49212-0), two Tsimshian (see figure I.11a and Musée du Quai Branly Jacques Chirac, cat. no. 71.1885.78.47), and four Haida (see figures I.9a, I.9b, I.13, I.15), and two Kwakwa̱ka̱'wakw (cat. nos. E129479, E129480) from Fort Rupert.

17. This includes the twenty-nine WCE house models, two others sold by Deans to the Provincial Museum (now the Royal British Columbia Museum, cat. nos. 224 and 232) in Victoria, and one acquired in 1894 in Victoria from Deans, now in the Fairbanks Museum and Planetarium in St. Johnsbury, Vermont. The frontal pole exhibited there can be attributed to John Robson.

ONE / Haida House Models in the White City

1. *Cultus* is the Chinook Jargon word for useless.

2. Oddly, the *Seattle Post Intelligencer* incorrectly reported: "Haida Indians for World's Fair. Vancouver, B.C. April 5 — Today fifteen Haida Indians, under the care of James Deans, leave here for Chicago to take part in the World's fair" (*Seattle Post Intelligencer*, April 5, 1893). In fact, all fifteen were Kwa̱kwa̱ka'wakw, not Haida.

3. The exact identities of the Kwakwa̱ka̱'wakw group who accompanied George Hunt is currently being researched by Judith Berman, University of Victoria (personal

communication, March 29, 2017). According to her research, also with the group were Mrs. George Hunt (Lucy); Mr. and Mrs. Wanukw and their eighteen-month-old son, Kostesalas; an eight-year-old girl named Koh-ste-sah-lass and her parents; as well as several others.

Several Kwakwa̱ka̱'wakw names were reported in some of the Chicago newspaper reports, but their creative spellings do not accurately reflect all of the names of the people now thought to have been there (*Chicago Sunday Post* 1893; *Chicago Times* 1893). Also, there were MalEte and Tom Hemasilaq (Jacknis 1991, 107–8) as well as John Drabble and his wife, Rachel (LaLahlew), from Nuwitti (Raibmon 2000).

4. F. W. Putnam Archives, Harvard University Archives 1717.2.14 Box 36.

5. A model of Chief Skidegate's house in the Milwaukee Public Museum was purchased by Barrett from the dealer Landsberg in Victoria in 1914. This model house had been exhibited in the WCE Anthropology Building in Landsberg's displays, separate from the Deans models, and for this reason had been erroneously credited to Deans's set of house models (Milwaukee Public Museum, cat. no. 16647a/4361; Cole 1985, 247).

6. Several of James Deans's relatives now live in Australia, descended from his brother Alexander Deans, who moved with their father, Alexander Deans, and brother Thomas to Coonabarabran, New South Wales, Australia (personal communication with Wanda Deans, August 11, 2005).

7. Many books with "White City" in the title have been written about the fair, perhaps none so widely read as Erik Larson's *The Devil in the White City: Murder, Magic, and Madness at the Fair That Changed America* (Larson 2003). This historical novel follows two storylines: one of a serial murderer who preyed on young women at the fair, and one of the architectural history of the WCE and the city of Chicago. While not comparable to the issues in this book, the two opposing storylines seem as opposite to each other within Larson's book as the story of the WCE and the Haida's Indigenous house models that were separated from their makers and their home to be dropped into a Euro-American "White City" in Chicago.

TWO / Hlg̱aagilda Llnagaay

1. Haida clans are identified here by the numbers used by John Swanton, with "R" designating a Raven clan and "E" an Eagle clan, the two matrilineal exogamous moieties of the Haida (Swanton 1905a, 268–76).

2. Many other Haida historians worked with Swanton, providing the stories from other villages and clans, including Mary Ridley and Henry Edenshaw (from Massett), Chief Skedans, Job Moody (E5a), Hai'as (E21c), Walter (Massett, R15a), Douglas (Klinkwan, E21), and in addition, the unnamed but listed "several old people" from Kayang, Kung, K'yuusda, and Yaak'u (Swanton 1905a, 282–95).

3. See, for instance, Steedman and Collison 2011.

4. In some cases marriage outside of the opposite side did and does occur, and when the mother is not Haida or of the opposite clan, adoptions can take place to remedy this situation. The Canadian government and Christian church, which are based on a patrilineal system, further complicated the situation when they arrived, recognizing the father as the head of household, and giving children the father's surname. Section 12 (1)(b) of the old Indian Act of 1884 stipulated that Native women and their children lost their Indian status if they married a "non-status" person. They had to leave the reserve and could not even gather or possess traditional foods. It was not until the Bill C-31 of 1985 was passed that these women could return to their reserves (Steedman and Collison 2011, 19).

5. Various other spellings include: Skutkiss (Ingraham 1791 in Kaplanoff 1971), Skediates (Hoskins 1791 in Howay 1990), Skitlekits (Burling 1799), Skidegat (Deans 1883c), Skidegas (Green 1915), Skid-a-ga-tees (Poole 1872, 107).

6. For an illustration of this labret, see Wright 2001b, 37, 39, figures 2.4–2.6. This labret was in the British Museum until the middle of the nineteenth century (King 1981, 61, plate 39).

7. The twelve-year-old son of Yeltatzie at Dadens had the name "Skitlekits" according to Samuel Burling (see Wright 2001b, 92), but given his age, this was not likely a chiefly name. The Haida traditionally had several names—those bestowed at birth and also other childhood honorary names that could be given at house-building potlatches of their father or funerary potlatches of the paternal grandfather. These honorary names might also be held by others at the same time and come from an opposite clan, so could not be passed on. These names differed from the more important ceremonial or "potlatch names" that were a mark of rank and power (Enrico 1991).

8. The honorific title "Captain" was sometimes used by chiefs in the late nineteenth century because the captains of ships were known as the highest-ranking foreign officials at the time.

9. P. Broughton, "Oregon Columbus Hastings (1846–1912)—Pioneer Astronomer of British Columbia," *Journal of the Royal Astronomical Society of Canada* 106, no. 5 (2012): 199 (accessed April 20, 2022); http://cameraworkers.davidmattison.com/getperson.php?personID=I187&tree=cw18581950.

10. "Dossetter, Edward William," *Camera Workers, 1858–1950*, and "Dossetter, Edward William," *Camera Workers, 1858–1950*, http://cameraworkers.davidmattison.com/getperson.php?personID=I187&tree=cw18581950 (accessed April 20, 2022).

11. This pole, called Sea Otter Pole, was located near where Verna Williams's house now stands. The pole was sold sometime between 1968 and 1970 and went to the Museum of Vancouver and repatriated to the Haida Nation in 2019. The name "Sea Otter" pole comes from the clan of Skiu'lun a'oga for whom it was raised, who belonged to the Qugaangaas or sea otter family of Ravens (R7) (see figure 3.82).

THREE / Model Houses, Poles, and Their Makers

1. Franz Boas wrote a letter to L. VanKoughnet, Deputy Superintendent General of Indian Affairs, Ottawa, March 11, 1893, asking if it was possible to send a tracing of the survey of the reservation of Skidegate so that he might install the house models and posts of the village in "as nearly as possible in their original locations" in a display that "will form an important part of the exhibit of this department from British Columbia" (Boas 1893c). I have found no evidence that he ever received such a tracing, as I haven't found one in his papers, and no other letters that refer to it. He did use the sketch of the village drawn by James Deans, with the houses numbered and the garden and geographical features drawn in, so I assume that was all he had to go by in the end. The installation did deviate a bit from Deans's sketch (see below).

Note that on both pages of Deans's map the direction north is at the top and south at the bottom, suggesting that the village was oriented in an east-west direction, with his House Model No. 1 at the left and No. 27 at the right. In fact, the village of Hlg̱aagilda is oriented primarily in a north-south direction as shown on Map 2. MacDonald indicates this north-south orientation on his map of Skidegate with his houses No. 1 (27 on Deans's map) located to the north and his house No. 30 (4 on Deans's map) located to the south, but curiously in his discussion of the houses starting at his No. 1, he has the heading "Houses at Skidegate from the east" (MacDonald 1983, 38, 44). In my discussion I'll use the north–south orientation to stay true to Map 2.

2. At the end of Boas's list he says there were two houses from Ninstints, but Deans describes only one from there (Boas 1893b, 133). Deans's note on the back of the map says to place No. 22 alongside of No. 5.

3. Boas places this Model No. 17 on his list between Thunderstorm House and House of Waves: "No. 17. House of the Earthquake" (Boas 1893a, 35), but it doesn't appear here in the installation photo.

4. Marius Barbeau photographed one of the four Tsimshian model houses collected by Odille Quintal Morison

in Chicago in 1916 (Field Museum, cat. no. 18003). It was mistakenly identified as Haida by Barbeau (Barbeau 1957, 66–67). The Tsimshian model house catalog numbers are: Field Museum, cat. no. 18000, 18001 (BKLN 05.589.7794, now missing), 18003, 17826 (xBKLN 05.589.7789); and the Nuxalk model house catalog numbers are: Field Museum, cat. nos. 18641, 18642, 18643, 18644, 18645. One of the Tsimshian house models, Field Museum, 17826 (BKLN 05.589.7789), was deaccessioned to the Museo Nacional de Antropologia, Mexico, in December 1959 (January 10, 2002, letter from Susan Kennedy Zeller, Assistant Curator, Arts of the Americas).

5. Ira Jacknis was working on a book on museum miniatures and dioramas at the time of his death in 2021, and it is hoped that this can be published posthumously.

6. December 13, 2001, and January 14, 2002, emails from William Wierzbowski, Assistant Keeper, University of Pennsylvania Museum of Archaeology and Anthropology, Philadelphia; *Bulletin of the Pennsylvania Museum*, no. 63 (October 1918): 49; March 21, 1919, and March 3, 1919, letters from Langdon Warner, Director of the Memorial Hall, and Charles Hart, Chairman of the Philadelphia Council of Boy Scouts; and February 14, February 25, and March 3, 1919, letters to G. B. Gordon, Director of the University Museum, Philadelpha, University of Pennsylvania Museum archives.

7. The fairgrounds were destroyed by fire in 1894, but this building, originally the Palace of Fine Arts, was the only fireproof building at the WCE. At the close of the fair it became the home of the Field Museum collections, then called the "Columbian Museum of Chicago," until the new Marshall Field Museum building was opened in Grant Park in 1921. The Palace of Fine Arts building fell into disrepair and was restored as the Museum of Science and Industry in 1933, one of the only WCE buildings that still stands.

8. See Field Museum neg. nos. 102222, 102224, 102225, 102226.

9. Information from Newcombe's notes from W. Woods, October 1906: "XAina. The pole sent to Ottawa belonged to Gwaitaitla of the NAstoqeg.awa.i [Naasduu K̲iiG̲awaay, R10a]. He owned the raven, tcAmaos & thunderbird. The top figure is his & the tcAmaos at the bottom. His common name is George Smith & he is still alive." A handwritten note here by Newcombe gives a reference to Swanton (1905a, 280), describing the village of Lā'na hī'ldAns at Rennel Sound, with the chief's name of Gwa-i t!ā'-iłda "one who moves the world as he walks," likely referring to the name of the owner of the Xaayna house (Newcombe 1900–1911: Add. Mss. 1077, vol. 55, folder 8).

Information from Moses McKay: "XAina. No. 6 (Swanton). This belonged to Chief NAngkilstlas, 'one who makes things happen by his word.' He belonged to the Tlgaxetgu lanas [HlG̲axiidgu Laanas, R9] & owned the moon, thunder-bird, killer, rinbow [*sic*] & sea-lion as crests. Those seen on the pole are the Thunder-bird at top, & the killer at the bottom. The name of the house was Skilk'iaeg.a ta ige, 'house waiting for property.' This pole was sent to Ottawa" (Newcombe 1900–1911: Add. Mss. 1077, vol. 38, folder 3).

Swanton records the name of this house (his no. 6) as Skil k!ia'oga tā'-igo ("house waiting for property"). Family: Łgā'xetgu lā'nas (R9) (Swanton 1905a, 289).

10. The Haida thunderbird is a blue hawk (Swanton 1905a, 108). Farther south on the coast, among the Kwak̲wa̲ka'wakw, the thunderbird is a supernatural eagle.

11. Newcombe 1900–1911: Add. Mss. 1077, vol. 38, folder 3.

12. Swanton also recorded this story (Swanton 1905a, 202–3).

13. There are several cases where an Eagle clan has Raven as a crest, such as the E6 in Skidegate (said to be the result of one of the clan being poisoned while eating clams while visiting the Tsimshian country, and a Raven hat was given to atone for it, after which the Raven became their crest), and also where Raven clans have crests that are on the Eagle side, such as the dogfish, used by R19 in Alaska and E6 in Skidegate (see Swanton 1905a, 107–17).

14. Many of attributions of argillite carvings to George Smith by Barbeau are incorrect. The argillite pipe attributed by Barbeau to George Smith was actually made by John Cross, which Barbeau would have learned if he had exam-

ined the pipe firsthand, since it is one of the few argillite pipes with the artist's name written on the bottom "made by John Cross of Skidegate Mission Q.C.Is. B.C." (see Barbeau 1957, 101, Museum of Vancouver, cat. no. AA2337; Wright 1985, 586–87).

15. SG̱ang Gwaay is a village on Anthony Island, known as Ninstints after the Chief Nunsdins name in the nineteenth and early twentieth centuries. The name has been spelled variously Sgang gwaii, sran gwaay, sgungwai, etc.

16. Newcombe 1900–1911: Add. Mss. 1077, vol. 35, folder 1, diary June 8 and September 21, 1901.

17. The only other Joshua from SG̱ang Gwaay was Joshua Price (b. 1859, d. 1904 at age forty-five) (see note 20).

18. Swanton's lists of houses often differs in sequence from both MacDonald's and Newcombe's lists.

19. The Field Museum catalog mistakenly gives description for "House No. 2" to Field Museum cat. no. 17802, which was placed between House No. 11 (cat. no. 17803) and House No. 13 (cat. no. 17800) in the WCE installation. Newcombe commented on this cataloging error in a handwritten note on Deans's typescript: "This description does not tally with model pole crests but is evidently house 17828 on p. 38. John Cross the maker's name is on the door—CFN." Unfortunately, Newcombe was unaware that the real House No. 2 had been sent to Vienna, and incorrectly guessed that it must be 17828, Food House, which has John Cross as the maker. But Deans's description for 17828 (otter/bear/whale/eagle) does not match 17802 either. House No. 2 has fin-backed whale, but no dogfish. On the Deans accession list next to No. 22—Model of Katkins Kien nas, Katkins point house, a handwritten note says "probably sent to Vienna in July 94" the Field Museum catalog number 178? is crossed out. This name "Katkin Kien nas," Katkins point house, probably actually refers to FM17802. SHIP spells the name of this house as G̱aahllns Kun Naas (SHIP email September 30, 2020).

20. Clew or New Clew (New Klue, New Kloo) is the town located at Church Creek (also known as Mathers Creek), where some of the residents of T'aanuu Llnagaay and K̲'uuna Llnagaay moved in 1887 before finally migrating to HlG̱aagilda Llnagaay in 1897 (Dalzell 1973, 250). There is only one Joshua (apparently single, no last name, age twenty-eight) listed in the Skidegate census report for 1891 (Family #375). This might be Joshua Price. There is a possibility that Joshua Tait and Joshua Price might have been the same person, but since Newcombe knew both families, his identification of Joshua Tait as the owner of the house next to T. Tait strongly suggests that these two Joshuas were different men. Joshua Price was married to Susan Price, who died in 1897. He may have also been married earlier to a woman named Minnie (1855–1889). Joshua and Susan had a stillborn child in 1888. Joshua Price was probably related to Tom Price (brother?), the last Chief Nang Sdins (b. ca. 1861, d. March 25, 1927), a well-known artist who worked in argillite, wood, and silver (Gessler 1981; Holm 1981). Thomas Price (E1) was living in Skidegate in 1891 (age thirty) with wife Ellen (twenty-nine) and Peter Kelly (age ten, a stepson) (Family #360). His father (listed in the death record) was James Price (BCA microfilm #13361).

21. The 1891 Skidegate census lists Captain Gold, age fifty-nine (Family #412) with his wife, Mary, age fifty-one, and son Johnny, age eleven. This Captain Gold would most likely be the nephew who built the house at HlG̱aax̱id Llnagaay.

22. Also known as a Chilkat robe.

23. Deans frequently uses the term "tuden skeel" to refer to the watchmen figures at the top of poles. It is likely that this is his spelling of the Haida term for a chief's hat with potlatch rings: daajing sgilgaay. "Sgil" refers to the basketry rings on spruce root chief's hats that symbolized wealth and status.

24. The Museum of Vancouver model of SG̱iidagiids X̱aad has been attributed to John Robson by Kwiaahwah Jones and Corey Bullpit (Musuem of Vancouver online catalog, https://openmov.museumofvancouver.ca/node/91592 (accessed April 25, 2022), and it is likely that the Royal British Columbia Museum model is by him as well, based on its style.

25. MacDonald identified the small human figure as a bat, then a frog and a killer whale above the frog, but it

would appear that the figure at the top with the frog in its mouth is the bat (MacDonald 1983, 56).

26. The Naa 'Yuuwans X̱aaydaG̱aay E6a crests are listed by Swanton as raven, 'WaasG̱uu (sea wolf), dogfish, weasel, eagle, sculpin, and halibut (Swanton 1905a, 273).

27. The 1891 Skidegate census (Family #359) lists "Nicholls, Jacobus," age twenty-five, living with a wife named Justine (age twenty-three) and a baby girl (age one). This family was living next door to Tom Price. It is possible that the census taker wrote down Jacobus for Zacherias and Nicholls for Nicholas.

28. Also attributed to him are a frontal pole from Ts'aahl (MacDonald 1983, 127, plate 172) and a T'aanuu house post (see Wright 2009, 71, figure 4; Holm 1981, 199, figure 57). For an attributed bentwood chest, see Wright 2009, 70, figure 3; and Holm 1981, 198, figure 55.

29. Paddles attributed to Zacherias include one in the DeYoung Museum cat. no. 67–10 (Holm 1981, 199, figure 56) and the University of British Columbia Museum cat. no. Nb1.738, and model poles include British Museum cat. no. Am1954,05.969; University of British Columbia Museum, cat. no. A2530 and A2529 (Wright 2009, 71, figure 5), and Sotheby's Auction Catalog, New York, May 21, 1996, no. 212.

30. American Museum of Natural History, cat. no. T22717 (see Wright 2009, 70, figure 2); there is also an argillite chest in the Berlin Museum (Staatliche Museen zu Berlin), cat. no. IV A 1125. Cowan's Auctions, April 5, 2008, lot 35, www.cowanauctions.com/lot/haida-argillite-boat-with-figures-carved-by-the-master-of-the-chicago-settee-53763 (accessed May 3, 2022).

31. See Bunn-Marcuse 2007, 118–20; and the chest face also illustrated in Holm 1981, 198, figure 53; and Wright 2009, 70, figure 2.

32. See Wright and Augaitis 2013, 173, figure 192; 178, figure 198; 180, figures 202, 204, 205; 182, figure 207; and 188–89, figure 217.

33. There is some confusion on Deans's part here if he is referring to the "the Great Skidegate" as "Skidegate the Great," whom he calls Skidegate I, since he referred to Skidegate the Great's "son" as Skidegate II (see Grave House No. 7). Yet he goes on to refer to him here as Skidegate III and to his brother Niisdaka.na as Skidegate IV, which would place them later in time. According to MacDonald's numbering system, Grave House No. 7 would have been for Skidegate III, and this grave house would have been for Skidegates IV and V (see Appendix I, Chronology of the SG̱iidagiids Town Chiefs).

34. Newcombe's letter points out that Swanton mistakenly described the mandA pictured in his book (figure 13) as having been collected from Moses McKay, however Newcombe wanted to correct this as he actually collected this "beaver" mandA and another representing a "toad" in Skedans. They belonged to Gidkun according to Captain Klew (Newcombe Add. Mss. 1077, vol. 5, folder 140, letter from Newcombe to Swanton, February 6, 1906; Swanton 1905a, 132).

35. Newcombe 1900–1911: Add. Mss. 1077, vol. 55, folder 10, Skidegate photo, Carpenter copy 17439:1, nearest small figures. Jags Brown currently holds the name Niisdaka.na.

36. Newcombe 1900–1911: Add. Mss. 1077, vol. 55, folder 10. Swanton's list has three more houses after house No. 19 (20–22), but these are said to have belonged to the Skidegate Eagle clan (E6a, 6b). One was located farther east, where Amos Russ's house was, and two were in Tlell (Swanton 1905a, 286).

37. This figure is identified as a whale holding an otter by MacDonald (1983, 55).

38. Newcombe 1900–1911: Add. Mss. 1077, vol. 55, folder 10: Victoria, BC, Skidegate House and Totem Poles, October 4th, 1906, 1. MacDonald spells the name Dseltgaragati, a shaman and his brothers, the description taken from Newcombe's description of SG̱aana Naas, even though he calls this fin house (MacDonald 1983, 55).

39. The 1881 census report for Skidegate lists three women living in the house that was at the far southern end of the village: Kittejen, age forty-two, Telgevtat, age forty, and a widow Ttluuce, age sixty-five. None of these women would have been old enough to have been the woman who built

the house in the early nineteenth century. It is unknown whether Owl or SG̱aana Naas was still standing at that time, but it may not have been habitable then.

40. Even though Deans numbered it House 22, his notes say: "It ought to have been placed on the list of houses as No. 3," no doubt meaning it should have been the third in the Skidegate section that started after "Moon House," since this is where it was placed in the installation (Deans 1893b in Newcombe 1900–1911: Add. Mss. 1077, vol. 38, folder 3, Haida Industry Notes: Section II, 51).

41. Newcombe 1900–1911: Add. Mss. 1077, vol. 55, folder 10, Victoria, BC, Skidegate House and Totem Poles, October 4, 1906, 3.

42. On Newcombe's copy of Swanton's list of Skidegate houses, he crossed out "eat anything" and wrote in "look up being ashamed it is so big" (Newcombe 1900–1911: Add. Mss. 1077, vol. 55, folder 10, Skidegate House Names, Swanton).

43. Newcombe 1900–1911, Add. Mss. 1077, vol. 43, folder 4, Notes on totem poles at Skidegate–Dawson photography. Newcombe also spells this name "Tlinit" and says he was the first Jefferson and also the owner of the house next door, Na agAn kil AdldAndas "always wanting more" (Newcombe 1900–1911: Add. Mss. 1077, vol. 55, folder 10, Skidegate Houses and Totem Poles, October 4, 1906: House #5). There was apparently no model made of that house for the WCE.

44. Newcombe 1900–1911: Add. Mss. 1077, vol. 55, folder 10, Skidegate Houses and Totem Poles &c. C Jefferson informant. October 1906, Victoria, BC, 3; Swanton 1901b, 1.

45. Likely meaning "Jacques," see Model Pole No. 1.

46. While marrying someone from the opposite moiety was a standard practice for the Haida, it was not always done, even before contact with Europeans. This practice, as well as many others, was discouraged after Chistian missionaries arrived, although in recent years has been revived.

47. MacDonald also repeated Deans's error, saying Jefferson took the whale crest of Skidegate the Great after his death (MacDonald 1983, 54).

48. Deans notes that these should be placed between houses 6 and 7. He must have meant in the sequence of the installation, rather than his own house numbers.

49. Newcombe 1900–1911: Add. Mss. 1077, vol. 43, folder 4, Notes on totem poles at Skidegate–Dawson photography; see also MacDonald 1983, 54.

50. Kaaniihl aawga means Kaaniihl's mother (SHIP September 18, 2007). Kaaniihl is name of James Young's sister Clara (James Young, personal communication, February 7, 2004).

51. Newcombe 1900–1911: Add. Mss. 1077, vol. 55, folder 10, Skidegate photo Carpenter copy 17439, by Henry Moody, 2.

52. Newcombe 1900–1911: Add. Mss. 1077, vol. 55, folder 10. Charles Jefferson (R6) died on February 19, 1930, age eighty-five (BC Archives GR 2951, vol. 14). Jefferson's mother was married to two of the chiefs called Gidkun (K̲'una K̲iiG̱awaay, E3), the last of whom drowned at Skidegate in 1903. These were the chiefs of the village of T'aanuu (Newcombe 1900–1911: Add. Mss. 1077, vol. 55, folder 9).

53. Thanks to Mary Malloy, who assisted in confirming this information.

54. Newcombe 1900–1911: Add. Mss. 1077, vol. 55, folder 10: 4. Skidegate Houses and Poles, C. Jefferson Informant.

55. Given the prominent wolves at the top of the pole and corner posts of this model, it is possible that the wife of the man who made the model and her family who had the original house were of the K'aaadas Gaa K̲'iiG̱awaay (R3) of T'aanuu, who have wolf, rainbow, killer whale, black bear, and Ts'aamus as crests (Swanton 1905, 114).

56. Newcombe 1900–1911: Add. Mss. 1077, vol .43, folder 4, 8.

57. Newcombe 1900–1911: Add. Mss. 1077, vol. 55, folder 10, Skidegate Houses and Totem Poles, C. Jefferson of the Tlgaiyu laanas informant, Victoria, BC, October 4, 1906, #12a.

58. Newcombe 1900–1911: Add. Mss. 1077, vol. 55, folder 10, Skidegate Houses and Totem Poles, C. Jefferson of the Tlgaiyu laanas informant, Victoria, BC, October 4, 1906, #12a.

59. MacDonald reported that the five-finned whale was a crest acquired by Chief Skedans from the Tsimshian people at Kitkatla (MacDonald 1983, 52). This crest is not listed by

Swanton as a Skedans (R4) crest (Swanton 1905a, 269). The five-finned killer whale is listed by Swanton as a q!ā'gawa-i (K'aaG̱waay), crest of the "Ninstints people, those born in the southern part of the islands (E2)" (Swanton 1905a, 272, 110). Chief Gidansda, Guujaaw, in an email dated July 28, 2017, confirms that the Skedans people have never claimed any rights to the five-finned killer whale. Today the K̲aay'ahl Laanas (E9) do hold this crest (Jisgang, Nika Collison, personal communication, July 12, 2022). On September 30, 2022, a pole with a five-finned whale was raised in Xaayna for the late Kaay'ahl Laanas Chief Gaahlaay.

60. Newcombe 1900–1911: Add. Mss. 1077, vol. 55, folder 10, Skidegate Houses and Totem Poles, C. Jefferson of the Tlgaiyu laanas informant, Victoria, BC, October 4, 1906, #13. MacDonald says that this house (his #25) is the same house listed by Swanton as "House Upon Which Thunder Roars" (Swanton's #8) owned by the Seaward Eagles (E11), but Swanton's house #8 is positioned much farther to the east in the village and probably refers to a different house, owned by Daniel Iljuuwaas (see "Thunder and Lightning House" below) (MacDonald 1983, 52; Swanton 1905a, 286).

61. Newcombe 1900–1911: Add. Mss. 1077, vol. 55, folder 10, Skidegate Houses and Totem Poles, C. Jefferson of the Tlgaiyu laanas informant, Victoria, BC, October 4, 1906, #9. The house called "Mountain House" by MacDonald matches more closely the model called "Wolf House" discussed earlier (MacDonald 1983, 51).

62. The Jiiaxwii Sk̲aahladasG̱aay (R5) ("Down the inlet [or seaward] sgwaahlaadaas") clan apparently has no surviving members, although the name Luuguud "Wave Eagle" was held by George L. (the "L" is for Luuguud) Young, Chief Cumshewa (St'awaas X̲aayadaG̱aay, E5) (Barbara Wilson, personal communication, August 24, 2006). There were several George Youngs in Skidegate. In addition to Chief Cumshewa, there was a George Young Sr. (gunyaa) (b. 1864, d. 1924) (E?), married to Eliza (R13), and a younger George Young, Chief Skedans (b. 1893, d. 1975) (R4).

63. Newcombe 1900–1911: Add. Mss. 1077, vol. 55, folder 10, Skidegate Houses and Totem Poles, C. Jefferson of the Tlgaiyu laanas informant, Victoria, BC, October 4, 1906, #9.

64. Newcombe 1900–1911: Add. Mss. 1077, vol. 55, folder 10, 1.

65. Later in the 1891 census, a Mr. Jackson, age twenty-five, is listed as the nephew of Peter Smith (Family #386). This man would have been twenty-six years younger than Phillip if his death date is correct, so likely not the same man. No other Jacksons are listed in the 1891 Skidegate census.

66. Newcombe identifies Lansing as Moses McKay in his copy of the Deans typescript. Swanton spells this name Lansin (Swanton 1905b, 132).

67. Newcombe 1900–1911: Add. Mss. 1077, vol. 43, folder 4, Notes on totem poles at Skidegate–Dawson photography, #10.

68. Newcombe also says this man was Amos Russ's father (Newcombe 1900–1911: Add. Mss. 1077, vol. 43, folder 4, Notes on totem poles at Skidegate–Dawson photography, pole #17). Newcombe also gave a second name for Amos Russ's father: Kunxakahalats of the nasagas family (E6b) (Newcombe 1900–1911: Add. Mss. 1077, vol. 55, folder 10, Skidegate Includes photos, pole #17). Another location in Newcombe's notes for his No. 16 house also references "Swanton bottom of p. 128," which is a description two inside house posts (RBCM cat. nos. 1 and 2) (Newcombe 1900–1911: Add. Mss. 1077, vol. 55, folder 10, Skidegate. Includes photos, pole #16). Swanton's information came from Tom Stevens and Amos Russ, who gave two different names for the owner of RBCM 1. Stevens reported the name of the owner was GA'nx̱uat, and Russ said the name was Do'gAanakiłas. Since RBCM cat. no. 1 was apparently inside the house to the east of "New House," Newcombe's reference to this Swanton information for his house No. 16 may be simply pointing to the name Do'gAnakilas, not suggesting that the post was inside this house. Later photos of the frontal pole show the inside house post was in the house to the east, revealed after the houses were dismantled (Swanton 1905a, 128–29).

69. Newcombe 1900–1911: Add. Mss. 1077, vol. 55, folder 10, Skidegate Houses and Poles, Victoria, BC, October 4, 1906, #16.

70. In the WCE installation this mortuary model was

placed between "New House" and "Raven House" and closer to "Raven House" (Field Museum, cat. no. 17806).

71. Newcombe 1900–1900: Add. Mss. 1077, vol. 55, folder 10: Carved Totem Pole at Skidegate Erected in Honor of Chief Skedans. This is according to notes supplied to Newcombe by the present (1906) Chief Skedans (Newcombe 1900–1911: Add. Mss. 1077, vol. 55, folder 10, p. 1). This would have been Henry Moody.

72. Newcombe 1900–1911: Add. Mss. 1077, vol. 55, folder 10, "Carved Totem Pole at Skidegate, Erected in honor of Chief Skedans, from notes supplied by the present Chief Skedans."

73. Deans reports that another "daughter" of Chief Skedans became the wife of the man who built the house of which No. 7 (G̱ud Ḵwiig̱a X̱iigangs) is a model, and she died before their house was finished (Deans 1893c, 89). Deans may have been confused here again, as he was likely referring here to the man who raised the five-finned pole that was placed on the Model House (No. 7). This pole was also put up by Jackson (Chief Sg̱iidagiids) for his wife's uncle after he died (Swanton 1901b: 3). He also belonged to G̱aag'yals Ḵiig̱awaay (R4). Newcombe said that this was put up for Skidegate's wife (Newcombe 1900–1911: Add. Mss. 1077, vol. 55, folder 10, p. 15, #12a) (see above).

74. This would be Skidegate VII, Dogangakillas, according to MacDonald's numbering system (see Appendix I, Chronology of the Sg̱iidagiids Town Chiefs); however, Deans calls him Niisdaka.naa here.

75. The word "brother" is handwritten and inserted after Nang djingwas in Newcombe's notes (Newcombe 1900–1911: Add. Mss. 1077, vol. 55, folder 10, p. 16, #17).

76. Newcombe 1900–1911: Add. Mss. 1077, vol. 55, folder 10, Skidegate Houses and Totem Poles, October 4, 1906, pole #17.

77. Newcombe 1900–1911: Add. Mss. 1077, vol. 55, folder 10, "House no. 17."

78. Swanton listed (his #21)—Nā'gi īLxagit k!ā'idAñgAns ("house chiefs peeped at from a distance [because it was too great to let them come near]") as one that stood at tele'l, and was owned, together with No. 22 (Swanton's), by the chiefs of Skidegate. Family: Nā yu'Ans xā'idAga-i (E6a) (Swanton 1905a, 286). This refers to an earlier house.

79. Based on Newcombe's comment and its style, I believe that Albert Edward Edenshaw probably carved this house post, although Wilson Duff attributed it to Charles Edenshaw (Wright 2001b, 219–20).

80. Deans misidentifies the dorsal fin of the dogfish as a whale held in the hands of the bear at the top, a crest of Nang Jingwas's second wife. This house was undoubtedly erected before Nang Jingwas married a second time, so the frontal pole would not have had a second wife's crest, and the dorsal fin clearly belongs to the dogfish.

81. Newcombe 1900–1911: Add. Mss. 1077, vol. 55, folder 10, Skidegate Houses and Totem Poles, Victoria, BC, October 4, 1906, pole #18.

82. This conflicts with Newcombe, who says Amos Russ's father was a brother to Nang Jingwas. (The uncle/grandfather relationship was often confused by non-Haida people.) (Newcombe 1900–1911: Add. Mss. 1077, vol. 55, folder 10, Skidegate Houses and Totem Poles, October 4, 1906, pole #17).

83. His first wife's headstone is possibly Jed ils was (jatilswuss) born 1819, died June 28, 1884. Though the age is off by twenty years, she is also likely listed as Tyatiljuwas, female forty-five in the 1881 census. Collison reports that she was "married" to Nang Jingwas's nephew when Collison visited Skidegate in 1876 and described his encounter with "Nangsinwass" and his two wives (Collison 1981, 122). The nephew and heir to a chief was often married to the chief's widow.

84. The current holder of the name Nang Jingwas is Russ Jones.

85. The Canadian Museum of History website identifies these men as "Chief Nanjingwas wearing a naval uniform (left) and another man, probably Chief Skidegate VII, stand before the Former's Raven crest at Chief's House in Skidegate." This information likely came from George MacDonald, though no reason is given for the identification of the man not in uniform (www.historymuseum.ca/cmc/exhibitions/aborig/haida/hvski02e.html, accessed April 20, 2022).

86. To the left near Nang Jingwas's house were two mortuary poles—one apparently erected between 1878 and 1881 with a hawk head on the panel that is very similar to the mortuary panel attached to Captain Gold's house, as well as to "Skidegate the Great's" mortuary pole, and an old one with a plain panel with two dorsal fins (see figure 2.2). To the right/east of this house and back a bit was another old mortuary pole that Newcombe's notes identify as the X̱aad of an old Nang Jingwas (Newcombe 1900–1911: Add. Mss. 1077, vol. 55, folder 10, p. 16). No models were made of these three mortuary poles for the WCE.

87. MacDonald (1983, 100) mistakenly said the meaning of Tliman is not known. The word for elk hide in the Chinook Jargon was spelled variously: tliman, cleman, clemmel, claman (Gibson 1992, 230).

88. MacDonald 1983, 50, house #20; Newcombe 1900–1911: Add. Mss. 1077, vol. 55, folder 10, Skidegate Houses and Totem Poles, Victoria, BC, October 4, 1906, house #19.

89. The 1881 Census Report (Canadian government records RG31 on file at the Union of BC Indian Chiefs, 342 Water Street, Vancouver, BC) for House #12 lists the residents as:

Elungquunice m. 65
Tyatstjuwas f. 21 w.
Kitquun m. 25
Kitakeetinga m. 42
Gardis f. 26

90. Richard Wilson thought the name Iljuuwaas could have moved between E7 and E11 (personal communication, 2006). Billy Stevens (K'aadaas Gaa K̲'iiG̱awaay, R3), the great-grandson of Daniel Iljuuwaas, held the name Iljuuwaas. Tyson Brown (E9) has that name today. According to Doris Shadbolt, Bill Reid (R3) was given the name "Iljuwas" by Billy Stevens's mother, Hazel Stevens, in the late twentieth century (Shadbolt 1998, 205).

Swanton reported that the name "I'ldjiwas" means "nobleman" (Swanton 1905b, 400fn19) in reference to a different man with this name who belonged to the Middle Gitans (E8b). In a story that most likely took place in the early nineteenth century, as told to Swanton by Richard (a member of the Middle Gitans [E8b] clan), this I'ldjiwas and his elder brother, Gi'tg.axi'lina, were both killed at Kaigani in a battle with the Yahgu Laanas (R19) (Swanton 1905b, 397–98).

In a different story told to Swanton by Abraham (of the K'aadaas Gaa K̲'iiG̱awaay—R3), the father of a man named I'ldjiwas fell in a battle fought together with the people of T'aanuu against the Giti'sda (Tsimshian). In a footnote, Swanton speculates that this man many have been the father of a chief from Skidegate named I'ldjiwas (Swanton 1905b, 447–48fn17).

Reno Russ of the Maaman Gitanee became Chief Iiljuwaas in 1984, hereditary town chief of Massett (Sparrow 2003, 45).

91. The Field Museum cat. no. 17802 is written next to "House Model No. 2 of a house in Ninstints Village." This model was never cataloged by the Field Museum before it was sent to Vienna. Newcombe recognized there was an error, but his handwritten note on Deans's typescript for House No. 2 says: "This description does not tally with model pole crests but is evidently house 17828 on p. 38. John Cross the maker's name is on the door—CFN." The model with John Cross's name on the door is Field Museum cat. no. 17802. Newcombe was wrong about the catalog number 17828, which is Food House and has John Cross as the maker, but Deans's description for 17828 (which has a whale with a single fin but no double-finned dogfish) does not match 17802 (Deans 1893b, in Newcombe 1900–1911: Add. Mss. 1077, vol. 38, folder 4, pp. 20–21, 38–39).

92. House Model No. 12 was placed between Model Nos. 9 and 10.

93. The house name "House Calling Out" was held by SG̱aana Jaads K'yaga X̱iigangs, Kathleen (Golie) Hans, matriarch of the Naa 'Yuuwans X̱aaydaG̱aay (E6a).

94. Newcombe 1900–1911: Add. Mss. 1077, vol. 55, folder 10, Skidegate Village Houses and Poles, Victoria, BC, October 1906, House, House #20.

95. See Emmons 1991, 403–4 for an account of this among the Tlingit.

96. Skun-doo (Sxandu?ú), a chief of the Chilkoot Tlingit, yis xá.n duwa?ú Wolf clan, was perhaps the most famous shaman on the Northwest Coast. He was imprisoned for his cultural practices and sent to McNeil's Island Prison, where he served three years. While there, his hair was forcibly cut, and he was forced to give up his shamanic practice. After his release from prison he earned a living by posing for photographers and providing information to collector George Emmons about shamanism. He also was paid to perform in the Eskimo Village on the Pay Streak at the Alaska Yukon Pacific Exposition in Seattle in 1909 (Emmons 1991, 411–12).

97. Barbeau published that Cross was in the same Eagle clan as both Charles Edenshaw and Isaac Chapman (Barbeau 1957: 123), but Charles Edenshaw was Staastas (E21) and Issac Chapman was Du.ugwaa tsiij git'anee (E17).

98. This "uncle Dan" might have been Daniel Iljuuwaas (see Genealogy Chart 8).

99. Hazel Stevens was married to Walter Stevens when Barbeau interviewed her in 1939. He later incorrectly described her (Mrs. Walter Stevens) as John Cross's niece (she was his daughter). Barbeau's notes were clearly muddled as in the very next paragraph in his discussion of John Cross, after he says that Cross had learned from Joshua Work, he talks about Work's daughter and jumps to saying "his" (Work's?) maternal uncles were "presumably" the T'aanuu artists "Kitkun and his brother Genés-kelos—a carver and tatooer," quoting James G. Swan's description of a tattoo drawing by Genés-kelos (Swan 1974: 5 and plate 3), but incorrectly and inexplicably inserting as the citation the plate and figure number from Swanton's *Contributions to the Ethology of the Haida* "Plate XXI, p. 5," which is a tattoo drawing by John Wi'ha (Barbeau 1957, 124).

100. In 1949, Mary Tulip showed Barbeau her gold bracelet depicting a grizzly bear made by John Cross (Barbeau 1916–1954, box 314, folder 11).

101. Newcombe 1900–1911: Add. Mss. 1077, vol. 55, folder 10, Skidegate Houses and Totem Poles. C. Jefferson, J. Wesley, A. Russ informants. Newcombe typed "Qamodi" on its own line above "Skidegates," suggesting this was the chief's name, not his wife's name. Elsewhere Newcombe says Qamodi was Nestaqana's name as a youth (Newcombe 1900–1911: Add. Mss. 1077, vol. 55, folder 10, Skidegate Village. Houses & Poles. C. Jefferson informant, Victoria, BC, October 1906, House #20).

102. MacDonald disagreed with Deans, Swanton, and Newcombe in describing the two-finned whale on this pole as a 'WaasG̱uu and the human figure holding the tail as the lazy son-in-law of this story (MacDonald 1983, 49, 18X2). While he says the 'WaasG̱uu is a crest of the wife, there is no other evidence to suggest this. The two-finned killer whale is also a crest of the Yahgu Laanaas in Northern Haida Gwaii and Alaska.

103. Newcombe 1900–1911: Add. Mss. 1077, vol. 55, folder 10, Skidegate Houses and Totem Poles. C. Jefferson, J. Wesley, A. Russ informants.

104. Macdonald speculated that it may have been the fifth Chief Skidegate who built this house around the middle of the nineteenth century, likely based on Deans's numbering system (MacDonald 1983, 48).

105. MacDonald incorrectly reports that there was an inside house post in this house (the one that is now at the Übersee Museum in Bremen, Germany) (MacDonald 1983, 49). Newcombe says that this inside house post was actually in the house next door, Daa.a Guu Ḵaahll (see Model House No. 15, Raven/Chief's House below). Newcombe doesn't even describe Naa S'aagas (Rotten House) in his list, probably since it doesn't show in the Maynard photo from which he was working at the time. It would have been Newcombe's house #21, but his list jumps from #20 to #22 (Newcombe 1900–1911: Add. Mss.1077, vol. 55, folder 10, Skidegate Village. Houses & Poles. Victoria, BC, October 1906). He does describe the inside house post later in the documents (Newcombe 1900–1911: Add. Mss. 1077, vol. 55, folder 10, Haida Totem Pole at the Städtisches Museum, Bremen, from Skidegate, Queen Charlotte Islands, BC).

106. Newcombe 1900–1911: Add. Mss. 1077, vol. 55, folder 10, "Skidegate Houses and Totem Poles, C. Jefferson, J. Wesley, A. Russ informants," Memorial Pole #21.

107. A letter from James Deans in the Newcombe archives reports that the model pole and/or the beak of the raven for House No. 15 was apparently missing in March 1893. It must have been found, as it appears in the photo of the installation, with the beak (Newcombe 1900–1911).

108. Newcombe 1900–1911: Add. Mss. 1077, vol. 55, folder 10, Skidegate Village. Houses & Poles. Victoria, BC, October 1906, House #22.

109. This may be the reason that MacDonald misunderstood which house this inside post came from in the Newcombe material, since he erroneously places the inside house post in Dug-Out House. MacDonald identified this house (his #17 as "Shining House" based on Swanton's house #15: X̱Ał ta-igo ("shining house") Family Naa yuuans (E6a). SHIP translates Xaahl TayG̱aaw as "Shining Sitting There House" (SHIP email, September 30, 2020) (MacDonald 1983; Swanton 1905a, 48–49). Note: Today the name Shining House is held by Jixaa, Gladys Vandal, of the Naa 'Yuuwans X̱aaydaG̱aay (E6a) (Jiixa, Gladys Vandal, personal communication, 2017).

110. Newcombe 1900–1911: Add. Mss. 1077, vol. 55, folder 10, Haida Totem Pole at the Stadtisches Museum, Bremen.

111. Newcombe 1900–1911: Add. Mss. 1077, vol. 55, folder 10, Skidegate. Includes photos, page 3 of Haida Totem Pole at the Stadtisches Museum, Bremen, "The large heraldic post which formerly stood outside Skidegate's house."

112. Newcombe reports Swanton's comment that the Yaku Gitanee had to leave Skidegate after one of them had shot a Skidegate chief, relocating to Ts'aahl Llnagaay (Swanton 1905a, 274). Newcombe also reports that all of the crests shown on the outside pole as well as the inside house post could be used by the Yaku Gitanee (Newcombe 1900–1911: Add. Mss. 1077, vol. 55, folder 10, Haida Totem Pole at the Stadtisches Museum, Bremen, from Skidegate, Queen Charlotte Islands, BC, page 1).

113. Newcombe 1900–1911: Add. Mss. 1077, vol. 55, folder 10, Skidegate Houses and Totem Poles. Victoria, BC, October 4, 1906, House #16.

114. The first Christian missionaries to settle on Haida Gwaii were Rev. William H. Collison and his family, who were Anglican, and came to Massett in 1876 (Wright 2001b, 233).

115. It is unknown how or why Amos Russ had the name Gedansd, the Skedans chief's name of the G̱aa K'yaals K̲iiG̱awaay (Swanton 1905b, 269). Sometimes names were given through the male side, but they remain a name of the clan. Amos Russ is listed among the first to be baptized in Skidegate (Chief Gidansda, Guujaaw, personal communication, July 20, 2017).

116. This was Chief Sdiihldaa, who died in 1877 (Collison 1981, 130–32).

117. It is possible that the girl called Ellen by Swan is actually Fanny, as their birth dates are close (see Genealogy Chart 8). We know that Swan was in the habit of giving young girls the name Ellen, and even shared the name Swan. During the time that Swan was living in Neah Bay (1859–66 and 1878–82), he became close friends ("he was like a father") with Ellen Swan Sikesy (Wa-ái-chitl or Archillu, b. 1867, d. 1887). She was listed as "Ellen Swan" in the 1885 and 1886 Makah censuses. She was the mother of Charlie Swan, who was the father of Helma Swan Ward (Goodman and Swan 2003, 263–65, 276n10). Swan's journal mentions "Ellen Swan Tow-hi-gen-das" during the time he was in Massett in July 1883. The Massett Ellen apparently practiced writing this new name in the back of Swan's diary (Swan 1883a, 28; Swan 1883c).

118. Deans's journal later reports that Sam was deaf.

119. It is interesting, given the discussion above of the other Iljuuwaas, Swanton reported that his clan, the Laana Tsaadas (E7), with the permission of the Gidins, could use any of the Gidins's crests except the 'WaasG̱uu (Swanton 1905a, 274).

120. UW Libraries have corrected the date on the front of the photograph from 1862 to 1882. According to the 1881 census, Suudaahl was seventeen in 1881, so born in 1864, but family records give her birth and death dates as born 1869, died 1932, clearly making the 1862 date for the photograph incorrect. Swan reported that the family visited him in Port Townsend two years before he visited them in Skidegate (Swan 1883a, 54, Thursday, August 28). We know that

during the winter of 1881, Daniel Iljuuwaas worked in Port Townsend making jewelry in a room rented by Swan with funds from Professor Baird at the Smithsonian provided for the National Museum collecting (McDonald 1972, 180).

A search for photographers in Port Townsend in 1881 revealed that Oregon Columbus (O. C.) Hastings reopened his studio there in November 1881, so the date of June 1882 for this photograph is most likely. Hastings also had a photography studio on Fort Street in Victoria and partners there with Stephen Allen Spencer (see figure 3.102). Reviewing the O. C. Hastings photographs at the Jefferson County Historical Society in Port Townsend revealed a photo of Miss Annie Reese with the same drapes, rug, and footstool seen in the Suudaahl photo (https://cdm16785.contentdm.oclc.org/digital/collection/p16785co1114/id/1291/rec/28) and the same footstool as well as the table and candlestick appear in a "Formal Portrait of Two Young Boys" (https://cdm16785.contentdm.oclc.org/digital/collection/p16785co1114/id/2451/rec/4) and Gertrude Willison (https://cdm16785.contentdm.oclc.org/digital/collection/p16785co1114/id/608/rec/5). So we know that this photograph was taken by O. C. Hastings in Port Townsend, likely in June 1882 when she was visiting there with her family. Suudaahl appears to be older than twelve here, more likely seventeen, putting her birthdate at 1864.

121. Josephine (Suudaahl) was the stepsister of Hazel's mother, Fanny (see Genealogy Chart 8).

122. Jisgang, Nika Collison (personal communication August 16, 2022).

123. Today Cindy Crosby has the name Suudaahl (Guujaaw, personal communication, July 28, 2017).

124. Samuel Ellsworth died in Queen Charlotte on March 3, 1946, age seventy-four (BC Archives microfilm #B13376). If this age is correct, he would have been nine at the 1881 census and nineteen at the 1891 census.

125. Newcombe recorded another house with this name, which was located at the far east (right) end of the village. The owner was named Daji kilstlas (R13), or Dats kilstlas, "like a small bird in good humour" (see Food House No. 14).

126. Newcombe 1900–1911: Add. Mss. 1077, vol. 55, folder 10, Totem Pole from Skidegate, Q.C.I., purchased for the Columbian Exposition by J. Deans.

127. Deans further confused the record, saying "I have in my collection a model of this house, No. 21," but there is no House No. 21 on his list (Deans 1893b, 44). This confused the record with another model house No. 2 (see Naa Gudgiikyagangs, House No. 2/21, p. 148). Boas called this other house model "No. 21 Katlinskien Nas. Katlins point house" [G̱aahllns Kun Naas, Cape Ball House], probably based on Deans description here, but Boas placed this house between Box House and House of Dishes and listed the full-size House of Waves as Deans did as No. 18, saying "Regarding the men at the end of the beams of the house, see description of house 18" (Boas 1893b, 112, 111).

128. Both Robson and Tl'aajaang quuna were of the Naay Kun K̲iiG̱awaay. Swanton lists the crests of the Naay Kun K̲iiG̱awaay (R13) as "Grisly bear, killer-whale, tcᴀ'maos, stratus-clouds, cirrus-clouds, hawk, sea-lion (recently adopted)" (Swanton 1905a, 270).

129. Swanton lists the crests of the Yahgu Laanaas (R19) as "Grisly bear, dog-fish, killer-whale, wolf, (recently) the moon, (in olden times) the raven" (Swanton 1905a, 271). Today the Yahgu Laanaas don't use the moon or wolf.

130. There are occasions when chiefly names did pass between the Eagle and Raven sides, such as at Old Massett when the Town Chief Wiiaa (Weah, K'aawas, E21a) passed his name to his son Sigai, a Raven chief (Ski'daoqao, R16), and he in turn passed the title to his son Stephen Wiiaa (Weah) (S[G]adjuu'ga.ahł Laanas, E14), who died in 1883 (Sparrow 1998, 216).

131. Newcombe 1900–1911: Add. Mss. 1077, Skidegate Totem Poles &c. continued C. Jefferson informant, Enlargement of Maynard's later photo, Pole O2.

132. The only two Skidegate houses that have been associated with the name Iljuuwaas are "Thunder & Lightning House" (House Model No. 16) and "House of Dolphins" (House Model No. 11). MacDonald also incorrectly identifies

the wife of Daniel "Eldjius" as Albert Edward Edenshaw's daughter, perhaps based on Deans's confusion (see above).

133. Newcombe 1900–1911: Add. Mss. 1077, vol. 55, folder 10: Skidegate Houses & Totem Poles &c. informants C. Jefferson & John Wesley, Maynard's later photo, enlarged Re east end, R, 1. The similarity between the names "Large Fallen Tree Limb" for Old Tl'aajaang quuna's wife and "Branches" for Tom Stevens's first wife suggests this may have been the same woman, and that Tom Stevens may have married his widowed aunt after the death of Old Tl'aajaang quuna, as was the custom. See John Robson, p. 140, and note 3.83.

134. Deans's confusion may in fact derive from the Haida themselves, since in the Haida way great-aunts can be called grandmother and great-uncles grandfather.

135. George MacDonald gives this pole the number 9X, saying it was a mortuary for a chief of the Point Town People (Kuun Laanas, R14). This does not agree with Newcombe's notes for the pole he numbers "R2 Xat" (MacDonald 1983, 46, 9X; Newcombe 1900–1911: Add. Mss. 1077, vol. 55, folder 10, Skidegate Houses & Totem Poles &c. Informants C. Jefferson & John Wesley,' R,2) Xat).

136. Roy Wilson has the name Dalskujas today (SHIP February 11, 2004).

137. This photograph was published in the book *Raven Travelling* in the chapter by Peter Macnair, who laments that the artist's name remains unknown and captions the portrait "the unfortunate Haida silver carver, ca. 1870" (Augaitis et al. 2006, 107, figure 78). The portrait had been identified as Waekus by Robert Brown in 1869 (see Frederick Dally photograph, BC Archives neg. no. G-06031, Bunn-Marcuse 2007, 17; Brown 1868–1869, 389).

138. Robert Brown reported that Waekus "went north and was shot by a chief in a drunken quarrel" (Brown 1868–1869, 389; Bunn-Marcuse 1998, 82; Drew and Wilson 1980, 86).

139. James Young told me that the name WiiG̱anad was later held by his mother, Fanny Blackstone Young. Her gravestone reads: "Fanny Chief Weenuts—in loving memory of our dear mother b. 1885 d. 1941." She was married to Henry Young (James Young, personal communication, February 7, 2004).

140. Deans spelled this "Chootsa Nass and Chooats ah Chlecha, Bear's Mouth House." One plank from the original carved and painted house front survives at the Royal British Columbia Museum (RBCM #1395).

141. Deans also states the owner of this house was related to Albert Edward Edenshaw, who gave the name of Gatlin (Giałins of Swanton) to his second son. George MacDonald repeated Deans's account and implied that the owner of the house was Albert Edward Edenshaw's son (MacDonald 1983, 45). In fact, Albert Edward Edenshaw's second son, Henry Edenshaw, did have this name as a child and was related to this clan through his sisters, who married into the Naay Kun K̲iiG̱awaay (R13), but he was not the owner of Xuuajii X̱iihlii Naas (see Wright 2001b, 353n6).

142. Florence Edenshaw Davidson was born in 1896 and went through her TaaG̱uunah seclusion when she was thirteen in 1909, but the distribution of gifts to the women of her father's lineage who assisted with this ritual was kept hidden from the missionary. Florence's sister Nora, who was three years younger, did not take part in this ceremonial seclusion (Blackman 1982, 92). See also Blackman 1982, 27–28; Dawson 1880 [1878], 130–31B.

143. Jisgang, Nika Collison and Aay Aay Gidins, personal communication, August 16, 2022; Elders of HlG̱aagilda X̱aayda Kil Naay 2016, 73, 168, 329.

144. Newcombe 1900–1911: vol. 55, folder 10, Skidegate Houses and Totem Poles. C. Jefferson Informant.

145. The older beaver memorial had apparently fallen by the time this photo was taken by Newcombe in 1897.

146. This beaver pole was mistakenly identified as a memorial to an uncle of Amos Russ by MacDonald (his 1M), and based on its position in figure 3.123, it is placed in the wrong position, switched with the pole described as 2M on his map of Skidegate (MacDonald 1983, 44, 38).

147. MacDonald speculated that this transfer occurred in the late 1860s (MacDonald 1996, 216), but this would have been when Robson was around twenty years old.

148. In 2001, I wrote in *Northern Haida Master Carvers* that "no further information about Robson's son, John, has been located as of this date." At that time I reported that Q'aaw quunaa died in 1896, 28 years before John Robson, and he apparently married a second time. This information comes from a letter written in 1911 to Newcombe by Robson, complaining that he had no children to help him when his wife was dying of cancer (Wright 2001b, 353fn9; Newcombe 1900–1911: Add. Mss. 1077, vol. 5, folder 124).

149. Barbeau thought these letters were "meaningless capitals" and attributed the chest to Charles Edenshaw (Barbeau 1957, 58), but Holm recognized the letters as being part of the name for John Robson, Gwaiskunagiatlens, recorded by Newcombe (Holm 1981, 191). The chest is now in the National Museum of Natural History, Smithsonian Institution, cat. no. 88999. For a discussion of the various interpretations of the name Gyaawhlnns, see Wright 2001b, 353fn7.

150. Charles Edenshaw also drew this story (American Museum of Natural History, Anthropological Archives, cat. no. Z/25 H).

151. MacDonald speculated that Edenshaw and Robson worked together on the five-finned whale pole that stood in front of Gud K̲wiiG̲a X̲iigangs, House upon which Storm Clouds Make a Noise, and also on Chief Skedans mortuary pole, both in Skidegate, but there is no evidence for this (MacDonald 1996, 216).

152. In a letter to Franz Boas, Swanton mentions the commission of poles, reporting that they will cost about nine dollars each (Swanton letter to Boas, January 16, 1901, American Museum of Natural History, Anthropological Archives). The differing styles of Robson and Edenshaw have been described by Bill Holm (1981, 181–92).

153. The name Skildoana (male eighteen) also appears in the 1881 census for Gold Harbour living in House 1, family 6.

154. Barbeau recorded information he got from Henry Young that David Shakespeare or Skowskeay (David Skilduunaas) was a Raven, and his Haida name was "Gyitsihlixalaxaté," and that David Shakespeare was the father of George Smith and had come to Skidegate from Ts'aahl Llnagaay and Xaayna Llnagaay (Barbeau 1916–1954, box 314, folder 13). Barbeau wrote that George Smith came to Skidegate from Chaatl and Xaina and was of the "Nastoq'iganaai" (R10a) clan (Barbeau 1957, 95). But we know that David Skilduunaas's clan was Naayii Kun K̲iiG̲awaay (R13) and his wife was Staastas (E21), so his relationship to George Smith might be questioned.

155. SHIP explained that the Haida words Taawt'a gaay naas means "food box house," and Ga taa naay means "come and eat house, like a restaurant," which may be the source of Deans's name (SHIP February 11, 2004).

156. Swanton gave this name for his house #9, Na'ga ga'ilas ("house to which the tide comes") (family: Naayii Kun K̲iiG̲awaay R13) (Swanton 1905a, 286).

157. Newcombe 1900–1911: Add. Mss. 1077, vol. 36, folder 13; Newcombe 1870–1955: vol. 55, folder 10, Notes on a Totem-pole sent by C. F. Newcombe to the National Museum, Melbourne.

158. Newcombe 1900–1911: Add. Mss. 1077, vol. 36, folder 13; McGowan 2003, 62.

159. Newcombe 1900–1911: Add. Mss. 1077: vol. 36, folder 13.

160. Regarding the north/south rather than east/west orientation of the two "easternmost" (northern) houses, see note 3.1.

161. In the Skidegate Haida dialect copper is spelled T'aaG̲uu; in X̲aad Kíl the Masset Haida dialect, ceremonial copper is spelled t'áa.u, and copper is spelled t'áaw in the Alaskan Haida dialect (HlG̲aagilda X̲aayda Kil Naay 2016: 199; https://xaad-kil.blogspot.com/2014/01/t-masset-haida-english_5.html; Lachler 2010, 530).

162. Newcombe 1900–1911: Add. Mss. 1077, vol. 38, folder 4; Deans 1893b, 94.

163. There were apparently only three mortuary poles in Skidegate that show three-dimensional bears heads on the panel. In addition to Tl'aajaang quuna's mortuary pole that stood in front of his house (see figure 3.112, 3.109, right),

and a pole that stood in front of Chief Skidegate's Dug-Out House, said to represent sea bear (see figures 3.87, 3.90), there was an older pole set back to the left of these (MacDonald 1983, 49,18X3; see figure 2.6, center). This pole had a double-finned whale carved on the pole below the panel, similar to Skidegate's wife's pole, and must have been for an older relative of these families.

164. Box of Supernatural Light is translated as guuda ga gaadaga; tluutl'xas is translated as a canoe coming in (SHIP February 1, 2004).

165. Newcombe 1900–1911: Add. Mss. 1077, vol. 38, folder 1.

166. Susan Grey also said that Charles Edenshaw was "like one of our own people." This may explain Young's use of the name "gunya" (gaanyaa), which has been variously spelled Cuneah, Coneehaw, Connehow, Connehaw, Cunneyah, Cania, Cunnea, Cunniha, Cunnyha, Cunneah, Cunniah, Coneyaw, gaanyaa, and Gunia. Gunya was the name of an eighteenth-century Eagle chief at K'yuusda (Wright 2001b, 339n10). It is listed as "Gunia" by Swanton, as the name of the chief of the Djus xade' (Juus xaade, E18) (Swanton 1905a, 275).

We know this man exchanged the name "Douglas" with Albert Edward Edenshaw. Douglas was acquired by gaanyaa from the British fur trader Captain William Douglas, and the name gaanyaa has been held by a number of men since then, including, in addition to George Young, Robert Ridley (1857–1937), Robert Davidson Sr. (E9, 1880–1969) (Wright 2001b, 40–41, 346n27, 351n44), and Rodney Scheck. Also, an extended Hydaburg family carries the name Gunya, which has moved between the Eagle and Raven clans as it is now used as a surname there.

167. Newcombe 1900–1911: Add. Mss. 1077, vol. 38, folder 1, Skidegate Totem Poles &c. continued. C. Jefferson informant, Maynard's Old, also Dawson's 34 & 36.

168. Deans called this "Model of Hat of Millas."

169. Robert Miller and Lovett Miller are the same man; since there is no "r" in the Haida language, "robert" was pronounced "lovett." Perhaps the "r" at the end of Miller also became "Millas" (Irene Mills, personal communication, September 2006).

170. Newcombe 1900–1911: Add. Mss. 1077, vol. 36, folder 13.

CONCLUSION

1. At least three other poles honoring women in Skidegate had no WCE models made of them (see figures 3.87, second pole from left, raised for the wife of a Chief Skidegate, MacDonald 1983, 49, 18X1; raised for one of Tl'aajaang quuna's wives, a beaver pole with raven on top, figure 3.109; and raised for Klaaskost, Jane Shakespeare, figure 3.125).

APPENDIX I

1. The term "town chief" is explained in chapter 2.

APPENDIX II

1. In the list quoted by Dawson, forty houses are assignated to Skidegate. The wife of Chief Skidegate said that the number was probably correct. Before the last row of houses was built, the houses stood farther back and were more numerous.

REFERENCES

Abbott, Donald, ed. 1981. *The World Is as Sharp as a Knife: An Anthology in Honour of Wilson Duff*. Victoria, BC: British Columbia Provincial Museum.

Arnold, C. D., and H. D. Higinbotham. 1893. Official Views of the World's Columbian Exposition, Department of Photography World's Columbian Exposition Company, Chicago.

Atkinson, Maureen. 2011. "The 'Accomplished' Odille Quintal Morison: Tsimshian Cultural Intermediary of Metlakatla, British Columbia." In *Recollecting: Lives of Aboriginal Women of the Canadian Northwest and Borderlands,* edited by Sarah Carter and Patricia A. McCormack, 135–56. Edmonton, AB: Athabasca University Press.

Augaitis, Diana, et al. 2006. *Raven Travelling*. Vancouver, BC: Vancouver Art Gallery; Douglas and McIntyre.

Barbeau, C. Marius. 1916–1954. Unpublished notebooks, notes, and correspondence. National Museum of Man, Canadian Centre for Folk Culture Studies, Ottawa.

———. 1950. *Totem Poles According to Crests and Topics.* Vol 1., Bulletin No. 119, Anthropological Series No. 30. Ottawa: National Museum of Canada.

———. 1953. *Haida Myths Illustrated in Argillite Carvings.* Bulletin No. 127. Anthropological Series No. 32. Ottawa: National Museum of Canada.

———. 1957. *Haida Carvers in Argillite*. Ottawa: Department of Northern Affairs and Natural Resources, National Museum of Canada.

———. 1958. *Medicine-Men on the North Pacific Coast.* Ottawa: National Museum of Canada.

Barrett, James. 1817–1821. *Log of the Ship Volunteer from Boston towards the Coast of North West America*. Boston Public Library.

Beck, David R. M. 2019. *Unfair Labor? American Indians and the 1893 World's Columbian Exposition in Chicago.* Lincoln: University of Nebraska Press. www.jstor.org/stable/j.ctvggx4fm. Accessed June 13, 2020.

Benedict, Burton. 1983. *The Anthropology of World's Fairs: San Francisco's Panama International Exposition of 1915.* Berkeley, CA: Lowie Museum of Anthropology; and London: Scolar Press.

Beresford, William. 1789. *A Voyage around the World; but More Particularly to the North-West Coast of America Performed in 1785, 1786, 1787, and 1788 in The King George and Queen Charlotte, Captains Portlock and Dixon*. London: George Goulding.

Blackman, Margaret B. 1981. *Window on the Past: The Photographic Ethnohistory of the Northern and Kaigani Haida.* Ottawa: National Museum of Canada.

———. 1982. *During My Time: Florence Edenshaw Davidson, a Haida Woman.* Seattle: University of Washington Press.

Boas, Franz. 1893a. Collections from the North Pacific Coast, Department of Ethnology, W.C.E.: The Haida

Indians, American Philosophical Society, Boas Collection; B.C. Archives Microfilm Reel A00238.

———. 1893b. The Exhibits from the North Pacific Coast. Putnam Papers, Peabody Museum, Harvard University. Cambridge, MA.

———. 1893c. Letter to L. VanKoughnet, March 11, 1893. Library and Archives Canada. Indian Affairs. NA, DIA, RG10, Vol. 3865, File 85,529.

Bolt, Clarence. 1992. *Thomas Crosby and the Tsimshian: Small Shoes for Feet Too Large*. Vancouver: University of British Columbia Press.

Boyd, Robert. 1999. *The Coming of the Spirit of Pestilence: Introduced Infectious Diseases and Population Decline among Northwest Coast Indians, 1774–1874*. Seattle: University of Washington Press.

British Colonist. 1862. "Amputated."

Broughton, P. "Oregon Columbus Hastings (1846–1912)—Pioneer Astronomer of British Columbia." *Journal of the Royal Astronomical Society of Canada* 106, no. 5 (2012): 199.

Brown, Robert. 1868–1869. *On the Physical Geography of the Queen Charlotte Islands*. Proceedings of the Royal Geographical Society, session 1868–1869.

Bunn-Marcuse, Kathryn. 1998. "Reflected Images: The Use of Euro-American Designs on Northwest Coast Silver Bracelets." Art History, School of Art, University of Washington.

———. 2000 . "Northwest Coast Silver Bracelets and the Use of Euro-American Designs." *American Indian Art Magazine* 25, no. 4: 66–73, 84.

———. 2007. "Precious Metals: Silver and Gold Bracelets of the Northwest Coast." PhD dissertation, Division of Art History, School of Art, University of Washington.

———. 2011. "Bracelets of Exchange." In *Objects of Exchange: Social and Material Transformation on the Late-Nineteenth Century Northwest Coast*. New York: Decorative Arts, Design History, Material Culture, Bard Graduate Center.

Bunn-Marcuse, Kathryn, and Jisgang, Nika Collison. 2018. "Gud Gii AanaaG̱ung: Look at One Another." *ab-Original: Journal of Indigenous Studies and First Nations and First Peoples' Cultures* 2, no. 2: 265–99.

Bunyan, Don. 1982. "James Deans—Pioneer Archaeologist." *Heritage West* (Spring): 14–15.

Burling, Samuel. 1799. *Journal of the Eliza*. Microfilm. Massachusetts Historical Society

Chicago Sunday Post. 1893. "Mr. Wanuck at Home. Quacquhl Indians Have a House-warming at the Fair. Ceremonies of an Odd Tribe." May 7, 1893.

Chicago Sunday Tribune. 1893. "Race Types at the World's Fair Sketched from Life." July 30, 1893.

Chicago Times. 1893. "With Savage Abandon. Quoc Queth Indians Give a Stirring Exhibition of the Minuet." April 21, 1893.

Chittenden, Newton H. 1984 [1884]. *Exploration of the Queen Charlotte Islands*. Vancouver, BC: G. Soules.

Cole, Douglas. 1985. *Captured Heritage: The Scramble for Northwest Coast Artifacts*. Seattle: University of Washington Press.

———. 2003. "Deans, James." In *Dictionary of Canadian Biography*. Vol. 13. Toronto: University of Toronto/Université Laval.

Cole, Douglas, and Ira Chaikin. 1990. *An Iron Hand upon the People: The Law against the Potlatch on the Northwest Coast*. Vancouer, BC: Douglas and McIntyre.

Cole, Douglas, and Bradley Lockner. 1989. *Journals of George M. Dawson: British Columbia, 1875–1878*. Vancouver: University of British Columbia Press.

———. 1993. *To the Charlottes: George Dawson's 1878 Survey of the Queen Charlotte Islands*. Vancouver: University of British Columbia Press.

Collison, William Henry. 1981. *In the Wake of the War Canoe*. Edited and annotated by Charles Lillard. Victoria, BC: Sono Nis Press.

Cracroft, Sophia. 1974. *Lady Franklin Visits the Pacific Northwest: Being Extracts from the Letters of Miss Sophia Cracroft, Sir John Franklin's Niece, February to April 1861 and April to July 1870*. Edited by Dorothy Blakeley Smith. Victoria Provincial Archives of British Columbia Memoir, no. 11.

Crosby, Thomas. 1914. *Up and Down the North Pacific Coast*. Toronto: The Missionary Society of the Methodist Church.

Daily Inter Ocean. May 7, 1893, 6.

Dally, Frederick. n.d. Frederick Dally MS/E/B/D 16M. BC Archives, Victoria.

Dalzell, Kathleen E. 1968. *The Queen Charlotte Islands, 1774–1966*. Vol. 1. Madeira Park, BC: Harbour Publishing.

———. 1973. *The Queen Charlotte Islands*. Vol. 2, *Places and Names*. Madeira Park, BC: Harbour Publishing.

Dawson, George M. 1880 [1878]. *Report on the Queen Charlotte Islands 1878, Geologial Survey of Canada*. Montreal: Dawson Brothers.

Deans, James. 1878. *Settlement of Vancouver Island*. BC Archives, Victoria.

———. 1887. "Inside View of a Huidah Dwelling." *American Antiquarian* 9, no. 5 (September): 309–10.

———. [1888?]. "What Befell the Slave-Seekers: A Story of the Haidahs on Queen Charlotte's Island, B.C." *Journal of American Folk-Lore*: 123–24.

———. 1890. "The Huida-Kwul-Ra, or Native Tabacco of the Queen Charlotte Haidas." *American Antiquarian* 12, no. 1 (January): 48–50.

———. 1892. "Antiquites of British Columbia." *American Antiquarian* 14, no. 1: 41–44.

———. 1893a. "Collections from North Pacific Coast, Department of Ethnology, World's Columbia Exposition, Haida Indians, Collection of James Deans." Field Museum of Natural History Archives, Accession 21.

———. 1893b. Model No. 1 of Haidah Houses in Skidegat (James Deans ms. with notes by C.F.N.). Add. Mss. 1077, Newcombe Family. Vol. 38, Folder 4, Haida Industry Notes: Section III. Pp. 15–95. BC Provincial Archives, Victoria, BC.

———. 1893c. Order of Haidah Houses as they used to stand in Skidegats Town, Q. C. Islands, B.C. Accession 21. Pp. 1–37. Anthropology Division, Field Museum of Natural History, Chicago.

———. 1895. "The Hidery Story of Creation." *American Antiquarian* 17: 61–67.

———. 1899a. *Legendary Lore of the Coast Tribes of Northwestern America*. Chicago: Archives of the International Folk-Lore Association.

———. 1899b. *Tales from the Totems of the Hidery*. Chicago: International Folk-Lore Association.

DeArmond, R. N., ed. 1981. *Lady Franklin Visits Sitka, Alaska 1870: The Journal of Sophia Cracroft, Sir John Franklin's Niece*. Anchorage: Alaska Historical Society.

Dexter, Ralph W. 1966. "Putnam's Problems Popularizing Anthropology." *American Scientist* 54, no. 3: 315–32.

Drew, Leslie, and Douglas Wilson. 1980. *Argillite: Art of the Haida*. Vancouver, BC: Hancock House Publishers, Ltd.

Duncan, Kate C. 2000. *1001 Curious Things: Ye Olde Curiosity Shop and Native American Art*. Seattle: University of Washington Press.

Elders of HlG̱aagilda X̱aayda Kil Naay. 2016. *HlG̱aagilda X̱aayda Kil K̲'aalang SHIP Xaayda Kil Glossary*. Haida Gwaii: HlG̱aagilda X̱aayda Kil Naay.

Emmons, George Thornton. 1991. *The Tlingit Indians*. Edited by Frederica de Laguna. Seattle: University of Washington Press; New York: American Museum of Natural History.

Enge, Marilee. 1993. "Treasure of the Tlingit Master Carver Modern-Day Carvers and Anthropologists Follow the Trail of a Tlingit Artist of Profound Vision and Skill." *Anchorage Daily News*, April 5, 1993, A1.

Enrico, John. 1991. "Names and Naming?" Unpublished manuscript.

Feest, Christian. 1987. *Indians and Europe: An Interdisciplinary Collection of Essays*. Aachen, Germany: Edition Herodot, Rader-Verlag.

Fogelson, Raymond D. 1991. "The Red Man in the White City." *In Columbian Consequences*. Volume 3, *The Spanish Borderlands in Pan-American Perspective*, edited by D. H. Thomas, 73–90. Washington, DC: Smithsonian Institution Press.

Foster, Hamar, and Megan Harvey. 2018. "Amos Russ." *In Dictionary of Canadian Biography*, Volume 16 (1931–1940). www.biographi.ca/en/bio/russ_amos_16E.html.

Garfield, Viola E. 1980 (1940). *The Seattle Totem Pole*. Rev. and exp. ed. Seattle: University of Washington Press.

Gessler, Trisha (Glatthaar). 1981. *The Art of Nunstins*. Queen Charlotte Islands Museum, Second Beach, Skidegate, BC.

Gibson, James R. 1992. *Otter Skins, Boston Ships, and China Goods: The Maritime Fur Trade of the Northwest Coast, 1785–1841*. Seattle: University of Washington Press.

Glass, Aaron, ed. 2011. *Objects of Exchange: Social and Material Transformation on the Late Nineteenth-Century Northwest Coast*. New York: Decorative Arts, Design History, Material Culture, Bard Graduate Center.

Goodman, Linda J., and Helma Swan. 2003. *Singing the Songs of My Ancestors: The Life and Music of Helma Swan, Makah Elder*. Norman: University of Oklahoma Press.

Green, Rev. Jonathan S. 1915. *Report of an Exploring Tour on the North-West Coast of North America in 1829*. New York: Charles Fred Heartman.

Gunther, Erna. 1966. *Art in the Life of the Northwest Coast Indians*. Portland, OR: Portland Art Museum.

Haida Gwaii Museum at Ḵay Llnagaay. n.d., Clans of Skidegate. Haida Gwaii Oral History Project.

———. 2014. *Gina Guuda Tl'l X̱asii: Came to Tell Something: Art and Artist in Haida Society*. Haida Heritage Centre at Ḵay Llnagaay. Skidegate, BC: Haida Gwaii Museum Press.

———. n.d. Skidegate Graves List. Skidegate, BC.

Hall, Michael D., and Pat Glascock. 2011. *Carvings and Commerce: Model Totem Poles, 1880–2010*. Seattle: University of Washington Press; Saskatoon, SK: Mendel Art Gallery.

Halligan, Jewell N. 1894. *Halligan's Illustrated World's Fair*. A portfolio of photographic views of the World's Columbian Exposition carefully selected by *Halligan's Illustrated World's Fair*. London, New York, Chicago, Paris, Berlin: Jewell N. Halligan Co., Pubs.

Hinsley, Curtis M., Jr., and David R. Wilcox, eds. 2016. *Coming of Age in Chicago: The 1893 World's Fair and the Coalescence of American Anthropology*. Lincoln: University of Nebraska Press.

Holm, Bill. 1981. "Will the Real Charles Edenshaw Please Stand Up?" In *The World Is as Sharp as a Knife: An Anthology in Honour of Wilson Duff*, edited by D. Abbott, 175–200. Victoria: British Columbia Provincial Museum.

Howay, Frederic W. 1990. *Voyages of the "Columbia" to the Northwest Coast 1787–1790 and 1790–1793*. Portland: Oregon Historical Society in cooperation with the Massachusetts Historical Society.

Jacknis, Ira. 1991. "Northwest Coast Indian Culture and the World's Columbian Exposition." In *Columbian Consequences*. Vol. 3, *The Spanish Borderlands in Pan-American Perspective*, edited by D. H. Thomas. Washington, DC: Smithsonian Insitution Press.

———. 2002. *The Storage Box of Tradition: Kwakiutl Art, Anthropologists, and Museums, 1881–1981*. Washington, DC: Smithsonian Institution Press.

———. 2016. "Refracting Images: Anthropological Display at the Chicago World's Fair, 1893." In *Coming of Age in Chicago: The 1893 World's Fair and the Coalescence of American Anthropology*, edited by C. M. Hinsely and D. R. Wilcox, 261–336. Lincoln: University of Nebraska Press.

Johnson, Rossiter, ed. 1898. *A History of the World's Columbian Exposition, Held in Chicago in 1893*. Vol. 2, *Departments*. New York: D. Appleton.

Jonaitis, Aldona, and Aaron Glass. 2010. *The Totem Pole: An Intercultural History*. Seattle: University of Washington Press.

Kaplanoff, Mark D., ed. 1971. *Joseph Ingraham's Journal of the Brigantine Hope, 1790–1792*. Barre, MA: The Imprint Society.

King, J. C. H. 1981. *Artificial Curiosities from the Northwest Coast of America: Native American Artefacts in the British Museum Collected on the Third Voyage of Captain James Cook and Acquired through Sir Joseph Banks*. London: British Museum Publications Ltd.

Krmpotich, Cara, and Laura Peers, with the Haida Repatriation Committee and Staff of the Pitt Rivers Museum and British Museum. 2013. *This Is Our Life: Haida Material Heritage and Changing Museum Practice*. Vancouver: University of British Columbia Press.

Lachler, Jordan. 2010. *Dictionary of Alaskan Haida*. Juneau: Sealaska Heritage Institute.

Larson, Erik. 2003. *The Devil in the White City: Murder, Magic, and Madness at the Fair That Changed America*. New York: Crown Publishers.

MacDonald, George F. 1983. *Haida Monumental Art, Villages of the Queen Charlotte Islands*. Vancouver: University of British Columbia Press.

———. 1994. *Haida Monumental Art: Villages of the Queen Charlotte Islands*. Vancouver: University of British Columbia Press; Seattle: University of Washington Press.

———. 1996. *Haida Art*. Seattle: University of Washington Press.

Malloy, Mary. 1998. *"Boston Men" on the Northwest Coast: The American Maritime Fur Trade, 1788–1844*. Fairbanks, AK: Limestone Press.

Mattison, David. 1980. "The Maynards: A Victoria Photographic Couple." *The Islander*, 3.

———. 1985. "Richard Maynard: Photographer of Victoria, B.C." *History of Photography* 9, no. 2: 109–29. DOI: 10.1080/03087298.1985.10442269.

McDonald, Lucile. 1972. *Swan among the Indians: Life of James G. Swan, 1818–1900*. Portland, OR: Binfords & Mort.

McGowan, Cynthia Lynne. 2003. *Seeing the Forest for the Trees: Catalogue of Totem Poles*. Collected by Charles F. Newcombe. Art History, School of Art, University of Washington.

Miles, George A. 2003. *James Swan, Cha-tic, of the Northwest Coast: Drawings and Watercolors from the Franz & Kathryn Stenzel Collection of Western American Art*. Beinecke Rare Book and Manuscript Library, Yale University.

Moore, Emily L. 2018. *Proud Raven, Panting Wolf: Carving Alaska's New Deal Totem Parks*. Seattle: University of Washington Press.

Morley, Alan. 1967. *Roar of the Breakers: A Biography of Peter Kelly*. Toronto: Ryerson Press

Neary, Kevin. 2003. "Newcombe, Charles Frederic." In *Dictionary of Canadian Biography*, volume 15. University of Toronto/Université Laval. www.biographi.ca/en/bio/newcombe_charles_frederic_15E.html. Accessed January 28, 2017.

Newcombe, Charles F. 1900–1911. Unpublished notes, Add. Mss. 1077—Newcombe Family Papers. BC Archives.

———. 1909. *Guide to Anthropological Collections in the Provincial Museum, Victoria, B.C.* Victoria, BC: Richard Wolfenden.

Neylan, Susan. 2003. *The Heavens Are Changing: Nineteenth-Century Protestant Missions and Tsimshian Christianity*. Montreal: McGill-Queen's University Press.

Pokagon, Simon. 1893. *The Red Man's Rebuke. World's Columbian Exposition*. Chicago: C. H. Engle.

Poole, Francis. 1872. *Queen Charlotte Islands; A Narrative of Discovery and Adventure in the North Pacific*. London: Hurst and Blackett.

Prevost, James C. 1853. Report to Rear-Admiral Fairfax Moresby, July 23, 1853. Public Record Office, London.

Pringle, Heather. 2015. "The Girl with the Shimmering Eyes." *Hakai Magazine*, May 27. www.hakaimagazine.com/article-short/girl-shimmering-eyes/.

Raibmon, Paige. 2000. "Theatres of Contact: The Kwakwa̱ka̱'wakw Meet Colonialism in British Coumbia and at the Chicago World's Fair." *Canadian Historical Review* 81, no. 2 (June): 157–90. https://search.proquest.com/docview/224238404?accountid=14784 (dated November 25 in online edition).

Ramsay, Heather. 2011. *gyaagang.ngaay: The Monumental Poles of Skidegate*. Skidegate: Haida Gwaii Museum Press.

Roe, Michael, ed. 1967. *Journal and Letters of Captain Charles Bishop on the Northwest Coast of America, in the Pacific, and in New South Wales, 1794–1799*. Cambridge, England: Hakluyt Society.

Ross, Matt. 2003. "Museum Releases Remains to Haida Gwaii." *Windspeaker* 21, no. 9: 13.

Rydell, Robert W. 1978. "The World's Columbian Exposition of 1893: Racist Underpinnings of a Utopian Artifact." *Journal of American Culture* 1, no. 2: 253–75.

———. 1980. "All the World's a Fair: America's International Expositions, 1876–1916." PhD dissertation, UCLA.

———. 1984. *All the World's a Fair: Visions of Empire at American International Expositions, 1876–1916*. Chicago: University of Chicago Press.

———. 1989. "The Culture of Imperial Abundance: World's Fairs in the Making of American Culture." In *Consuming Visions: Accumulation and Display of Goods in America, 1880–1920*, edited by S. J. Bronner. New York: W. W. Norton for the Henry Francis du Pont Winterthur Museum.

Savard, Dan. 2010. *Images from the Likeness House*. Victoria: Royal British Columbia Museum.

Shadbolt, Doris. 1998. *Bill Reid*. Vancouver, BC: Douglas and McIntyre.

Smith, Harlan I. 1893. "Man and His Works: The Anthropological Building at the World's Columbian Exposition." *American Antiquarian and Oriental Journal* 15: 115–17.

Sparrow, Kathy Bedard. 1998. "Correcting the Record: Haida Oral Tradition in Anthropological Narratives." *Anthropologica* 40, no. 2: 215–22. DOI: 10.2307/25605898.

———. 2003. "A Haida Writing: About Chief Wiiaa." MA thesis, Department of Anthropology and Sociology, University of British Columbia.

Steedman, Scott, and Jisgang, Nika Collison, eds. 2011. *That Which Makes Us Haida: The Haida Language*. Haida Heritage Centre at K̲ay Llnagaay. Skidegate, Haida Gwaii: Haida Gwaii Museum Press.

Sunday Inter Ocean. 1893. "Before Colon Came. Primitive Life among the North American Indians. Congress of Aborigines. Tribes Are in Camp from All Parts of the Country. In Their Ancestors' Houses Scenes from Aboriginal Life Will Be Depicted." July 9.

Swan, James G. 1869. *Diary for 1869*. Swan diaries. Swan Papers, Special Collections, University of Washington Libraries.

———. 1874. *The Haidah Indians of Queen Charlotte's Islands, British Columbia with a Brief Description of Their Carvings, Tattoo Designs, etc.* Washington, DC: Smithsonian Institution.

———. 1883a. Extract from "Diary of a Cruise to Queen Charlotte Islands, B.C. for the Smithsonian Institution." Swan Papers, Special Collections, University of Washington Libraries.

———. 1883b. Swan's Letters from QCI [Queen Charlotte Islands]. UW Microfilm A8576, Reel 3 A.1.6. Swan Papers, Special Collections, University of Washington Libraries.

———. 1883c. Swan Diary, UW Microfilm #203. Swan Papers, Special Collections, University of Washington Libraries.

———. n.d. [1883]. *Journal of a Trip to Queen Charlotte Islands, B.C.* Microfilm. Swan Papers, Special Collections, University of Washington Libraries.

Swanton, John Reed. 1901a. "Explanation of Totem Poles Carved by Charlie Edenshaw." Anthropology Archives, American Museum of Natural History, New York.

———. 1901b. "Poles Carved by John Robson of Skidegate." Anthropology Archives, American Museum of Natural History, New York.

———. 1905a. *Contributions to the Ethnology of the Haida*. Leiden: E. J. Brill; New York: G. E. Stechert.

———. 1905b. *Haida Texts and Myths, Skidegate Dialect*. New York: Bureau of American Ethnology.

Twigg, Alan. 2005. "Deans, James." BC Bookworld Author Bank. https://abcbookworld.com/writer/deans-james/. Accessed August 9, 2022.

Van den Brink, J. H. 1974. *The Haida Indians: Cultural Change, Mainly between 1876–1970*. Leiden: E. J. Brill.

Victoria Daily Colonist. 1892a. "Mr. James Deans Secures a Splendid Collection for the World's Fair." May 28, 2.

———. 1892b. "Skidegate Curios." September 9.

Vowell, A. W. 1892. Letter, October 19, 1892. NA, DIA, RG10, Vol. 3865, File 85,529. Library of Canada Collections.

Wade, Stuart C., and Walter S. Wrenn. 1893. *The Nut Shell: The Ideal Pocket Guide to the World's Fair and What To*

See There. Every Important Exhibit or Sight Accurately Located with Ground Plans. Chicago: The Merchant's World's Fair Bureau of Information Co.

Walsh, Jane MacLaren. 2002. "Collections as Currency." In *Anthropology, History, and American Indians: Essays in Honor of William Curtis Sturtevant*, edited by W. L. Merrill and I. Goddard, 201–9. Washington, DC: Smithsonian Institution Press.

Watson, Petra. 1996. "Hannah Maynard: Pioneer British Columbia Photographer." In *Raincoast Chronicles.* Vol. 17, *Stories and History of the British Columbia Coast*, edited by Howard White, 20–26. Madeira Park, BC: Harbour Publishing.

Weissenborn, von J. 1908. *Der Totempfahl der Haida im Stadtischen Museum fur Natur, Volker, und Handelskunde*, 18–25. Bremen, Germany: Jahrbuch der Bremischen Samnlungen.

Wilks, Claire Weissman. 1980. *The Magic Box: The Eccentric Genius of Hannah Maynard.* Toronto: Exile Editions.

Wilson, Barbara J. (Kii'iljuus), and Heather Harris. 2005. "Tllsda Xaaydas K'aaygang.nga: Long, Long Ago Haida Ancient Stories." In *Haida Gwaii: Human History and Environment from the Time of Loon to the Time of the Iron People,* edited by Daryl W. Fedje and Rolf W. Mathewes, 121–39. Vancouver, BC: University of British Columbia Press.

Wright, Robin K. 1977. "Haida Argillite Pipes." MA thesis, University of Washington.

———. 1979. "Haida Argillite Ship Pipes." *American Indian Art Magazine* 5, no. 1 (Winter): 40–47.

———. 1980. "Haida Argillite Pipes: The Influence of Clay Pipes." *American Indian Art Magazine* 5, no. 4 (Autumn): 42–47, 88.

———. 1982. "Haida Argillite Carved for Sale." *American Indian Art Magazine* 8, no. 1 (Winter): 48–55.

———. 1985. "Nineteenth Century Haida Argillite Pipe Carvers: Stylistic Attributions." PhD dissertation, Division of Art History, School of Art, University of Washington.

———. 1986. "The Depiction of Women in Nineteenth Century Haida Argillite Carving." *American Indian Art Magazine* 11, no. 4 (Autumn): 36–45.

———. 1987. "The Traveling Exhibition of Captain Samuel Hadlock, Jr.: Eskimos in Europe 1822–1826." In *Indians and Europe: An Interdisciplinary Collection of Essays*, edited by C. F. Feest, 215–33. Aachen, Germany: Edition Herodot, Rader-Verlag.

———. 1992. "Kadashan's Staff: The Work of a Mid-Nineteenth Century Haida Argillite Carver in Another Medium." *American Indian Art Magazine* 17 , no. 4 (Autumn): 48–55.

———. 2001a. "Nineteenth Century Haida Argillite Carvings: Documents of Cutural Encounter." In *Art and the Native American: Perceptions, Reality, and Influences*, edited by Mary Louise Krumrine and Susan Clare Scott, 224–25. Papers in Art History 10. University Park: Pennsylvania State University.

———. 2001b. *Northern Haida Master Carvers.* Seattle: University of Washington Press.

———. 2009. "Zacherias and the Chicago Settee: Connecting the Masterpiece to the Master." *American Indian Art Magazine* 35, no. 1 (Winter): 68–75.

Wright, Robin K., and Daina Augaitis, eds. 2013. *Charles Edenshaw*. London: Black Dog Publishing; Vancouver, BC: Vancouver Art Gallery.

Wyatt, Victoria. 1984. *Shapes of Their Thoughts: Reflections of Culture Contact in Northwest Coast Indian Art*. Norman: University of Oklahoma Press.

Zeller, Suzanne, and Gale Avrith-Wakeam. 2003. "Dawson, George Mercer." In *Dictionary of Canadian Biography.* Vol. 13. University of Toronto/Université Laval, 2003.

INDEX

Page numbers in *italics* refer to illustrations and charts